# TÁHIRIH IN HISTORY
Perspectives on Qurratu'l-'Ayn
from East and West

Studies in the Bábí and
Bahá'í Religions

Volume Sixteen

# Studies in the Bábí and Bahá'í Religions
(formerly *Studies in Bábí and Bahá'í History*)

ANTHONY A. LEE, General Editor

*Studies in Bábí and Bahá'í History,* Volume One,
edited by Moojan Momen (1982)

*From Iran East and West*, Volume Two,
edited by Juan R. Cole and Moojan Momen (1984)

*In Iran*, Volume Three, edited by Peter Smith (1986)

*Music, Devotions and Mashriqu'l-Adhkár*, Volume Four,
by R. Jackson Armstrong-Ingram (1987)

*Studies in Honor of the Late H. M. Balyuzi*, Volume Five,
edited by Moojan Momen (1989)

*Community Histories*, Volume Six, edited by Richard Hollinger (1992)

*Symbol and Secret: Qur'an Commentary in Bahá'u'lláh's Kitáb-i Íqán*,
Volume Seven, by Christopher Buck (1995)

*Revisioning the Sacred: New Perspectives on a Bahá'í Theology*,
Volume Eight, edited by Jack McLean (1997)

*Modernity and the Millennium: The Genesis of the Baha'i Faith in the
Nineteenth-Century Middle East*, by Juan R. I. Cole, distributed as Volume Nine,
Columbia University Press (1999)

*Paradise and Paradigm: Key Symbols in Persian Christianity
and the Bahá'í Faith,* by Christopher Buck, distributed as Volume Ten,
State University of New York Press (1999)

*Religion in Iran: From Zoroaster to Baha'ullah*, by Alessandro Bausani,
distributed as Volume Eleven, Bibliotheca Persica Press (2000)

*Evolution and Bahá'í Belief: 'Abdu'l-Bahá's Response to
Nineteenth-Century Darwinism*, Volume Twelve, edited by Keven Brown (2001)

*Reason and Revelation*, Volume Thirteen,
edited by Seena Fazel and John Danesh (2002)

*Bahá'ís in the West*, Volume Fourteen, edited by Peter Smith (2004).

*Search for Values: Ethics in Bahá'í Thought*, Volume Fifteen,
edited by John Danesh and Seena Fazel (2004)

*Táhirih in History: Perspectives on Qurratu'l-'Ayn from East and West*,
Volume Sixteen, edited by Sabir Afaqi (2004)

*Táhirih: A Portrait in Poetry*
Volume Seventeen, edited by and translated Amin Banani (2004)

THE *CHADOR,* IRANIAN WOMEN, 1880
all wearing street dress (the veil). Two of the women have cast aside their white face coverings for the photograph. Note, however, that they cover their mouths and keep their eyes closed. The young girl (right) is not yet obligated to wear a *chador* over her indoor clothes.

Studies in the Bábí and Bahá'í Religions
Volume Sixteen

Anthony A. Lee
General Editor

# TÁHIRIH IN HISTORY
Perspectives on Qurratu'l-'Ayn
from East and West

Edited by Sabir Afaqi, Ph.D.

with the assistance of Jan Teofil Jasion

Kalimát Press
Los Angeles

Copyright © 2004 by Kalimát Press

Manufactured in the United State of America

All Rights Reserved

**Library of Congress Cataloging-in-Publication Data**

Táhirih in history: perspectives on Qurratu'l-'Ayn
from East and West / edited by Sabir Afaqi; with the
assistance of Jan Teofil Jasion.
  p. cm. – (Studies in the Bábí and Bahá'í religions; v. 16)
  Includes bibliographical references.
  ISBN 1-890688-35-5 (pbk.)
  1. Qurrat al-'Ayn, 1817 or 1814-1852. 2. Bahais—Iran—Biography.
  I. Sabir Afaqi, 1933- II. Jasion, Jan T., 1945- III. Series.
  BP395.Q87T34 2004
  297.9'3'092--dc22
        2004018717

Kalimát Press
1600 Sawtelle Blvd., Suite 310
Los Angeles, CA 90025

www.kalimat.com
orders@kalimat.com

# Table of Contents

Preface
*Sabir Afaqi*
x

Acknowledgements
xii

Note on Translation
xiii

### Bahá'í Sources

'Abdu'l-Bahá
*Jináb-i Táhirih*
3

Shoghi Effendi
*Valiant Táhirih*
15

### Eastern Impressions

Sabir Afaqi
*Qurratu'l-'Ayn Táhirih in Urdu Literature*
23

Muhammad Iqbal
From the *Javid-nama:*
*The Sphere Of Jupiter* (Excerpts)
45

M. Hidayat Hosain
*A Female Martyr of the Babi Faith*
51

Mohammad Ishaque
*Qurratu'l-'Ayn—a Bábí Martyr*
57

Mohammad Ali Siddiqui
*Qurratu'l-Ayn: A Profile In Courage*
67

Masudu'l Hasan
*Qurratu'l-Ayn Tahira*
71

Khwaja Masud
*The Cry of Tahira*
75

Süleyman Nazif
Passages from: *Nasiruddin Shah ve Babiler*
79

**Western Considerations**

Edward G. Browne
*Kurratu'l-'Ayn*
85

A.-L.-M. Nicolas
*Qourrèt-oul-Aïne*
97

Abbas Amanat
*Qurrat al-'Ayn: The Remover of the Veil*
113

Farzaneh Milani
*Becoming a Presence: Tahereh Qorratol'Ayn*
159

Susan Stiles Maneck
*Táhirih: A Religious Paradigm of Womanhood*
185

Negar Mottahedeh
*Ruptured Spaces and Effective Histories:
The Unveiling of the Bábí Poetess Qurrat al-'Ayn-Táhirih
in the Gardens of Badasht*
203

Jan Teofil Jasion
*Táhirih on the Russian Stage*
231

## The Writings of Qurratu'l-'Ayn
Denis MacEoin

*The Writings of Qurrat al-'Ayn Qazvini (Táhira)*
241

*A Prayer of Táhirih*
253

*A Gathering of the Poems*
257

Bibliography
265

Contributors and Translators
280

Poems of Táhirih in the Original Languages
281

# Preface

Qurratu'l-'Ayn—more commonly known as Táhirih—the poetess, the writer, the celebrated woman who lived and died for the cause she believed was good for the people and for the upliftment of humanity, is a matchless figure in the annals of history. She was courageous, she was bold, she was straightforward, and she had the integrity to say "no" to what she knew was wrong. She challenged the harmful traditions that had gathered over centuries and took practical steps to liberate the women of her country, to show them new ways to achieve honor, freedom, and prosperity.

She was the first woman to embrace the Faith of Sayyid 'Alí-Muhammad, the Báb, in the mid-nineteenth century. Not only did she accept it, but she also arose to promote it far and wide—from her native Qazvin in Iran to Karbala in Iraq, and from Iraq to Mazandaran. She proclaimed the new message of the Báb to every strata of society—from the layman to the shah of Persia, and even to the highest clergy of Persian society. She was the first woman who unfurled the banner of the equality of the sexes and removed the veil from her face.

Her devotion to her a mission, her selfless sacrifices, her unquenchable thirst for the truth, her unmatched detachment from worldly pomp and show, the thoughts she expressed in her poems and essays, and the revolutionary model that she presented have inspired millions of people of many generations in both the East and West. Scholars have written books or essays on Qurratu'l-'Ayn's person, message, and works in many languages. And she has inspired poets, writers, and social reformers all over the world. Qurratu'l-'Ayn has been a model for many movements aimed at the education, the rights, and the progress of women.

Besides the Báb and Bahá'u'lláh, 'Abdu'l-Bahá and Shoghi Effendi also have paid high tribute to this great lady who was among the first eighteen persons who championed the new cause of the Báb.

As women in every part of the world are still struggling for their rights and place in society, I believe that the life and work of Qurratu'l-'Ayn will serve as a model and source of encouragement, guidance, and inspiration to many of them. With this conviction, I thought it necessary to make a compilation of a number of articles written by different writers of the past and present generations. These articles were scattered in different magazines, periodicals, and books which are now not easily available to the common reader. This book contains some of these articles. Also included is a collection of Táhirih's poems in their original languages. English translations of a few of Qurratu'l-'Ayn's poems—three of them translated by Prof. E. G. Browne—are also included.

It is worth mentioning that the first biography on Qurratu'l-'Ayn was written by an American writer Martha L. Root. She had stayed long enough in Persia to investigate the details of Qurratu'l-'Ayn's life. This book entitled *Táhirih the Pure* was first published in Karachi in 1938. Since then, many books and articles have been published on Qurratu'l-'Ayn in many languages: Persian, English, Urdu, Italian, Azerbaijani, German, Arabic, French, Afrikaans, Russian, Polish, Dutch, Turkish, etc., and in many countries around the world from New Caledonia to Brazil, from Sweden to South Africa. Her poems have also appeared in numerous recordings—sung, chanted, and recited.

I present this book as a source of encouragement and inspiration to those who are engaged in movements for education and social upliftment throughout the world. Several of these even bear names such as The Táhirih Association for the Advancement of Women, The Táhirih Justice Center, and the Táhirih College of Education in Brazil, to mention just a few.

The articles presented here were previously published in a variety of books and periodicals over a considerable length of time. Each article bears the imprint of its own time with regard to style, spelling of names, and systems of transliteration. The editors have only made changes in the notes and combined the bibliographies at the back of the book in order to ease the reader's task of further research. All works mentioned in the articles will also be found in the bibliography.

Sabir Afaqi, Ph.D.<br>Pakistan, 2004

# Acknowledgments

Extracts from the following works are reprinted by permission: "Jináb-i Táhirih" from *Memorials of the Faithful*, by 'Abdu'l-Baha Copyright © 1971, 1997 by the National Spiritual Assembly of the Bahá'ís of the United States. "Valiant Táhirih" from *God Passes By*, by Shoghi Effendi Copyright © 1944 by the National Spiritual Assembly of the Bahá'ís of the United States. "Qurratu'l-'Ayn: The Remover of the Veil" from *Resurrection and Renewal: The Making of the Babi Movement in Iran*, 1844-1850, by Abbas Amanat Copyright © 1989 by Cornell University. "Becoming a Presence: Tahereh Qorratol'Ayn" from *Veils and Words: The Emerging Voices of Iranian Women Writers* Copyright © 1992 by Syracuse University Press. "The Writings of Qurrat al-'Ayn Qazvini" from *The Sources for Early Bábí Doctrine and History: A Survey* Copyright © 1992 by E. J. Brill.

The editors warmly acknowledge permissions received to reprint various articles: From Susan Stiles Maneck for "Táhirih: A Religious Paradigm of Womanhood"; from Negar Mottahedeh for "Ruptured Spaces and Effective Histories"; from Juan R. I. Cole for a portion of his "A Prayer of Táhirih Qurratu'l-'Ayn: Text and Translation."

The editors are grateful to the staff at the Bahá'í International Library, Haifa, Israel, and to the Bibliothèque Baha'ie de France, Paris, for their assistance. A special thanks is due to Annie-Joëlle Hurvy-Jasion for the French translations and for her support for this project.

## Note on Transliteration

Over the last one hundred and fifty years, a number of systems have been used by writers and academics to render Persian and Arabic names and words into the Latin alphabet. The essays in this volume reflect this diversity, and Persian and Arabic words appear here as the various authors chose to present them. No effort has been made to standardize spellings or to reduce the various systems of transliteration to one uniform code. So the reader will find the name "Solace of the Eyes," for example, in many forms: Qurratu'l-'Ayn, Kurratu'l-'Ayn, Qourrèt-oul-Aïne, Qorratol'Ayn, etc.

For the most part, these variations are easily recognizable and should cause little confusion.

The exceptions to the rule of faithful reproduction of various systems of transliteration are two. These changes, unfortunately, have been forced upon us by the limitations of the word processing programs currently available to our computers:

1) All sublinear diacritical marks have been removed;
2) Flat macrons used above the vowels a, i, and u, have been replaced with acute accents. So, the letters ā, ī, and ū, appear here as á, í, and ú.

The editors regret these changes and would have preferred to reprint all of the passages in this book exactly as they appeared in the original essays.

# TÁHIRIH IN HISTORY
## Bahá'í Sources

COURT LADY
One of the wives of Nasiru'd-Dín Sháh, probably Fatimih Khanúm, Anísu'd-Dowlih, c. 1865. This photo shows the indoor dress of women in the royal harem of this time.

# Jináb-i Táhirih

by 'Abdu'l-Bahá

A woman chaste and holy, a sign and token of surpassing beauty, a burning brand of the love of God, a lamp of His bestowal, was Jináb-i-Táhirih.[1] She was called Umm-Salmá; she was the daughter of Hájí Mullá Sálíh, a mujtahid of Qazvín, and her paternal uncle was Mullá Taqí, the Imám-Jum'ih or leader of prayers in the cathedral mosque of that city. They married her to Mullá Muhammad, the son of Mullá Taqí, and she gave birth to three children, two sons and a daughter; all three were bereft of the grace that encompassed their mother, and all failed to recognize the truth of the Cause.

When she was still a child her father selected a teacher for her and she studied various branches of knowledge and the arts, achieving remarkable ability in literary pursuits. Such was the degree of her scholarship and attainments that her father would often express his regret, saying, "Would that she had been a boy, for he would have shed illumination upon my household, and would have succeeded me!"[2]

One day she was a guest in the home of Mullá Javád, a cousin on her mother's side, and there in her cousin's library she came upon some of the writings of Shaykh Ahmad-i-Ahsá'í.[3] Delighted with what he had to say, Táhirih asked to borrow the writings and take them home. Mullá Javád violently objected, telling her: "Your father is an enemy of the Twin Luminous Lights, Shaykh Ahmad and Siyyid Kázim. If he should even dream that any words of those two great beings, any fragrance from the garden of those realities, had come your way, he would make an attempt against my life, and you too would become the target of his wrath." Táhirih answered: "For a long time now, I have thirsted after this; I have yearned for these explanations, these inner truths. Give me whatever you have of these books. Never mind if it angers my father." Accordingly, Mullá Javád sent over the writings of the Shaykh and the Siyyid.

One night, Táhirih sought out her father in his library, and began to speak of Shaykh Ahmad's teachings. The very moment he learned that his daughter knew of the Shaykhí doctrines, Mullá Sálih's denunciations rang out, and he cried: "Javád has made you a lost soul!" Táhirih answered, "The late Shaykh was a true scholar of God, and I have learned an infinity of spiritual truths from reading his books. Furthermore, he bases whatever he says on the traditions of the Holy Imáms. You call yourself a mystic knower and a man of God, you consider your respected uncle to be a scholar as well, and most pious—yet in neither of you do I find a trace of those qualities!"

For some time, she carried on heated discussions with her father, debating such questions as the Resurrection and the Day of Judgment, the Night-Ascent of Muhammad to Heaven, the Promise and the Threat, and the Advent of the Promised One.[4] Lacking arguments, her father would resort to curses and abuse. Then one night, in support of her contention, Táhirih quoted a holy tradition from the Imám Ja'far-i-Sádiq;[5] and since it confirmed what she was saying, her father burst out laughing, mocking the tradition. Táhirih said, "Oh my father, these are the words of the Holy Imám. How can you mock and deny them?"

From that time on, she ceased to debate and contend with her father. Meanwhile she entered into secret correspondence with Siyyid Kázim, regarding the solution of complex theological problems, and thus it came about that the Siyyid conferred on her the name "Solace of the Eyes" (Qurratu'l-'Ayn); as for the title Táhirih ("The Pure One"), it was first associated with her in Badasht, and was subsequently approved by the Báb, and recorded in Tablets.

Táhirih had caught fire. She set out for Kárbilá, hoping to meet Siyyid Kázim, but she arrived too late: ten days before she reached that city, he passed away. Not long before his death the Siyyid had shared with his disciples the good news that the promised Advent was at hand. "Go forth," he repeatedly told them, "and seek out your Lord." Thus the most distinguished of his followers gathered for retirement and prayer, for fasts and vigils, in the Masjid-i-Kúfih, while some awaited the Advent in Kárbilá. Among these was Táhirih, fasting by day, practicing religious disciplines, and spending the night in vigils, and chanting prayers. One night when it was getting along toward dawn she laid her head on her pillow, lost all awareness of this earthly life, and dreamed a dream; in her vision a youth, a Siyyid, wearing a black cloak and a green turban, appeared to her in the heavens; he was standing in the air, reciting verses and praying with his hands upraised. At once, she memorized one of those verses, and wrote it down in her notebook when she awoke. After the Báb had declared His mission, and His first book, "The Best of Stories,"[6] was circulated, Táhirih was reading a section of the text one day, and she came upon that same verse, which she had noted down from the dream. Instantly offering thanks, she fell to her knees and bowed her forehead to the ground, convinced that the Báb's message was truth.

This good news reached her in Kárbilá and she at once began to teach. She translated and expounded "The Best of Stories," also writing in Persian and Arabic, composing odes and lyrics, and humbly practicing her devotions, performing even those that were optional and supernumerary. When the evil 'ulamás in Kárbilá got wind of all this, and learned that a woman was summoning the people to a new religion and had already influenced a considerable number, they went to the Governor and lodged a complaint. Their charges, to be brief, led to violent attacks on Táhirih, and sufferings, which she accepted and for which she offered praise and thanks. When the authorities came hunting for her they first assaulted Shamsu'd-Duhá, mistaking her for Táhirih. As soon, however, as they heard that Táhirih had been arrested they let Shams go—for Táhirih had sent a message to the Governor saying, "I am at your disposal. Do not harm any other."

The Governor set guards over her house and shut her away, writing Baghdád for instructions as to how he should proceed. For three months, she lived in a state of siege, completely isolated, with the guards surrounding her house. Since the local authorities had still received no reply from Baghdád, Táhirih referred her case to the Governor, saying: "No word has come from either Baghdád or

Constantinople. Accordingly, we will ourselves proceed to Baghdád and await the answer there." The Governor gave her leave to go, and she set out, accompanied by Shamsu'd-Duhá and the Leaf of Paradise (the sister of Mullá Husayn) and her mother. In Baghdád she stayed first in the house of Shaykh Muhammad, the distinguished father of Áqá Muhammad-Mustafá. But so great was the press of people around her that she transferred her residence to another quarter, engaged night and day in spreading the Faith, and freely associated with the inhabitants of Baghdád. She thus became celebrated throughout the city and there was a great uproar.

Táhirih also maintained a correspondence with the 'ulamás of Kazímayn; she presented them with unanswerable proofs, and when one or another appeared before her she offered him convincing arguments. Finally she sent a message to the Shí'ih divines, saying to them: "If you are not satisfied with these conclusive proofs, I challenge you to a trial by ordeal."[7] Then there was a great outcry from the divines, and the Governor was obliged to send Táhirih and her women companions to the house of Ibn-i-Álúsí, who was muftí of Baghdád. Here she remained about three months, waiting for word and directions from Constantinople. Ibn-i-Álúsí would engage her in learned dialogues, questions would be asked and answers given, and he would not deny what she had to say.

On a certain day the muftí related one of his dreams, and asked her to tell him what it meant. He said: "In my dream I saw the Shí'ih 'ulamás arriving at the holy tomb of Imám Husayn, the Prince of Martyrs. They took away the barrier that encloses the tomb, and they broke open the resplendent grave, so that the immaculate body lay revealed to their gaze. They sought to take up the holy form, but I cast myself down on the corpse and I warded them off." Táhirih answered: "This is the meaning of your dream: you are about to deliver me from the hands of the Shí'ih divines." "I too had interpreted it thus," said Ibn-i-Álúsí.

Since he had discovered that she was well versed in learned questions and in sacred commentaries and Texts, the two often carried on debates; she would speak on such themes as the Day of Resurrection, the Balance, and the Sirat,[8] and he would not turn away.

Then came a night when the father of Ibn-i-Álúsí called at the house of his son. He had a meeting with Táhirih and abruptly, without asking a single question, began to curse, mock and revile her. Embarrassed at his father's behavior, Ibn-i-Álúsí apologized. Then he said: "The answer has come from Constantinople. The King has commanded that you be set free, but only on condition that you leave his realms. Go then, tomorrow, make your preparations for the journey, and hasten away from this land."

Accordingly Táhirih, with her women companions, left the muftí's house, saw to arranging for their travel gear, and went out of Baghdád. When they left the city, a number of Arab believers, carrying arms, walked along beside their convoy. Among the escort were Shaykh Sultán, Shaykh Muhammad and his distinguished son Muhammad-Mustafá, and Shaykh Sálíh, and these were mounted. It was Shaykh Muhammad who defrayed the expenses of the journey.

When they reached Kirmansháh the women alighted at one house, the men at another, and the inhabitants arrived in a continuous stream to seek information as to the new Faith. Here as elsewhere the 'ulamás were soon in a state of frenzy and they commanded that the newcomers be expelled. As a result the kad-khudá or chief officer of that quarter, with a band of people, laid siege to the house where Táhirih was, and sacked it. Then they placed Táhirih and her companions in an uncovered howdah and carried them from the town to an open field, where they put the captives out. The drivers then took their animals and returned to the city. The victims were left on the bare ground, with no food, no shelter, and no means of traveling on.

Táhirih at once wrote a letter to the prince of that territory, in which she told him: "O thou just Governor! We were guests in your city. Is this the way you treat your guests?" When her letter was brought to the Governor of Kirmansháh he said: "I knew nothing of this injustice. This mischief was kindled by the divines." He immediately commanded the kad-khudá to return all the travelers' belongings. That official duly surrendered the stolen goods, the drivers with their animals came back out of the city, the travelers took their places and resumed the journey.

They arrived in Hamadán and here their stay was a happy one. The most illustrious ladies of that city, even the princesses, would come to visit, seeking the benefits of Táhirih's teaching. In Hamadán she dismissed a part of her escort and sent them back to Baghdád, while she brought some of them, including Shamsu'd-Duhá and Shaykh-Sálih, along with her to Qazvín.

As they traveled, some riders advanced to meet them, kinsmen of Táhirih's from Qazvín, and they wished to lead her away alone, unescorted by the others, to her father's house. Táhirih refused, saying: "These are in my company." In this way they entered Qazvín. Táhirih proceeded to her father's house, while the Arabs who had formed her escort alighted at a caravanserai. Táhirih soon left her father and went to live with her brother, and there the great ladies of the city would come to visit her; all this until the murder of Mullá Taqí,[9] when every Bábí in Qazvín was taken prisoner. Some were sent to Tihrán and then returned to Qazvín and martyred.

Mullá Taqí's murder came about in this way: One day, when that besotted tyrant had mounted his pulpit, he began to mock and revile the great Shaykh Ahmad-i-Ahsá'í. Shamelessly, grossly, screaming obscenities, he cried out: "That Shaykh is the one who has kindled this fire of evil, and subjected the whole world to this ordeal!" There was an inquirer in the audience, a native of Shíráz. He found the taunts, jeers and indecencies to be more than he could bear. Under cover of darkness he betook himself to the mosque, plunged a spearhead between the lips of Mullá Taqí and fled. The next morning they arrested the defenseless believers and thereupon subjected them to agonizing torture, though all were innocent and knew nothing of what had come to pass. There was never any question of investigating the case; the believers repeatedly declared their innocence but no one paid them any heed. When a few days had passed the killer gave himself up; he confessed to the authorities, informing them that he had committed the murder because Mullá Taqí had vilified Shaykh Ahmad. "I deliver myself into your hands," he told them, "so that you will set these innocent people free." They arrested him as well, put him in the stocks, chained him, and sent him in chains, along with the others, to Tihrán.

Once there he observed that despite his confession, the others were not released. By night, he made his escape from the prison and went to the house of Ridá Khán—that rare and precious man, that star-sacrifice among the lovers of God—the son of Muhammad Khán, Master of the Horse to Muhammad Sháh. He stayed there for a time, after which he and Ridá Khán secretly rode away to the Fort of Shaykh Tabarsí in Mazindarán.[10] Muhammad Khán sent riders after them to track them down, but try as they might, no one could find them. Those two horsemen got to the Fort of Tabarsí, where both of them won a martyr's death. As for the other friends who were in the prison at Tihrán, some of these were returned to Qazvín and they too suffered martyrdom.

One day the administrator of finance, Mírzá Shafí, called in the murderer and addressed him, saying: "Jináb, do you belong to a dervish order, or do you follow the Law? If you are a follower of the Law, why did you deal that learned mujtahid a cruel, a fatal blow in the mouth? If you are a dervish and follow the Path, one of the rules of the Path is to harm no man. How, then, could you slaughter that zealous divine?" "Sir," he replied, "besides the Law, and besides the Path, we also have the Truth. It was in serving the Truth that I paid him for his deed."[11]

These things would take place before the reality of this Cause was revealed and all was made plain. For in those days no one knew that the Manifestation of the Báb would culminate in the Manifestation of the Blessed Beauty and that the law of retaliation would be done away with, and the foundation-principle of the Law of God would be this, that "It is better for you to be killed than to kill"; that discord and contention would cease, and the rule of war and butchery would fall away. In those days, that sort of thing would happen. But praised be God, with the advent of the Blessed Beauty such a splendor of harmony and peace shone forth, such a spirit of meekness and long-suffering, that when in Yazd men, women and children were made the targets of enemy fire or were put to the sword, when the leaders and the evil 'ulamás and their followers joined together and unitedly assaulted those defenseless victims and spilled out their blood—hacking at and rending apart the bodies of chaste women, with their daggers slashing the throats of children they had orphaned, then setting the torn and mangled limbs on fire—not one of the friends of God lifted a hand against them. Indeed, among those martyrs, those real companions of the ones who died, long gone, at Kárbilá—was a man who, when he saw the drawn sword flashing over him, thrust sugar candy into his murderer's mouth and cried, "With a sweet taste on your lips, put me to death—for you bring me martyrdom, my dearest wish!"

Let us return to our theme. After the murder of her impious uncle,

Mullá Taqí, in Qazvín, Táhirih fell into dire straits. She was a prisoner and heavy of heart, grieving over the painful events that had come to pass. She was watched on every side, by attendants, guards, the farráshes, and her foes. While she languished thus, Bahá'u'lláh dispatched Hádíy-i-Qazvíní, husband of the celebrated Khátún-Ján, from the capital, and they managed, by a stratagem, to free her from that embroilment and got her to Tihrán in the night. She alighted at the mansion of Bahá'u'lláh and was lodged in an upper apartment.

When word of this spread throughout Tihrán, the Government hunted for her high and low; nevertheless, the friends kept arriving to see her, in a steady stream, and Táhirih, seated behind a curtain, would converse with them. One day the great Siyyid Yahyá, surnamed Vahíd, was present there. As he sat without, Táhirih listened to him from behind the veil. I was then a child, and was sitting on her lap. With eloquence and fervor, Vahíd was discoursing on the signs and verses that bore witness to the advent of the new Manifestation. She suddenly interrupted him and, raising her voice, vehemently declared: "O Yahyá! Let deeds, not words, testify to thy faith, if thou art a man of true learning. Cease idly repeating the traditions of the past, for the day of service, of steadfast action, is come. Now is the time to show forth the true signs of God, to rend asunder the veils of idle fancy, to promote the Word of God, and to sacrifice ourselves in His path. Let deeds, not words, be our adorning!"

The Blessed Beauty made elaborate arrangements for Táhirih's journey to Badasht and sent her off with an equipage and retinue. His own party left for that region some days afterward.

In Badasht, there was a great open field. Through its center a stream flowed, and to its right, left, and rear there were three gardens, the envy of Paradise. One of those gardens was assigned to Quddús,[12] but this was kept a secret. Another was set apart for Táhirih, and in a third was raised the pavilion of Bahá'u'lláh. On the field amidst the three gardens, the believers pitched their tents. Evenings, Bahá'u'lláh, Quddús and Táhirih would come together. In those days the fact that the Báb was the Qá'im had not yet been proclaimed; it was the Blessed Beauty, with Quddús, Who arranged for the proclamation of a universal Advent and the abrogation and repudiation of the ancient laws.

Then one day, and there was a wisdom in it, Bahá'u'lláh fell ill; that is, the indisposition was to serve a vital purpose. On a sudden, in the sight of all, Quddús came out of his garden, and entered the pavilion of Bahá'u'lláh. But Táhirih sent him a message, to say that their Host being ill, Quddús should visit her garden instead. His answer was: "This garden is preferable. Come, then, to this one." Táhirih, with her face unveiled, stepped from her garden, advancing to the pavilion of Bahá'u'lláh; and as she came, she shouted aloud these words: "The Trumpet is sounding! The great Trump is blown! The universal Advent is now proclaimed!" [13] The believers gathered in that tent were panic struck, and each one asked himself, "How can the Law be abrogated? How is it that this woman stands here without her veil?"

"Read the Súrih of the Inevitable,"[14] said Bahá'u'lláh; and the reader began: "When the Day that must come shall have come suddenly... Day that shall abase! Day that shall exalt!. . ." and thus was the new Dispensation announced and the great Resurrection made manifest. At the start, those who were present fled away, and some forsook their Faith, while some fell a prey to suspicion and doubt, and a number, after wavering, returned to the presence of Bahá'u'lláh. The Conference of Badasht broke up, but the universal Advent had been proclaimed.

Afterward, Quddús hastened away to the Fort of Tabarsí[15] and the Blessed Beauty, with provisions and equipment, journeyed to Níyálá, having the intention of going on from there by night, making His way through the enemy encampment and entering the Fort. But Mírzá Taqí, the Governor of Ámul, got word of this, and with seven hundred riflemen arrived in Níyálá. Surrounding the village by night, he sent Bahá'u'lláh with eleven riders back to Ámul, and those calamities and tribulations, told of before, came to pass.

As for Táhirih, after the breakup at Badasht she was captured, and the oppressors sent her back under guard to Tihrán. There she was imprisoned in the house of Mahmúd Khán, the Kalántar. But she was aflame, enamored, restless, and could not be still. The ladies of Tihrán, on one pretext or another, crowded to see and listen to her. It happened that there was a celebration at the Mayor's house for the marriage of his son; a nuptial banquet was prepared, and the house adorned. The flower of Tihrán's ladies were invited, the princesses, the wives of vazírs and other great. A splendid wedding it was, with instrumental music and vocal melodies—by day and night the lute, the bells and songs. Then Táhirih began to speak; and so bewitched were the great ladies that they forsook the cithern and the drum and all the pleasures of the wedding feast, to crowd about Táhirih and listen to the sweet words of her mouth.

Thus she remained, a helpless captive. Then came the attempt on the life of the Sháh;[16] a farmán was issued; she was sentenced to death. Saying she was summoned to the Prime Minister's, they arrived to lead her away from the Kalántar's house. She bathed her face and hands, arrayed herself in a costly dress, and scented with attar of roses she came out of the house.

They brought her into a garden, where the headsmen waited; but these wavered and then refused to end her life. A slave was found, far gone in drunkenness; besotted, vicious, black of heart. And he strangled Táhirih. He forced a scarf between her lips and rammed it down her throat. Then they lifted up her unsullied body and flung it in a well, there in the garden, and over it threw down earth and stones. But Táhirih rejoiced; she had heard with a light heart the tidings of her martyrdom; she set her eyes on the supernal Kingdom and offered up her life.

Salutations be unto her, and praise. Holy be her dust, as the tiers of light come down on it from Heaven.

**Notes**
Reprinted from: 'Abdu'l-Bahá, *Memorials of the Faithful*; translated from the original Persian text and annotated by Marzeih Gail (Wilmette, Ill.: Bahá'í Publishing Trust, 1971) pp. 190-203.

1. Pronounced Tá-heh-reh.
2. Cf. Nabíl-i A'zam, *The Dawn-Breakers: Nabíl's Narrative of the Early Days of the Bahá'í Revelation*; translated and edited by Shoghi Effendi (Wilmette, Ill.: Bahá'í Publishing Committee, 1932) p. 81, note 2, and p. 285, note 2. Certain lines, there translated by Shoghi Effendi, are incorporated here.
3. The first of the two founders of the Shaykhí School.
4. Qur'án [*The Koran*; translated by Rev. J. M. Rodwell. London: J. M. Dent,1933] 17:1; 30:56; 50:19; etc.
5. The sixth Imám.
6. The "Ahsánu'l-Qisás" [Qayyumu'l-Asmá], the Báb's commentary on the Súrih of Joseph, was called the Qur'án of the Bábís, and was translated from Arabic into Persian by Táhirih. Cf. Shoghi Effendi, *God Passes By* (Wilmette: Bahá'í Publishing Trust, 1970) p. 23.

7. Qur'án 3:54. "Then will we invoke and lay the malison of God on those that lie!" The ordeal was by imprecation.
8. Qur'án 21:48; 19:37, etc. In Islam, the Bridge of Sirat—sharp as a sword and finer than a hair—stretches across Hell to Heaven.
9. Cf. Nabíl-i-A'zam, *The Dawn-Breakers*, p. 276. The murderer was not a Bábí, but a fervent admirer of the Shaykhí leaders, the Twin Luminous Lights.
10. Cf. Nabíl-i A'zam, *The Dawn-Breakers*, p. 278.
11. This refers to the doctrine that there are three ways to God: the Law (*sharí'at*), the Path (*taríqat*), and the Truth (*haqíqat*). That is, the law of the orthodox, the path of the dervish, and the truth. Cf. R. A. Nicholson "Commentary" in Jalál al-Dín Rúmí. *The Mathnawí of Jalálu'ddín Rúmí*; ed. with critical notes, translation & commentary by Reynold A. Nicholson (London: Luzac, 1925-1940) s.v.
12. The eighteenth Letter of the Living, martyred with unspeakable cruelty in the market place at Barfurúsh, when he was twenty-seven. Bahá'u'lláh conferred on him a station second only to that of the Báb himself. Cf. Nabíl-i-A'zam, *The Dawn-Breakers*, pp. 408-15.
13. Cf. Qur'án 74:8 and 6:73. Also Isaiah 27:13 and Zechariah 9:14.
14. Qur'án, Súrih 56.
15. A systematic campaign against the new Faith had been launched in Persia by the civil and ecclesiastical authorities. The believers, cut down wherever they were isolated, banded together when they could, for protection against the government, the clergy, and the people. Betrayed and surrounded as they passed through the forest of Mazindarán, some three-hundred believers, mostly theological students, built the Fort of Shaykh Tabarsí and held out against the armies of Persia for eleven months. Cf. Nabíl-i A'zam, *The Dawn-Breakers*, chapters 19 and 20; Shoghi Effendi, *God Passes By*, p. 37 ff.
16. On August 15, 1852, three Bábí youth wounded the sháh with shot from a pistol. The authorities thereafter carried out a wholesale massacre of the Báb's followers, its climax described by Renan as "a day perhaps unparalleled in the history of the world." Cf. George Nathaniel Curzon. *Persia and the Persian Question* (London: Longmans, Green, 1892) pp. 501-502, and Shoghi Effendi, *God Passes By*, p. 62 ff.

PERSIAN WOMEN AND GIRLS WEARING INDOOR DRESS, C. 1880.
Perhaps a woman (center) in a wealthy harem with her children and a servant (seated right).

# The Valiant Táhirih

by Shoghi Effendi

While Bahá'u'lláh was being so odiously and cruelly subjected to the trials and tribulations inseparable from those tumultuous days, another luminary of the Faith, the valiant Táhirih, was swiftly succumbing to their devastating power. Her meteoric career, inaugurated in Kárbilá, culminating in Badasht, was now about to attain its final consummation in a martyrdom that may well rank as one of the most affecting episodes in the most turbulent period of Bahá'í history.

A scion of the highly reputed family of Hájí Mullá Sálíh-i-Baraqání, whose members occupied an enviable position in the Persian ecclesiastical hierarchy; the namesake of the illustrious Fátimih; designated as Zarrín-Táj (Crown of Gold) and Zakíyyih (Virtuous) by her family and kindred; born in the same year as Bahá'u'lláh; regarded from childhood, by her fellow-townsmen, as a prodigy, alike in her intelligence and beauty; highly esteemed even by some of the most haughty and learned 'ulamás of her country, prior to her conversion, for the brilliancy and novelty of the views she propounded; acclaimed as Qurrat-i-'Ayní (solace of my eyes) by her admiring teacher, Siyyid Kázim; entitled Táhirih (the Pure One) by the "Tongue of Power and Glory;" and the only woman enrolled by the Báb as one of the Letters of the Living; she had, through a dream, referred to earlier in these pages, established her first contact with a Faith which she continued to propagate to her last breath, and in its hour of greatest peril, with all the ardor of her unsubduable spirit. Undeterred by the vehement protests of her father; contemptuous of the anathemas of her uncle; unmoved by the earnest solicitations of her husband and her brothers; undaunted by the measures which, first in Kárbilá and subsequently in Baghdád, and later in Qasvín, the civil and ecclesiastical authorities had taken to curtail her activities, with eager energy she urged the Bábí Cause. Through her eloquent pleadings, her fearless denunciations, her dissertations, poems and translations, her commentaries and correspondence, she persisted in firing the imagination and in enlisting the allegiance of Arabs and Persians alike to the new Revelation, in condemning the perversity of her generation, and in advocating a revolutionary transformation in the habits and manners of her people.

She it was who while in Kárbilá—the foremost stronghold of Shí'ah Islam—had been moved to address lengthy epistles to each of the 'ulamás residing in that city, who relegated women to a rank little higher than animals and denied them even the possession of a soul–epistles in which she ably vindicated her high purpose and exposed their malignant designs. She it was who, in open defiance of the customs of the fanatical inhabitants of that same city, boldly disregarded the anniversary of the martyrdom of the Imám Husayn, commemorated with elaborate ceremony in the early days of Muharram, and celebrated instead the anniversary of the birthday of the Báb, which fell on the first day of that month. It was through her prodigious eloquence and the astounding force of her argument that she confounded the representative delegation of Shí'ah, of Sunní, of Christian and Jewish notables of Baghdád, who had endeavored to dissuade her from her avowed purpose of spreading the tidings of the new Message. She it was who, with consummate skill, defended her faith and vindicated her conduct in the home and in the presence of that eminent jurist, Shaykh Mahmúd-i-Álúsí, the Muftí of Baghdád, and who later held her historic interviews with the princes, the 'ulamás and the government officials residing in Kirmánsháh, in the course of which the Báb's commentary on the Súrah of Kawthar was publicly read and translated, and which culminated in the conversion of the Amír (the governor) and his family. It was this remarkably gifted woman who undertook the translation of the Báb's lengthy commentary on the Súrah of Joseph (the Qayyúmu'l-Asmá) for the benefit of her Persian co-religionists, and exerted her utmost to spread the knowledge and elucidate the contents of that mighty Book. It was her fearlessness, her skill, her organizing ability and her unquenchable enthusiasm which consolidated her newly won victories in no less inimical a center than Qasvín, which prided itself on the fact that no fewer than a hundred of the highest ecclesiastical leaders of Islám dwelt within its gates. It was she who, in the house of Bahá'u'lláh in Tihrán, in the course of her memorable interview with the celebrated Vahíd, suddenly interrupted his learned discourse on the signs of the new Manifestation, and vehemently urged him, as she held 'Abdu'l-Bahá, then a child, on her lap, to arise and demonstrate through deeds of heroism and self-sacrifice the depth and sincerity of his faith. It was to her doors, during the height of her fame and popularity in Tihrán, that the flower of feminine society in the capital flocked to hear her brilliant discourses on the matchless tenets of her Faith. It was the magic of her words which won the wedding guests away from the festivities, on the occasion of the marriage of the son of Mahmúd Khán-i-Kalántar—in whose house she was confined—and gathered them about her, eager to drink in her every word. It was her passionate and unqualified affirmation of the claims and distinguishing features of the new Revelation, in a series of seven conferences with the deputies of the Grand Vizir commissioned to interrogate her, which she held while confined in that same house, which finally precipitated the sentence of her death. It was from her pen that odes had flowed attesting, in unmistakable language, not only her faith in the Revelation of the Báb, but also her recognition of the exalted and as yet undisclosed mission of Bahá'u'lláh. And last but not least it was owing to her initiative, while participating in the Conference of Badasht,[1] that the most challenging implications of a revolutionary and as yet but dimly grasped Dispensation were laid bare before her fellow-disciples and the new Order permanently divorced from the laws and institutions of Islám. Such marvelous achievements were now to be crowned by, and attain their final consummation in, her martyrdom in the midst of the storm that was raging throughout the capital.

One night, aware that the hour of her death was at hand, she put on the attire of a bride, and anointed herself with perfume, and, sending for the wife of the Kalantar, she communicated to her the secret of her impending martyrdom, and confided to her last wishes. Then, closeting herself in her chambers, she awaited, in prayer and meditation, the hour which was to witness her reunion with her Beloved. She was pacing the floor of her room, chanting a litany expressive of both grief and triumph, when the farráshes of Azíz Khán-i-Sardár arrived, in the dead of night, to conduct her to the Ilkhání garden, which lay beyond the city gates, and which was to be the site of her martyrdom. When she arrived the Sardár was in the midst of a drunken debauch with his lieutenants, and was roaring with laughter; he ordered offhand that she be strangled at once and thrown into a pit. With that same silken kerchief which she had intuitively reserved for that purpose, and delivered in her last moments to the son of Kalantar who accompanied her, the death of this immortal heroine was accomplished. Her body was lowered into a well, which was then filled with earth and stones, in the manner she herself had desired.

Thus ended the life of this great Bábí heroine, the first woman suffrage martyr, who, at her death, turning to the one in whose custody she had been placed, had boldly declared: "You can kill me as soon as you like, but you cannot stop the emancipation of women." Her career was as dazzling as it was brief, as tragic as it was eventful. Unlike her fellow-disciples, whose exploits remained, for the most part unknown, and unsung by their contemporaries in foreign lands, the fame of this immortal woman was noised abroad, and traveling with remarkable swiftness as far as the capitals of Western Europe, aroused the enthusiastic admiration and evoked the ardent praise of men and women of divers nationalities, callings and cultures. Little wonder that 'Abdu'l-Bahá should have joined her name to those of Sarah, of Ásíyih, of the Virgin Mary and of Fátimih, who, in the course of successive Dispensations, have towered, by reason of their intrinsic merits and unique position, above the rank and file of their sex. "*In eloquence,*" 'Abdu'l-Bahá Himself has written, "*she was the calamity of the age, and in ratiocination the trouble of the world.*"[2] He, moreover, has described her as "*a brand afire with the love of God*" and "*a lamp aglow with the bounty of God.*"

Indeed the wondrous story of her life propagated itself as far and as fast as that of the Báb Himself, the direct Source of her inspiration. "Prodige de science, mais aussi prodige de beauté" is the tribute paid her by a noted commentator on the life of the Báb and His disciples.³ "The Persian Joan of Arc, the leader of emancipation for women of the Orient . . . who bore resemblance both to the mediaeval Heloise and the neo-platonic Hypatia,"⁴ thus was she acclaimed by a noted playwright whom Sarah Bernhardt had specifically requested to write a dramatized version of her life.⁵ "The heroism of the lovely but ill-fated poetess of Qasvín, Zarrín-Táj (Crown of Gold) . . ." testifies Lord Curzon of Kedleston, "is one of the most affecting episodes in modern history."⁶ "The appearance of such a woman as Qurratu'l-'Ayn," wrote the well-known British Orientalist, Prof. E. G. Browne, "is, in any country and any age, a rare phenomenon, but in such a country as Persia it is a prodigy—nay, almost a miracle. . . . Had the Bábí religion no other claim to greatness, this were sufficient . . . that it produced a heroine like Qurratu'l-'Ayn."⁷ "The harvest sown in Islámic lands by Qurratu'l-'Ayn," significantly affirms the renowned English divine, Dr. T. K. Cheyne, in one of his books, "is now beginning to appear . . . this noble woman . . . has the credit of opening the catalogue of social reforms in Persia. . . ."⁸ "Assuredly one of the most striking and interesting manifestations of this religion" is the reference to her by the noted French diplomat and brilliant writer, Comte de Gobineau. "In Qasvín," he adds, "she was held, with every justification, to be a prodigy." "Many people," he, moreover has written, "who knew her and heard her at different periods of her life have invariably told me . . . that when she spoke one felt stirred to the depths of one's soul, was filled with admiration, and was moved to tears."⁹ "No memory," writes Sir Valentine Chirol, "is more deeply venerated or kindles greater enthusiasm than hers, and the influence which she wielded in her lifetime still inures to her sex."¹⁰ "O Táhirih!" exclaims in his book on the Bábís the great author and poet of Turkey, Sulaymán Nazím Bey, "you are worth a thousand Násiri'd-Dín Sháhs!"¹¹ "The greatest ideal of womanhood has been Táhirih" is the tribute paid her by the mother of one of the Presidents of Austria, Mrs. Marianna Hainisch, ". . . I shall try to do for the women of Austria what Táhirih gave her life to do for the women of Persia."¹²

Many and divers are her ardent admirers who, throughout the five continents, are eager to know more about her. Many are those whose conduct has been ennobled by her inspiring example, who have committed to memory her matchless odes, or set to music her poems, before whose eyes glows the vision of her indomitable spirit, in whose hearts is enshrined a love and admiration that time can never dim, and in whose souls burns the determination to tread as dauntlessly, and with that same fidelity, the path she chose for herself, and from which she never swerved from the moment of her conversion to the hour of her death.

**Notes**

Reprinted from: *God Passes By* (Wilmette: Bahá'í Publishing Trust, 1999) pp. 72-77.

1. For Shoghi Effendi's description of the Conference at Badasht. See *God Passes By*, pp. 31-33.
2. 'Abdu'l-Bahá, *A Traveller's Narrative: Written to Illustrate the History of the Báb*; edited in the original Persian, and translated into English, with an introduction and explanatory notes by Edward G. Browne (Cambridge: The University Press, 1891) Vol. 2, p. 20.
3. A. L. M. Nicolas, *Seyyèd Ali Mohammed, dit le Bâb: histoire* (Paris: Dujarric, 1905) p. 273.
4. Jules Bois, "Babism and Bahaism," *Forum* (Concord, N.H.), Vol. 74 (July 1925) pp. 1-10.
5. Originally the playwright Catulle Mendès (1841-1909) was asked. When he failed to produce a script, the writer Jules Bois (1871-1943) was asked.
6. George Nathaniel Curzon, *Persia and the Persian Question* (London: Longmans, Green, 1892) Vol. 1, p. 497, note 2.
7. Edward Granville Browne in 'Abdu'l-Bahá, *A Traveller's Narrative*, Vol. 2, Note Q, p. 213.
8. T. K. Cheyne, *The Reconcilliation of Races and Religions* (London: A. & C. Black, 1914) pp. 114, 115.
9. Arthur, comte de Gobineau, *Les Religions et les Philosophies dans l'Asie Centrale* (Paris: Didier, 1865) pp. 136-137, 150. English translation in Emily McBride Perigord. *Translation of French Foot-Notes of the Dawn-Breakers* (Wilmette, Ill.: Bahá'í Publishing Trust, 1977) p. 76.
10. Valentin Chirol, *The Middle Eastern Question* (London: J. Murray, 1903) p. 124.
11. Süleyman Nazif, *Nasiruddin Shah ve Babiler* (Istanbul: Kanaat Kütuphanesi, 1923). English translation in: Süleyman Nazif, "Translation of Passages on Tahirih . . . pp. 35, 44-49" appendix to Necati Alkan, "Süleyman. Nazif's *Nasiruddin Shah ve Babiler*: An Ottoman Source on Babi-Baha'i History," *Research Notes in Shaykhi, Babi and Baha'i Studies*, Vol. 4, no. 2 (November, 2000). http://www.h-net.org/~bahai/notes/vol4/nazif.htm
12. Quoted in Martha L Root, *Táhirih the Pure, Iran's Greatest Woman* (Karachi: Root, 1938) p. 112. Reprinted as *Táhirih the Pure* (Los Angeles: Kalimát Press, 1981 [2000]). Marianne Hainisch (1839-1936) was the founder in 1901 of the Bund Österreichescher Frauenvereine and the mother of Michael Hainisch (1858-1940), President of Austria, 1920-1928.

# TÁHIRIH IN HISTORY
## Eastern Impressions

**WINTER INDOOR COSTUME**
of Persian women in the late nineteen century. The woman on the left holds a water pipe.

# Qurratu'l-'Ayn Táhirih in Urdu Literature

by Sabir Afaqi

Qurratu'l-'Ayn Táhirih occupies a noble station in the annuals of the history of the religions of the world. This matchless lady, who was given the title "Khatun-i 'Ajam" (The Lady of Persia) by Muhammad Iqbal, is that brave and courageous woman of the nineteenth century that rose from the horizon of Persia and captured the hearts and minds of the writers and poets with the perfection of her knowledge and distinction of her poetry. Both her friends and foes are admirers of her accomplishments and moral eminence.

In Urdu too, as in Persian, Arabic, English, and scores of other languages, much has been written on the personality and poetry of Táhirih. It is still being written.

Táhirih was a devoted teacher of a new religion and introduced a new poetry. She had such a deep knowledge of the Qur'an, the Holy Traditions, Islamic jurisprudence, and principles of religion that her contemporary ulama used to benefit from her. She was the daughter of a mujtahid (a doctor of religion), and had she not been a woman, she would herself have been a mujtahid.

"Khatun-i 'Ajam" was born in Qazvin, Persia, in 1819. In the bloom of her youth she became famous in other towns and cities of Persia for her learning and art. She accepted the Bábí religion and was among the first eighteen souls who had accepted the Báb and were given the title of "The Letters of the Living." She acquired Islamic education and knowledge in Qazvin and in Iraq and taught her newfound Faith in Baghdad, Kirmanshah, Qazvin, Tehran, and Mazandaran. She was made to suffer imprisonment for seven years before she was martyred (strangled to death) in the Ílkhání garden of Tehran in 1852. Then she was thrown into a dry well and covered with dust and stones. Her last words to her executioners were: *"You can kill me as soon as you like, but you cannot stop the emancipation of women."*[1]

Táhirih is the first woman who raised the call for the liberation of women and the equality of men and women in Asia. Her family, Baraghání, was famous for learning and accomplishments during the Qájár dynasty. Three brothers of this family—Mullá Muhammad Taqí, Mullá Muhammad Sálih, and Mullá Muhammad 'Alí were not only renowned and learned but also mujtahids of their time.

Qurratu'l-'Ayn was the daughter of Hájí Mullá Sálih Baraghání. After she completed her education, Táhirih was married to her first cousin Mullá Muhammad. This resulted in the birth of two sons and one daughter. The daughter passed away after the martyrdom of her mother—Táhirih. A grandson of Táhirih's son, Sheikh Muhammad Ismail was a famous Bahá'í poet named Nematullah Warta (d. 1342 A.H.). Warta's mother was Sheik Muhammad Ismail's daughter Masooma Khanum. Another son of Táhirih, Muhammad Ibrahim, went to Iraq and became a famous religious scholar.

Táhirih is a matchless lady of that age. She earned the admiration of the famous personalities of the East and of the West for her genius and prudence, her courage and boldness, her knowledge and sobriety.

Táhirih, who was an embodiment of piety, chastity, and dignity, was equally praised by Sayyid 'Alí Muhammad (the Báb), Bahá'u'lláh, 'Abdu'l-Bahá, and Shoghi Effendi.

One can see how famous Táhirih is by the fact that in almost all the books written, in any language, on the history of Persia, on the Bábí movement, or about women's liberation we can find references to Táhirih. Among the famous persons of the West who have mentioned Táhirih with great admiration and respect, the names of Lord Curzon,[2] Joseph Arthur, comte de Gobineau,[3] Prof. T. K. Cheyne,[4] Sir Francis Edward Younghusband,[5] Arminius Vambery,[6] Edward Granville Browne,[7] A.-L.-M. Nicolas,[8] Martha L. Root,[9] Laura Dreyfus Barney,[10] Clara A. Edge,[11] Alessandro Bausani,[12] Marzieh

Gail,[13] John S. Hatcher,[14] Jan Rypka,[15] and Annemarie Schimmel[16] are worth mentioning.

In the Indo-Pakistan subcontinent the names of Muhammad Iqbal,[17] Sheikh Abdul Qadir,[18] Khavaja Hasan Nizami,[19] Suleman Nazim Beg, Sarojini Naidu,[20] M. Hidayat Hossein,[21] 'Abdulhalím Sharar,[22] Aziz Ahmad,[23] Zahír Káshmírí,[24] Habib Jalib,[25] Jamílah Háshmí,[26] Intezar Husain,[27] Abr Ahsani Ginnaori,[28] Ra'is Amrahvi,[29] and Kishvar Nahid[30] top the list of the famous persons who were impressed by the life and poetry of Táhirih.

The life and poetry of Táhirih has influenced many of the writers, poets and academics of the Indo-Pakistan subcontinent. Right from the very beginning of this century, the poetry of Táhirih captured the hearts of the educated section of the people of the subcontinent. Her poetry has been a source of courage and hope for every courageous and devoted woman.

Qurratu'l-'Ayn was a great scholar, an enchanting debater, and a penetrating poetess. She had equal command of Persian, Arabic, and Turkish. She used to communicate, through letters, with her contemporary religious scholars on issues of philosophy and spirituality in these languages. Alas! Like most of her poetic works, most of these letters and communications have been lost. However, some of these letters have been preserved in the book *Tarikh-i Zuhúru'l-Haqq*.[31] These letters are some of those written to the Bábu'l-Báb, Mullá Husayn-i Bushrú'í (1813-1849); to the Mufti of Baghdad, Mullá Javád-i Qazvíní; and to Hájí Karím-i Kirmání. All of these letters are in fluent Arabic and Persian.

Qurratu'l-'Ayn Táhirih became famous in the world due to her knowledge and certitude; her devotion and sobriety; her sacredness and purity; her chastity and modesty; her writings and poetry; her courage and boldness; her high morality and sweet words; her beauty and charm; her patience and steadfastness, and last but not the least for her martyrdom.

There were more than a hundred clerics present in Qazvin at the time of Táhirih. But they were helpless before her knowledge and couldn't defeat her. She fought the learned in her own family. She criticized the beliefs that were current in her society. She started inviting people by announcing the advent of the long awaited Mahdi in Karbala, which was a center of knowledge and spirituality. She was imprisoned. She was stoned. She was banished. She was declared an infidel. Her belongings were looted. She was offered the position of Queen of Persia. But Táhirih was neither perplexed by these atrocities nor tempted by those offers of power and position. She rather became triumphant by defeating death. It is this very courage and steadfastness where lies the secret of her greatness.

In the poetry of Táhirih there is light and thunder, like that of lightening, and roar and flow, like that of a stream that comes down from uphill during the rainy season. In fact, she is the founder of a new cadence and inventor of a new mode of poetic expression. This cadence and mode of expression has become characteristic of Bábí, and later of Bahá'í, poetry. Táhirih's poetry is the witness of the vastness of her outlook, the sincerity of her art, the force of her utterances, and the depth of her feelings.

Táhirih was a preacher and a promoter of modernism in society. In poetry, she also seems to be a supporter of experiments and changes. In the light of these examples, we can regard Táhirih as the founder of modern Persian poetry, a poetry that was perfected by later generations of poets in Iran. Modern Persia has produced four great poetesses Qurratu'l-'Ayn Táhirih, Simin Bahbahani (b. 1924), Parvin E'tesamii (1906-1941), and Forough Farrukhzad (1938-1967). But Táhirih's stature is very high among them. No sooner is her name mentioned before us than our eyes are filled with twinkling stars and our heads instinctively bow in respect and devotion for her.

The abandonment of rites, the promotion of new positive values, the unity of humankind, the enlightenment of women, and the establishment of world peace were the high ideals and pious values for which Táhirih offered up her life.

Before presenting a review of the impact of Táhirih's life and poetry on Urdu literature, let us ponder a while on this point: What is the reason that Táhirih has earned such fame in the world at large, and particularly in the subcontinent? This is a question that is frequently asked whenever I deliver a lecture on Táhirih, or whenever I have some article or essay published on her life and work. There may be many reasons for this popularity. However the more I ponder this question, the more it becomes evident to me that the following are some very distinct reasons:

(1) During the Mogul period, close literary and cultural relations were established

between Persia and the subcontinent. In the Mogul period, dozens of Persian poets visited India and were received with much honor and love in literary circles. It is in keeping with the same cultural norm that when Táhirih's name and poems reached India around 1880, the poets and writers of India received that poetess with reverence and welcomed her poetry eagerly.

(2) Other than the Mogul Princess Zebunnisa Makhfi (1638-1702), Persia and the subcontinent had not produced till 1819, any poetess worth mentioning. When Táhirih's voice rang in that vacuum, it attracted all lovers of poetry and literature and everyone recognized and admired her greatness.

(3) Martyrdom has remained a symbol of pride and honor in all ages and in every religion. The dazzling example of the martyrdom of al-Husayn ibn Mansur Hallaj (858-922) in Baghdad and Sarmad Shahid (1618-1660) in the subcontinent remains in the consciousness of the people. When Táhirih offered up her life and retraced the path set by those martyrs, both the Arab and non-Arab world became attracted to her.

(4) If a person is not prominent and his mission is not great his martyrdom does not become a big event or tragedy. But Táhirih was a great scholar and poetess of her age. She had the mission of the renewal of the world in front of her, and her martyrdom took place in very tragic circumstances. All these three elements have made her live forever. She has become immortal.

(5) In Eastern society, a woman is a symbol of timidity. No great accomplishment or sacrifice is expected of her. It is common to say about a timid man that he bears a womanish heart. In this society Táhirih offered up her life for a great and noble Cause. This courage and sacrifice became another reason for the fame of Táhirih.

(6) It has always been a cherished dream of men to become king, and for women, to become queen. People have always tried hard to gain that position, even at the cost of their honor and prestige. But Táhirih's was a different case. The shah of Persia invited her to become his queen, but she refused to accept it. This detachment and contentment also attracted the heart of the people, and they became admirers of Táhirih.

(7) Another reason of Táhirih's station being so distinct is that she was among the first eighteen souls who had welcomed and embraced the new religion. Thus she no longer remained just a poetess, but was elevated to a position of holiness and sanctity. These qualities helped in making her popular and revered.

(8) A further reason of her fame in the subcontinent may be that when Bahá'í teachers from Iran visited this land beginning in the early nineteenth century, they did, perhaps, use the poems of Táhirih as an introduction and expanded on this base their presentation of the Bahá'í Faith. Thus Táhirih became famous as a poetess among the educated and literary circles of the subcontinent. Rather, it can be safely said that Táhirih was more famous than the Faith itself on the Indo-Pakistan subcontinent.

(9) The great philosopher-poet Iqbal was an admirer of Táhirih, and he mentioned her name with deep adoration in one of his collections *Javed Namah*[32] and quoted a full poem of hers in that book. This gesture of Iqbal's produced two benefits: Iqbal became famous among Bahá'ís, and Táhirih gained fame through the *Javed Namah*.

However, in my view the greatest reason for Táhirih's fame and popularity is her poetry. She was not a professional poet, i.e., she was not like other poets who engage in thinking over their poems for hours and collect them into a book. Rather, she was a natural poet. Whenever her love for the Báb and longing for the new Cause of God inspired her, she would express herself in songs. She has composed poems and odes. She could easily compose poems in Arabic, Persian, and Turkish. A few years back a non-Bahá'í researcher in Baku, Azerbaijan published in her book some of poems of Táhirih in the Turkish language.[33]

The period of Táhirih was a time of carnage, spoliation, and terror. It is understood that the enemies of the Faith destroyed most of her poems. But the two-dozen poems and odes that have been saved for posterity are so deep in meaning, zealous in style, and fluent in language that an equal to them can hardly be found in the whole of Persian poetry. This is why the lovers of poetry in Iran, Pakistan, India, Bangladesh, Afghanistan, and Kashmir have placed her poems and odes close to their hearts. Like the couplets of Baba Tahir Uryan (d. 1019?), the poems of Táhirih became commonplace. Some jealous men in Iran, having noted this popularity and fame of Táhirih, started saying and writing that some of the odes and poems ascribed to Táhirih are not her creations. However, they could not prove to which poet or poetess they belonged. If they are from any other poet, then why did they not become famous with his or her own name?

I believe that the thing that has given fame and prestige to Táhirih and kept her alive is her great poetry, her love for the newborn Faith, and her martyrdom for her mission.

The living and strong spirit of Táhirih, is even today, inspiring millions of Bahá'í men and women who are engaged, hand in hand, in promoting world peace, the unity of humanity, and prosperity for all. As Iqbal said:

> Behold the light of Táhirih in the cities and deserts.
> Don't think that she has left this world.

It was around 1870, when a few Bábís came to Bombay (today Mumbai), India, and started teaching the new Faith. It is through them that the name of Táhirih started gaining fame on the subcontinent for its association with the Báb and his movement. The grace of her personality, the greatness of her character, her poetry, and her martyrdom made Qurratu'l-'Ayn Táhirih a much loved and admired figure in the eyes of the learned circles of the subcontinent.

The first mention of Qurratu'l-'Ayn Táhirih is found in the account of Persian poets compiled by 'Abdulghafur Nassakh (1834-1889). This book, titled *Tazakaratu'l-Ma'asareen*, was published in Calcutta. Táhirih was martyred in 1852. Thus one may deduct that her name and poetry reached Calcutta in just thirty-seven years. The book *Tazakaratu'l-Ma'asareen* was compiled alphabetically and published only once. At present one copy of that book is preserved in the Dhaka University Library, and a second copy is the property of Dr. Jamil Jalebi (of Karachi). Dr Jalebi has graciously provided me with a photocopy of page 193 of that book for which I am thankful to him. Nassakh writes: "Tooti was a woman famous as Qurratu'l-'Ayn Babi a follower of Mohammad Ali the Bab . . ." It is noteworthy that Nassakh identifies Táhirih as "Tooti" and the name of Sayyid 'Alí Muhammad as "Mohammad Ali."[34]

According to my research, the first researcher who wrote about Táhirih on the subcontinent was Prof. M. Hidayat Hossein, the secretary of the Royal Asiatic Society, Calcutta. His article was published in the *Journal of the Asiatic Society of Bengal*. It is said that the professor had also written a separate book on the Bahá'í Faith.

One of the Letters of the Living (the first disciples of the Báb) was Shaykh Sa'íd-i Hindí of Multan. But apart from him there are also other teachers who visited India from the beginning of the Bábí Movement (1844). Some of the teachers who visited the Indo-Pakistan subcontinent from 1844 to 1920, were Jamal Effendi, Mírzá Mahmúd-i Zarqání, Munir Nabil Zadeh-i Ghazvini, and Mirza Mahram. Mirza Mahram was among the friends of Maulana Abul Kalam Azad (1888-1958)—the famous learned politician of India. Maulana Azad used to say: "I have learnt the art of using appropriate verses and stanzas from poetic works in appropriate occasions, from Mirza Mahram."

In the year 1902, Mírzá Mahmúd-i Zarqání visited Lahore and started teaching the Bahá'í Faith. His residence was in the Anarkali district. Thus Muhammad Iqbal soon came into contact with him, and they became good friends. It was through Zarqání that Iqbal came to know about Táhirih and her poetry. By the year 1915, Táhirih's poems had reached several countries of the world. Therefore, Martha Root (1872-1939) writes: "In whichever country I went before my visit to Iran I noticed that people knew about Táhirih."[35] It is worth mentioning that Root was a famous Bahá'í scholar and teacher. She traveled throughout world and delivered lectures on the Bahá'í Faith at over four hundred universities.

Root first visited the subcontinent in the year 1915, but she passed through Mumbai (then called Bombay) and returned through Rangoon (present name: Yangon). During the period between 1915 and 1930, several persons in the subcontinent wrote about Táhirih. One of them is Maulana 'Abdulhalím Sharar (1860-1926). The Maulana wrote a booklet in Urdu titled *Qurratu'l-Ayn*.[36] He, after quoting Táhirih's verses, writes:

> These are a few verses of the Zarrin Taj (Táhirih). You will not find any match of this taste even if you go through the all the pages of all the collections of Persian poetry. What a zeal, what a taste, what a fluency and maturity is found in them? What an exalted thought and what a grandeur is present in these verses? You name a poetic quality and it is present with all its perfection in her poetry.[37]

In 1930, Martha Root visited Iran and completed her paper on the life, poetry, and accomplishments of her beloved poetess Qurratu'l-'Ayn Táhirih. This American lady reached Karachi in June 1930, from Persia and stayed here for four months. During this period Isfandyár Bakhtiyárí of Karachi had a collection of several odes of Táhirih printed under the title of *Tuhfah-i Tahirah* and widely distributed it.

Root, along with Isfandyár Bakhtiyárí and Prof. Pritam Singh (1881-1959) of Dial Singh College, Lahore, met the famous poet-philosopher Muhammad Iqbal and presented him with a copy of *Tuhfah-i Tahirah*. Let it be remembered that both Prof. Pritam Singh and Dr. Muhammad Iqbal were from the same city (Sialkot) and were good friends. There friendly relations continued till Iqbal's death in 1938.

Root met Iqbal for the second time on 24 June 1930. Bakhtiyárí writes that Iqbal seemed happier this time. He showed deep reverence to this American lady, and they had a long conversation. It was during this conversation that the poet Iqbal said that he wanted to mention Táhirih in a book he was writing. Later on, he mentioned Táhirih in his book *Javed Namah* (published in 1932) with much reverence and included in it one of her famous *ghazals* that starts with the verse: "*Gar ba to uftadam mazar chehre-ba-chere, ru-ba-ru*" (If I were to meet you face to face . . .).[38]

Iqbal, in the journey he recounts in *Javed Namah*, passes through the skies of the Moon, Mercury, Venus, and Mars; he reaches the planet Jupiter; and comes into contact with three glorious souls—Mansur Hallaj, Ghalib, and Qurratu'l-Ayn Táhirih. The restlessness and revolutionary spirit in each of these three souls impressed Iqbal very much. Iqbal beautifully portrays the details of this journey. In brief, he stood before these three holy souls, who had a fire in their hearts that could consume the earth. They wore red dresses, and their faces were glowing. These personalities were glorious and intoxicated with the wine of their own songs. On that occasion Iqbal's guide, Maulana Rumi calls him and says:

> You should also be resurrected through the souls of these passionate singers. If you have not seen passion (wine), behold it now; and if you have not witnessed the power of "Sahba," then experience it here. Mirza Ghalib, Hallaj, and Táhirih have filled the atmosphere of the enclosure with agitation. Their songs bestow constancy to the souls because their songs drive their heat from the universe of inner-heat.

Iqbal is a national poet who speaks of progress and sacrifice. This is why he pays homage to Ghalib, Hallaj, and Táhirih.[39] Continuing on, he says that owing to the new courage of a person with enthusiasm, a new universe is coming into being. His unbound passion and love is tearing down veils, removing the scenes of ancient hoariness. His presence can be witnessed in the cities and villages:

> Think you not Táhirih has left this world.
> Rather she is present in the very conscience of her age.

In 1930 Root met, besides Iqbal, many other famous personalities of the subcontinent, such as Sir Abdul Qadir, Sarojini Naidu, Mirza Qalich Beg (1853-1929), Sir Tej Bahadur Sapru (1875-1949), Rabindranath Tagore (1861-1941), and Bhupendrasingh

Rajindersingh, the Maharaja of Patiala (1891-1938). In that very year Root also visited Kashmir and Burma. She writes: "Many learned persons of India have memorized verses of Táhirih."

Root visited the subcontinent for the third time in 1937-1938. During this visit, she printed three thousand copies of her English book *Táhirih the Pure* and distributed them free. She posted many copies of this book to the scholars of the East and the West. Then the late Abbas Ali Butt translated this book into Urdu. His translation was first published in Delhi before the establishment of Pakistan. The second edition was published in Karachi in 1966. The third edition was also published in Karachi in 1974. I have included in the third edition some more poems of Táhirih and translated them into Urdu.[40]

Much has been written about Táhirih in various languages of the Indo-Pakistan subcontinent. It is not possible to collect all these references in this article. In 1933, a conference was held by Idara-i Ma'arif-i Islamia Lahore. Prof. M. Hidayat Hossein of Calcutta presented a research paper in English in that conference. Its title was "The Female Martyr of the Bábí Faith."[41] A famous Urdu writer and researcher Prof. Aziz Ahmad (d. 1978) has written a story titled "Zarrin Taj." It was published in the monthly *Savera* of Lahore. In that story, Ahmad says in the words of Zarrin Taj (i.e., Táhirih): "I am Zarrin Taj—a woman of Persia who is borne once in centuries and surprises the men."[42] A dramatic presentation of this story was broadcast by Radio Pakistan, Rawalpindi, in 1963.

Prof. Mohammad Ishaque of Calcutta had written a book in English entitled *Four Eminent Poetesses of Iran*. This book was published in Calcutta in 1950.[43] The writer and historian of Pakistan, Maulana Ghulam Rasul Mihr (1895-1971) has mentioned Táhirih in his book *Matalib-i Zarb-i Kalim*.[44]

Another writer Akhtar Aziz writes in his book, *Larkian Jo Mashhoor Hu'in* (The women who became famous):

> In such an age, a brilliant and talented lady was born in Iran. This lady was besides her other qualities, the foremost poetess of Iran. In her verse is found a flow like that of the verses of the Qaani. But in respect of magnificenct words, zeal and passion, she is far superior to Qaani. As long as the Persian language loves, her name will endure.[45]

The poetry of Qurratu'l-'Ayn has also affected the high clergy. For example, Maulana Anwar Shah Kashmiri (d. 1933) of the religious school Dar al-'Ulum at Deoband has written a *ghazal* in the style of Táhirih.⁴⁶

Aneesa Kirmani wrote an article titled "Zarrin Taj—Quratu'l-'Ayn" in which she recounted the incident in which the King of Persia, Násiru'd-Dín Sháh, wrote a letter telling Táhirih that he wanted to make her his queen. Táhirih showed such courage and strength that she wrote this verse from one of her poems on the back of the letter of the king and returned it to him:

> Thou and thine kingdom, pomp and kingship,
> me the ways and means of hermits;
> If that be good, keep it for yourself,
> and if this be bad, its my lot.⁴⁷

The monthly *Sang-i Meel* of Karachi has published, in one of its 1964 issues, a poem by Pervez Wasti that is in the style of one of Táhirih's famous poems.⁴⁸ Shad Kashmiri, the editor of *Nawa-i Kashmir* (Gujranwala) has written a eulogy in the memory of Táhirih Qurrat'ul-'Ayn that consists of twenty-two verses. In 1962, the poet Azim Qureshi paid his tribute to three great poetesses—Sifu, Meera Bai (1500-1546), and Qurratu'l-'Ayn in a publication issued in Peshawar.⁴⁹

The famous short story writer Sheikh Manzoor Elahi wrote a story "Qurratu'l-'Ayn." It was first published in the monthly *Naqoosh* (Lahore) in 1965,⁵⁰ and then in the collection of his essays *Dard-e-Dilkusha*.⁵¹

Dr. Inam'ul-Haque Kaosar wrote an informative article entitled "Qurratu'l-'Ayn Táhirih " and had it published in the daily *Imroze* (Lahore) in 1966. In this article, it is mentioned that the great philosopher-poet Iqbal was much impressed by the zeal and love of Táhirih. In fact he recognized the reflection of his ideals of self and love in her life. Iqbal termed Táhirih as "Sahib-i Junun" (one intoxicated with love) who has caused the sea of life to surge, has broken the false idols of religion, and presented the philosophy of progress. Iqbal counted the "Khatoon-i Ajam" as the best example of the women of the world.⁵² Likewise the interpreter of Iqbal's verses, Prof. Yúsuf Salím Chishtí, writes: "Táhirih did not love any mortal human being rather she continued teaching her Faith till her last breath."

The monthly *Saiyara Digest* published in August 1968, an article written by Siraj Nizami. The writer has portrayed the life of Táhirih and praised her poetry and services for the Bábí religion.[53] In the Urdu Encyclopedia of Islam (*Urdu da'irah-i ma'arif-i Islamiya*), published in 1964, details regarding the life of Qurratu'l-'Ayn have been given.[54]

The well-known Bahá'í poet Abr Ahsani Ginnauri Badayuni, who was a guide to hundreds of poets in the subcontinent, was a great admirer of Táhirih. One of his poems on Táhirih has been published in the *Bahá'í Magazine* (Lahore).[55] Ghulamali Ismail Naji has recorded the events of the life of Táhirih in his book *Zihra Bano* (Karachi, 1972).[56] Another well-known Bahá'í poet and journalist, the late Sayyid Mahfúzulhaq 'Ilmí, has translated one of the poems of Táhirih into Urdu.[57]

Memorial meetings on the life and work of Táhirih are held in different towns and places of Pakistan in which researchers and poets present their views to enrich the knowledge of their audiences. The report of such a gathering that was held on 22 February 1976 in Karachi has been published in the *Bahá'í Magazine*. Famous writers such as Dr. Ghulam Sarwar (b. 1926), Shan'ul-Haq Haqqi (b. 1917), Dr. Alia Imam, and Prof. Sahar Ansari were present in that gathering to pay their tribute to Táhirih.

My younger brother Mukhlis Vijdani, who himself is a poet in the Urdu and Gorji languages, has translated one of the famous poems of Táhirih into Urdu. This translation was published in *Wah Karigar*, June 1969 issue.[58] Vijdani has also written a poem about Táhirih.

Dr. Syed Chiragh Hussain Shah of Peshawar has written a book on Táhirih and Iqbal, *Iqbal Aur Qurratu'l-'Ayn*.[59] M. Ghulam Mustafa (Saqib Hazeen) (b. 1930) has written a book *Bábí wa Bahá'í* in which he has discussed the poetry of Táhirih.[60] The great Urdu poet, the late Ra'is Amrahvi, has written a poem in the pattern of a famous poem by Táhirih, and it is included in his collection.[61] Likewise the famous poet of Pakistan John Elia (b. 1931) has also translated a poem of Táhirih into Urdu. John Elia is a lover of Táhirih's poetry and admirer of her personality. He has written about this in the forward to the collection of his own works *Sháyad*.[62]

A student at the Department of Literature of the University of the Punjab, Sayyeda Akhtar Sultana, has mentioned Táhirih Qurratu'l-

'Ayn in her Master's thesis. This thesis is entitled *Makalamat-e Iqbal Ka Tajzia* (An analysis of Iqbal's conversations).⁶³ Another student of the same University of the Punjab, Khanum Asmat Afza, has mentioned Táhirih in her paper on "The Perspectives of Women in the Ideological System of Iqbal" (in Urdu).⁶⁴ A. D. Baloch presented his Master's thesis to the University of the Punjab titled "Iqbal and Iran."⁶⁵ One can find details regarding Táhirih's life in this thesis. All these three papers are unpublished, but are available at the Library of the University of the Punjab.⁶⁶

'Abulqasim Rafiq Dilavari has written about Táhirih in the second volume of his book *Á'imah-yi tablís* and included five of her poems. Dilavari has praised the eloquence, maturity, high thoughts, and glorious words of Táhirih.⁶⁷ In the April 1980 issue of the *Al-Ilim* (Karachi), a poem by Hakim Matiur Rahman Qureshi was published. The title of the poem is "Tazmeen bar Qurratu'l-'Ayn Baha'i." This is actually a poem written on the style of one of Táhirih's most famous poems "*Gar ba to uftadam nazar . . .*"⁶⁸ Sayyid Amjad Altaf has written a *naat* (a poem to praise the Prophet Muhammad) in the style of the same poem of Táhirih.⁶⁹

The Bahá'í community of Lahore published a booklet entitled *Tajalli* in 1974.⁷⁰ A brief but useful essay regarding the life of Táhirih is included in that booklet. Jamílah Háshmí has written a novel *Chihra bachihrah rúbarú* on the tumultuous life of Táhirih. A poem of Táhirih appears on the cover of the book, written in the hand of the famous artist Sadiqain.⁷¹ Maqbool Anwar Dawudi has mentioned Táhirih in his book *Matalib-i Iqbal*.⁷² A famous poet of Pakistan, Tabish Dihlavi (b. 1911), has beautifully translated a poem of Táhirih's into Urdu, and published it in *Hashr Badaman* (Karachi, 1982).

S. M. 'Umar Fáruq (b. 1915) dedicated his book *Tavásín-i Iqbál* to Shaykh Bashir Ahmad by quoting a verse from a poem of Táhirih.⁷³ The well-known poet and writer Prof. Shaukat Wasti, referring to Táhirih in his autobiography *Kahta hun Sac* (1995), writes:

> . . . Qurratu'l-'Ayn has imbued such romance and freshness into Persian poetry that the account of this movement is still alive in the literary discourse.⁷⁴

In the Urdu encyclopedia published by Firozsanz in 1984 Táhirih Qurratu'l-'Ayn is mentioned under the letter "Qaf." The compilers comment: "To summarize she was matchless in the art of poetry."[75]

This writer (Sabir Afaqi) in his long poem "Talu-i-Sahar" (1985)[76] has written some verses to pay tribute to Táhirih. The *Nigár-í Pákistán* of Karachi has published my detailed article in Urdu on the life and works of Táhirih.[77]

Laura Clifford Barney (1879-1974) was a famous Bahá'í writer living in France. She wrote a play titled *God's Heroes*[78] (Paris, 1910). This play consists of five acts, and it depicts the story of Táhirih's life and her tragic death. Sadiqulkhair has translated it into Urdu with the title of *Hashr Badaman*.[79]

Distinguished short story writer Intezar Hussain has written about Táhirih's poetry in his comments on *Hashr Badaman* in his column in the daily *Mashriq* (Lahore).[80] Habib Jalib was one of the most popular poets of Pakistan, who wrote for the common people. He has compiled his poetry under the title *Harf-i Sar-idar* (Words spoken on the cross). This compilation was published simultaneously in London and Lahore. He writes:

> For a long time I wanted to write about poets who stood to fight the anti-people rulers, for example Qurratu'l-'Ayn Táhirih and those poets of Qajar dynasty who said when burning candles were being forced into the holes made in his flesh: "Happy that lover who knows not whether he should lay down his turban or head."

Habib Jalib calls himself a poet of the order of Mansur Hallaj and Qurratu'l-'Ayn. He has used several verses from the *ghazals* of Táhirih as the titles of his poems.[81]

Prof. Jagannath Azad, an authority on Iqbal writes in the narrative of his travels in America titled *Kolambas ke das men* (In the country of Columbus):

> When I reached the Mashriqu'l-Adhkar of Chicago, I was charmed by the atmosphere and freshness of its gardens. My friend Iftekhar Nasim chanted for me the poem of Qurratu'l-'Ayn Táhirih "*Gar ba tu Uftadam Nazar . . .*" and I lost myself in its melody and felt the same feeling that she cherished for the founder of the Bahá'í Faith.[82]

The detailed dissertation of Prof. Mohammad Irshad was published in the monthly *Fanun* (Lahore) in two installments. The title was *"Du Aahu-i Tishna Dar Namakzaar—Habatia and Qurratu'l-'Ayn"* (Two thirsty deers in the saline land—Hypatia and Qurratu'l-'Ayn). Irshad has compared the life and beliefs of Hypatia of Egypt (d. 415 A.D.) with those of Qurratu'l-'Ayn of Persia. He writes:

> Qurratu'l-'Ayn was highly accomplished in Arabic and Persian poetry although her poetic life was no longer than five years. It was not necessary for her to practice, poetic verses were revealed to her. And Ghalib was her contemporary. But she said such verses that are in no way inferior to those of Maulana Rumi in impromptu-ness and simplicity, ecstasy and control. Some of her poems are in Persian, the others in simple and fluent Arabic and yet some are in Arabic-influenced Persian.[83]

Dr. Muhammad Riyáz writes in his book *Jávednáma: Tahqíq o tauzíh* (*Javed Namah*: research and exposition)[84] that the courage and sacrifice of Táhirih had attracted and impressed Iqbal. In the collection of the poetry of Siyyid Qamar Hashmi there are poems in which tribute has been paid to some great personalities of the subcontinent. Among those personalities are included Amir Khursaw Dihlavi of Delhi (1253-1325), Shah Abdul Latif Bhitai (1689-1752), Táhirih, Ghalib (1796-1869), and Iqbal. It is important to note that Qamar Hashmi has placed the poem on Táhirih just following Amir Khursaw Dihlavi of Delhi and Shah Abdul Latif Bhitai. He printed a portrait of Táhirih in the book. I asked the late Qamar Hashmi about the source of this portrait. He said that he had obtained it from a museum in France.[85]

The *Sang-i Meel* published in 1988, a collection of analytical essays of Prof. Dr Sohail Ahmad under the title of *Tarfain*. In one of his analyses of the stories of Aziz Ahmad, he writes specially on Aziz Ahmad's story "Zarrin Taj." He writes that "Zarrin Taj is well loved among these stories, and the reason for its popularity is that it depicts an episode that is known. Queen Noor Jahan and Qurratu'l-'Ayn are already fully present in our consciousness."[86]

Distinguished writer and dictionary compiler Nasim Amrohvi (1908-1987) writes in *Farhang-i Iqbal* that Iqbal has chosen Qurratu'l-'Ayn Táhirih to be one of his "great souls" because she was so steadfast and staunch in her beliefs that she lost her life but did not recant her faith. Táhirih was peerless in her learning and mental capacities. Her literary station is very high.[87]

Mirza Maqbúl Beg Badakhshání writes in his *Adab námah-yi Írán*: "The verses of Qurratu'l-'Ayn are the best examples of fluency and maturity."[88]

My elder brother Maulana Abdul Rahim Nadeem is a cleric and poet in the Urdu and Gojri languages. He has written a poem on Táhirih. Short story writer and critic Dr. Akhtar Hussain Raipuri (1912-1992), who had lived in Tehran for a few years during his service with UNICEF, said in his autobiography *Gard-i Rah* that he had collected information on the famous Persian poetess Qurratu'l-'Ayn Táhirih and was very much impressed by it.[89] Kabir Ahmad Jai'si (b. 1936) has copied a poem of the famous Iranian poet, Abul Qasim Lahuti (1887-1957), which was written in the style of one of Táhirih's Arabic poems. Lahuti wrote this poem in Tabríz in 1922. Jai'si writes:

> When we read this poem we feel that somewhere in the back of the mind of Lahooti lies that poem of Qurratu'l-'Ayn some verses of which are being quoted here. In spite of the similarity of style the differences noticed in the verses of Qurratu'l-'Ayn and Lahooti is due to the differences in the personalities. Like Lahooti, Táhirih also did her utmost for what she felt was right. Due to this attitude she became a target of wrath of the clerics of the Qajar King and at last was killed. It is an interesting fact that seventy-one years after Táhirih's murder Lahooti is bringing the memory of Táhirih's song to life.[90]

Masaud Javed has written an article "Khatoon-i Ajam" that has been published in the monthly *Rujhan* (Karachi, 1991). Masaud Javed writes:

> Táhirih is a shining gem among the poets of Iran. She has impressed the poets and writers right up to now. She has endeared a world due to the warmth of her speech and depth of her knowledge. Umm-i-Salma Qurratu'l-'Ayn Táhirih Zarrin Taj of the nineteenth century who was born in the land of Persia is far more astonishing than Joan of Arc . . .[91]

Renowned critic and journalist Dr. Mohammad Ali Siddiqui (b. 1938) writes in the daily *Dawn* (Karachi):

> Táhirih is the first bearer of the standard of the equality of man and woman

in the nineteenth century. There would be seldom any poet of the Urdu language who would have not said a poem following the style of Táhirih.[92]

Khálid Sharíf is a well-known poet. The study of the third edition of his poetic collection, titled *Nárasá'í*, shows that the poet read Táhirih's works and was impressed by them.[93] The late Karam Haideri (b. 1918) writes in the introduction of the collective work *Nuquoosh Arzu* (compiled by Raisuddin Tahoor Jaferi): "There are two names in the Persian language—Baba Tahir and Qurratu'l-'Ayn Táhirih—that will shine forever in the skies of literature and poetry."

Sáqib Razmí has given, in his book *Ázádí-yi nisvánkánayá saverá* (Dawn of the liberation of women),[94] a message in the voice of Táhirih. The learned writer of the book *Iqbal aur aorat* (Iqbal and women), Khádim 'Alí Jáved, has included an essay by Prof. Jilani Kamran (Ghulam Jilani) (b. 1926) in which tribute has been paid to Qurratu'l-'Ayn Táhirih.[95] Nilam Farzanah in her book *Urdú adab kí ahamkhavátín návil nigár* (The women who became famous novelists) mentions Táhirih with reference to Jamila Hashmi's novel.[96]

A poet from Sialkot, Asim Sahbai, has written a poem in praise of Táhirih and read it in a memorial meeting for Táhirih. It is published in my book *Khátún-i 'ajam*. Renowned poet, writer, critic, and journalist Shabnam Romani has sent me a very beautiful poem on Táhirih that has been published in my above-mentioned book.

In the evening of 19 April 1993, a meeting was held in Hotel Avari in Lahore to commemorate "Táhirih Day." Prof. Mohammad Akram Ekram, Prof. Zahooruddin Ahmad, Saira Hashmi, Kaleem Akhtar, and others read papers on the personality, mission, and poetry of Qurratu'l-'Ayn Táhirih. I read my paper titled "*Khatoon-i Ajam aur Iqbal*." The chief guest of this function was Dr. Javed Iqbal (b. 1924). He gave a very impressive lecture. He said that Asia has not yet produced a lady as great as Táhirih. Recounting the events leading to her martyrdom, Javed Iqbal was carried away by emotion and the eyes of the audience also became wet. Khahid Ahmad writes about this seminar:

> Dr. Annemarie Schimmel had quite recently delivered a lecturer on the personality of Táhirih with reference to the collection titled *Javed Namah of Iqbal* in the University of Bonn. I told her that Dr. Javed Iqbal has recently given a lecture regarding Táhirih in Lahore which is a very bold

step considering our circumstances. Dr. Schimmel said that Dr. Javed Iqbal was due in Bonn shortly and that she would have an exchange of ideas on his lecture. I informed her that in Pakistan even orthodox Muslim women are very much admirers of Táhirih, but they do not express their views openly . . ."

In the August 1994 issue of the *Qaomi Digest* (Lahore) an essay titled "*Charaghan-i Rafta*," written by Prof. Dr. Altaf Ali Qureshi, was published. It depicts the stories of famous personalities. Mr Qureshi writes: "Beautiful, attractive and young Qurratu'l-'Ayn Táhirih was an active propagandist of the Bahá'í movement. She was also a great poetess."[97] He then relates the story that how Násiru'd-Dín Sháh Qájár invited her to become his queen and how Táhirih rejected his proposal.

*Samanzaar-i Sher Farsi wa Hindi* is an important book written by Prof. Zia Ahmad Badayuni. He has mentioned Qurratu'l-'Ayn Táhirih in that book and published one of her poems with its Urdu translation.[98]

In 1995, a large volume *Khátún-i 'ajam* compiled by this writer (Sabir Afaqi) was published by the Maqbal Academy of Lahore.[99] Articles written by thirty-seven established writers of the Urdu language are collected here. Poems by twenty-three poets have also been included in this volume. All these essays and poems are in honor of Táhirih. *Khátún-i 'ajam* also includes the Persian poems of Táhirih, written in the hand of the famous Pakistani calligrapher Abd-ur Rasheed Butt and their Urdu translation by this humble one. Under the title "*Kitab Nama-i Táhirih*" a list of sources on Táhirih has also been included in this book. *Khosha Haa-i-Ilm-o-Adab Switzerland*, provided this list of sources. *Khátún-i 'ajam* is gaining popularity in the literary and academic circles of this subcontinent. Its publication opened a new chapter in the introduction of Táhirih Qurratu'l-'Ayn. The following Urdu poets have paid homage to Táhirih, and their poems have been included in *Khátún-i 'ajam*: Raghib Massud Asadi, Rafiq Khawar (b. 1908), Kishwar Naheed, S. Mohammad Zia, Khaliq Ibrahim Khaliq (b. 1932), Saqib Razmi, Khalida Bano Shama, and Fletkar Mughal.

Another major work to make the eventful life and brilliant poetry of Táhirih known to the public in Pakistan has been undertaken by the translation of a novel on the life of Táhirih into Urdu. This novel was originally written by an American lady, Clara A. Edge, and was published under the title *Táhirih* in 1964, in Grand Rapids, Michigan. Shamsheer Ali has translated the novel into Urdu and the translation was published by the monthly *Sputnik* (Lahore) in book form in 1998, and was posted to all its readers and sold in the bookshops. This has helped a lot in making the message of Táhirih public.[100]

This brief review of the Urdu essays, articles, poems, and books written on Táhirih in Pakistan sufficiently shows that with the passage of time the name of the brave "Lady of Persia" is becoming more and more emblazoned in the hearts and minds of the people of the land. How true was Hafiz when he said:

> The one whose heart is pure and is made alive by love, can never die, our eternity has been written in the register of the world.

**Notes**
This essay is published for the first time in this volume.

1. Shoghi Effendi, *God Passes By*, New ed. (Wilmette, Ill.: Bahá'í Publishing Trust, 1974) p. 75.
2. George Nathaniel Curzon, *Persia and the Persian Question*, 2 vols. (London: Longmans, Green, 1892).
3. Joseph Arthur, comte de Gobineau, *Les Religions et les Philosophies dans l'Asie Centrale* (Paris: Didier, 1865).
4. Thomas Kelly Cheyne, *The Reconciliation of Races and Religions* (London: A. & C. Black, 1914).
5. Sir Francis Edward Younghusband, *The Gleam* (London: J. Murray, 1923).
6. Arminius Vambery. *Reise in Mittelasien von Teheran durch die Turkmanische Wöste an der ostköste des Kaspischen Meeres nach Chiwa, Bochara und Samarkand*, 2. aufl. (Leipzig, F. A. Brockhaus, 1873).
7. Edward Granville Browne, "The Bábís of Persia. II. Their Literature and Doctrines," *Journal of the Royal Asiatic Society* (London), Vol. 21 (1889) pp. 881-1009.
8. A. L. M. Nicolas, *Seyyèd Ali Mohammed, dit le Bâb: histoire* (Paris: Dujarric, 1905).
9. Martha L. Root, *Táhirih the Pure, Iran's Greatest Woman* ([Karachi: Root], 1938).
10. Laura Clifford Barney, *God's Heroes, a Drama in Five Acts* (London: K. Paul, Trench, Trübner, 1910).
11. Clara A. Edge, *Tahirih* (Grand Rapids, Mich.: Edgeway Publisher, 1964).
12. Alessandro Bausani, *Persia religiosa: da Zaratustra a Bahá'u'lláh* (Milan: Il saggiatore, 1959).
13. Marzieh Gail, "The White Silk Dress," *World Order* (Wilmette, Ill.), Vol. 7 (November 1941) no. 8, pp. 261-74.
14. Qurratu'l-'Ayn, *The Poetry of Táhirih*; [trans.] by John S. Hatcher and

Amrollah Hemmat (Oxford: George Ronald, 2000).
15. Jan Rypka, *Dějiny perské a tádžické literatury* (Prague, 1956).
16. Annemarie Schimmel, *Gabriel's Wing: A Study into the Religious Ideas of Sir Muhammad Iqbal* (Leiden: E. J. Brill, 1963).
17. Sir Dr. Muhammad Iqbal (1877-1938), poet and philosopher.
18. Sir Sheikh 'Abd ul-Qadir (1872-1950), essayist, magazine editor and statesman.
19. Khvajah Hasan Nizami (1878-1955), Islamicist, belletrist, and Sufi.
20. Sarojini Naidu (1879-1949), Indian poet and political leader.
21. M. Hidayat Hosain, "A Female Martyr of the Babi Faith," *Proceedings of the Idara-i-Maarif-i-Islmia* (Lahore: [s. n.],1933). See pp. 51 in this volume.
22. 'Abd-ul Halim Sharar (1860-1926), fiction writer, magazine editor and historian.
23. Aziz Ahmad (1914-1978), fiction writer, historian, poet, and translator.
24. Zahir Kashmiri (1919-1994), poet and journalist.
25. Habib Jalib (1928-1993), poet and political activist.
26. Jamílah Háshmí (1929-1988), fiction writer.
27. Intezar Husain (b. 1925), novelist.
28. Abr Ahsani Gunnauri (1898-1973), poet.
29. Ra'is Amrahvi (1914-1988), poet and journalist.
30. Kishvar Nahid (b. 1940), poet, translator and magazine editor.
31. Mírza Asadullah Fádil-i Mázandaráni, *Tarikh-i-Zuhúru'l-Haqq*, Vol. 3. (Tehran: [s. n.], 1944).
32. Muhammad Iqbal, *Javidnama* (Lahore: [s. n.], 1932); and *Javid-nama: ma'ahu farhang* (Hyderabad: [s. n.], 1946) [With Persian-Urdu glossary]. English translation: *Javid-nama*; translated from the Persian by Arthur J. Arberry (London: Allen & Unwin, 1966).
33. 'Azizǎ Cǎfǎrzadǎ, *Zǎrr'intac Tah'itǎ* (Baku: Göytürk, 1996).
34. Abdulghafur Nassakh, *Tazkaratu'l-Ma'asareen* (Calcutta) p. 193.
35. Martha L. Root, *Táhirih the Pure, Iran's Greatest Woman* ([Karachi: Root], 1938).
36. Lucknow: Dilgudaz Press, Karha Begkhan, 1923.
37. 'Abdulhalím Sharar, *Qurratu'l-'Ayn* (Lucknow: Dilgudaz Press, 1923).
38. Sabir Afaqi, *Najm-i-Durri* (Karachi: [National Spiritual Assembly of the Bahá'ís of Pakistan], 1964).
39. Muhammad Iqbal, *Kulliyát-i-Iqbál Urdú* (Lahore: Ghullam Ali & Sons, 1973).
40. Martha L. Root, *Táhirih, Qurratu'l-'Ayn*; trans. by Abbas Ali Butt (Delhi:[s. n.], n. d.); 2nd ed. (Karachi: Bahá'í Publishing Trast, 1966); 3rd ed. (Karachi: Bahá'í Pablishing Trust, 1974).
41. M. Hidayat Hosain, "A Female Martyr of the Babi Faith," *Proceedings of the Idara-i-Maarif-i Islmia* (Lahore, 1933).
42. Aziz Ahmad, "Zarrin Taj," *Savera* (Lahore), 1963.
43. Mohammad Ishaque, "Qurratu'l-'Ayn: A Bábí Martyr," in *Four Eminent Poetesses of Iran* (Calcutta: Iran Society, 1950) pp. 28-35. See pp. 59of this volume.
44. Ghulam Rasul Mehr, *Matalib-i Zarb-i Kalim* (Lahore: Shaikh Ghulam 'Ali, 1976).
45 Akhtar Aziz, *Larkian Jo Mashhoor Hu'in* (Lahore).
46. Maulana Anwar Shah Kashmiri, in *Dar al-'Ulum* (Deoband number), 1957.

47. Aneesa Kirmani, "Zarrin Taj—Qurratu'l-'Ayn," *Bahá'í Magazine* (Lahore).
48. Pervez Wasti, in *Sang-i Meel* (Karachi), 1964.
49. Azim Qureshi, in *Mahnama Ihsas* (Peshawar), 1962.
50. Manzoor Elahi, "Qurratu'l-'Ayn," *Naqoosh* (Lahore), 1965, no. 140, p. 532.
51. Idem., "Qurratu'l-'Ayn," in his *Dard-e*-Dilkusha (Lahore).
52. Inam'ul-Haque Kaosar, "Qurrat'ul-Ayn Táhirih," *Imroze* (Lahore), 23 April 1966.
53. Siraj Nizami, in *Saiyara Digest* (Lahore), Aug. 1968.
54. *Urdu Encyclopedia of Islam* (*Urdu da'irah-i ma'arif-i Islamiya*), Vol. 2 (Lahore: Punjab University, 1964) p. 16.
55. Abr Ahsani Ginnauri Badayuni, in *Bahá'í Magazine* (Lahore), July 1972.
56. Ghulamali Ismail Naji, *Zihra Bano* (Karachi, 1972); English version: Ghulamali Ismail Naji, *Zehra Bano*, trans. by Raza Husain Baroywal (Karachi: Peermahomed Ebrahim Trust, 1973).
57. Sayyid Mahfúzlhaq 'Ilmí, *Tajalli* (Lahore: Bahá'í Publishing Trust, 1972).
58. Mukhlis Vijdani, in *Wah Karigar* (Peshawar), June 1969.
59. Chiragh Hussain Shah, *Iqbal aur Qurratu'l-'Ayn* (Peshawar).
60. Saqib Hazeen, *Bábí wa Bahá'í* (Peshawar).
61. Ra'is Amrahi, *Kulliyat-i Ra'is Amlrahvi* (Karachi: Velkam Buk Port, 1995).
62. Jaun Eliyá, *Sháyad* (Karachi: Eliyá Akádimyá, 1990).
63. Sayyeda Akhtar Sultana, "*Makalamat-e-Iqbal Ka Tajzia*," Master's thesis, University of the Punjab (Lahore) pp. 238-43.
64. Khanum Asmat Afza, "*Iqbal kay fikri nazam maen aurat ka maqam*" (The perspective of women in the ideological system of Iqbal), research paper, University of the Punjab (Lahore). See pp. 165-69.
65. A. D Baloch, "*Iqbal aur Iran*," Master's thesis, University of the Punjab (Lahore).
66. Sayyid Mu'ínurrahmán, *Jámi'át men Iqbál kátahqíqí and tanqídímutála'ah* (Lahore: Iqbál Akádmí, 1977).
67. 'Abúlqásim Rafíq Dilávarí. *Á'imah-yi tablí*, Vol. 2 (Lahore: Maktabab-yi Ta'imír Insáyyat, 1978).
68. Hakim Matiur Rahman Quershi, "*Tazmeen bar Qurratu'l-'Ayn Baha'i*," *Al-Ilm* (Karachi), April 1980.
69. Siyyid Amjad Altaf, "Sham-o-Sahar," *Naqsh Sani* (Lahore), Jan.-Feb. 1982, p. 20.
70. *Tajali* (Lahore: [Bahá'í Community], 1974).
71. Jamílah Háshmí, *Chihra bachihrah rúbarú* (Lahore: Rá'i'tarz Buk Klab, 1977; 1983).
72. Maqbood Anwar Dawudi, *Matalib-i Iqbal* (Lahore: Feroze Sons, 1984).
73. Es. Em. 'Umar Fáruq, *Tavásín-i Iqbál* (Lahore: Iqbál Akádimí Pákistán, 1987).
74. Shaukat Wasti, *Kahta hun Sac* (Islamabad: Idar-i-Ilm wa Fun, 1991).
75. "Qurratu'l-'Ayn," in *Urdú insá'iklopídiya*, 3rd ed. (Lahore: Firozsanz, 1984).
76. Sabir Afaqi, *Talu-i-Sahtar* (Karachi: Baha'i Publishing Trust, 1985).
77. Sabir Afaqi, "Qurratu'l-'Ayn Táhirih," *Nigár-í Pákistán* (Karachi), April 1986, pp. 54-67.
78. Laura Clifford Barney, *God's Heroes, a Drama in Five Acts* (London: K. Paul, Trench, Trübner, 1910).

79. Barney, Laura Clifford, *Hashr Badaman: Qurratul'ain ke 'uruj o zaval kikarbnak tamsil*, [trans. by] Sadiqulkhair (Karachi: Shahnaz Buk Klab, 1986).
80. Intiz'ar Husain, [review of *Hashr Badaman*], in *Mashriq* (Lahore), 1986.
81. Habíb Jalib, *Harf-i sar-idár* (Lahore: Vanguard, 1987).
82. Jagannath Azad, *Kolambas ke das men: Safar námah* (New Delhi: Maktabah-yi Jámi'ah, 1987).
83. Mohammad Irshad, "Du Aahu-i-Tishna Dar Nanakzar—Habatia aur Qurratu'l-'Ayn," *Fanun* (Lahore), Nov.-Dec., 1986.
84. Muhammad Riyáz, *Jávednáma: Tahqíq o tauzíh* (Lahore: Iqbál Akádimí Pákstán, 1988).
85. Siyyid Qamar Hashmí, *Tamasha Talab Aazaar* (Karachi, 1988).
86. Sohail Ahmad, *Tarfain* (Lahore: Sang-i Meel, n.d.).
87. Nasím Amrohví, *Farhang-i* Iqbál (Lahore: Izhár Sanz, 1984).
88. Maqbúl Beg Badakhshání, *Adab námah-yi Írán*, Vol. 1 (Lahore: Nígárishát, 1989).
89. Akhtar Hussain Raipuri, *Gard-i*-Rah (Karachi: Af Kaar, 1989).
90. Kabír Ahmad Já'isí, *Jadid Taik i* Shu'ara (Aligarh: Idarah-yi 'Ulum-i Islamiyah, 'Aligarh Muslim Yunivarsiti, 1990).
91. Masaud Javed, "*Khatoon-i Ajam*," *Rujhan* (Karachi), 1991.
92. Mohammad Ali Siddiqui, "Qurratu'l-Ayn: A Profile in Courage," *The Daily Dawn* (Karachi), 4 March, 1973.
93. Khálid Sharíf, *Nárasá'í* (Lahore: Mávará, 1989).
94. Sáqib Razmí, *Ázádí-yi nisvánkánayá saverá* (Lahore: Maqb-ul Ikaidamí, 1991).
95. Khádim 'Alí Jáved, *Iqbal Aur Aorat* (Lahore).
96. Nílam Farzánah, *Urdú adab kí ahamkhavátín návil nigár* (Aligarh: Ejúkeshanal Buk Há'ús, 1992).
97. Altaf Ali Qureshi, "Charaghan-i-Rafta," *Qaomi Digest* (Lahore), Aug. 1994.
98. Zia Ahmad Badayuni, *Samanzaar-i-Sher Farsi wa Hind* (Delhi: Arjuman-i-Taraqqi-i-Urdu, n.d.).
99. Sábir Áfáqí, *Khátún-i 'ajam* (Lahore: Maqbál Akai'damí, 1995).
100. Clara A. Edge, *Qurratu'l-'Ayn Táhirih*, trans. by Shamsheer Ali (Lahore: Sputnik, 1998).

# From the Javid-Nama

by Muhammad Iqbal

### The Sphere Of Jupiter
*The noble spirits of Hallaj,[1] Ghalib,[2] and Qurrat al-Ain Tahira[3] who disdained to dwell in Paradise, preferring to wander forever.*

> Let me be a ransom for this demented heart
> which every instant bestows on me another desert;
> whenever I take up a lodging, it says, 'Rise–up!'
> The self-strong man reckons the sea as but a pool.
> Seeing that the signs of God are infinite
> where, traveller, can the high-road end?
> The task of science is to see and consume,
> the work of gnosis is to see and augment;
> science weighs in the balance of technology,
> gnosis weighs in the balance of intuition;
> science holds in its hand water and earth,
> gnosis holds in its hand the pure spirit;
> science casts its gaze upon phenomena,
> gnosis absorbs phenomena into itself.
> In quest of continuous manifestations
> I travel through the skies, lamenting like a reed;
> all this is by the grace of a pure-born saint
> whose ardour fell upon my soul.

The caravan of these two scanners of existence
presently halted by the shores of Jupiter,
that world, that earth not yet complete,
circling about it moons swift of pace;
the glass of its vine was still empty of wine,
desire as yet had not sprouted from its soil.
Midnight, a world half day in the moon's gleam,
the air thereof neither chill nor torrid.
As I lifted my gaze towards heaven
I saw a star closer to me;
the awful prospect robbed me of my senses—
near and far, late and soon became transformed.
I saw before me three pure spirits
the fire in whose breasts might melt the world.
They were clad in robes of tulip hue,
their faces gleamed with an inner glow;
in fever and fervour since the moment of Alast,
intoxicated with the wine of their own melodies.
Rumi said, 'Do not go out of yourself so,
be quickened by the breath of these songs of fire.
You have never seen intrepid passion; behold!
You have never seen the power of this wine; behold!
Ghalib and Hallaj and the Lady of Persia
have flung tumult into the soul of the sanctuary.
These songs bestow stability on the spirit,
their warmth springs from the inmost heart of creation.'

## The Song Of Hallaj

Seek from your own earth a fire as yet unseen,
another's apparition is unworthy of your demand.
I have so fastened on myself my gaze, that though the beauty
    of the Beloved
fills all the world, I am left no time to contemplate.
I would not give for Jamshid's realm that verse of Naziri[4]:
'He who is yet unslain belongs not to our tribe.'
Though reason whose trade is wizardry mustered an army,
your heart will not be dismayed, for Love is not alone.
You know not the way and are uninformed of the stage;

what melody is there that is not in Sulaima's lute?⁵
Tell a tale of the hunting and fettering of sharks:
do not say, 'Our skiff knows not the face of the sea.'
I am disciple of the zeal of that wayfarer who never set foot
on any high-road that ran over mountains, deserts and seas.
Be partner with the ring of wine-bibbing dissolutes;
beware of allegiance to a Master who is not a man of tumult.

## The Song Of Ghalib

Come, let us change the rule of heaven,
let us change fate by revolving a heavy measure of wine;
though the police-captain makes trouble, we will not worry,
and if the king himself sends a present, we will reject it.
Though Moses converse with us, we will not say a word;
though Abraham be our host, we will decline him.
Battling, the tribute-snatchers of the grove
we will turn away from our garden's gate with empty basket;
peacefully, the birds that flutter their wings at dawn
we will send back from the grove to their nests.
You and I are of Haidar, so no wonder would it be
if we turn back the sun towards the East.

## The Song Of Tahira

If ever confronting face to face my glance should alight on you
I will describe to you my sorrow for you in minutest detail.
That I may behold your cheek, like the zephyr I have visited
house by house, door by door, lane by lane, street by street.
Through separation from you my heart's blood is flowing
    from my eyes
river by river, sea by sea, fountain by fountain, stream by stream.
My sorrowful heart wove your love into the fabric of my soul
thread by thread, thrum by thrum, warp by warp, woof by woof.
Tahira repaired to her own heart, and saw none but you
page by page, fold by fold, veil by veil, curtain by curtain.
The ardour and passion of these anguished lovers
cast fresh commotions into my soul;
ancient problems reared their heads
and made assault upon my mind.

The ocean of my thought was wholly agitated;
its shore was devastated by the might of the tempest.
Rumi said, 'Do not lose any time,
you who desire the resolution of every knot;
for long you have been a prisoner in your own thoughts,
now pour this tumult out of your breast!'

## Hallaj

The sound of the Last Trump was in my breast;
I saw a people hastening to the tomb,
believers with the character and colour of infidels
who cried 'No god but God' and denied the Self.
'God's bidding' they called a vain image[6]
because it was bound to water and clay.
I kindled in my self the fire of life
and spoke to the dead of the mysteries of life.
The whole world has been founded on Selfhood,
love therein has been compounded with violence;
Selfhood is everywhere visible, yet invisible,
our gaze cannot endure to look on Selfhood;
within its light many fires lurk hidden,
from its Sinai creation's epiphanies shine.[7]
Every moment every heart in this ancient convent
discourses, albeit secretly, of the Self;
whoever has not taken his share of its fire
has died in the world, a stranger to himself.
India and Iran alike are privy to its light,
but few there are who also know its fire.
I have spoken of its light and its fire;
confidant of my secret, see now my crime.
What I have done you too have done; beware!
You have sought to resurrect the dead: beware!

## Tahira

From the sin of a frenzied servant of God
new creatures come into being;
unbounded passion rends veils apart,
removes from the vision the old and stale,

and in the end meets its portion in rope and gallows
neither turns back living from the Beloved's street.
Behold Love's glory in city and fields,
lest you suppose it has passed away from the world;
it lies concealed in the breast of its own time—
how could it be contained in such a closet as this?

**Notes**

Reprinted from: Muhammad Iqbal, *Javid-nama*; translated from the Urdu by Arthur J. Arberry (London: Allen & Unwin, 1966) pp. 90-93, 96.

1. The celebrated mystic-martyr Hallaj, executed on a charge of blasphemy in A.D. 922, wrote a book entitled 'The Book of Tawasin.' *Tawasin* is the plural of *Tasin*, a mysterious symbol prefixed to Koran XXVII.
2. Ghalib (1797-1869) was the greatest Persian poet of India in his times.
3. Qurrat al-Ain, Persian poetess and martyr of the Babi movement, was executed in 1852.
4. Naziri (d. 1612) was a famous Persian poet born in Nishapur who passed most of his active life in India. Jamshid was one of the greatest kings of ancient Persia.
5. Sulaima is a symbol of the beloved.
6. "God's bidding" : a reference to Koran XVII 87: They will question thee concerning the Spirit. Say: "The Spirit is of the bidding of my Lord."
7. It was on Sinai (Koran VII 139) that Moses witnessed the effects of the Divine epiphany.

**PERSIAN WOMAN IN TEHRAN**
posed in a studio putting on her outdoor dress (*chador*), that would include baggy trousers, a full black covering (right, on the floor), and a white veil to cover her face (left, on stand). See p. ii, for photo of the full costume.

# A Female Martyr of the Babi Faith

by M. Hidayat Hosain

Many noblemen have sacrificed their precious lives for the sake of the religion that they held to be true. The annals of the civilized world abound with such instances. In *Tarikh-ul Islam*[1] there is the record of many such heroes of imperishable fame but few among them belong to the fair sex. Whatever may be the reason for this dearth of names of female martyrs in our history it is not a fact that Moslem ladies have been behind in championing the cause of religion. Below is given a short sketch of the life and deeds of a most cultured lady of wide reputation who gave up her life for the sake of the Babi faith[2] which she believed with her whole heart and preached with great fervour.

The name of this illustrious lady is Umm-i-Salima, better known as "Tahira" or "Qurrat-ul-Ain." Zarrin Taj is another name which is attributed to her. Her father was Haji Mulla Salih[3] of Qazvin who was a brother of Mulla Taqi,[4] called by the Shi'ites "Shahid"—the third martyr. Tahira was married[5] to her cousin, Mulla Muhammad, son of Mulla Taqi, and bore a daughter and two sons. A very erudite scholar was appointed to educate Tahira when she was young. She attained such a very high degree of proficiency in literature that her father wished she were his son so that he might nominate her as his successor.

One day Tahira was the guest of her cousin (son of an aunt), Mulla

Jawad. In the library of her host she chanced to notice some books written by Shaikh Ahmed Ahsa-i[6] which appealed to her very much. She felt inclined to get possession of them, Mulla Jawad warned her saying that if she would read the books her father would try to kill him as he was against the views mentioned in those books. Far from being dissuaded by the warning, Tahira prevailed on Mulla Jawad to make over the books to her. When she had thoroughly grasped the contents of the books, Tahira spoke of the views and religious beliefs of Shaikh Ahmad Ahsa'i to her father. He thought that some of the religious views of Shaikh Ahmad had been put into her head by Jawad and he therefore told her that she had been misled by Mulla Jawad. She replied that she had read the works of Shaikh Ahmad Ahsa-i and that there were the edicts of Imams to prove the validity of the Shaikh's doctrines. She then expressed her doubts as to the justice of the claims of her father and uncle to be God-knowing men. Her father naturally desired to bring the erring child back to the fold of the faithful not by force but by persuasion. He therefore held with her prolonged discussions on such topics as "The Day of Resurrection," "Prophethood of Muhammad of Arabia," "Mi'raj" (Ascension of the Prophet to Heaven), "Hell and Heaven," and the "Advent of the Twelfth Imam." Once Tahira quoted an authority from Imam Ja'far Sadiq,[7] which was laughed away by her father; and she retorted that such an authority should not have been set aside so abruptly and after this incident she never spoke to him on any doctrinal question.

Now she commenced to receive light on various points from Saiyid Kazim[8] of Rasht by correspondence, who gave her the title of "Qurrat-ul-Ain." The title was approved of by Bab also. Her thirst for knowledge now increased and she went to Karbala to see Saiyid Kazim in person, who however unluckily died a week prior to her arrival.

Just before his death Saiyid Kazim had spoken to his disciples that the advent of the promised Imam (Twelfth Imam) was very near. So his disciples waited for the advent of the Imam in the mosque at Kufa, and others did so at Karbala. At this time Tahira fasted at daytime and used to keep awake at night for prayer and meditation. One night she dreamed that a youth with a green turban and black mantle was offering his prayers while he was standing on the air. He was muttering a verse which Tahira learnt by heart and noted down in a book. When Bab appeared and his book *Ahsan-ul-Qisas*[9] was out, Tahira was astonished to find the same verse in this book. She then believed in the validity of Bab's "Imamhood," and henceforward she devoted herself to the preaching of Babism. She now began to write notes and exposition of *Ahsan-ul-Qisas*. She also poured forth her feelings and prayers in verses and odes which are still very popular. She was so much given to piety and prayer that she never ignored even the minute rituals.

The 'ulama of Karbala heard about Tahira's preaching a new faith which was gaining ground every day and wrote to the Government. As a result various obstacles were put in her way and in the end she offered herself for arrest to relieve another lady of the Babi faith, Shams-ud-duha, who was put under police custody by mistake. The house of Tahira was surrounded by the police and her communication with people outside the house was stopped. This continued for about three months, but on her petition to Government she was allowed to proceed to Constantinople via Baghdad. Tahira along with Shams-ud-duha and her mother, Waraqat-ul-Firdaus, went to Baghdad and put up in the house of Agha Muhammad Shibl. People began to flock there to have an interview with her. She therefore changed the house and set herself to preaching and soon became known to one and all at Baghdad. One day she sent words to the Shi'a 'ulama to take recourse to "Mubahila," that is, to establish a belief by which two parties curse each other with the hope that the weaker will go to the wall, if arguments were of no avail. This upset the whole group of 'ulama and the Government had to send her and her companions to the house of the Mufti of Baghdad, 'Allama Ibn Alusi, were she for three months awaited the orders of the Turkish Government.

During this period of internment, Ibn Alusi talked with her on different topics and was simply astonished at her smart replies. Once he said to her that he had dreamt that the Shias were removing the corpse of Imam Husain out of his grave, and he stopped them from doing so by throwing himself on the body of Imam Husain. She said that the dream meant that he would very soon rescue her from the troubles caused to her by the Shi'a 'ulama. The Allama spent most of his time in discussing with her various religious topics, viz; "Life after death," "Weighing of Sin and Virtue," etc. One day it so happened that the father of 'Allama Ibn Alusi came to Tahira and talked with her harshly which put the 'Allama to shame.

She was later on told that she was ordered to leave the Turkish borders. Consequently, Tahira with other ladies left Baghdad for Persia. She however continued to preach during her journey and converted the following dignitaries to the Babi faith: Shaikh Salih the Arab, Shaikh Tahir, Mulla Ibrahim of Mahallat, and Shaikh Sultan the Arab. At length she entered Kirmanshah with these personages. The ladies were lodged in one house and the rest in another. The people of this place also flocked around her which provoked the local 'ulama, and they ordered them to leave the city. The leader of the locality collected his men, looted their articles and forced them out of the town unveiled. The helpless group had to pass their days in jungle, from where they submitted to the Governor of the place a petition mentioning their helplessness and the tyrannies perpetrated on them. The governor of Kirmanshah who had no information about this act of tyranny, asked his men to see that the articles of which they had been robbed were restored to them. This order was carried out, and Tahira with her party went to Hamadan. Here she was well received by the royal ladies who embraced her new faith. Tahira then went to Qazvin and preached her religion.

In the meantime Mulla Taqi of Qazvin was murdered, for which many persons professing the Babi religion were arrested, Tahira being one of them. But Agha Hadi managed the flight of Tahira to Teheran where she stayed in the house of Baha'ullah and from where she went to Badasht in Khurasan. Here a great meeting took place. After this meeting, the Government sent her back to Tehran and interned her in the house of the Kalantar. But she never ceased to preach religious tenets which were very closely listened to even by aristocratic ladies. Some time later, a marriage ceremony took place at the house of Kalantar. On this occasion, Tahira preached her religion. The preaching dampened the merriment of the occasion, and ladies of different ranks listened to her with rapture. This was too much for the authorities. They again had her arrested, and this time she was tried on a charge of having conspired with other Babis against the life of the Shah of Persia and sentenced to her execution. But as Tahira had been in strict confinement for a long time she could not possibly have had any concern with the conspiracy. She therefore gave up her life only for the sake of her faith.

The end came on Wednesday, September 15, 1852. Just before her execution she dressed herself decently and applied scent to her body. She was then taken to a garden. As the executioner hesitated to use his fatal axe, a Negro slave rushed forward, thrust a kerchief down into her throat and strangled her to death. Her body was thrown into a well in the garden and it was filled up with dust, earth, and stone. Tahira looked very cheerful till the very end.

"The appearance of such a woman," says E. G. Browne, "as Qurrrat-ul-Ain is in any country and any age a rare phenomenon, but in such a country as Persia it is a prodigy nay, almost a miracle. Alike in virtue of her marvelous beauty, her rare intellectual gifts, her fervid eloquence, her fearless devotion, and her glorious martyrdom, she stands forth incomparable and immortal amidst her countrywomen. Had the Babi religion no other claim to greatness, this were sufficient that it produced a heroine like Qurrat-ul-Ain."[10]

Qurrat-ul-Ain was a great poetess. The specimens of her poems given by Browne[11] will serve to indicate her great poetic talent.

**Notes**
Reprinted from: *Proceedings of the Dá'ir-yi ma'árif-i Islámiyya* (Lahore, 1933).

1. Muhammad ibn Ahmad Dhahabí, *Tárikh-al Islám wa-wafayát al-masháhrwaír-wa-al-'lám* (Beirut: Dár al-Kitáb al-Arabí, 1987-1993) in 38 vols. The early collective biography of Islam, published in various editions.—Ed.
2. The Babi religion has its own beliefs, and conceptions of a new state of society. The founder of this new faith is Saiyid Ali Muhammad of Shiraz who called himself Bab, or the gateway of knowledge of Divine truth. Born on 1 Muharram 1236 (26 March 1819), the son of a merchant, he became an orphan and early occupied himself with religious questions. At the age of 25 he began to preach his new doctrine as a result of which he and his disciples were put to severe persecution by the Government of Persia. After a brief career of six years Ali Muhammad was executed on July 8, 1850, but his disciples—the Babis who spread in different parts could not all be suppressed. One of them Baha-ullah founded a new sect which has made besides Persians some converts among Americans and Europeans.

    According to the Babi doctrine God is one and 'Ali-Muhammad is the mirror in which He is reflected and in which every one can regard Him. "You ought to make mirrors of yourselves and your deed so that you shall only see in these mirrors the sun which you love," says the Bayan.

    The Babis do not consider as we do Muhammad, the Prophet of Islam, peace be upon him, as the last prophet, nor the Qur'an as the final revelation from God.
3. He was an erudite doctor and the sage of Qazvin.
4. Haji Mulla Taqi was the eldest of three brothers, of whom the second Haji Mullah Salih, was also a divine and jurisconsult, while the third, Haji Mulla Ali, was first a disciple of Shaikh Ahmad Ahsa-i and afterwards a partisan of the Bab. Haji Mulla Taqi detested Shaikh Ahmad and his doctrines, and was indeed

the first among the Shi-ite clergy to denounce him as a dangerous heretic; but if his detestation of the Shaikhis was great, much bitterer and more violent was his hatred of the Babis. The fact that not only his youngest brother, Haji Mulla 'Ali but also his niece and daughter-in-law Zarrin Taj or better known as Qurrat-ul-Ain, had embraced the doctrines which he so abhorred, must have greatly conduced to an intensification of this hatred, which rose to such a pitch that he was during the last year of his life chiefly engaged in violent public denunciation of the Bab and his religion. This cost him his life, for at length certain Babis stung by his words into uncontrollable anger, fell upon him early one morning as he was praying in the mosque, and with knives and daggers inflicted on him eight wounds, from the effects of which he expired two days later. He was buried at Qazvin in the precincts of the Shahzada Husain.

5. This marriage after adoption of the Babi religion proved a most unhappy one, and she refused to reconcile herself to her husband on the ground that he (husband) was unclean as he rejected God's religion while she was pure. "Between us there can be naught in common nor any equality," she said.
6. Shaikh Ahmad Ahsa-i was the son of Shaikh Zain-ud-Din Ahsa-i and was born in A.H. 1166/A.D. 1752 and died in A.H. 1242/A.D. 1826. He is the author of a large number of books. For details see Nujam as-Sama, p. 367, and 'Abdu'l-Bahá, *A Traveller's Narrative: Written to Illustrate the Episode of the Báb*; edited in the original Persian, and translated into English, with an introduction and explanatory notes by Edward G. Browne (Cambridge: The University Press, 1891) Vol. 1, p. 234.
7. Imam Ja'far Sadiq was the sixth Imam of the Shi'a sect. He died in A.H. 148/A.D. 765. See Prince Dará Shikúh, *Safinat-ul-Auliya* (Cawnpore, 1884) p. 25.
8. Shaikh Ahmad Ahsa-i was succeeded at his death by his disciple Saiyid Kazim of Rasht. His family were merchants of repute. His father was named Aqa Saiyid Qasim. When twelve years old he was living at Ardabil near the tomb of Shaikh Safi-ud-Din Ishaq, the descendant of the seventh Imam Musa Kazim and the ancestor of the Safavi kings. One night in a dream it was signified to him by one of the illustrious progenitors of the buried saint that he should put himself under the spiritual guidance of Shaikh Ahmad Ahsa-i, who was at this time residing in Yazd. He accordingly proceeded thither and enrolled himself among the disciples of Shaikh Ahmad, in whose doctrine he attained such eminence that on the Shaikh's death he was unanimously recognized as the leader of the Shaikhi school. He died at Baghdad ere he had attained his fiftieth year A.H. 1259/A.D. 1843-1844. His works are said to exceed 300 volumes.
9. It is a commentary of the Sura of Joseph. It is named in allusion to the Qur'an 12:3 where the history of Joseph is thus characterized. For details of works by Bab see Edward G. Browne, in 'Abdu'l-Bahá, *A Traveller's Narrative,* Vol. 2, p. 335.
10. Ibid, p. 309. (See pp. 88 of this volume.—Ed.)
11. Ibid., p. 315.

# Qurratu'l-'Ayn—A Bábí Martyr

by Mohammad Ishaque

The early part of the reign of Násiru'd-Din Sháh witnessed the birth of a new religion, viz., the Bábí religion. The adherents of the new faith gradually increased in number. Some of the Bábís being suspected of an attempt upon the life of the Sháh, the Bábís were subjected to terrible persecution and the atrocities which were committed upon them beggar description. But by the fortitude and calmness with which they faced the persecutions inflicted on them, they won the sympathy and admiration of the feeling hearts. Qurratu'l-'Ayn suffered in common with them and was executed.

The real name of Qurratu'l-'Ayn is Umm-i Salmá.[1] She was the only daughter of Hájj Mullá Sálih, the erudite doctor known as the sage of Qazvín. She was born in 1230-31 A.H./1814-15 A.D. and was married to her uncle's son Mullá Muhammad.[2] She had three children, two sons and one daughter.

She was an educated lady, well-versed in Arabic, the science of the traditions, and exegesis of the Qur'án. She was endowed with brilliant eloquence, and it is said that she used to give learned discourses on theology in public without a veil. Browne says that he asked Subh-i Azal (The Morning of Eternity) whether it was true that Qurratu'l-'Ayn had discarded the veil. His reply was: "It is not true that she laid aside the veil. Sometimes, when carried away by her eloquence, she would allow it to slip down off her face, but she would always replace it after a few moments."³ At first she was a follower of the doctrines of Sayyid Kázim 'Alí Rashtí,⁴ the spiritual director of the Báb. She was in correspondence with him about the intricacies of his doctrines. The Sayyid recognized her ability and in his letters used to address her as Qurratu'l-'Ayn (Coolness for the Eye) by which appellation she is best known. On the death of Sayyid Kázim 'Alí Rashtí, she embraced the new doctrines of Mírzá 'Alí Muhammad, the Báb.⁵ By her eloquent preachings, she made many converts to the new faith.

She visited Karbalá during the lifetime of Sayyid Kázim 'Alí Rashtí. There she became acquainted not only with the Sayyid but also with his chief followers, including Mullá Husayn of Bushrúyih, the first apostle of the Báb. When Mullá Husayn set out for Shíráz after the death of Sayyid Kázim, she wrote to him begging that if he would succeed in finding the spiritual guide, he should at once inform her. After conversion to the faith of the Báb, Mullá Husayn made over her letter to the Báb who recognized the rare qualities of the writer whom he included among the eighteen "'Living Letters" (*Hurúfát-i hayy*)⁶ who formed the "First Unity" of the Bábí hierarchy.

Qurratu'l-'Ayn remained sometime in Karbalá where from behind a curtain she used to preach to the followers of the late Sayyid Kázim 'Alí Rashtí. The Governor intended to arrest her. So she hastily left Karbalá and went to Baghdád where she defended, with great ability, her creed before the chief Muftí. The question of whether she should be allowed to preach her faith was submitted first to the Páshá of Baghdád and then to the Central Government of Turkey, with the result that she was ordered to leave the territory of Turkey. On her return journey from Baghdád to Kirmánsháh and Hamadán she continued preaching and made some converts. Some Bábís did not like that a woman should publicly preach to men and referred the mater to the Báb who not only sanctioned her preaching but gave her the title of Janáb-i Táhirah (Her Holiness the Pure) which confirmed her high position in the Bábí church.

From Hamadán, Qurratu'l-'Ayn wanted to go to Tehran. It is said that she hoped to be able to convert Muhammad Sháh himself to her new faith. Her father became aware of her object and sent servants to intercept her and to bring her home to Qazvín. Her marriage with her cousin probably took place after her return to Qazvín, though the exact date of the event is not known. The marriage was a most unhappy one because her husband had, like his father, a bitter hatred for the Shaykhís and the Bábís, and finally Qurratu'l-'Ayn refused to live with her husband. Her position became perilous in the highest degree when her uncle and father-in-law was killed by certain Bábís. It was hinted by some that she was privy to the assassination. Her husband charged her before the Governor of Qazvín for complicity in the murder of his father, but she was acquitted.

Though acquitted, it became impossible for her to live in Qazvín. So she set out by way of Tehran for Khorasan. She was present at the celebrated meeting of the Bábí chiefs at Badasht, from where she turned towards Mázandarán with Mullá Muhammad 'Alí of Bárfurúsh and his party. We know nothing as to what happened to Qurratu'l-'Ayn after she separated from Mullá Muhammad 'Alí and his followers, until she was brought a captive to Tehran.

In 1852 A.D., one day Násiru'd-Din Sháh was passing through Tehran on horse-back when four Bábí rebels shot at him. One of them killed himself on the spot and another threw himself into a well and the remaining two were taken prisoners by the attendants of the Sháh. An enquiry was set up and a Bábí conspiracy was unearthed. Qurratu'l-'Ayn was given up to the authorities and sent to Tehran where she was placed in custody in the garden of Mahmúd Khán, the Kalántar, in a house without stairs. There she remained a prisoner till her death. There is nothing to prove the complicity of Qurratu'l-'Ayn in the conspiracy, nor do we know the circumstances under which she was made over to the authorities. It is said that on the occasion of the marriage of Mahmúd Khán's son, she was taken to his house where the wives of the city magnates were present. She, by her speech, made a good impression on the ladies, none of whom, however, ventured to say anything in her favour. It is said that the king wrote to her saying that if she would cease to be a Bábí, the king would take her into his harem. She is said to have written the following verses in reply on the back of the letter:

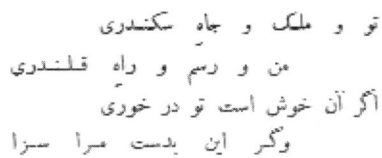

Sikandar's[7] pomp and display be thine,

> the Qalandar's[8] habit and way be mine;
> That, if it please thee, I resign,
> while this, though bad, is enough for me.

Her gaoler was completely under the influence of her eloquence and requested her to abjure her faith, hoping to secure her release. But she refused. At last, by the order of the authorities, she met a cruel and lingering death,[9] with calmness and fortitude, which excited the admiration of Dr. Polak who witnessed her death.[10]

Though Qurratu'l-'Ayn has considerable fame as a poetess, the authorship of the poems generally attributed to her has been doubted.[11]

The following ghazal in the Kámil metre is commonly attributed to her:[12]

لَمَعَاتُ وَجْهِكَ اَشْرَقَتْ وَ شُعَاعُ طَلْعَتِكَ اعْتَلَى
ز چه رو اَلَسْتُ بِرَبِّكُم نزنی بزن که بلی بلی
بجواب طبل الست تو ز ولا چه کوس بلا زدند
همه خیمه زد بدر دلم سپه غم و حشم بلا
من و عشقِ آن مه خوبرو که چو شد صلای بلا برو
بنشاط و قهقه شد فرو که اَنَا الشَّهِیدُ بِکَربَلا
چو شنید نالهٔ مرگ من پی سازِ من شد و برگِ من
فَمَشَى اِلَىَّ مُهَرْوِلاً وَ بَكَى عَلَىَّ مُجَلْجِلا
چه شود که آتشِ حیرتی زنیم بقلهٔ طور دل
فَكَّكْتَهُ وَ دَكَّكْتَهُ مُتَدَكْدِكًا مُتَزَلْزِلا
پی خوانِ دعوتِ عشقِ او همه شب ز خیلِ کروبیان
رسد این صفیر همیشی که گروه غمزدهٔ الصَّلا
تو چه فَلسِ ماهیِ حیرتی که زنی ببحرِ وجود دم
بنشین چو طاهره دم بدم بشنو خروشِ ننگِ لا[a]

The effulgence of thy face flashed forth and the rays of thy visage arose on high;
Then speak the word, *"Am I not your Lord?"* and *"Thou art, Thou art!"* we will all reply.
The trumpet-call *"Am I not?"* to greet how loud the drums of affliction beat!
At the gates of my heart there tramp the feet and camp the hosts of calamity.

That fair moon's love is enough, I trow, for me, for he laughed at the hail of woe,
And triumphant cried, as he sunk below, "The Martyr of Karbalá am I.
When he heard my death-dirge drear, for me he prepared, and arranged my gear for me;
He advanced to mourn at my bier for me, and o'er me wept right bitterly.
What harm if thou wilt the fire of amaze should'st set my Sinai-heart ablaze,
Which thou first mad'st fast in a hundred ways but to shake and shatter so ruthlessly?
To convene the guests to his feast of love all night from the angel host above
Peals forth this summons ineffable, "Hail, sorrow-stricken fraternity!"
Can a scale of the fish of amaze like thee aspire to enquire of Being's Sea?
Sit mute like Táhira, hearkening to the whale of "No" and its ceaseless sigh.[13]

But Áyatí (formerly surnamed Ávára) is definitely of the opinion that this poem is the composition of an earlier poet Muhammad Báqir *Suhbat* of Lár, in whose díván the whole poem with certain variants occurs with the pen-name "Suhbat" in the second hemistich of the last couplet.[14]

The following ghazal, also in Kámil metre, is said to be from her pen:

جَذَبَاتُ شَوقِكَ ٱلجَمَعَت بِسَلاسِل ٱلغَم وَ ٱلبَلا
همه عاشقان شکسته دل که دهد جان بره ولا

اگر آن صنم ز سر ستم پی کشتن من بیگنه
لَقَد استَقَامَ بِسَيفِه فَلَقَد رَضِيتُ بِمَا رَضَا

سحر آن نگار ستمگر قدی نهاد ببسترم
وَ إِذَا رَأَيتُ جَمَالَهُ طَلَعَ الصَّبَاحُ كَأَنَّمَا

نه چو زلف غالیه بار او نه چو چشم فتنه شعار او
شده نافة همه ختن شده کافری همه خطا

تو که غافل از می و شاهدی بی مرد عابد زاهدی
چه کنم که کافر جاحدی ز خلوص نیّتِ اصفیا

بمرادِ زلف معلّق پی اسپ و زین معرّق
همه عمر منکرِ مطلق ز فقیر فارغ و بی نوا

تو و ملک و جاه سکندری من و رسم و راه قلندری

اگر آن خوش است تو در خوری وگر این بد است مرا سزا

بگذر ز منزل ما و من بگزین بملک فنا وطن

فَإِذَا فَعَلْتَ بِمِثْلِ ذَا فَلَقَدْ بَلَغْتَ بِمَا تَشَا

The thralls of yearning love constrain in the bounds of pain and calamity
These broken-hearted lovers of thine to yield their lives in their zeal for thee.
Though with sword in hand my Darling stand with intent to slay, though I sinless be,
If it please him, this tyrant's whim, I am well content with his tyranny.
As in sleep I lay at the break of day that cruel charmer came to me,
And in the grace of his form and face the dawn of the morn I seemed to see.
The musk of Cathay might perfume gain from the scent those fragrant tresses rain,
While his eyes demolish a faith in vain attacked by the pagans of Tartary.
With you, who contemn both love and wine for the hermit's cell and the zealot's shrine,
What can I do, for our Faith divine you hold as a thing of infamy?
The tangled curls of thy darling's hair, and thy saddle and steed are thy only care;
In thy heart the Absolute hath no share, nor thought of the poor man's poverty.
Sikandar's pomp and display be thine, the Qalandar's habit and way be mine;
That, if it please thee, I resign, while this, though bad, is enough for me.
Pass from the station of "I" and "We", and choose for thy home Nonentity,
For when thou hast done the like of this, thou shalt reach the supreme Felicity.[15]

Browne also cites a masnaví poem for the kind known as *Sáqi-náma* and is inclined to believe, for reasons not quite convincing, to be her composition.[16]

The following ghazal is also ascribed to Qurratu'l-Ayn. Áyatí[17] in his Kawákibu'd-Durriyyah attributes the poem to her.[18] But afterwards he changed his opinion.[19]

During my second sojourn at Tehran in 1934, on the occasion of the Firdausí Millenary Celebrations, I had the honour of being acquainted with Áyatí and had the pleasure of talking with him on various phases of Persian poetry. At that time, Áyatí gave out as his decided opinion that this poem was not the composition of Qurratu'l-Ayn, but of Mullá 'Abdu'l-Wahháb of Qazvín, poetically surnamed Hazín. He said that the last distich which contained the pen-name "Hazín" was interchanged with an intermediate distich in the poem with the insertion of the surname "Táhirah" in it. The explanation is rather ingenious, but the opinion is dogmatic and does not carry conviction.[20]

گر بتو افتـدم نظر چهـره بچهـره دو برو
شرح دهم غم ترا نکتـه بنکتـه مو بمو
از پی دیدن رخت همچو صبـا فتاده ام
خانه بخانه در بدر کوچـه بکوچـه کو بکو
دور دهـان تنـگ تو عارض عنبـرین خطت
غنچـه بغنچـه گل بگل لاله بلاله بو ببو
میرود از فراق تو خـون دل از دو دیدهام
دجله بدجله یم بیم چشمه بچشمه جو بجو
مهر ترا دل حزین بافتـه بر قمـاش جان"
رشتـه برشتـه نخ بنخ تار بتـار پو بپـو

If I happen to see thee before me face to face, I shall tell thee of my
  pangs in minute details;
To see thy face, like unto Zephyr I passed from house to house, door
  to door, street to street, lane to lane;
The circuit of thy tiny mouth and thy cheeks with down of amber
  gris (are luxuriant) with buds, roses, tulips and fragrance;
On account of thy separation, my heart's blood flows forth from my
  eyes (like) many a Tigris, many a sea, many a brooklet,
  many a stream.
The dejected heart hath knit thy love on the web of life thread by
  thread, fibre by fibre, warp by warp, woof by woof;
*Táhirah* entered her heart and found nothing save thee (searching)
  page by page, fold by fold, screen by screen, layer by layer..

A booklet *Tuhfah-i Táhirah*[21] professing to contain the poems of Qurratu'l-'Ayn has been published by Isfandyár Bakhtiyárí. It contains three other poems of which no mention has been made by Browne or Áyatí.

Thus we have only a few poems attributed to her. Of these poems at least one cannot be her composition, while the authorship of the rest is doubted. On what then, does the fame of Qurratu'l-'Ayn rest? Certainly not on poetic gifts of which we possess very little proof. The cause of her fame should be sought elsewhere. We learn from the works of different writers that she was a profound theologian and preacher of great eloquence. Her audiences were charmed by her eloquent discourses and heard her with rapt attention. To her deep knowledge of theology and her persuasive eloquence, we are inclined to think, her fame must be due.

Whether these poems are from the pen of Qurratu'l-'Ayn or not, they are characterized by unity of thought and uniformity of style. They are, as a rule, interspersed with bombastic and unfamiliar Arabic lines and phrases which, however, do not disturb the spontaneous flow. The graceful ease, magnificent diction and charming rhythm have rendered the poems musical and inspiring.

**Notes**

Reprinted from: Mohammad Ishaque, *Four Eminent Poetesses of Iran* (Calcutta: Iran Society, 1950) pp. 28-35.

1. According to Mahmúd Effendí Álúsí her real name is Hind and Umm-i Salmá is her *kuniyya* (see 'Abdu'l-Husayn Ayati "Ávárih," *Al-Kavákibu'd-Durriyyih fí Ma'áthiri'l al-Bahá'iyah* [Cairo: Matba`at as-Sa`adah, 1342/1923] Vol. 1, pp. 63-64). She is also known by the name Zarrín Táj.
2. The following genealogical table will clearly explain her family relationships:

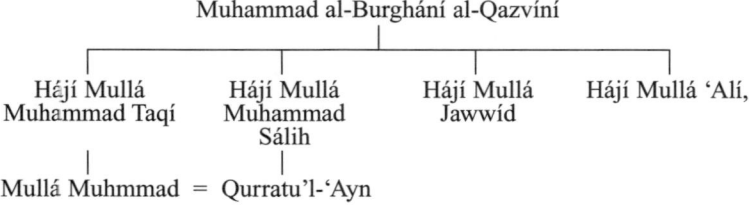

3. Edward Granville Browne, quoted in 'Abdu'l-Bahá, *A Traveller's Narrative: Written to Illustrate the History of the Báb;* edited in the original Persian, and translated into English, with an introduction and explanatory notes by Edward G. Browne (Cambridge: The University Press, 1891) Vol. 2, p. 314.
4. b. A.H. 1205/A.D. 1790; d. A.H. 1251 or 1259/A.D. 1835 or 1843.
5. Born at Shíráz in 1820; proclaimed himself the Báb (the Gate), 23 May 1844; executed in Tabríz, July, 1850.
6. Eighteen of the earliest chosen disciples of the Báb. The Báb described them as "Eighteen Living Letters" and himself as The Point. These eighteen chosen disciples were specially trained how to instruct others and prepare the way for

receiving one who was about to reveal himself.
7. Alexander the Great.
8. A kind of religious mendicant.
9. The accounts of her death are quite conflicting and it is difficult to say which version is correct. Gobineau says she was burned after the executioner had first strangled her. According to one version she was cast into a dry well in the garden of the palace called Nigáristán and the well was then filled up with stones. Anyhow the fact remains that a cruel death was inflicted on her. She suffered martyrdom on 17 August 1852.
10. Jakob Eduard Polak, *Persien: das Land und seine Bewohner* (Leipzig: F. A. Brockhaus, 1865) Vol. 1, p. 333.
11. 'Abdu'l-Husayn Ayati "Ávárih," *Al-Kavákibu'd-Durriyyih fí Ma'áthiri'l al-Bahá'íyah,* Vol. 1, p. 309; also 'Abdu'l-Husayn Ayati "Ávárih," *Kashfu'l-Hiyal* (Tehran: Kitabfurushi-yi `Ilmi, 1346/1947) Vol. 2, p. 46.
12. In Qurratu'l-'Ayn, *Tuhfah-i Tahirah,* ed. by Isfandyár Bakhtiyárí (Karachi: Bakhtiyárí, 1930) (see infra); this ghazal forms the ending part of a bigger poem comprising twenty-one distichs, of which the *matla'* runs thus:

مه ای گروه عـایـان بکشیـد طلـة ولا    که طیور دلیر ما میان شده فانی و ظاهر و زملا

13. Edward Granville Browne, *Materials for the Study of the Babi Religion* (Cambridge: The University Press, 1918) pp. 350-51.
14. Muhammad Báqir Suhbat Lárí, *Dívan-i Suhbat Lárí* (Tehran: Shirkat-i taba-i kitab, 1317/1938-39) p. 130.
15. Edward Granville Browne, *Materials for the Study of the Babi Religion,* pp. 348-49.
16. Ibid., pp. 343-47.
17. Muhammad Ishaque, *Sukhanvarán-i Irán dar 'Asr-i Házir* (Calcutta, 1933-1937) Vol.2, pp. 8-14.
18. See 'Abdu'l-Husayn Ávárih, *Al-Kavákibu'd-Durriyyih fí Ma'áthiri'l al-Bahá'íyah,* p. 308.
19. 'Abdu'l-Husayn Ávárih, *Kashfu'l-Hiyal* (Tehran) Vol. 2, p. 48 (footnote).
20. In Qurratu'l-'Ayn, *Tuhfah-i Táhirah,* p. 4, there occurs before this verse the following extra distich:

ابرو و چشم و خال تو صید نموده مرغ دل    طبع بطع و دل بدل مهر بمهر و خو بخو

21. Lithographed at Karachi on 1 Núr 87 of the Bábí year/6 June 1930.

STUDIO PHOTOGRAPH, TEHRAN, 1880s.
This posed photo shows a Persian woman's indoor costume under a print *chador* that can be used to cover her whole body when outside. She is holding a water pipe.

# Qurratu'l-Ayn:
# A Profile In Courage

by Mohammad Ali Siddiqui

Qurratu'l-Ayn Tahira is a great name in Persian literature. Her influence is felt in Urdu poetry as well. She gave vent to a rare lyrical impulse which leaps over geographical barriers. She is loved, respected, and emulated throughout the world for her radiating wisdom, courage, and beauty.

Hardly any account of Iran of the last century fails to mention her. That all histories, journals, travelogues, and diplomatic correspondence testify to her greatness of heart and spirit is a rare phenomenon. Be it Lord Curzon's Persian Odyssey,[1] or Sir J. Malcolm's travelogue,[2] or French diplomat Comte de Gobineau's *Les Religions et les Philosophies dans l'Asie Centrale*,[3] a common feature of admiration and sympathy for the creed Qurratu'l-Ayn believed in is always there.

Her magic lies in lifting others to her level of super-consciousness. Her poetry is miraculous in its portents. One may disagree with what the poetess believes in, but the sheer music and earnestness of her lines renders one immune to what is spun round by her religious polemicists.

Even the uncharitable Czarist ambassador's account of Bab and his followers, so assiduously translated under the title *Bab-o-Abha Ra Beshanansid* and published in Hyderabad, Deccan, some twenty-three years ago, could not deny the poetess the honour of being the foremost champion of women's liberation. One is entitled not to accept her faith, but the magic of her poetry is so universal that all those who have been able to study the story of the Bahai faith have to admit that it is quite seldom that exquisite beauty, highly lyrical poetry, and polemical finesse have converged into one individual in so right a measure.

Iran of her times was ruled by a tottering monarchy given to all manner of corruptions. Superstitions, poverty, and religious fanaticism ruled supreme; and there was not even a whiff of modernism, which the sub-continent was exposed to in the pre-1857 period.

Urdu poet Ghalib was cognizant of the supremacy of British technology and was so much overawed by the steam engine, electricity, telegraph, and the Enfield gun that he is found exhorting his countrymen to adapt themselves to the change and give up the old ways of life. He discards the social and political laws of the Great Moghuls in favour of Western laws. He favours the founding of Delhi College (later Arabic College) in 1824. But his Iranian contemporary Qa'ani doesn't seem to be mindful of the Czarist intrigues going on in the Court or the changes wrought by the Western science and technology.

Ghalib's greatness lies in the fact that he prepared his countrymen for seizing the dilemma by the horns. He may have erred by writing Qasidas here and there but Ghalib was such a designing artist that he couldn't lull us into a false sense of compliance. His prescription was simple: Imbibe as much of British virtues as possible in order to compete with them in fields where they are stronger. There is no shortcut to national emancipation except in assimilating the best that one can have from any quarter.

But Tahira did a novel service. She saw the immobility of her womenfolk with a feeling of anguish and worked for their emancipation with a gusto that took the whole of Iran by storm. She was stoned, molested, and beaten but she went on with her work undaunted.

No prize was as high as the emancipation of the Iranian womenfolk, and it is not strange that Iran has little to boast of her literature of the last century by Qurratu'l-Ayn. She symbolizes Iran like Florence Nightingale and Joan of Arc do for England and France in the changes which they came to release forth by virtue of their examples. Their fields may be different, but they are the milestones of human greatness. They have proved to be specimens of courage, devotion, and brightness.

Tahira was born in 1819 or 1820, in Qazvin, Iran, in the orthodox family of a religious scholar, Haji Mulla Salih. As a child she was so intelligent and eager for knowledge that she could floor even the learned scholars by her great gift of polemics. She was a great student of Quranic and Hadith studies.

She had gone to Karbala to learn Islamic jurisprudence and philosophy; and it was her teacher there, Syed Kazim Rashti, who gave her the title of Qurratu'l-Ayn, meaning "consolation of the eyes."

Tahira is also a title given to her by Baha'u'llah whereas her real name is Zarrin Taj. She was married to a scholar, but when Mirza Ali Mohammad declared himself to be the Bab she joined the new sect. It took some years before this Shiite sect broke away from Islam and became Babi after the name of Mirza Ali Mohammad Bab.

Qurratu'l-Ayn's mettle shone brilliantly after the abortive attempt on the life of Nasiruddin Shah on 15 August 1852, in retaliation for Bab's execution at Tabriz on 9 July 1850. A frightful persecution followed and, in the words of E. G. Browne in the *Literary History of Persia*,[4] twenty-eight more or less prominent Babis, including the beautiful and talented poetess Qurratu'l-Ayn suffered death with horrible tortures.

There is some disagreement about the way she was put to death. Dr. Jakob Polak, the then physician to the Shah of Iran, reports in his book *Persien: das Land und seine Bewohner*[5] that she was executed and that he was a witness to her super human fortitude.

The French ambassador Gobineau; in his book *Les Religions et les Philosophies dans l'Asie Centrale*, also published in 1865, writes that Tahira was first strangled and then burned in full view of the spectators. Her remains were thrown into a dry well which was subsequently filled up with earth and stones. What a tyranny!

Qurratu'l-Ayn is a highly respected artist. Allama Iqbal discusses her greatness in *Javid Nama*[6] and regards her as one of the Great Souls along with Rumi, Mansur Hallaj, and Urdu poet Ghalib. Marie Von Najmajer's great epic poem *Gurret-ül-Eyn*[7] is one of the charming classics in the German language.

The Turkish poet Nazim Hekmat has paid her rare tribute: "O Tahira, a thousand Nasiruddin Shahs have died with you. O glowing flame of human liberty."[8]

One can glean respect and admiration for her in Lord Curzon's book *Persia and the Persian Question*, Valentin Chirol's *The Middle*

*Eastern Question*,[9] and Sir Francis Younghusband's book *The Gleam*[10]; but the tribute paid by Edward G. Browne, famous for his *A Literary History of Persia*, should always serve as the most authoritative one for hardly any other Orientalist has studied Persian literature as feelingly as he did. He writes:

> The appearance of such a woman as Tahirih in any country and in any age, is a rare phenomenon, but in such a country as Iran it is a prodigy . . . nay, almost a miracle . . . Alike in virtue of her marvelous beauty, her rare intellectual gifts, her fervid eloquence, her fearless devotion, and her glorious martyrdom, she stands incomparable and immortal amidst her countrywomen. Had the religion of the Bab no other claim to greatness, this were sufficient that it produced a heroine like Qurratu'l-Ayn Tahira."

**Notes**
Reprinted from: *Dawn*, Karachi, 4 March 1973. All footnotes by the editor.

1. George Nathaniel Curzon, *Persia and the Persian Question* (London: Long mans, Green, 1892).
2. The author could not have meant Sir John Malcolm, *A Sketch of Persia* (London: J. Murray, 1827); perhaps he confused him with Napier Malcolm, *Five Years in a Persian Town* (London: Murray, 1905), which also sympathetically relates the persecution of the Bábís.
3. Paris: Didier, 1865.
4. Edward Granville Browne, *Literary History of Persia: Modern Times,1500-1924* (Cambridge: The University Press, 1924 [1959]) p. 154.
5. Leipzig: F. A. Brockhaus, 1865.
6. Muhammad Iqbal, *Javid-nama*; translated from the Persian by Arthur J. Arberry (London: Allen & Unwin, 1966). See excerpts included in this volume. pp.
7. Marie von Najmajer, *Gurret-ül-Eyn. Ein Bild aus Persiens Neuzeit in 6 Gesängen* (Vienna: Rosner, 1871).
8. Süleyman Nazif, *Nasiruddin Shah ve Babiler* (Istanbul: Kanaat Kütuphanesi, 1923). English translation in: Süleyman Nazif, "Translation of Passages on Tahirih . . ., pp. 35, 44-49," appendix to Necati Alkan, "Süleyman. Nazif's *Nasiruddin Shah ve Babiler*: An Ottoman Source on Babi-Baha'i History," *Research Notes in Shaykhi,Babi and Baha'i Studies* (East Lansing), vol. 4, no. 2 (November, 2000). <http://www.h net.org/~bahai/notes/vol4/nazif.htm>
9. Valentin Chirol, *The Middle Eastern Question; or, Some Political Problems of Indian Defence* (London: J. Murray, 1903).
10. Sir Francis Edward Younghusband, *The Gleam* (London: J. Murray, 1923).

# Qurratu'l-Ayn Tahira

by Masudu'l Hasan

Qurratu'l-Ayn Tahira was the most remarkable woman of the nineteenth century. Iqbal calls her "Khatoon-i-Ajam." Her original name was Zarin Taj. She was the daughter of Mulla Salih, an eminent theologian of Qazvin. She was highly educated, intelligent, and talented. She was an eloquent speaker. She was an embodiment of beauty, and her long hair reached to her knees.

She was married to Mulla Muhammad. He was the son of the elder brother of the father of Qurratu'l-Ayn Tahira. The marriage was blessed with three children, and in the early years the couple was happy with each other.

When the Bab proclaimed his new creed Qurratu'l-Ayn became his devoted follower. That caused a rift between the husband and the wife. Qurratu'l-Ayn went to Karbala and Baghdad, and openly preached the new creed. The Government ordered her extradition from Baghdad. She returned to Iran, and in the course of her journey she delivered lectures in favor of Babism at wayside stations. She was so beautiful and eloquent that large crowds were attracted to hear her, and she made many converts.

Back in Qazvin, her father-in-law took her to task for straying from the right path. Within a week her father-in-law was murdered by a Babi. That led to the persecution of the Babis. Qurratu'l-Ayn also appeared in the court of the Persian Shah Nasir-ud-Din Qajar.

Seeing her, he was struck by her beauty. He ordered "Leave her; she is so beautiful."

Thereafter Nasir-ud-Din Qajar sent her a message that if she recanted her faith in the new creed, he was prepared to marry her and make her the most favorite queen. In reply she sent him the following message in verse:

> You are fond of power and empire;
> I am fond of faith and poverty;
> If power and empire are to be preferred
> Be blessed with them.
>  And if the way of the Dervish is to be deprecated
> I don't mind the punishment.

At this reply the Shah was silenced. The Babis intensified their activities, and an attack was made on the life of the Shah. The Shah escaped, and in the trial that followed, the Bab, the founder of the new faith, was executed in 1850. His death was regarded by his followers as martyrdom. An element of passion entered into the movement and the Bábís rose to avenge the death of their Master. The Government ordered vigorous measures against the Babis. Qurratu'l-Ayn Tahira was also arrested, but before she could be regularly tried she was put to death by the soldiers of the Shah.

In *Javid Nama*[1] Iqbal encounters the spirit of Tahira on Jupiter in the company of Hallaj and Ghalib—the trio who disdained to dwell in paradise preferring to wonder forever.

To Iqbal, Tahira is an embodiment of true love. Iqbal quotes her Ghazal:

> O Beloved, if I am admitted to your presence
> I will tell Thee in detail of the grief that I suffer because of Thy
>    separation,
> In order to get a glimpse of your face, I am moving like zephyr
>    From door to door, and street to street
> Because of Thy separation the blood of my heart flows as tears
>    From my eyes, like fountains, streams and rivers;
> Your love is woven into the fabric of my soul;
>    Thread by thread, warp by warp, and woof by woof.
> In the book of my heart, there is naught but you
>    In every word, every sentence, and every page.

Like Hallaj, Tahira regards herself as a frenzied servant of God. In the frenzy of love, Hallaj or Tahira may act in a way which is not in accordance with accepted norms of law or religion, but such frenzy is creative. It unveils the mystery of love, so that the lover takes his pleasure to the gibbet.

The point that Iqbal highlights is that creativity is another name for love. You cannot create a new world unless you have the frenzy of love and are determined to give your life for the fulfillment of your aim.

**Notes**
Reprinted from: *Stories and Biographies from Iqbal* (Lahore: Ferozsans, 1978) pp. 167-69.

1. Muhammad Iqbal, *Javidnama* (Lahore: [s. n.], 1932).

THREE NOMAD WOMEN FROM LORESTAN
c. 1890. The women wear a long tunic over very baggy trousers. Their heads are covered with a length of material secured with a tightly bound headscarf. The woman in the middle also wears a checkered *chador* (the full body veil).

# The Cry Of Tahira

by Khwaja Masud

> *If I could only raise my eyes,*
> *face to face, in front of you,*
> *I would narrate grief for you,*
> *point by point, word to word.*

These are the first lines of Tahira's poem—one of the sublimest poems ever written. No one, not even with the stoniest heart, could express what Tahira had to go through in her life—a life entirely dedicated to the love of God and wholly committed to the emancipation of women during the nineteenth century. Another woman, a great Russian poet, Anna Akhmatova, had spoken about a fellow poet:

> For filling earth with new throb
> Of stanzas echoing in new cosmos,
> She has been granted eternal childhood
> Generosity, luminescent vision,
> All earth is the heritage
> That she has shared with all.

If any poet deserves these words, it is Tahira. Baha'u'llah named her Tahira which means the "pure one." Her teacher at Karbala, Syed Kazim Rashti, called her Qurrat-ul-Ayn, which means "consolation of the eyes." Another name by which she was known is Zarrin-Taj, or "one crowned with gold." She was also addressed as "Nuqta" which means "the point." The name her father had given her is never used.

As she trod the untrodden path, she had to endure what all non-conformists endured in their life. Socrates had to drink hemlock, because he was accused of worshipping one deity. Mansur was crucified, because he cried out: "*An Al Haq*" (I am the Truth). Joan of Arc was burnt alive, because she led the troops to free her country from the clutches of the British. Tahira was the first Muslim woman to dare to lay aside the veil and converse with men at conferences. Addressing the Badasht conference, she said: "Rise, brothers, the Qur'an is fulfilled and a new era has begun. Am I not your sister, and you my brother? Can you not look upon me as a real friend? If you cannot put out of your mind evil thoughts [because it was unheard of in that age not to hide her face behind a heavy veil] how will you be able to give your lives for a great cause? Are you aware that this custom of veiling the face was not enjoined by Muhammad (peace be upon him) so rigorously as you seem to observe? Do you not remember that in some matters he used to send his disciples to go and ask his wife? Let us emancipate our women and reform our society. Let us rise out of our graves of superstition and egoism and pronounce that the Day of Judgment is at hand; then shall the whole earth respond to freedom of conscience and new life! The blast of this trumpet of Resurrection, it is I."

As a child, Tahira was so intelligent and so eager for knowledge that she devoured all the lessons that her father, one of the most learned priests of Iran, taught her. Few men in her day knew the Qur'an and its meanings, the traditions, and the Islamic law as well as she did. On her own, she studied the books written by two eminent scholars—Sheikh Ahmad Ahsai and his pupil Sayed Kazim-i-Rashti. The teachings of Sheikh Ahsai went against orthodoxy. Tahira compared them with the inner principles of the Qur'an and felt they did not contradict them. One of the Sheikh's beliefs was about the resurrection of the body. He taught that the body would not rise but disintegrate, while the spirit would dwell in the presence of God.

Tahira, the spiritual young woman of Qazvin, had been corresponding with Sayed Rashti, asking him profound questions about religion. It was he who gave her the name Qurratu-ul-Ayn.

She longed to go to Karbala to study with Shaikh Kazim. Her uncle supported her, and she got the permission to make the pilgrimage to the sacred shrines at Karbala and Najaf. The journey was undertaken in 1843, when she was twenty-three years old and the mother of two sons and one daughter. She remained at Karbala for three years. When her teachers died, she replaced them and began to deliever lectures.

No thinking man or woman wishes to die without having done something for humanity. The finest quality in Tahira was her fidelity in searching for truth. She began her search for truth while still a small girl, and she never gave it up until her martyrdom.

Her lectures began to attract big audiences. She was eloquent. She was sincere. She was treading a new path. She broke the shackles of orthodoxy. As her lectures struck at the very root of the supremacy of the priests, they were alarmed. They wanted to get rid of her. She had to leave Baghdad for Iran. There she was driven from one town to another. Only in Hamadan was she welcomed. Prof. Edward Browne has paid a rare tribute to Tahira: "The appearance of such a woman as Tahira in any country and in any age, is a rare phenomenon, but in such a country as Iran it is a prodigy, nay almost a miracle."

Tahira's father pronounced her a heretic and her husband divorced her. Only her mother stood by her. When imprisoned, she said, "You can kill me any moment you like but you cannot stop the emancipation of women." Meanwhile an attempt was made on the life of the shah. The fate of Tahira was sealed. She was taken to a garden where she was strangled and thrown into a well. Until the last moment of her life, she wore a smile on her face. Iqbal once said:

> Let me tell you how a person of faith reveals himself,
> There is a smile on his face when he faces death.

By that Iqbalian standard, she remained loyal to her faith to the last.

In Allama Iqbal's magnum opus *Javaid Nama*,[1] he pays tribute to Tahira in two poems fully devoted to her. In one, Iqbal quotes the greatest poem by Tahira, with whose first few lines I began my homage to her. In this poem *"Nawai Tahira"* (The Cry of Tahira), Iqbal ends with the following verses:

> The passion of long suffering lovers
> Creates a new tumult in any soul,
> It takes away my old griefs,
> But envelopes me with storms at night.

> My thoughts deep as the ocean confront a new agony,
> Overflowing the coast with a tidal wave.
> Rumi said: Have a firm grip over time,
> If you want to untie the knots (of secrets)
> Be a prisoner of your own new thoughts,
> If you are keen to relieve your conscience
> From hellish anguish.

In the second poem, Iqbal addresses Tahira as the epitome of all that is best in a human being.

> From a sinner, mad in passion,
> Emerges a new universe.
> Unlimited commitment tears apart all veils,
> Orthodoxy is left crest-fallen,
> The scaffold and hangman's noose is her destiny,
> For a lover never comes out alive from the beloved's abode.
> You still see her in full glory, everywhere,
> Let no one think even for a moment that
> She is no longer in our world!
> She has enveloped herself by *zeitgeist*
> Within her is a treasure without any bounds.

Iqbal places Tahira in the company of Mansur, Al-Hallaj, and Ghalib, saying that their exalted souls could not sit still in paradise and are in constant commotion. He calls Tahira "the woman of the East" (*khatoon-i-ajam*), he says: "Ghalib, Hallaj, and Khatoon-i-Ajam have created a tumult within the precincts of 'harem.'"

No greater homage could be paid to Tahira than that Iqbal confers on her the title of Khatoon-i-Ajam. She stands out as a beacon to all women, to the whole of mankind, beckoning them to a future where they will be fully emancipated from orthodoxy and conformity, and can forge a new world of liberty, equality, and fraternity. This will be a world where women will march shoulder to shoulder with men to wipe off the tears of a grieved humanity.

**Notes**
Reprinted from: *The News* (Rawalpindi), 13 November 1995.

1. Muhammad Iqbal. *Javidnama*. Lahore: [s. n.], 1932.

# Passages from
*Nasiruddin Shah ve Babiler*

by Süleyman Nazif

Translated by Necati Alkan

A young woman accepted Babism and became the disciple of the new Messiah. Her name was Zarrin Taj. But the people, being attracted to her countless virtues, gave her the title "Qurratu'l-'Ayn" [solace of the eyes]. This exceptional woman who was extraordinarily intelligent, erudite, a poetess, mature, eloquent and resolute, also was, with regard to her chastity and decency, uncorrupted—even to the extent that she forced her enemies to confirm and admit [her eminence]. Her first followers conferred upon her the attribute "Tahirih" [the pure]; she was addressed and remembered by this name. Among the masters of poetry in Iran, the poems of Qurratu'l-'Ayn in our day no doubt rank high. The minds and thoughts of those hesitating to support Babism were bewildered and captivated in the presence of Tahirih by her desire-inflaming beauty, her indisputable excellence, her particular eloquence and firmness and courage. She entered every place unveiled, and through her sermons about the new sect, in a brief time established a community with numerous members. . . .

This exceptional woman, in my opinion, is the world's staunchest and most virtuous lady. When this exceptional woman was born, her parents gave her the name "Zarrin Taj" [golden crown]. She indeed was a golden crown. She was born with a diadem of beauty and grace and an endless treasure of talent for knowledge. After dedicating her merits and virtues, whether inherited or acquired, for the salvation of the people, they deemed the title "Qurratu'l-'Ayn" as worthy for her. Zarrin Taj became a light of gladness and a flame of hope for every weary eye. In addition to such beauty and courage, she was so chaste and decent that even her most pitiless arch-enemies could not question the attribute "Tahirih" conferred upon this exceptional woman by those gathered under the banner of her judgment, and those intending to kill her received confirmation and were treated with respect in the presence of her fame and honour. This symbol of chastity that valiantly and enthusiastically associated with everyone remained unstained from the corruption of passion.

Like the eloquence of her discourse that dominated the minds and consciences, her desire-inflaming beauty and grace consisted only of the excitement of her love for an eternally worshipped One who was her object and holy goal, in whose path she ultimately gave up her life.

Not only were the abandoned, the down-trodden, and those people in need of help enchanted by her virtues, but also the great ones of that time. Even the highest rank police commander in Tehran was earnestly striving to mitigate the incarceration of this unique heroine and to liberate her completely. However, resolute and dignified as she was, Qurratu'l-'Ayn rejected this proposed amnesty and, as she was faithful to her own honour, remained loyal to her noble principles. In the palace, the vicinity of which the plot against Nasiru'd-Din Shah took place, a great multitude of princes, important officials and notables was present while Zarrin Taj was being interrogated. At the same time that she was once again in the presence of these people declaring, without fear or doubt, her adherence and attraction to the Babi sect, she did not hesitate to include in her confession that she was ready to give up her life for the sake of her religion. Nothing could weaken her determination, neither her executioners' threat nor the requests and tears of her husband and father who were present. The history of the world has hardly ever recorded [the story of] a woman, or even a man, who died such a tragic death with such fortitude. Zarrin Taj was born beautiful, and Qurrat'ul-Ayn wanted to die a great death.

Zarrin Taj was burned alive at the fortress in Tehran, and they threw her ashes into the winds of the horizons.

Qurratu'l-'Ayn illustrated the last page of her life in this verse. Who knows, she might have recited these two lines at that historical moment:

> Be a salamander, be a moth, I do not say;
> Yet brave, if you wish to be burned, stay.

This verse composed in two languages [Persian-Arabic] shows what eternal rapture for divine love she was in:

> The gleaming of your cheeks has risen;
> And the light of your countenance arisen.
> Why don't you cry out "Am I not your Lord?"
> Cry out, "Yea, yea."

Whether a sect or a religion; whether based on illusions or superstitions; whether resulting from the need of the age for renewal and development, it is very likely that Babism will revive—either in its old condition or in another form. And again it is very likely that it will totally perish in the narrow ditch kicked into it by the Iranian shahs. But Qurratu'l-'Ayn's name and memory is always alive and fascinating. Nothing whatsoever, no might and no onslaught can destroy this name. If the goal for the sake of which she gave up her life is destined to be windswept and annihilated, it is written on her grave; but if life and power is promised and facilitated by God, then Zarrin Taj's dream and name will eternally flash like lightning on her glorious and noble stone.

She is more authentic, more genuine and more eminent, and a greater heroine than Jeanne d'Arc, so much so that from Eve to the last of Eve's daughters to be born, every member of the noble community [the Muslims], when remembering this youthful Turkish woman from Qazvin, will be moved to tears and swell with pride. Ah! Alas, Qurratu'l-'Ayn! You were worth a thousand Nasiru'd-Din Shahs . . . a thousand Qajar dynasties. The executioners have not scattered your ashes to the horizons of Tehran, but from those horizons into the hearts of mankind. Every heart is your shrine, Tahirih! . . .

During Qurratu'l-'Ayn's interrogation, the other imprisoned Babis were also present. All, including the young girls and boys among the arrested, were happy and at ease. They witnessed how Tahirih left for the place of execution without saying a word, not even words of farewell. When these wretched ones' turn came, both those involved in the plot and those not involved, without exception, admitted that they were Babis and, blessing moreover the name of the Bab, Ali Muhammad Shirazi, whom they addressed as "*Hazrat*" [His Holiness], and the names of the other Babi disciples and martyrs and adding their plea "May God sanctify them," said that they were ready to face everything. . . .

The uprising in Mazindaran [Shaykh Tabarsi] and Qurratu'l-'Ayn's impetus were the greatest cause for these sudden changes. Zarrin Taj passed only a few month of this interval for the propagation of the sect and spent most of the time in prison. If she had been free and in more favourable circumstances, Iran for sure would have seen much better days.

**Notes**

From Süleyman Nazif, *Nasiruddin Shah ve Babiler* (Istanbul: Kanaat Kütüphanesi, 1923) pp. 35, 44-49. Translated by Necati Alkan. Translation published in: *Research Notes in Shaykhi, Babi and Baha'i Studies* (East Lansing), v. 4, no. 2, November 2000 <http://www.h-net.org/~bahai/notes/vol4/nazif.htm>

# TÁHIRIH IN HISTORY
## Western Considerations

ARMENIAN CHRISTIAN WOMEN
From northern Iran, wearing indoor clothing. Unmarried women wear a skullcap; married women add a headscarf. The clothing of Christian women is markedly different from the clothing of Muslim women.

# Kurratu'l-'Ayn

by Edward Granville Browne

I

The appearance of such a woman as Kurratu'l-'Ayn is in any country and any age a rare phenomenon, but in such a country as Persia it is a prodigy—nay, almost a miracle. Alike in virtue of her marvellous beauty, her rare intellectual gifts, her fervid eloquence, her fearless devotion, and her glorious martyrdom, she stands forth incomparable and immortal amidst her countrywomen. Had the Bábí religion no other claim to greatness, this were sufficient—that it produced a heroine like Kurratu'l-'Ayn.

In this note I do not propose to repeat facts with which everyone who has studied the subject is acquainted, neither shall I attempt to re-tell a tale which has been already set forth by Gobineau in language far more eloquent than I can command. My purpose is merely to add such new particulars as I have been able to glean from the *Táríkh-i-Jadíd* and from oral tradition. Before proceeding to do this, I wish once more to call attention to the graceful poem by Marie von Najmájer whereof Kurratu'l-'Ayn is the heroine.[1]

The following table, taken in conjunction with the remarks [previously made] will sufficiently serve to indicate Kurratu'l-'Ayn's family relationships:

The following particulars are derived from the *Táríkh-i-Jadíd*. During the life of Hájí Seyyid Kázim of Resht Kurratu'l-'Ayn visited Kerbelá, where she became acquainted not only with Seyyid Kázim himself, but with many of his chief followers, including Mullá Huseyn of Bushraweyh. When, on the death of Seyyid Kázim, Mullá Huseyn set out for Shíráz, Kurratu'l-'Ayn wrote a letter to him beg-

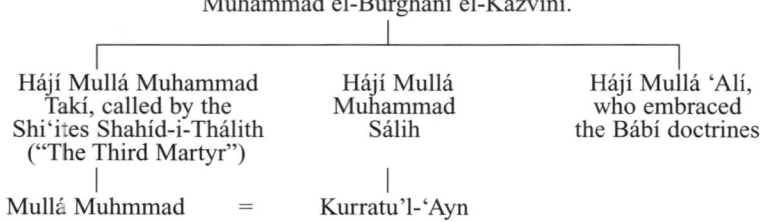

ging that should he succeed in finding the spiritual guide whom they were expecting[2] he would at once inform her. This letter Mullá Huseyn on his conversion placed in the hands of the Báb, who, recognizing the rare qualities and attainments of which it gave evidence, included its writer amongst the eighteen "Letters of the Living" *Persian text* who composed the "First Unity" of the Bábí hierarchy.

Kurratu'l-'Ayn continued for some time at Kerbelá, where, seated behind a curtain, she used to lecture and preach to the disciples of the late Seyyid Kázim. The governor, becoming aware of this, wished to arrest her, but she hastily quitted Kerbelá without a passport and went to Baghdad, where she proceeded directly to the house of the chief Muftí, before whom she defended her creed and her conduct with great ability. The question whether she should be allowed to continue her teaching was submitted first to the Páshá of Baghdad and then to the central government, the result being that she was ordered to leave Turkish territory. During her journey from Baghdad to Kirmánsháh and Hamadán she continued to preach, and made several converts to the Bábí faith, amongst these being Sheykh Sálih the Arab, Sheykh Táhir, Mullá Ibrahím of Mahallát, and Sheykh Sultán the Arab. Certain of the Bábís, however, were at first disposed to regard her efforts with disapproval, and some of these even wrote to the Báb asking whether it was seemly for a woman to preach publicly to men. In reply the Báb not only sanctioned her preaching and applauded her zeal, but bestowed on her the title of *Jenáb-i-Táhira* (Her Excellency the Pure), whereupon those who had been disposed to censure her expressed contrition and penitence, and her high position in the Bábí church became uncontested.

From Hamadán Kurratu'l-'Ayn intended to go to Teherán, hoping, it is said, to be able to convert Muhammad Sháh himself; but her father Hájí Mullá Muhammad Sálih, being apprized of this plan, sent servants to intercept her and bring her home to Kazvín. Perhaps it was on her return thither that she was married to her cousin Mullá Muhammad the son of Hájí Mullá Muhammad Takí, but of the date when this marriage was contracted I can find no indication. At all events the marriage must have been a most unhappy one, for Mullá Muhammad seems fully to have shared his father's hatred of the Sheykhís and Bábís, and finally Kurratu'l-'Ayn refused to live with him any longer.

The position of Kurratu'l-'Ayn, sufficiently irksome and even precarious already, was rendered perilous in the highest degree by the death of her uncle at the hands of certain Bábís[3]. Some have hinted that Kurratu'l-'Ayn was privy to this assassination, but of this there is absolutely no proof, and we may be sure that, had there been any evidence of her complicity, the Musulmáns would not have failed to make use of it to rid themselves of one who was well known to be amongst the most zealous supporters of the Báb. As it was, she was brought before the governor of Kazvín, charged by her husband with complicity in the murder of his father, and acquitted. Several of the Bábís were arrested and tortured, until finally one—Mírzá Sálih of Shíráz, according to the *Táríkh-i-Jadíd*, Sálih Táhir according to Subh-i-Ezel—confessed that he, alone and unabetted, had compassed the death of the murdered *mujtahid*, in proof of which he described in detail how the murder had been committed, and where the blood-stained knife with which the deed was done might be found. This Sálih was sent to Teherán with several others suspected of complicity, but he succeeded in making his escape, fettered as he was, to Mázandarán, where he was subsequently killed at Sheykh Tabarsí. As to the others arrested, *Táríkh-i-Jadíd* and Subh-i-Ezel are not completely in accord. Both agree, however, that Sheykh Sálih the Arab and Mullá Ibrahím of Mahallát (who, as we have already seen, were amongst the first proselytes gained by Kurratu'l-'Ayn) were of their number. The first of these was killed at Teherán; the second was taken back to Kazvín, where, in company with another (Sheykh Táhir according to the *Táríkh-i-Jadíd*, Hájí Muhammad 'Alí according to Subh-i-Ezel), he was cruelly done to death by the populace. These were the first Bábís who were put to death in Persia. The *Táríkh-i-Jadíd* adds the name of another—an old man called Hájí Asadu'lláh—who died of cold and fatigue during his conveyance to Teherán.

Although Kurratu'l-'Ayn had been acquitted of all share in her uncle's death, it was clearly impossible for her to remain in Kazvín any longer, even had she desired to do so, which scarcely seems probable. She accordingly set out by way of Teherán for Khurásán, and was present at the celebrated meeting of the Bábí chiefs at Badasht.⁴ From Badasht she turned back with Mullá Muhammad 'Alí of Bárfurúsh and his party towards Mázandarán. At this point the narrative of the *Táríkh-i-Jadíd* breaks off, neither is it, in spite of the author's promise, again renewed; while all other written histories are equally silent as to what befell Kurratu'l-'Ayn from the time that she separated from Mullá Muhammad 'Alí and his followers to the time when she was brought captive to Teherán and placed in the custody of Mahmúd Khán the *Kalántar*. From Subh-i-Ezel, however, I learned the following particulars. After separating from the Bábís who went to form the garrison of Sheykh Tabarsí, Kurratu'l-'Ayn went to Núr, where she remained unmolested till the final suppression of the Mázandarán insurrection. She was then delivered up to the government authorities by the people of Núr and sent to Teherán. On her arrival there she was brought before Násiru'd-Din Sháh, who, on seeing her, said:

از هیئتش خوشم می آید بگذار باشد

"I like her looks: leave her, and let her be."

She was accordingly placed under the custody of Mahmúd Khán the *Kalántar*, and in his house she remained till her execution in August A.D. 1852. Her imprisonment was not very rigorous, and she was occasionally seen by different Bábís under various pretexts.

Her life, indeed, was in no jeopardy till the disastrous attempt on the Sháh's life by certain Bábís[5] made the mere profession of the Bábí faith a crime deserving not death only, but the most horrible tortures, and gave rise to that reign of terror which has been so vividly described by Gobineau,[6] Lady Sheil,[7] Polak,[8] and Ussher.[9] Even then Kurratu'l-'Ayn might, by abjuring her faith, have escaped death, and exchanged glorious martyrdom and immortal fame for a few brief years of life; but this her noble spirit scorned to do. That she met the cruel fate reserved for her with "superhuman fortitude" is a fact to which Dr Polak, who actually witnessed her execution, testifies in the following words: "*Ich war Zeuge von der Hinrichtung der Kurret el ayn, die vom Kriegsminister und seinen Adjutanten vollzogen wurde; die schöne Frau erduldete den langsamen Tod mit übermenschlicher Stärke.*"[10] In what manner death was inflicted I have not been able to learn. Gobineau says that she was burned, but that the executioner first strangled her. Subh-i-Ezel says that the accounts of her death are various, one being that she was strangled with the bowstring in the Bágh-i-Íl-Kání; some with whom I conversed in Persia stated that she was killed in the Bágh-i-Lálé-zár; others that she was cast into a dry well in the garden of the palace called Nigáristán, which well was then filled up with stones. However this may be, we have it on Polak's authority that her death was painful and lingering, and that she met it as a heroine should do.

I was anxious to discover from Subh-i-Ezel whether it was true, as has often been alleged, that Kurratu'l-'Ayn discarded the veil. His reply, so far as I can remember, was as follows: "It is not true that she laid aside the veil. Sometimes, when carried away by her eloquence, she would allow it to slip down off her face, but she would always replace it after a few moments."

Kurratu'l-'Ayn's fame as a poetess is great, but during my sojourn in Persia I only succeeded in obtaining three of the poems attributed to her, viz. two short but very beautiful *ghazals* and a long *masnaví*. Of one of these *ghazals* I published the Persian text with a translation into English verse in my second paper on the Bábís in the *J. R. A. S.* for 1889.[11] I now give the second, which, though its authorship is more disputed, certainly savours strongly of Bábí doctrines and modes of expression.

ط

هو المحبوب

لمعات وجهك اشرقت و شعاع طلعتك اعتلا
زچه رو اَلَستُ بِرَبِّكم نزد بزن كه بَلَى بَلَى
بجواب طبل الستِ تو ز ولا چه كوس بلى زدند
همه خيمه زد بدر دلم سپه غم و حشم بلا
من و عشق آن مه خوبرو كه چو زد صلاى بلا برو
بنشاط و قهقهه شد فرو كه انا الشهيد بكربلا
چو شنيد الٰهُ مرگ من پئ ساز من شد و برگ من
فمشى الى مَهرَوِلاً و بكى على مُحَلحَلاً
چه شود كه آتش حبرق. زنيم بقلهٔ طور دل
فسكـكـتَـهُ و دكـكَتَهُ متدكدكاً متزلزلاً
پئ خوان دعوت عشق او همه شب ز خيل كرويان
رسد اين صفير مهيمنى كه گروه غمزده الصلا
تو چه قلس ماهى حبرق چه زنى ز بحر وجود دم
نشين چو طاهره دم بدم بشنو خروش نهنگ لا

The effulgence of thy face flashed forth and the rays of thy visage arose on high;
Why lags the word "*Am I not your Lord?*" "*Yea, that thou art*" let us make reply.12
"*Am I not's*" appeal from thy drum to greet what "*Yeas*" do the drums of devotion beat;
At the gate of my heart I behold the feet and the tents of the host of calamity.13
That fair moon's love for me, I trow, is enough, for he laughed at the hail of woe,
And exulting cried as he sank below, "The Martyr of Kerbelá am I."14
When he heard my death-wail drear, for me he prepared, and arranged my gear for me,
He advanced to lament at my bier for me, and o'er me wept right bitterly.
What harm if thou with the fire of amaze should'st set my Sinai-heart ablaze.
Which thou first mad'st fast in a hundred ways but to shake and shatter so ruthlessly?15
To convene the guests to his feast of love all night from the angel-host above

Peals forth this summons ineffable 'Hail, sorrow-stricken community!'
Can a scale of the fish of amaze like thee aspire to sing of Being's Sea?
Sit still like Táhira, hearkening to what the monster of 'No' doth cry."[16]

## II

Turning from the Báb, there is another figure amongst those who took part in this sad drama which irresistibly commands our attention. I mean the beautiful and accomplished Kurratu'l-'Ayn, the heroine poetess, nay, almost the prophetess, of the new faith, distinguished by the title of *Jenáb-i-Táhiré*, "Her Excellence the Pure." Anxious as I was to obtain some of her poems, I only met with a very limited amount of success. None of the Bábís at Shíráz whom I conversed with had any in their possession, and they said that Kazvín and Hamadán, where Kurratu'l-'Ayn had preached, and Teherán, where she had suffered martyrdom, would be the most likely places to obtain them. However, at Yezd I saw copies of two short poems (*ghazals*) attributed to her authorship. Both of these are in the same metre (*kámil*), and have the same rhyme; and of each of them I obtained a copy for myself. I wrote to one of my friends at Shíráz, and asked his opinion on their authenticity. He replied that one of them, beginning,

> '*Lama 'átu wajhika ashrakat, wa shi'á'u tal'atika' 'tilá:*
> *Zi ché rú* '*Alasta bi-Rabbikum?*' *na-zaní? Bi-zan ki* '*Balá!*
> *Balá!*'

was not by Kurratu'l-'Ayn, but by a Súfí poet called Suhbat, of Lár. Although I have on several occasions heard the latter spoken of by dervishes and others in Persia with the highest approbation, I have neither been able to obtain his works, nor to discover any particulars about him; for he is not mentioned in any of the Biographies of Poets (*Tazkirés*) which I have been able to consult, not even in the *Riyázu'l-'A'rifín* of the learned *Rizá-Kulí Khán,* published a year or two ago at Teherán.

The second poem attributed to Kurratu'l-'Ayn, beginning,

> *Jadhabátu shawkika aljamat bi-salásili'l-gham wal'l-balá*
> *Hama 'áshikán-i-shikasté-dil, ki dihand ján bi-rah-i-walá,*

was thought by my friend, and pronounced with certainty by others, to be undoubtedly the work of Kurratu'l-'Ayn.

In a small work on Persian grammar called *Tanbíhu'l-Atfál*, composed by Hájí Mírzá Huseyn Khán, Persian Consul at Trebizonde, and printed in Constantinople in A.H. 1298 (A.D. 1881), the first verse of the first of these two poems, which I have quoted above, is cited as an example, and its author is stated to be the above-mentioned Suhbat (Mullá Muhammad Bákir) of Lár. Further on in the same work a verse occurring in the second poem is quoted, and attributed to Mírzá 'Abdu'l-Karím, whose *takhallus* was Símá; Although these poems, especially the first, can only be referred very doubtfully to the authorship of Kurratu'l-'Ayn, it must be borne in mind that the odium which attaches to the name of *Bábí* amongst Persian Muhammadans would render impossible the recitation by them of verses confessedly composed by her. If, therefore, she were actually the authoress of poems, the grace and beauty of which compelled an involuntary admiration even from her enemies, it would seem extremely probable that they should seek to justify their right to admire them by attributing them to some other writer, and this view is supported by an assertion which I have heard made by a learned Persian with whom I was acquainted in Teherán, and who, though not actually a Bábí, did not lack a certain amount of sympathy for those who were such, to the effect that many poems written by Kurratu'l-'Ayn were amongst the favourite songs of the people, who were for the most part unaware of their authorship. Open allusions to the Báb had, of course, been cut out or altered, so that no one could tell the source from whence they came.

Without pretending to assert positively, then, that either of these two poems is by Kurratu'l-'Ayn, I venture to give a translation of the second of them, which I have attempted to versify in imitation of the original metre, so as to afford a better idea of its style than could be given by a literal rendering in prose. In this I have endeavoured to adhere as closely as possible to the sense of the original, even though the English may have suffered thereby. I have chosen the second rather than the first poem, because there is a stronger consensus of opinion in favour of its being the work of Kurratu'l-'Ayn. The text of the poem will be found appended at the end of this paper.

## TRANSLATION OF THE POEM BEGINNING
*Jadhabátu shawkika aljamat,* etc.

> The thralls of yearning love constrain in the bonds of pain and calamity
> These broken-hearted lovers of thine to yield their lives in their zeal for thee.
> Though with sword in hand my Darling stand with intent to slay, though I sinless be,
> If it pleases him, this tyrant's whim, I am well content with his tyranny.
> As in sleep I lay at the break of day that cruel Charmer came to me,
> And in the grace of his form and face the dawn of the morn I seem to see.
> The musk of Cathay might perfume gain from the scent of those fragrant tresses rain,
> While his eyes demolish a faith in vain attacked by the pagans of Tar tary.
> With you, who contemn both love and wine for the hermit's cell and the zealot's shrine,
> What can I do? for our Faith divine you hold as a thing of infamy?
> The tangled curls of thy darling's hair, and thy saddle and steed are thy only care,
> In thy heart the Absolute hath no share, nor thought of the poor man's poverty,
> Sikandar's pomp and display be thine, the Kalandar's habit and way be mine,
> That, if it please thee, I resign, while this, though bad, is enough for me.
> The country of "I" and "We" forsake; thy home in Annihilation make,
> Since fearing not this step to take, thou shalt gain the highest Felicity.

Besides these poems, I have a copy of a Masnaví of about 570 couplets in the same metre as the Masnaví of Jalálu'd-Dín Rúmí (*Ramal-i-musaddas-i-mahzúf*) attributed to Kurratu'l-'Ayn. That this latter is a Bábí poem I have no doubt, but I have not yet had a time to examine it carefully with a view of determining whether it may not be a later production in praise of Behá rather than the Báb. For this reason, and also on account of its length, I leave it for future consideration.

**Notes**
I. Reprinted from "Note Q" of ['Abdu'l-Bahá], *A Traveller's Narrative: Written to Illustrate the Episode of the Báb; composed a.d. 1886 being an authentic description of the Persian Bábí movement, Babism, c. 1844-1886*; trans. and ed. Edward

G. Browne. 2nd ed. (Cambridge University Press, 1891 [Amsterdam: Philo Press, 1975; Los Angeles: Kalimat Press, 2004]).

II. Reprinted from "The Bábís of Persia. II. Their Literature and Doctrines," *Journal of the Royal Asiatic Society* (London) Vol. 21 (1889) pp. 934-37.

The form of the notes has been slightly altered and expanded to conform with the rest of the book.—Ed.

1. See *supra* p. 207. (The page numbers here and below refer to Browne's translation of *A Traveller's Narrative*, and not to the pages in this book.—Ed.)
2. See pp. 239-240 *supra*.
3. See p. 198 *supra*.
4. See Joseph Arthur, comte de Gobineau, *Les Religions et les Philosophies dans l'Asie Centrale* (Paris: Didier, 1865) pp. 180-84.
5. See Note T *infra* and pp. 49-50 *supra*.
6. Gobineau, *Les Religions,* pp. 301-03.
7. Mary Sheil, *Glimpses of Life and Manners in Persia* (London: J. Murray, 1856) pp. 273-82.
8. Jakob Eduard Polak, *Persien: das Land und seine Bewohner* (Leipzig: F. A. Brockhaus, 1865) Vol. 1, pp. 352-53.
9. John Ussher, *A Journey from London to Persepolis. . .* (London: Hurst and Blackett, 1865) pp. 627-29.
10. "I was a witness to the execution of Kurret el Ayn, by the war minister and his assistant; the beautiful woman endured her slow death with superhuman fortitude."—Ed.
11. Edward Granville Browne, "The Bábís of Persia. II. Their Literature and Doctrines," *Journal of the Royal Asiatic Society* (London), Vol. 21 (1889) pp. 936-37 and 991.
12. That is, "Why do you hesitate to lay claim to a divine nature? Were you to do so, all of us would admit your claim." See Kur'án vii. 171, and B. ii., pp. 917-18 and note [*The Koran*; trans. by George Sale. London: Thomas Tegg, 1825—Ed.]
13. The following lines from a poem attributed to Nabíl express a similar idea:–

    چو کسی طریق مرا رود    کنمش ندا که خبر شود
    که هر انکه عاشق من شود    نرهد ز محنت و ابتلا

    If one should choose my path to go I will cry to him that he well may know
    That none shall escape from grief and woe who is once afflicted with
    love for me.
14. That is, Imám Huseyn, with whom the Báb repeatedly declares himself to be identical in essence.
15. That is, "You first strengthened my heart with knowledge, and inspired it with zeal and enthusiasm; then you crushed and subdued it with love. Were it not well if you would now kindle on it, as on Mount Sinai, that fire whence comes the cry إنی انا الله 'Verily I am God'?" Cf. Kur'án xxviii. 30, and vii. 139.

16. That is, "How can you, who are but as a scale on some little fish which swims wonderingly in the vast expanses of the sea, speak fittingly of the Ocean of Being? Sit still then, as I, Kurratu'l-'Ayn (*Jenáb-i-Táhira*), do, and listen to the roar of the monster, whale, crocodile, or Leviathan which continually cries لا اله الا انا 'There is no God but me'." Some versions of this poem have بنشین چو طوطی و دم بدم "Sit still like a parrot" &c. at the beginning of the second hemistich of this couplet.

NASIRU'D-DIN SHAH IN HIS HAREM
c. 1870, photographed here with seven of his wives, wearing indoor dress.

# Qourrèt-oul-Aïne

by A.-L.-M. Nicolas
Translated by Peter Terry

## I
### The Council of Bedecht

Molla Saléh had, among his children a girl, Zarrine Tadj—the crown of gold—who called attention to herself from earliest childhood. Instead of devoting herself to games and amusements like her peers did, she spent hours listening to the theological discourses of her parents. Her lively intelligence quickly assimilated all of Islamic science, without floundering, and soon she took part in discussing the most obscure and esoteric points. The traditions [*hadith*] held no secrets for her. Her reputation was quickly established in the town, and her fellow townsmen considered her a true prodigy.

A prodigy in knowledge, but also a prodigy in beauty: for the child grew up and became a young girl whose face gleamed with such radiant beauty that she was given the surname of Qourrèt-oul-Aïne—which M. de Gobineau translates "Consolation of the Eyes."

Her brother, Abd oul Vahhab Qasvini, who inherited the learning and reputation of his father, has himself stated, even though he remained (in appearance at least) a Muslim: "All of us, her brothers, her cousins, we did not dare to speak in her presence, so much did her knowledge intimidate us; and if we hazarded to express an hypothesis on a contested point of doctrine, she demonstrated to us that we were taking the wrong route in such a clear, precise, and peremptory fashion that we retired, all confused."

She attended the classes of her father and of her uncle in the same room as two or three hundred students, but concealed behind a curtain; and more than once, she refuted the explanations that these two elders proposed for this or that question.

Her reputation became immense among the learned of Persia and the highest ulama consented to adopt some of her hypotheses and her opinions. This fact is even more remarkable inasmuch as the Shiite Muslim religion has placed woman almost at the rank of the animal: she does not have a soul and exists only for reproduction.

While still very young, she married the son of her uncle, Mohammed Qasvini, who was the Imam Jomé [leader of the Friday prayers] of the town and, afterwards, she went to Kerbélah where she assisted in the lessons of Seyyed Kazem Rechti. She shared the ideas of her teacher with passion, ideas which she knew of previously, Qasvine having become a center for the Cheikhies [Shaykhí] doctrines.

She possessed, as we will see, an ardent temperament, a clear and lucid intelligence, a marvellous composure, and an indomitable courage.

All these qualities together were to bring her to occupy herself with the Báb, whom she heard about after her return to Qasvine. What she learned about him interested her so intensely that she entered into correspondence with the Reformer and, soon convinced by him, she made her conversion known to one and all. (1848)

The scandal was immense and the clergy were dismayed. In vain her husband, her father, and her brothers counseled her to renounce this dangerous foolishness, but she remained inflexible and loudly proclaimed her faith.

It is perfectly untrue that she, from this moment, rejected the usage of the veil and that she appeared in assemblies with an uncovered face. So complete a rejection of all the most sacred laws would have been promptly and severely punished. Prejudice is too strongly rooted in the spirit of the Persians for her to have dared to do so, and it would have served no purpose. Furthermore, up until the time of the council of Bedecht, the command for those who knew the secret thoughts of the Báb was to announce that the promises contained in the Qoran were being realized, that the hidden Imam was manifest, and that he was going to submit the whole world to the religion of Islam. It would have been a singular aberration to act in contradiction to the laws which one announced as deemed to be so soon triumphant.

These two reasons suffice to demonstrate the error which M. de Gobineau made. Furthermore, we will soon see where and how Qourrèt-oul-Aïne appeared for the first time before a crowd with an uncovered face.

In any case, the scandal went on, growing every day; and it was with a sigh of relief that her family accepted the proposition she made to them that she return to Kerbélah. It was hoped on the one hand that her absence would make her forget [her folly], and on the other that the majesty of the sacred shrines would cause her to return to her senses. But it was in vain that she accomplished the pilgrimage; for, in the midst of the illustrious tombs of the martyrs [of Shí'í Islam—the Imam 'Alí and the Imam Husayn], she remained as resolute a Bábí as she had been in Qasvine. So before her attitudes caused some grave consequence in the very center of fanatical Shiism, her family believed they must affect her return.

Hadji Mohammed Hammami was chosen for this mission, along with several servants from the house. This is how he described his journey:

> I arrived in Kerbélah and immediately went to see Qourrèt-oul-Aïne. I gave to her the letters that had been entrusted to me by her father, her husband, and her uncle. I begged her to obey the orders that they contained, and I ended up convincing her by my insistence. I prepared a conveyance for her, and we set off. Some Bábís accompanied her until we reached a forest of date palms which was close by, where they took leave of her.
>
> I was very happy to have succeeded in my mission, and I thought only of the joy of returning. Suddenly, after having passed the said forest, I was joined by some riders who approached the conveyance, respectfully saluted Qourrèt-oul-Aïne, and took up escorting her.
>
> When we arrived at the way station, it was they who installed her at a certain distance from us and who devoted themselves to her service.
>
> It was like this all through the journey. When we arrived in Qasvine, the riders dispersed in all directions.
>
> I conducted Qourrèt-oul-Aïne to the house of her father and told him what I had seen. Hadji Molla Taghi who was present at the meeting, showed

himself to be very irritated, and ordered all the servants to prevent this woman from leaving the house under any circumstances, and to permit no one without an authorization expressly from himself, to visit her.

These orders given, he visited the traveler and hoped by persuasion to convince her of the error in which she was engaged. He could not do so, and furious before her calm and conviction, he could not restrain himself from cursing the Bab and showering him with insults.

Qourrèt-oul-Aïne looked him in the face then and said to him: "Alas for you, for I see your mouth filled with blood."

After that, she was closely watched and spent her days walking in what now became her prison, singing psalms and sacred songs.

One night, armed men forced entry into the house. The prisoner received them, had them enter, and delivered a sermon that lasted for more than two hours. When this became known, Hadji Molla Taghi was informed. Giving free reign to his temper, he insulted his niece, and beat her.

Thereafter, excitement grew every day in the town. The Babis of Qasvine could not repress their enthusiasm, and these signs of happiness further increased the fury of the Muslims. There was nothing but heated debates, mutual insults, and the renewal of troubles without ceasing. Qourrèt-oul-Aïne, always in correspondence with the Bab, had just received an order from him to go forth and evangelize the provinces.

Seyyed Ali Mohammed was at this time imprisoned in [the fortress of] Makou. This precipitated further events, for it became urgent to take counsel. The imprisonment of the Prophet could be the prelude to a bloody end. Already in various places, isolated Babis had been massacred and persecution was always menacing. If they did not take immediate and forceful measures, they risked seeing all this agitation collapse as it was being born, and the new religion drowned in rivers of blood. And this very religion, was it not now finally necessary to unveil it before the eyes of its followers, so they might follow it without doubting what it was in reality and where it could lead them? Was it not necessary to finally consider a means of removing the Bab from the painful and dangerous situation in which he was found? All of these questions were the subject of an active correspondence among the various Babi leaders, and it was precisely in order to find the solution that it was decided to convene a general convocation, which we have called the Council of Bedecht.

It was therefore necessary that Qourrèt-oul-Aïne find a way to leave Qasvine. But before this she had to punish the heretic who had dared, in her presence, to proffer a curse upon the Bab.

Molla Mohammed Taghi had a habit of going out before sunrise to say his morning prayers in the mosque. There he saw nobody but the servants charged with the upkeep of the temple and two or three beggars. That morning, he had just entered the mosque when an individual struck him in the mouth with the blow of a lance, fulfilling thus the prediction which his niece had made. Five or six other assassins threw themselves upon him and dispatched him with blows of saber and knife. This deed accomplished, each left for his own place, leaving the victim where he fell.

The tumult was frightful in the town. This bold sacrilege made the hearts of all the Muslims tremble. They solemnly proclaimed Molla Mohammed Taghi a martyr of the Islamic faith and loudly called for the punishment of the guilty ones. The governor arrested all those whom he suspected of being Babis, and he referred the matter immediately to Mohammed Chah. In the meantime, an Arab, Cheikh Saleh, declared himself to be solely responsible for the assassination.

Qourrèt-oul-Aïne was closely watched, but the investigation was long, and one lovely night the Babis came and took her away. She was mounted on a horse and the troop left the town through a breach in the city walls. Naieb Quli, who afterwards became the agent of the shah, tells of this escape thus:

> I was among the servants who accompanied this woman. As soon as we had left the town, we abandoned the main road and followed that of Zah'ra of Qasvine. We arrived by traveling in this way at Enderman, near the Chahzadeh Abd Oul Azim. Having arrived there, she gave me a letter and commanded that I carry it to Téhéran, to the house of Mirza Bouzourg Nouri,[1] where I was to give it to Mirza Housseïn Ali.[2]
>
> I arrived in the town early in the morning and remitted my letter into the hands of its destined recipient. He ordered me to return to Endermane and to announce that he would arrive there himself in the afternoon. In fact, about five hours before sunset, Mirza Housseïn Ali, accompanied by some riders holding saddled horses by the reins, came to join us. Qourrèt-oul-Aïne retired to change clothes and mounted a horse whose bridle was made of gold. We each one of us mounted one of the horses that had been brought, and we set off, one hour before sunset. Two hours later, we were

in the house of Mirza Housseïn Ali. We remained there for several days during which Qourrèt-oul-Aïne received numerous visitors.

About five days after our arrival, I was surprised to see that there was only one single servant left in the house. He served me tea and announced that a horse was saddled for me in the stable. He told me to go to Mesker Abad, near Sourkh Eçar. I arrived in this village before lunch, and I saw lots of people and numerous tents. Qourrèt-oul-Aïne summoned me, and asked me if I wanted to convert to Babism. Upon my refusal, she gave me several handfuls coins and said to me: "Tonight you are still my guest, but tomorrow morning you will leave for Téhéran."

After dinner she left with her people, and the next morning I returned to the town with some servants who did not wish to follow her. I learned afterwards that she had gone to Khorassan.

This was, in fact, the route that she took to arrive at Bedecht where she found herself with Molla Husseïn Bouchrouyéhi—the Bab el-Bab, Mirza Housseïn Ali, Quouddous and others, who had arrived before her.

These persons discussed amongst themselves certain obscure points over which they were not in accord. They chose as arbitrator the one who hads just arrived, who gave her responses in writing, which all accepted.

The imprisonment of the Bab was the object of the first consultation. They agreed to organize a pilgrimage to the mountain of Makou. Their missionaries were to spread out over the land, recruit as many pilgrims as possible, and as soon as their troop was formed present themselves at the prison of the Prophet. Even though no history says it, even though oral tradition is mute on this subject, it is certain that—in the final analysis—this was to result in the liberation of the prisoner. I certainly hope that it was decided in principle not to make recourse to violence, but I am convinced that this mass of pilgrims would have waited for the outcome of events and, if the Government had decided upon the death of the Bab, they would have opposed the execution of the sentence by force. Perhaps they even had the idea that, in case too many troops should attack them, they could easily escape into Russia.

Their action on behalf of the prisoner thus decided, the new doctrine was examined in all its aspects. They were all unanimous on this point: that Seyyèd Ali Mohammed was a new prophet greater than those who had preceded him and that, even as Jesus had abrogated the law of Moses, even as Muhammad had abrogated that of

Christ, the Bab had abrogat[3]ed the Qoran, which [doctrine] was represented by this formula—"God has manifested himself and the earlier religion is abrogated; the old law is uprooted; we must disseminate the new among men."

Qourrèt-oul-Aïne declared then that it was right and fair to inform the ignorant Babis of this fundamental teaching.[4] Quouddous observed that their followers were sincere Muslims, that their natural fanaticism had been even more excited by their predictions, and that it was actually dangerous to disillusion them.

Qourrèt-oul-Aïne replied that to postpone the explanations [of these teachings] until later would only delay the inevitable; that furthermore the danger would only grow with the exaltation of their fellows, and that it would be better—before a drop of blood be spilled—to be assured of the conscious devotion of those who wished to follow them.

Would there be any? This was the heart of the question, and all besides Qourrèt-oul-Aïne were of the view that, at the first words they would hear pronounced against the Qoran, their adherents would be appalled by the blasphemy, and would cover them with maledictions and insults; and that might not be the worst of it. They could not imagine without trembling the rage that would follow the shock [in the hearts of] these unknowing Babis. Perhaps for the first time, they understood the responsibility they had in having sought to attract human beings to such a terrible adventure without making them aware of what they were engaged in.

Things were at great risk of turning out badly when Qourrèt-oul-Aïne thought of a strategy.

To understand this plan, one must know that the Shiite religion condemns every apostate [from the religion of Islam] to death without remission. No excuse is accepted, and even if the transgressor returns to Islam, he cannot stop or suspend the sentence pronounced against him by the law. But it is not so for women. They are just reproducing animals; they are not responsible for their acts. Also, if one of them happens to change religion, she cannot do so except unconsciously—one must then reason with her, instruct her, make her understand her crime, and bring her back to Islam. Her return to her original religion assures forgiveness for her mistake. Only if she persists in her deadly error, it is then, and only then, that she merits death.

It was by stressing this distinction of Shi'i law that Qourrèt-oul-Aïne convinced her coreligionists to attempt the adventure. "We will convene," she said, "all those who have come here with us. Quouddous will not attend the gathering. When our faithful ones have assembled, I will unveil all the truth to them. I will make them understand the manifestation of God and the abrogation of the Qoran. If these men accept, we will have attained our aim without difficulty; if on the contrary they are scandalized and revolt, they will certainly go to inform the only one of their leaders who did not take part in the meeting. Quouddous then will renounce me, will declare me an unbeliever, and will try to make me return to Islam. This will take some days, during which we will have time to calm the excitement and convince our people. If we are not successful, then I will appear to accept the arguments of Quouddous, and I will pretend to return to the Qoran."

After having maturely reflected upon this proposition, the leaders understood that it was the best means to arrange things. As it was necessary to make this proclamation, it was better to make it immediately and in a fashion that would not compromise them all.

All these dispositions having been taken and determined, the Babis were summoned to a sermon, as was done every day in the camp. Everyone knew that Her Highness the Pure [Táhirih] was to speak. Everyone came to the meeting except Quouddous, who found a way to make his absence and explained it by an illness which obliged him to take to bed.

Qourrèt-oul-Aïne had, conforming to the usage she had adopted, caused a light piece of cloth to be suspended from two cables like a curtain. It was always from behind this veil that she spoke. That day she dressed in her most beautiful garments and her richest adornments. She ordered that her two maidservants stand a little behind her, armed with scissors. At a sign that she would make, the two of them together were to cut the cords holding the cloth, which would fall in a single motion.

She began forthwith her lecture: the adventure she had planned, the very natural emotion which she felt, the hope of success, the fear of a failure excited her to such a point that never before had she been so eloquent or so persuasive. The listeners, charmed by her voice and by her talent, listened to her with profound attention—no one moved.

At the moment when she pronounced these words: "You must today all know that God has manifested himself and the Qoran is abrogated: a new book has descended to us from heaven, a new law is given to us," she made the agreed upon sign. The maidservants obeyed her, the curtain fell, and resplendent she appeared to the eyes of her listeners. She returned for one second to her maidservants as if to ask them to take account of what had happened, and immediately she faced the crowd: "What does this accident matter?" she said. "This has no importance—am I not your sister and are you not my brothers? And what sister has ever hidden her face from her brother?"

But the effect produced was overwhelming. Some hid their faces with their hands, others prostrated themselves, others enveloped their heads in their garments so as not to see the face of Her Highness the Pure One. If looking at the face of an unknown woman who passes in the street is a serious sin, what a crime was this for one's eyes to rest upon the saint that she was?

She tried to convince them, walking among them and calling them her brothers, telling them that the Qoran being abrogated, and the law which ordained that women be veiled existed no longer. But she could not succeed. Some, very few, looked at her. Mirza Husseïn Ali Beha, understanding that the scene had lasted long enough and that it might turn towards the tragic, threw his overcoat, called an *aba*, over the head of Qourrèt-oul-Aïne and conducted her to his tent.

The meeting ended in the midst of an indescribable tumult. Insults poured down upon a woman so indecent as to show herself in this way, with an uncovered face. Some said that she had suddenly gone mad, others that it was a provocation, others—very few—took her defense. The discussion intensified to the point of violence, and in the end it was decided to go inform Quouddous of the scandal which had just happened. Only those who had defended her installed themselves around the tent of Her Highness Tahéré.

Quouddous received the malcontents and had them describe the affair in minutest detail. He could thus see for himself the horror that was inspired in these fanatical Muslims by the act of Qourrèt-oul-Aïne. Not wishing to deflate the emotions which had exploded with such force, and thinking to reserve this in the future, he declared: "The fact in itself is incomprehensible and confuses me. If in acting and in speaking as she has Her Highness Tahéré has really expressed her conviction, she is an unbeliever and you must hereafter consider her such. But perhaps there is in all of this a hidden significance."

As the speaker had hoped, these last words fully preoccupied the imagination of those who had heard them. They sought with passion the inner purpose, the mysterious significance [of these events], and from then on, a basis for discussion was found.

Every day Quouddous drove deeper into the spirit of his adherents the doubt which he had so deftly seeded. "Certainly," he said, "the veil is more a custom than a law; the wives of the Prophet did not veil themselves except after an Arab had the impudence to wish to buy Aïcha from Muhammad, and one can think that the commands of the Qoran concern only these sacred wives. But this custom is venerable in its antiquity and, furthermore, protects the modesty of our wives and the sanctity of the family. Certainly, if the contrary usage established itself, men would get used to it very quickly and, from thereon, they would respect those with whom it is forbidden for them to have commerce. This might even improve the debauched customs of our large cities. But how dare anyone say that the Qoran is abrogated and wish to substitute a new law? The Mahdi must explain all that is obscure in the Divine Book, but he must amplify it, not destroy it. Qourrèt-oul-Aïne is a heretic."

Having thus reconciled them to so unexpected an act of Qourrèt-oul-Aïne, he deftly insisted on the obscurities and the inconsequentials of the Qoran, all the while renewing every day her excommunication. When he thought he had sufficiently prepared them, he informed his associates to attempt a final test.

Qourrèt-oul-Aïne did not remain inactive. When she was informed of the excommunication pronounced against her, she assembled those who had remained faithful to her, whose number had increased since the earliest days. She explained to them the new doctrine, demonstrated to them the divinity of the Bab, and excommunicated in his turn Quouddous and his adherents. Her unmatched talent won over the conviction of those whom the marvelous beauty of her face did not predispose altogether in her favor. When Quouddous let her know that the hour had come to try a last assault, she asked for two men who were ready to die. Two young men presented themselves, and she gave them her instructions.

They went to the enemy camp and arrived there at the moment

when Quouddous made his daily address. They interrupted him and shouted: "Her Highness the Pure reproaches you for saying bad things about her without daring to debate her in person. She thus challenges you to come into our camp and to dispute with her according to reason and true arguments, and this publicly. That if you triumph over her, she will acknowledge this and will obey you; if, on the contrary, it is she who triumphs over you, it will be for you to incline yourself towards her and to submit."

"No," said Quouddous, "This woman has apostatized her religion: I want neither to see her, nor to speak with her."

"Certainly," they replied, "we will not bring back a response so offensive to her. Therefore, here are the three alternatives that she has left us: either we must bring you to her willingly; or, if you refuse, bring her your head; or, if we do not succeed, ourselves be killed in seeking to succeed in this. These are the orders which we have received, and we are here to execute them. So then, choose: Come, be killed, or kill us."

Quouddous turned towards his companions and said to them: "It is you that must reply: if you say to me *kill*, I will kill; if you say *die*, I will die; if you say *go*, I will go."

There was a lively discussion, but the decision was not long in coming; it was formulated thus: "Go find Qourrèt-oul-Aïne and speak with her; it is better than killing or being killed."

Quouddous then arose and, followed by all his people, went to the camp of Tahéré. When all the people had taken their places, our heroine came to sit opposite her adversary and the discussion immediately began. By deft citations from the Qoran and the *hadith*, she successfully demonstrated what the task of the hidden Imam was to be: that he was charged with speaking all the divine truths ordained in the name of God, and that before the grandeur of this role the stations of all the prophets gone before, including Muhammad, were completely effaced.

Defeated, Quouddous arose and proclaimed loudly: "That which she says is the Truth, and what she did it well done." He then turned towards her and asked her forgiveness for his errors and his blasphemies. All his people imitated him, and the new religion was thus founded in the midst of universal enthusiasm and happiness.

After some days given to joy and mutual congratulations, the leaders separated in order to search for pilgrims [willing to go to Mákú]. Mollah Houssein Buchrouyehi retraced his way towards the interior of Khorassan. Quouddous directed himself towards Mazanderan. And Qourrèt-oul-Aïne, after having been escorted for some days by the apostle of Mazanderan [Bahá'u'lláh], separated from him and seems to have directed herself to Qasvine, passing of course through Nour [Bahá'u'lláh's home region]. We will return to her around 1266.

## II
### The Execution of Qourrèt-oul-Aïne

It is certain that Qourrèt-oul-Aïne returned to Qasvine,[5] because it was then that she was arrested and taken to Téhéran where she was imprisoned in the house of Mahmoud Khan, the Qalenter [mayor].

She remained there for a long period, receiving numerous visits from men as well as women. She impressed the latter by demonstrating the abject role that Islam had assigned to them, and she captivated them in showing the liberty and respect accorded to them by the new religion. There were, as a result, many domestic scenes from which the husbands did not always exit victorious.

These discussions could have lasted for a long time if Mirza Agha Khan Nouri had not been appointed the Sadr A'azam. The prime minister gave the order to Hadji Molla Mirza Mohammed Endermani and Hadji Molla Ali Kéni to interview her in order to examine her convictions. There were seven meetings between the two men and the prisoner. She discoursed with passion and affirmed that the Bab was the promised and awaited Imam. Her interviewers remarked to her that, according to the prophecies, the promised Imam must come from [the heavenly cities of] Djab oul Qa and Djab oul Sa. She replied to them with vehemence that this was not true, that these were false traditions, that these two cities did not exist, and that this was only a superstition worthy of an ailing mind. She proclaimed the new doctrine, bringing forth the truth, but they continued to clash with her citing the same argument referring to Djab oul Qa.

Impatient with them, she said, "The arguments that you give are those of an ignorant and stupid child. When will you stop these insanities, these lies? When will you lift your eyes to the Sun of Reality?"

Infuriated by this blasphemy, Hadji Molla Ali arose and addressed his companion, saying: "What would it profit us to have more discussions with an infidel?" They returned to the home of one of them and drew up the verdict that, affirming her apostasy and her refusal to make penitence, condemned her to death in the name of the Qoran!

One of the women, a Muslim maidservant in the house of the Qalenter, describes the sojourn of Qourrèt-oul-Aïne there in this fashion:

> The prisoner's habit was to rise at the time of the *séhèr* (a little before dawn), while everyone else was still asleep. She made her ablutions, all the while softly chanting prayers and spontaneous praises of God. During the day she did not leave the room in which she was installed, which she kept in a state of scrupulous cleanliness. Nobody was admitted to her presence without having first obtained her permission. Alone, she was always carefully dressed and held herself as if she was in the midst of assembled company without letting anything go. Sometimes she arose and walked in her room while praying. The women who came to see her, after having received clearance, were all captivated by the charm of her beauty and her eloquence; they were won over and transported in their admiration of her.
>
> While she was a prisoner, the marriage of the son of the Qalenter was held at the house. All the wives of the important personages in the town were naturally invited. But, no matter how much the family tried to entertain the guests with all the diversions that are encountered in these circumstances, with great cries the guests called for Qourrèt-oul-Aïne to be brought in. Finally she presented herself, and she began to speak. Musicians and dancers were sent in, but forgetting all the sweet things of which they are so fond, the women had eyes and attention only for Qourrèt-oul-Aïne.
>
> Finally, one night she left her room, as she was accustomed to doing. I was awake and I saw her go into the courtyard where she washed her whole body. Then she returned to her room, where she changed into all white clothing. She perfumed herself while singing, and I had never seen her so content and so joyous. She spoke to all the women of the household and begged them to pardon the discomforts which her presence had brought upon them and the wrongs she had committed towards them. She acted, in a word, exactly like someone who is going to undertake a great journey. We were all surprised, asking ourselves what this meant. The evening having arrived, she wrapped herself in a *tchagehour*. Her joy, in acting this way was so strange that we began to weep, for we loved her on account of her goodness and her inexhaustible benevolence. But she smiled at us and said: 'Tonight I am going to undertake a great, a very

great voyage.' At that moment, there was a knock on the door to the street. 'Run and open it,' she said. 'It is me they have come for.'

It was the Qalenter who entered. He came into her room and said to her: 'Come, madam, for you have been summoned.'

'Yes,' she said, 'I know where I will be taken; I know what will be done to me. But, remember well, a day will come when your master will in turn kill you.' (This prediction was realized in short order.)

She thus went out with the Qalenter, dressed as she was. We did not know where they were taking her and did not learn until the next day that she had been executed.

One of the nephews of the Qalenter gives the following details on the death of Qourrèt-oul-Aïne:

When the juridical sentence of Hadji Molla Mirza Mohammed Endermi and Hadji Molla Ali Kéni, condemning to death the Babi apostle was submitted to the shah, His Majesty ordained her execution. The secret was carefully guarded and was known only to two government functionaries. Already some days before, my uncle had given me the order to attentively watch the police and by frequent patrols to assure myself that the policemen were actually at their posts. An ordinance was published forbidding the inhabitants of the city from remaining in the streets later than three hours after sunset, the hour after which it was forbidden for anyone to leave his dwelling. That night I received the order to establish a cordon of policemen from the house of the Qalenter to the garden of Ilkhani. I made excuses to my men as best I could and ordered them to fire upon whoever would present himself who was not of our administration. Four hours after sunset, the Qalenter asked if all the measures had been taken and, based on the assurances I gave him, he conducted me to his house. He entered alone into the enderoun [women's quarters] and returned soon afterwards accompanied by Qourrèt-oul-Aïne. He gave me a sealed envelope saying: "Conduct this woman to the garden of Ilkhani and deliver the proof of her receipt to Aziz Khan Serdar."

A horse was brought and Qourrèt-oul-Aïne was mounted upon it. But, afraid that the Babis might have been alerted to what was happening, I threw my coat over her in such a way that she was taken to be a man. With a well-armed escort, we set off through the streets. Notwithstanding the precautions I had taken and the large number of troops that I had with me, I am convinced that, had we been attacked, all of them would have fled, so much did the Babis inspire terror.

I let out a sigh of relief when we entered the garden. I had my prisoner placed in a room, which was found under the corridor of the entryway, and ordered my soldiers to carefully guard the door while I went to the first floor to find the *serdar*.

He was alone and awaited me. After having read the letter that I gave him, he asked me, "Nobody knows who you have brought here?" "Nobody," said I, "and now that I have fulfilled my mission, give me the release form for my prisoner." "No," he said, "you must assist in the execution, and I will then give you your receipt."

He summoned a Turkish domestic manservant in his employ, a young man with a very handsome face. The *serdar* gave him many compliments and said to him, "You have been in my service for a long time, and I have been mistaken not to take note of you. Nevertheless, I love you well and I want to reward you. Take these twenty pieces of gold, spend them as you wish, and soon I will find you a good job. But while waiting, take this silk handkerchief and go down with the officer. He will conduct you into a room where you will find a young infidel woman who turns away the believers from the path of Muhammad. Strangle her with this handkerchief—in this way you will render a great service to God, and I will recompense you generously.

The valet responded and left with me. I conducted him to the room in which I had left my prisoner. I found her prostrated and praying. The young man approached her to execute the order he had received. Then she raised her head, looked him straight in the eye, and said to him, "Young man! It would be unworthy for your hand to soil itself with this murder."

I don't know what happened in the soul of this domestic servant, but he ran off like a madman. I ran after him, and we arrived together before the *serdar* to whom he declared that it was impossible for him to accomplish the act that had been assigned to him. "I will lose your protection," he said. "I will lose myself. Do with me whatever you wish, but I will not touch this woman."

Aziz Khan chased him off and thought for a few minutes. He then called for one of his horsemen who, being punished for his bad behavior, had been made to serve in the kitchen. When this man entered, he chided him amiably: "So, son of a dog, bandit, philanderer, I hope that your chastisement has made you reflect and that you will be wiser in the future. You should be disgusted now to engage in follies, and I think you are worthy of winning back my affection. It must have very much bothered you to go so long without being able to drink spirits. Here, take a large glass and drink, I give you leave." He then gave him a new handkerchief and repeated the order that he had previously given to the young Turk.

We arrived together in the room. As soon as he entered, he attacked Qourrèt-oul-Aïne, put the handkerchief around her neck and pulled it several times. Unable to breathe, the woman fell to the ground. Then he put a knee on her back and pulled on the handkerchief with all his might. As he was roused up and afraid, he did not allow her time to exhale. He took her up in his arms in a swoon and carried her behind the wall of the icehouse. There was a well there into which he pitched her alive. We called some men, and we hastily filled up the well, because dawn was approaching.

Opposite the British Legation and the Embassy of Turkey, there was a fairly large yard which disappeared after 1893. Towards the middle of this yard, but alongside the street, there were five or six trees that marked the spot where the Babi heroine died, because at that time the garden of Ilkhani extended to that place.

Upon my return [to Tehran], in 1898, the yard had disappeared, invaded by modern construction, and I do not know whether the new owner honored those trees, which a pious hand had planted.[5]

**Notes**
Translated from: A.-L.-M. Nicolas, *Seyyèd Ali Mohammeddit le Bâb* (Paris: Dujarric & Cie, Editeurs, 1905) pp. 273-87 and pp. 446-52.

1. Bahá'u'lláh's father—Ed.
2. The future Bahá'u'lláh.
3. Bouchrouyéhi joined thus with Hadji Mollah Ali and Quourrèt-oul-Aïne who had left Khorassan before him. They had private meetings where they occupied themselves with the details of the religion. Finally, they lifted curtain and Quourrèt oul Aïne ascended the dais and took off her veil, crying forth: "O my brothers, these very days are days of the interregnum. There are no more obligations. These prayers, these fasts signify nothing any more. When the Bab will have conquered the seven climates and reunited all the religions, he will bring a new doctrine and will propagate his Qoran among men, and all obligations he then will indicate, one will have to accomplish. But for the moment, do not make useless difficulties [for yourselves]. All women are common [property] for you, common for you are all good things." When she was heard thus to speak, those who were Muslims abandoned Babism, but the others who possessed nothing good, no woman, abandoned Islam. (*Mutanabiyyin*)
4. According to Mirza Djani, she went to Barfourouch, and from there with Soubh-i-Ezel to Nour.
5. I don't know to whom M. de Gobineau makes allusion when he speaks on page 313 of his work of a woman named "Djenab Motcherreh." I that that Qourrèt-oul-Aïne, Djenab Tahérèh, left poems extremely valued by the Persians.

# Qurrat al-'Ayn: The Remover of the Veil

by Abbas Amanat

Not long after the captivity of Mullá 'Alí Bastámí, the small group of Babi sympathizers in Iraq found a new leader in the person of Qurrat al-'Ayn. Between 1260/1844 and 1263/1847, she built up a sizeable body of support among those who were demoralized by earlier setbacks. Though largely the result of an independent quest, Qurrat al-'Ayn's conversion and her rise to leadership aptly characterized the messianic ethos around which the entire Babi movement was formed. She was a woman of great talent, with the outlook of a mystic and aspirations of revolutionary. The part she played in shaping the movement is comparable only to the roles of Mullá Husayn Bushrú'í and Mullá Muhammad 'Alí Báfurúshí Quddús. Her career illustrates the way the new Babi alternative gave scope to the otherwise suppressed aspirations of those whose experiences, both intellectual and emotional, brought them to near rejection of society's sanctified norms.

For Qurrat al-'Ayn, a woman of vigor and vitality, the road between the secluded enclosure of the Baraghání house in Qazvin and her unveiled appearance at the Badasht gathering of 1246/1848 was a long one, crossing many barriers of social restriction and religious taboo.

## Background and Family

Fátima Zarrín Táj Baraghání, surnamed Umm Salma—called Qurrat al-'Ayn (the solace of the eye) by Rashtí and Táhira (the pure) by the Bab[1]—was born in Qazvin in 1231/1814 to a well-known family of 'ulama.[2] Her father Mullá Muhammad Sálih, and his two brothers were originally from the village of Baraghán, in the Sávujbulágh district east of Qazvin, and came to Qazvin in the first decade of the nineteenth century. Later, the two elder brothers moved to Qum, Isfahan, and then the 'Atabát, where they studied under well-known Usúlí teachers and acquired their authorization.[3] On their return to Qazvin, despite their humble background and earlier poverty, both Muhammad Taqí and Muhammad Sálih were soon acclaimed as first-rank mujtahids, accumulating large fortunes, and were able to establish religious control over certain quarters in the city. In the early decades of the century, Qazvin was a thriving trade center between north and south. The Baraghání brothers were beneficiaries of this commercial success as well as being frequent recipients of royal favor.

Fátima's father, remembered chiefly for his scholarly works in Qur'ánic exegesis and jurisprudence as well as his elegies on the tragedies of Karbalá'[4] was also known for his zeal for the execution of legal punishments. As Tunkábuní, who was his student, related: "He was rigid and firm in enjoining the good and prohibiting the evil,"[5] which probably meant active opposition to consumption of wine and other irreligious acts. In his later life, however, he seems to have been more devoted to scholarship than to participation in public affairs. His brother Mullá Muhammad Taqí, a more typical Usúlí jurist,[6] owed his fame not merely to his scholarship but to his ambition to overcome his rivals in Qazvin and later to his denunciation of Ahsá'í and his successor. The youngest brother Mullá 'Alí, on the other hand, became a devout follower of Rashtí. He was a prolific writer with mystical leanings, and his works are the best testimonies of the development of a non-Sufi mysticism within the Shaykhi school.[7]

Fátima and her younger sister, Marzíya, were brought up in a strictly religious yet affluent environment. In her early youth, because of her talent ("a prodigy of knowledge") and her father's tolerant view toward her education, Fátima managed to further her studies beyond the elementary level, a novelty for women of her time. Under her father and her uncles she completed her elementary studies in theology, jurisprudence, and literary sciences. She reportedly surpassed many of her father's students.[8] Sipihr wonders how a woman of her beauty could also be "highly accomplished in Arabic literature, in memorizing the hadíth, and in esoteric interpretations of Qur'ánic verses."[9] Her father, we are told, lamented: "If she were a boy, she would have illuminated my house and come to be my successor."[10]

In spite of her promising literary and poetic talents,[11] she could not escape the family pressure that at the age of fourteen obliged her to marry, perhaps against her will, her cousin Mullá Muhammad Baraghání, son of Mullá Muhammad Taqí and later imám jum'a of Qazvin.[12] Soon after, in 1244/1828, she and her husband left Qazvin for the 'Atabát, where Mullá Muhammad was to continue his studies under the celebrated Usúlí Mullá Muhammad Báqir Qazvíní. For close to thirteen years the couple resided in Karbalá'. Though Fátima gave birth to two sons, Ibráhím and Ismá'íl,[13] it appears that almost from the start the marriage was not free from domestic quarrels. She became acquainted with Shaykhi teachings through her maternal cousin Mullá Jawád Valíyání, who gave her samples of Ahsá'í's works.[14] She may have also attended Rashtí's circle, against her husband's objections. In Qazvin, she must have heard her elder uncle's antagonistic denunciation of Shaykhism and her other uncle's veneration of Rashtí.

The years of Karbalá' were crucial for broadening Fátima's intellectual horizon. But her inclination toward Shaykhism inevitably gave an ideological dimension to the couple's private differences.[15] On their return to Qazvin in 1257/1841, although she still hesitated to express her views in public, her elder uncle, her husband, and her father all rebuked her in private for showing devotion to Shaykhism and dissuaded her from any further pursuit of her studies.[16] However, she seems to have had some support from her younger uncle, Mullá 'Alí, and later her brother-in-law, Mullá Muhammad 'Alí Qazvíní (son of Mullá 'Abd al-Wahháb Qazvíní and later Letter of the Living). Through them Fátima secretly corresponded with Rashtí and sent him a treatise she had composed in vindication of some Shaykhi tenets. In reply Rashtí praised her as "the delight of my eye and the soul of my heart."[17] No doubt Rashtí was impressed by the young woman's talent, and he must have also been pleased that in addition to Mullá 'Alí he had found another ally among the Baraghánís. Mullá Muhammad, Fátima's husband, whose loyalty to his father was unwavering, must have found it taxing to compete with an independent-minded woman whose intellectual interests went beyond the standards of her time. Though she never received her authorization because "it was not customary to give ijáza of ijtihád to women,"[18] Fátima's scholastic accomplishment seems to have qualified her as a mujtahid. There is evidence that at least Rashtí, if not her own father, Mullá Sálih, saw her as fit for the honor.[19]

As her marriage deteriorated, Qurrat al-'Ayn decided to leave her husband and children and return to the 'Atabát. Her father apparently could not discourage her from separation. His second daughter, Marzíya, had married the son of Mullá 'Abd al-Wahháb, the prominent Shaykhi in Qazvin,[20] and Mullá Sálih himself did not seem to approve of his elder brother's public condemnation of the Shaykhis. Shortly afterward, with the advice and assistance of her uncle Mullá 'Alí, Fátima decided to join the Shaykhi circle in Karbalá'.[21]

Together with Marzíya, she set out for the 'Atabát toward the end of 1259/1843.[22] Her latter collaboration with Mullá Husayn and his friends, as well as her own remarks, confirm that she was watchful for some form of messianic revelation.[23] It is not clear whether she left Qazvin after Rashtí's death or whether indeed she was aware of it. In her risála in reply to Mullá Jawád Valíyání, she stated that "at the beginning of his excellency's [the Bab's] cause I was in Qazvin, but as soon as I heard of this cause, even before reading the holy commentary [*Qayyúm al-Asmá'*] or *Sahífat al-Makhzúníya*, I recognized it."[24] This statement only makes sense if we assume that she heard of the Bab before 1260 in Qazvin, possibly through her brother-in-law, Mullá Muhammad 'Alí Qazvíní.

## Conversion and Leadership

When Qurrat al'Ayn arrived in Karbalá' in the last days of 1259/1844, shortly after Rashtí's death,[25] she found herself embroiled in the controversy that divided the Shaykhi students. Reports regarding her participation in the Kúfa retreat cannot be wholly dismissed,[26] but what is certain is that from the start she supported Mullá Husayn. She was apparently informed of the proclamation of the Bab through a letter delivered to her by Mullá Muhammad 'Alí Qazvíní, in reply to an earlier petition she had presented to the unknown Bab when Mullá Husayn was departing from the 'Atabát.²⁷ *Nuqtat al-Káf* stresses that after receiving the writings of the Bab, "she reached the state of intuitive certitude;"²⁸ perhaps an illusion to the fact that Qurrat al-'Ayn was never able to meet the Bab in person. The Bab's "immediate response to her declaration of faith was "an exalted ordinance revealed in her honor."²⁹

In Karbalá', Qurrat al-'Ayn resided in the house of Rashtí and became acquainted not only with his widow and the other women of the household but also with his former students and followers.³⁰ By allying herself with the more radical elements, she was able to organize a chorus of support with ultimate loyalty to the Bab. In creating this united front, she was faced with the challenge of three groups that between 1844 and 1847, constantly hindered her efforts: the conservative Shaykhis, headed by Gauhar and aided by defectors from the Babi ranks; the conservative Babis, headed by Mullá Ahmad Hisárí, who despised her anti-Sharí'a radicalism; and the Islamic orthodox establishments, both Shi'ite and Sunni, who were happy to see the growing animosity among the Shaykhis, but were increasingly wary of Qurrat al-'Ayn's potential as a charismatic leader.³¹

Between Muharram 1260/January 1844 and Sha'bán 1262/August 1846, while in Karbalá',³² Qurrat al-'Ayn was able to broaden her popular following. By complying with the policy of prudence that prevailed over the activities of the Babi sympathizers, particularly after the captivity of Bastámí, she partially avoided intrigues and open hostility. Yet even from the start, she did not hesitate to air views contradictory to the interpretations of Rashtí's senior students. Holding regular gatherings in Rashtí's house, she spoke to large audiences from behind a curtain.³³ In the inner quarters she also held classes for women. Her personality, theological knowledge, and mastery of Arabic impressed Arabs and Persians alike. Shaykhi 'ulama of some rank and seniority, such as Shaykh Muhammad Shibl (father of Muhammad Mustafá al-Baghdádí), saw in her, if not signs of intuitive inspiration, at least a determined leadership. The Qurratíya, as her followers came to be known in Iraq, were successful in transmitting her message to the Shi'ite public beyond Karbalá', thus causing excitement in the 'Atabát and anxiety for the Shaykhi and Usúlí leaders alike.³⁴

In Sha'bán 1262/August 1846, Qurrat al-'Ayn and her followers temporarily moved to nearby Kázimayn, presumably as a result of pressure from Gauhar's quarter, which obliged her to seek refuge with the Kázimayn Babi 'ulama.[35] Here she stayed for the next six months as their guest, continuing her public sermons with greater vigor and freedom.[36] An eyewitness confirms that "a large number of people attended her teaching circles and prayed behind her. As she spoke, they listened with great astonishment in their hearts and were moved by her speeches."[37]

The thrust of Qurrat al-'Ayn's debate was based on Shaykhi ideas, but with a distinct messianic overtone. In many respects, she went beyond the limits that hold Shaykhism within the boundaries of Islamic theology. Some sources report that she even assumed the title of "the Point of the Divine Knowledge," which implies that she may have envisaged some revelatory status for herself.[38] The fact that she had her own views contradictory to the Islamic law and legal injunctions, combined with the fact that she adopted certain ascetic practices like devotional prayers[39] and eschewing meat and cooked food,[40] underscores her independent religious stance. Clearly, her commitment to the Bab provided her with a framework for the propagation of many of her preconceived views. At the earlier stages it is difficult to say how far her commitment to Babism was purely a consequence of messianic expectations. Only from 1262/1846, is it certain that she was fully aware of the ideas of the Bab as they were reflected in his writings.

The surviving samples of Quarrat al-'Ayn's works from this early period testify to her skill in making use of the Qur'án and hadíth for arguing the theme of progressive revelations.[41] In a treatise written in 1266/1846, in reply to her cousin Jawád Valíyání (who first became a follower of the Bab but later, following the events of 1845-1846 defected to the anti-Babi camp), she discussed the legitimacy of the new Zuhúr. The position of Sayyid 'Alí Muhammad the Bab in relation to that of Ahsá'í and Rashtí was a critical question that preoccupied many of the Shaykhi converts. She argues that the Grand Divine Proof, the title by which she refers to the Bab, is the ultimate fulfillment of Shaykhi thought. Those who had not grasped the essence of Shaykhism to the extent that Rashtí expected are naturally foreign to the continuous process of unfolding revelation:[42] "This is not to say that the two gates [*bábayn:* i.e., Ahsá'í and Rashtí] were in darkness and that their words were imperfect. All in all today in the face of the universe [the position] of those two revered souls has not been recognized except by the point in the circle of the being [the Bab]."[43]

She states that Rashtí himself regarded his position as being above the Four Gates of the period of the Lesser Occultation, a sign that after him the process will continue to result in a revelation of a greater magnitude. There is no evidence "from the word of God or that of the guardians of the faith" or "the gates to the Infallibles" (i.e., Ahsá'í and Rashtí) that prevents the occurrence of such complimentary revelations.[44] To acknowledge this unfolding process, she points out, it is necessary to bear in mind that "the divine norm" basically differs from "the human norm" and indeed from the habits of the past, and therefore "the norms for testing the truthfulness of the proof of God are not apparent to the people."[45] To recognize the proof, only an inner awareness of the divine norm would lead the seeker to the right path. This, she insisted, is the essence or "the secret of the secrets" in the new revelation.[46]

To experience this "secret of the secrets," she suggests the teachings of Ahsá'í and Rashtí should be used as the keys for unraveling the complexities of the revelatory process. Here she distinguishes two complementary concepts and prescribes *mujáhada* (spiritual endeavor) as opposed to *mujádala* (rational argumentation) as the essential approach to the truth.[47] This implies that, contrary to her rejection of the contemporary Sufis, in some respects she is influenced by their intuitive methods. The truthfulness of the Bab, as indeed that of the prophets of the past, is conceivable only "by insight of the inner heart and [search] in the true essence of one's existence."[48]

But in Qurrat al-'Ayn's view, this intuitive approach is inseparable from the proof of wisdom (*dalíl-i hikmat*)[49] Such rational proof, according to her, is complementary to spiritual endeavor for acknowledgment of the fact that "in every age there is a necessity for a bearer and interpreter who would supervise all matters."[50] Passionately, Qurrat al-'Ayn argues that she herself came to recognize the Bab when in a moment of intuitive insight she grasped the unceasing necessity for divine revelation:

> With an insight free from intruders, I observed God's power and omnipotence [and realized] that this great cause most definitely needs a locus of

manifestation for after God made His Fourth Pillar and His encompassing sign and His manifested locality known to people, and [thus] brought them close to His presence and showered them from His high exalted Heaven with His [spiritual] nourishment, then by proof of wisdom it is incumbent upon Him, whose status is high, not to leave the people to themselves as it is necessary for His grace to increase, His benevolence to broaden and His blessing to mature since [in the past] His norm always rested upon this. And day after day the cycle of universe is in progress (*kaur dar taraqqíst*) and "there is no suspension in his emanation." Praise to God and our prayer and gratitude [to Him] that the cause is everlasting.[51]

The theme of spiritual evolution in this passage conveys an unmistakable historical dynamism that is absent even from the nonorthodox currents of the time. The rule of benevolence makes continuous divine emanation an unsuspending responsibility. This is reminiscent of the Mu'tazilite theology of the past, but it also tends to go a step beyond Sufi and even Ismá'ílí thoughts, as it implies that "the unfolding destiny" of mankind necessitates an evolutionary perfection in successive revelations. It is as if Qurrat al-'Ayn has elaborated this view on her own initiative and as a result of a personal inquiry that employed both "the intuitive endeavor" and the "proof of the wisdom."

This was a significant step forward in the Shaykhi-Babi thinking that employed hikma (in the sense of rational endeavor) in conjunction with intuition to explain a continuous spiritual progress of mankind, and hence to conclude that "the unceasing emanation of God" would inevitably evolve into a new prophesy. The logical outcome was the notion of spiritual progress that the Bab, and Babi writers like Qurrat al-'Ayn, adapted in support of their liminal relation with Islam. Here the maxim "The cycle is in progress," viewing the forward movement of man in the rotation of celestial spheres as a historical process, expresses one of the most essential breakthroughs in Babi thought. Distinguishing between the past and the present, Qurrat al-'Ayn alludes to a sense of betterment in the course of time. Such a view was essentially irreconcilable with the doctrine of prophethood in orthodox Islam. Human progress was thus her prime concern in seeking a new revelation in the Bab. At the basis of the Bab's theory of successive resurrections[52] lay a vision of the future that could only materialize if a break occurred with the past religious legacy. Perhaps this very desire to break with the past should be taken as the origin of a widening difference between the orthodox Shi'ite and the Babi worldviews.

Qurrat al-'Ayn's actions complemented her theological position. On the one hand, she questioned and in many instances rejected the soundness of the practices of past generations in the matter of legal injunctions (*furú'*); on the other, by emphasizing the imminent advent of a new prophetic cycle, she sharpened the distinction between believers and denouncers. In what amounted to a symbolic protest, she enjoined her followers not to buy food from the market, because people who denounced the Bab were infidels and therefore eating their food was unlawful—no doubt a defensive response to the pressure on the Babis, who were now rejected as unbelievers.[53] She justified her new prohibition on the basis of the Bab's assertion that since in the state of "initial truth" of the Fourteen Infallibles she stands as the manifestation of Fátima, the daughter of the Prophet, her sight is purifying. She ordered the Babis to bring all the food to her, so that by her purifying sight she could make it suitable for use. The eyesight of the clan of God, of which the daughter of the Prophet is one, is symbolic of their will, upon which rests the prohibition of confirmation of religious commands. Nuqtat al-Káf notes: "This was the first breach of the religious code . . . among those people."[54]

But not all the "infringements of the religious injunctions" were limited to the Babis' relations with their adversaries. Perhaps her most daring act was her appearance, unveiled, at a gathering of her followers. The gesture was utterly unacceptable, even to some of the Babis in the 'Atabát.[55] Still more blasphemous was her belief that the Islamic compulsory obligations, including the daily prayers, should be lifted altogether, because the interregnum prior to the advent of the next dispensation had begun. The use of the Islamic concept of fatra (an interval between two successive messengers) in a new historical context connotes Qurrat al-'Ayn's interpretation of her own age, not simply as a period of slackening the rules of shari'a, but as an age of willing transition toward the final break. Similar to the unitarians (Hunafá') of the pre-Islamic times, she viewed her own mission, and those of the other early Babis, as a precursory vigilance. Thus the infringement of the legal and devotional boundaries was a necessary distancing from the customary norms of the community in order to grasp the signs of the new Zuhúr. Such messianic certitude was to be achieved not by devotional acts and religious duties but by spiritual endeavor combined with the proof of wisdom.

Publication of such controversial doctrine at a time when every infringement of the religious norms met with strongest opposition was hazardous, especially for a woman. As the first Persian woman in modern times who advocated unveiling on her own initiative and as a result of an intellectual quest, Qurrat al-'Ayn was bound to be concerned with the inferior role assigned to women in the society of the time. Her challenge to men on a ground traditionally closed to women must have had a strong appeal to the small circle of women that formed around her,[56] who appear to have achieved a nascent feminist consciousness defined by Qurrat al-'Ayn's personality and inspired by her words and deeds. Coming from different social backgrounds, they were all later distinguished for their Babi commitment. Kurshíd Bagum, called Shams al-Duhá, wife of Mírzá Muhammad 'Alí Nahrí,[57] and Qurrat al-'Ayn's sister, Marzíya, were both deeply influenced by her. Also known to us are Mullá Husayn's mother, a poetess; Bibi Kúchak, later called Warqat al-Firdaus, Mullá Husayn's sister and the wife of another Babi, Shaykh Abú Turáb Ishtihárdí;[58] Rashtí's wife, who was originally from Shiraz,[59] and Qurrat al-'Ayn's maid Káfiya.[60] In the later years in Qazvin, daughters of Hájjí Asadulláh Farhádí, Khátún Ján, Shírín, and Sáhiba also became her faithful followers. It was Khátún Ján who assisted Qurrat al-'Ayn in her escape from Qazvin.[61] On her return from the 'Atabát in 1263/1847, Qurrat al-'Ayn also attracted the wives of local notables in Kirmánsháh and Hamadan, two in particular: Zubayda Khánum, better known as Firishtih, the daughter of Fath 'Alí Sháh and the mother of the válí of Kurdistan, Muhammad Husayn Khán Hisám al-Mulk Qaraguzlú, who was a poetess with the pen name Jahán[62]; and the wife of Mahmúd Khán Násir al-Mulk.[63] Qurrat al-'Ayn's influence is also seen in another Babi poetess, Shams Jahán, the daughter of Muhammad Rizá Mírzá, with the pen name of Fitna. In her lyric masnaví Fitna gave an account of her first acquaintance with Qurrat al-'Ayn when she was imprisoned in the house of Mahmúd Khán Kalántar, the chief of police of Tehran, between 1266/1850 and 1268/1852.[64]

Even before her return to Karbalá' in February 1847, Qurrat al-

'Ayn's casting off of her facial veil in the presence of men aroused strong misgivings inside the Babi community.⁶⁵ In the first of Muharram of 1262/30 December 1845, the annual month of mourning for the Shi'ite martyrs, she instructed the Babis to joyfully celebrate the anniversary of the Bab's birthday in Rashti's house. Ignoring the custom of wearing black during Muharram, she herself dressed in color and appeared in the feast without wearing a veil.⁶⁶ This open disregard for the Shi'ite mourning rites, even though performed at a gathering of the Babis, enraged some Babi 'ulama, such as Mullá Ahmad Hisárí and Sayyid Bushr Kázimayní, who still tended to see the Bab and his da'wa as the continuation of Shi'ite traditions. The manner in which Qurrat al-'Ayn implicated the Bab's mission as being a manifestation independent from Islam and thus criticized the traditional-minded Babis for their failure either to appreciate "the state of the inner heart" or to grasp the participatory role of the early believers, the Sábiqín, doubtless troubled many who joined the movement with very different expectations.

Already in 1262/1846, Jawád Valíyání returned from Shiraz to Qazvin utterly disenchanted with the Bab and his voluntary isolation. Staging a vigorous anti-Babi campaign, Valíyání questioned the Bab's referral of worldly affairs to Mullá Husayn and attacked the exclusive status the former bestowed upon the Sábiqín. In her letters from Karbalá', Qurrat al-'Ayn tried in vain to vindicate reasons for deputations in a Shaykhi context and to clarify the hierarchical structure of the early believers envisaged by the Bab. Valíyání soon defected to Kirmání's side,⁶⁷ yet many of the questions he raised troubled other loyal Babis such as Mullá Ahmad Mu'alim Hisárí, who could not easily come to terms with the fast-changing message of the movement.

Hisárí, a tutor of Rashti's son Ahmad,⁶⁸ was the representative of the conservative Babis of the 'Atabát. For ideological and personal reasons, contrary to Qurrat al-'Ayn, he advocated conformity and prudence. In collaboration with Mullá Husayn, and with the tacit support of Muhít and Gauhar, he was able for a while to exercise some control over the Díwán and the household of Rashtí.⁶⁹ Some twenty-three students, mostly his own relatives, constituted the core of his support and attended his teaching circle in the Rashti's house.⁷⁰ His risála *'Aqá'id al-Shaykhíya*⁷¹ is harshly critical of

Qurrat al-'Ayn and her supporters, accusing among others, Mullá Muḥammad Báqir Tabrízí, one of the Sábiqín and a Letter of the Living, of deliberate misrepresentation of "cognition of the Imam" in order to elevate Qurrat al-'Ayn to deputyship or even gateship, on a level with Mullá Ḥusayn.[72] He chastised "the daughter of evil" (*bint-i tálih;* a pun for *bint-i sálih*) not only for disregard of taqíya, recommended by the Bab, but for propagating the end of the Islamic era, the abrogation of sharí 'a, and misrepresentation of the Zikr as an independent revelation. To vindicate his views, Mullá Aḥmad, amid a growing hostility, sent letters of inquiry to leading Babis and to the Bab himself in Isfahan.[73]

Qurrat al-'Ayn and her supporters were equally uncompromising. Shaykh Sulṭán Karbalá'í, one of Qurrat al-'Ayn's closest companions, accuses Mullá Aḥmad of hypocrisy, unjustified compromise, personal ambition, collaboration with Shaykhi and Uṣúlí adversaries, conspiracy against Qurrat al-'Ayn, and slander.[74] It was Mullá Aḥmad's shameless allegations, Karbalá'í declares, that poisoned the minds of Kázimayn Babis and turned them against Qurrat al-'Ayn.[75]

Indeed, Sayyid 'Alí Bushr and other Babis of Kázimayn, already enraged by Qurrat al-'Ayn's behavior, were appropriately encouraged by Mullá Aḥmad to write to the Bab asking his opinion of her conduct, her status, and her advocacy of termination of Islamic sharí'a. Baghdádí reports that her critics insisted: "[The Bab] has not abrogated the old sharí'a and did not renew any command but increased [observation] of the religious injunctions and emphasized [the necessity] of prayers and fasting and prohibited smoking and now this woman Qurrat al-'Ayn has exceeded the limit and abrogated the sharí'a that we inherited from our fathers and grandfathers without the mandate of his holiness the Exalted One [i.e., the Bab]."[76]

The Bab defended Qurrat al-'Ayn and her position publicly and unequivocally, entitling her *Táhira* (the Pure) to emphasize his disapproval of the charges of immorality. He not only approved of Qurrat al-'Ayn and her leadership over the Babis of the 'Atabát but significantly acknowledged the progressive tendency in the movement, even at the expense of losing some of the traditionalist followers.[77] The Bab "emphasizes: "Concerning what you have inquired about that mirror which has purified its soul in order to reflect the word by which all manners are solved; she is a righteous, learned, active, and pure woman; and do not dispute al-Táhira in her command for she is aware of the circumstances of the cause and there is nothing for you but submission to her since it is not destined for you to realize the truth of her status."78 Perhaps for the first time, the Bab openly approved the ideas and actions of his most outspoken and radical disciple. The fact that the matter was referred to the judgment of the Bab underscores his significance as the movement's core and supreme authority.

When his reply was read to a gathering of seventy Babis in Kázimayn, a number of followers, seeing it as an open breach of the Islamic code, declined to accept his command and left the Babi ranks.79 Later, in a commentary on Súrat al-Hamd that is probably addressed to Bushr and his faction, the Bab confirmed his approval of Táhira, at the same time urging the defectors to set themselves free of these "nonessential matters."80

The Bab also answered Mullá Ahmad's inquiries. He tried not to alienate the zealous Babi for his criticism of Qurrat al-'Ayn, yet he remained unreservedly praiseful of "the pure leaf." Approving even her claim of "being a proof of God," the Bab says: "Let none of those who are my followers repudiate her, for she speaks not save with evidence that have shown forth from the people of sinlessness [the Imams] and tokens that have radiated from the people of truth."81 Even such strong endorsement of Qurrat al-'Ayn did not dissuade Mullá Ahmad from further criticism. Nor did her conciliatory gestures and offers of cooperation bridge the widening ideological gap between the two.82

Apparently it was during this period that Qurrat al-'Ayn, who seems not to have been apprehensive of the recurrence of anti-Babi feeling, first invited the Usúlí mujtahids to an open debate and, when none responded to her challenge, called upon them to stand with her for mubáhala.83 Naturally the mujtahids were not prepared to risk an encounter that in the eyes of the public would lend credibility to a heretic. An angry mob, outraged by her open vilification of sharí'a and incited by the Shaykhi elements, attacked Rasti's house and arrested her. She was detained in the house of Hájjí Mahdí Kamúna.84 To prevent any further disturbance, the Ottoman governor of the city interfered, making her release contingent on a ruling from Baghdad.85 Defending herself, she explained that she advanced no claim save that of learning. "Assemble the doctors both Sunni and Shi'ite, that we many confer and dispute, so the truth and falsity of either side, and the wisdom of both parties may be made apparent to all persons of discernment."[86]

While in temporary detention, she summoned Mullá Ahmad for the last time. To him she clearly stated her intention to move to Baghdad, where she would "lift the taqíya and prove the veracity of the Zikr.""[87] After some three days she was released, apparently on condition that she leave Karbalá' immediately.[88] The departure of Qurrat al-'Ayn and her followers was a victory for the Shaykhis, Babi conservatives, and Usúlís alike, successfully frustrating the Babis' last chances for mass conversion in the Shi'ite centers of learning.

The news of Qurrat al-'Ayn and the rumors about her "immoral" acts must have soon reached Qazvin and caused great anxiety for the Baraghánís. In the face of "all the ado, incitement, and malicious defamation," Qurrat al-'Ayn, in a letter to her father, defended herself: "I plead with you! This humblest of people is your daughter. You know her, and she has been brought up and educated under your supervision. If she had, or has, a worldly love, that could not have remained a secret to you. If you want to inquire into her affairs, God who holds the scale and is the remover of the veils would testify for her."[89] She reminds him that last year her "declaration of the word of God" received no response except "accusations of disbelief and paganism [*shirk*]." Whoever ignores the "glorious cause of the great living Imam," she warns, will see all his deeds end in sorrow and will no more be saved than the Khárijites who rejected 'Alí. She criticizes the literalists' trivial preoccupation with the appearance of the Bab's words and urges upon her father to heed their spirit instead. She ends on a note of sympathy and concern: "Dear father! So many times when I visit the holy shrine of the Imam, may peace be upon him, in the flood of my tears I pity you and pray for you that perhaps you may be saved."[90] Other letters reecho the same urgency and admonition: "If you fail to recognize the cause, there will be no benefit for you in all your acts of devotion."[91]

It is not known how Mullá Sálih received his daughter's letters, but they could have been instrumental in convincing the Baraghánís to dispatch a special envoy, Mullá Muhammad Hammámí, to Iraq to bring back the rebellious Qurrat al-'Ayn.[92]

Residing in the house of Shaykh Muhammad Shibl in Baghdad, Qurrat al-'Ayn again renewed her activities. The public was curious to learn about the woman who was proclaiming the advent of a new revelation.[93] Her rising fame in Baghdad faced the válí, Najíb Páshá, once more with a Babi menace and the risk of factional unrest if she continued preaching. Mullá Hasan Gauhar, who apparently carried some weight with Najíb Páshá, helped arouse his concern.[94] But this time, contrary to Bastámí's case, instead of calling for a tribunal Najíb simply summoned Qurrat al-'Ayn and questioned her about her beliefs. The details of this interrogation are not known, nor are the names of those present, but it appears that Najíb, and possibly his aides, could find no convincing evidence of her heretical or even non-Islamic beliefs.[95] Perhaps it was for the purpose of further investigation by the chief muftí that he then ordered her transfer to the house of Shaykh Mahmúd Álúsí, the leading man in Bastámí's trial, in the meantime referring her case to the Sublime Porte.[96] The pasha's milder response to the renewal of Babi activities may have resulted from the fact that in the case of Bastámí, the only definite result of the trial was the tacit victory of the Shi'ites, who wisely caused Bastámí's banishment from the 'Atabát. To put a woman on trial was unprecedented, and particularly ill advised when neither the evidence nor the laws of apostasy, as applied to women, showed any prospect of a definite verdict.[97] If there was a trial, Qurrat al-'Ayn's oratory might work in her favor and publicize her views even further.

Ground for these speculations can be found in a passage attributed to Álúsí, who seems, in passing a verdict on Qurrat al-'Ayn, to reserve his praise for her:

> She was one of those who followed the Bab after the death of Rashtí, but later even disagreed with Rashtí in many matters such as on the question of the religious duties [takálíf]. Some people alleged that Qurrat al-'Ayn believes in the total abolition of all duties but I do not see any truth in this though she stayed in my house about two months and so many discussions took place between me and her in which there was no taqíya or apprehension. Verily, I saw in her such a degree of merit and accomplishment as I rarely saw in men. She was a wise and decent woman who was unique in virtue and chastity. I have referred to my discussions with her on another occasion; if one became aware of them, one would realize that there is no doubt about her knowledge. It became obvious to me that Bábíya [Babis]

and Qurratíya [Qurratis] are the same. They believe that the time for five times obligatory prayers is over and that revelation is unsuspended and therefore the Perfect [Man] will have [further] revelations. However, these revelations are not canonical but are for explanations of what has been previously laid down. This is similar to the ideas of the Sufis . . . Some of [the Babis] are vigilant at nights with prayers and devotion. They are [all] opposed to the Ithná 'Asharís and they denounce them and avoid them.[98]

The Sunni scholar's tone implies that during Qurrat al-'Ayn's stay in his house there was an exchange of views. (Perhaps it was this sympathetic dialogue that prompted the Bab, some months later, to write to Álúsí calling upon him to recognize his mission.[99]) Apparently while Qurrat al-'Ayn was in the house a gathering was held there, attended by the Sunni 'ulama. The details of such an assembly are not known.[100]

A number of observations can be made on the above passage. Most striking is that, even in the presence of the muftí who had condemned her coreligionist Mullá 'Alí Bastámí to death, Qurrat al-'Ayn unhesitatingly declared her allegiance to the Bab. Equally noteworthy is the fact that her compelling propagation of her views caused one of the most revered Sunni scholars of the time to admire her intelligence and make some unbiased assessment of her beliefs. Third, Álúsí's remarks contain an apparent contradiction, for although the Sunni muftí did not detect that Qurrat al-'Ayn abrogated all duties, he reports her rejection of the obligatory daily prayers. This suggests that Qurrat al-'Ayn still regarded the Bab's claim, as Álúsí puts it, a "noncanonical revelation" complementary to the previous Islamic revelation. This the muftí identifies as similar to the Sufi doctrine of the Perfect Man.

Two months later orders came from Istanbul for Qurrat al-'Ayn's deportation. The contents of the Porte's instruction are not known, but Álúsí gives some insight into the situation that finally persuaded the pasha to arrange for her banishment and that of her followers: "And thus appeared in that time [early 1260/1844] a group of Shi'ite extremists [*ghulát*] calling themselves Bábíya . . . . All those who possess wisdom would testify to their blasphemous beliefs. A group of them would have remained in Iraq if it had not been for the endeavors of Najíb the válí, about whose zeal and religiosity there is a consensus. He humiliated them, may God support him, and disturbed their assembly and became furious at them, may God be content with him, and upset their activities, may God repay him with his benevolence."[101] The mufti's remarks sound contradictory to his praise for Qurrat al-'Ayn if one does not consider his apprehension of the Babi threat, for the removal of which he praises Najíb Páshá so effusively. The second passage was written in circa 1265-1266/1849-1850, when the Babi uprising in Iran made it appropriate for Álúsí to make public his resentment at the resurgence of Shi'ite extremism lest it spill over to Iraq, whereas the first passage regarding Qurrat al-'Ayn was probably written in 1270/1861-1862, two years after the final defeat of the movement and Qurrat al-'Ayn's execution.

Hájjí Mullá Muhammad Hammámí, the envoy dispatched by Baraghánís, met Qurrat al-'Ayn in the house of Álúsí, and discussed with him the release of the "chaste women" whom he argued had been "overwhelmed with satanic temptations." He reported to her uncle Mullá Muhammad Taqí, that Álúsí agreed to intercede with the válí for Qurrat al-'Ayn's release. He also stated that Qurrat al-'Ayn was particularly angry at Gauhar, presumably for his mischievous calumny. Moreover, he observes: "The entire nobility and the 'ulama of Baghdad greatly respect her and confer on her highest praises. Whatever has been relayed to you and rumored [about her] is slander and fabrication."[102]

## En Route to Qazvin

Sometime in Rabi' al-Thani 1261/March 1847, accompanied by an Ottoman officer Qurrat al-'Ayn was sent to Khánaqín on the Persian border. With her traveled about thirty of her followers. As Álúsí rightly observed, her deportation was the end of the effective presence of the Babis in the 'Atabát for the next five years, before the arrival of Bahá'u'lláh and his party, who were exiled to Iraq toward the middle of 1269/1853. Her journey from Baghdad to Qazvin took about three months, in the course of which she passed through Karand, Kirmánsháh, and Hamadan before reaching Qazvin toward the middle of 1263/1847. All along the way, accompanied by her Persian and Arab disciples, led by Mullá Ibráhím Mahallátí, Mullá Sálih Karímávi, and Shaykh Sultán Karbalá'í, she publicly advocated the new Zuhúr[103] and in numerous gatherings entered into discussions with mujtahids, Sufis, and notables. In spite of her disappointments in the 'Atabát, she seems to have been in high spirits throughout and did not flinch from the violent reactions that she and her followers frequently encountered during the journey.

In Karand, a large Kurdish village west of Kirmánsháh, and later in Sahna, halfway to Hamadan, Qurrat al-'Ayn received a warm welcome from the Ahl-i Haqq population, who reportedly even gave her their allegiance.[104] The enthusiasm shown by the villagers and their chiefs is a clear indication of the potential support in rural sectarian communities of western Iran, communities that were often harassed and persecuted[105] but maintained their messianic spirit untouched by the religion of the large cities. The fact that Qurrat al-'Ayn declined the offer of the people of Sahna to participate in the march—all twelve thousand of them[106]—signals her unwillingness to organize the popular backing into anything beyond preliminary conversion. At this stage, the main issue was "conveyance of the word."

Upon arrival in Kirmánsháh, Qurrat al-'Ayn set up a center of public preaching, where her disciples recited the Bab's commentary on Súrat al-Kauthar, and she answered queries and challenged the 'ulama to public debate.[107] In the early part of her forty-day stay, she conversed with the governor of the province, Muhibb 'Alí Khán Mákú'í,[108] his wife, and some notables. Her activities seemed to have created enough excitement among the population, predominantly Kurdish with strong Ahl-i Haqq presence, to alarm the 'ulama and oblige the chief Usúlí mujtahid Shaykh 'Abdulláh Kirmánsháhí (one of the Bihbahání clan, great-grandson of Áqá Muhammad Báqir and grandson of Muhammad 'Alí, the famous Súfí Kush[109]), to plead with the governor for expulsion of the troublesome heretic and her more than thirty Arab and Persian disciples. The governor willingly transmitted to the mujtahid the two options that Qurrat al-'Ayn proposed: to debate or to stand for mubáhala.[110] Obliged to choose between the undesirable and the irrational, Shaykh 'Abdulláh wrote for assistance to Qurrat al-'Ayn's father and uncles. With 'Abdulláh's advice, the dispatched party from Qazvin, in collaboration with the chief officer of the local garrison, a rival of Muhibb 'Alí, bypassed the governor and ordered the troops to storm the dwellings of Qurrat al-'Ayn and her retinue by night. The Babis were battered, their belongings were looted, and some twenty-five of the Arab followers were detained while she and her close companions were forced out of the city.[111] By the governor's intervention the next day, the detainees were released and their belongings recovered, but Qurrat al-'Ayn, humiliated by the harrowing treatment, declined to return to the city.

Despite family pressure demanding her hasty return to Qazvin, Qurrat al-'Ayn was determined to carry her public declaration to Hamadan. At her request, and presumably through the good offices of the influential women of Quraguzlú nobility,[112] the governor, Khánlar Mírzá Ihtishám al-Daula, a brother of the shah and an effective member of the princely ruling elite[113] convened a gathering of local divines and scholars representative of all tendencies[114] in his quarters.[115] The invited parties chose Hájjí Mírzá 'Alí Naqí Hamadání, better known as Jannat 'Alí Sháh, son of Mullá Rizá Hamadání and head of the Kausar 'Alí Sháh suborder,[116] as their spokesman. Speaking from behind a curtain, Qurrat al-'Ayn set three rules for disputation: reliance on prophecies; abstinence from smoking—a strict Babi prohibition; and most significantly, adopting decent language and avoiding abuse and execration.[117] She unequivocally reiterated the basic themes of the early Babi doctrine: everlasting divine guidance, the progressive cycle of revelation, need for a new creed to meet the challenge of a changing age, and the legitimacy of the Bab as the sole recipient of divine inspiration.

Hájjí Mírzá 'Alí Naqí can hardly have missed Qurrat al-'Ayn's underlying mystical themes, yet her messianic dynamism must have appeared too far-fetched. Reports on his response range from sheer dismissal to, more plausibly, tacit conviction.[118] Whatever his reaction, it must have been difficult for him as a mystic of some repute, to challenge her main argument concerning the necessity of divine revelation. The omnipresence of the Perfect Man, the pivotal tenet of Sufism,[119] was turned upside down by words of an eloquent preacher to relay messianic consequences far beyond what any contemporary Sufi, even the celebrated Núr 'Alí Sháh, the spiritual guide of 'Alí Naqí's father, had dared to entertain, even in the privacy of his own mystical experience. [120] But if 'Alí Naqí hesitated to quarrel with Qurrat al-'Ayn, others did not—a mujtahid named Mullá Husayn[121] struck up a violent argument with her. The governor angrily reproached the intruder and dispersed the meeting.

Later, when Mullá Ibráhím Mahallátí presented a risála by

Qurrat al-'Ayn to the chief mujtahid of the city, the ra'ís al'ulamá,[122] he was showered with abuse, severely battered, and then thrown out.[123] Perhaps fearing an attack by the mujtahid's supporters, Qurrat al-'Ayn took refuge in the house of a sympathetic Jewish rabbi, Hákhám Ilyáhú, whose son, Il'ázár, had already been attracted by her passionate preaching.[124] The next day she moved to the Qaraguzlú-owned village of Shavarín, on the outskirts of Hamadan, and from there accompanied her relatives to Qazvin. Only a few of her adherents, mostly Persians, followed her. The rest were ordered by Qurrat al-'Ayn to return to the 'Atabát.[125]

As in other cities, the mujtahids of Kirmánsháh and Hamadan emerged as the chief adversaries of the Babis. Once they sensed government hesitation, they had no reservations about resorting to intimidation and violence. Curiosity aside, the local authorities' main motive for allowing religious debates was to remind the 'ulama that if need be, they could be challenged on their own grounds; a prospect that the 'ulama found particularly repellent. The chief mujatahids of both Kirmánsháh and Hamadan rejected invitations to debates. The people of the cities were curious bystanders, leaving the lútís, the tulláb, and occasionally the troops to implement the will of the mujtahid. For Qurrat al-'Ayn, still a believer in dialogue and debate, these were days of mixed feelings—short-lived hopes and growing frustration. A year later (1264/1848), in Tehran, she was sufficiently disappointed with the prospects of "accomplishing the proof" and "delivering the word" to advise Sayyid Yahyá Vahíd Dárábí to abandon the old policy and demonstrate his commitment by action instead.[126] This recommendation was in anticipation of the Bab's open declaration of Qá'imíya. It aptly grasped the changing mood within the Babi community in the wake of the Badasht conference and armed resistance in Tabarsí. In a famous ode, she had already expressed an urge to hear the "tale of woe" for which, she declared, she would give her passionate assent:

> The effulgence of thy face flashed forth and rays of thy visage arose on high;
> Then speak the word, "Am I not your Lord?" and "Thou art, thou art!" we will all reply.
> Thy trumpet-call "Am I not?" to greet how loud the drums of affliction beat!

At the gates of my heart there tramp the feet and camp the hosts
   of calamity.[127]

## Captivity, Revolt, and Death

The arrival of Qurrat al-'Ayn in Qazvin, accompanied by her brothers,[128] after three years of residence in Iraq, again exposed her to family tensions and doctrinal conflicts, which had sharpened since her departure. She had left as a Shaykhi devotee and returned as a Babi leader. During the two troubled months of her stay in the city (Sha'bán-Ramadán 1263/July-September 1847), she was drawn into a series of events that led ultimately to the assassination of her uncle Mullá Muhammad Taqí by a militant Babi and her subsequent flight from Qazvin—events that had their roots not only in the quarrels within the Baraghání family, but also in the ongoing factional disputes in Qazvin.

The divisions within the family seemed inevitable now that both sons of Mullá 'Abd al-Wahháb Qazvíní, Mullá Hádí and Mullá Muhammad 'Alí, Marzíya's husband, had become devotees of the Bab. Mullá 'Abd al-Wahháb himself remained safely distant, but nevertheless sympathetic to the Bab.[129] The vacuum that was created in Qazvin after his death in 1263/1847,[130] further weakened the Shaykhi constituency. Mullá 'Alí Baraghání, Qurrat al-'Ayn's Shaykhi uncle "confessed submission" to the Bab and testified to "the veracity of the Great Remembrance," but publicly remained noncommittal.[131] Being a mystic and a scholar, his clerical influence in the city seems to have been overshadowed by that of his elder brothers. Qurrat al-'Ayn's father, deeply affectionate toward his daughter, was hopelessly trying to close the widening breach in the family by maintaining a middle course, while her elder uncle, Muhammad Taqí, now in his eighties, aided by his son Mullá Muhammad (Qurrat al-'Ayn's deserted husband), were publicly denouncing the Shaykhi creed, its initiators, and its recent offshoot: the Babi heresy. The relation between the two elder brothers was further complicated over the issue of Qurrat al-'Ayn's divorce. She strongly resisted Mullá Muhammad's demands that she return to his living quarters (presumably to maintain a closer watch over her activities). She told her father, tormented by the submission of his articulate daughter to a "Shírází lad," that she considered her marriage unilaterally dissolved, for the practice of the Prophet dictates that the bond of marriage with unbelievers, among whom she counted her husband, must be broken without divorce.[132] . . .

Even before the arrival of Qurrat al-'Ayn, the introduction of the new Babi element had already brought Shaykhi-Usúlí tension to a new pitch. Mullá Ja'far Qazvíní relates that when the writings of the Bab first reached Qazvin, Mullá Jawád Valíyání (then still a supporter of the Bab) was exhilarated by the news, exclaiming: "Now the time has arrived for us to take revenge on Baraghání." The next day he ascended the pulpit and proclaimed the Advent of the Bab, calling for the support of believers. After forty days, in company with a large group of followers, he set out for the 'Atabát.[133] Mullá 'Alí Baraghání, 'Abd al-Wahháb Qazvíní's two sons, Muhammad 'Alí and Muhammad Hádí, and others joined the Babi ranks. Among them were three from Rudbár region: Mullá Taqí, Mullá Ja'far (the author of an important narrative), and Mullá 'Abd al-Husayn Qazvíní. Shaykh Muhammad Nabíl Qazvíní, a student of Rashtí who after his studies preferred to continue his father's trade, was another important early Babi.[134] Conversions in Qazvin were chiefly due to the efforts of Mullá Jalíl Urúmí but also Mullá Yúsuf Ardabílí, and Qurrat al-'Ayn.[135]

These conversions were bound to provoke a reaction from Muhammad Taqí's quarter. The physical punishment of 'Abd al-Jalíl by order of the powerful mujtahid began a new phase of hostility in Qazvin. The small but active band of Babis, who were now recruiting among merchants, traders, and artisans, in the city was determined to retaliate.[136] Residing in her father's inner quarter, Qurrat al-'Ayn, was meanwhile pressured by her family to disown her Babi followers. Her repeated pleas with the remaining 'Atabát adherents to leave Qazvin and join other Babis in Tehran and Khurasan, were reluctantly obeyed.[137]

The heightening of tension seems to have been related to rumors of Qurrat al-'Ayn's alleged unchastity and immoral conduct. The stories originated in Qurrat al-'Ayn's strong views on the need for abrogation of Islamic law particularly on the issue of unveiling in public. Most sources agree that before the Badasht conference, she never unveiled publicly, and some even doubt that she did so on that occasion.[138] Her conversations with men were often conducted from behind a screen.[139] In gatherings of the Babi adepts in Karbalá', however, as indicated earlier, she felt secure in casting off her facial veil.[140] Such an act, or even hints of its desirability, was considered an anathema of the gravest nature. As we were told by a contemporary observer, facial unveiling in the presence of any male except members of the immediate family, even for the purpose of medical examination, was regarded as no less sinful than prostitution.[141]

Even if Qurrat al-'Ayn had never unveiled in public, her controversial views on Islamic sharí'a and the very presence of a large body of male companions who followed her from Karbalá' to Qazvin were enough to arouse suspicion.[142] The allegations of Qurrat al-'Ayn's unchastity and sexual liberty were widespread enough to reach court chronicler, Siphir, who rendered a wildly fictitious account of the "moonfaced" Qurrat al-'Ayn and her relations with the "wandering Babis" long deprived of their homes and wives. Siphir takes a prurient pleasure in reporting that Qurrat al-'Ayn not only believed in unveiling but endorsed the marriage of one wife to nine husbands.[143] The Qajar chronicler goes on:

> She would decorate her assembly room like a bridal chamber and her body like a peacock of Paradise. Then she summoned the followers of the Bab and appeared unveiled in front of them. First she ascended a throne and like a pious preacher reminded them of Heaven and hell and quoted amply from the Qur'án and the Traditions. She would then tell them: 'Whoever touches me, the intensity of Hell's fire would not affect him." The audience would then rise and come to her throne and kiss those lips of hers which put to shame the ruby of Rammán, and rub their faces against her breasts, which chagrinned the pomegranates of the garden.[144]

The pictorial details are figments of Siphir's wild imagination. The sexual tone, however, is typical of the way Qurrat al-'Ayn's wish to unveil was perceived.

Such allegations obviously were damaging to the Baraghánís' reputation. Qurrat al-'Ayn's above mentioned allusions "to slanderous defamation" and her denial of entertaining "worldly love" presumably refer to accusations that horrified her relatives. Nevertheless her father does not seem to have believed the rumors, and indeed he may not have remained unmoved by his daughter's sincerity and fortitude. Even after the assassination of Mullá Muhammad Taqí later that year, Mullá Sálih was confident enough of his daughter's innocence to deny categorically the accusations of immortality brought against her by the imám jum'a of Qazvin in a gathering of prominent 'ulama of the city. In response the sarcastic imám jum'a mockingly read a verse: "No glory remains on that house / From which the hens crow like the cocks." Mullá Sálih, remained silent, tears running down his cheeks to his beard.[145] Bitter reproaches of this kind eventually forced him to emigrate from Qazvin and retire in the 'Atabát, where he died in 1283/1866.[146]

Mullá Muhammad Taqí seems to have been even more humiliated by the infamous rumors. This was another reason for him to react ever more harshly and intensify his attacks on those who he believed had brought ill repute on his house.[147] His criticism and harassment, however, were to cost him his life. In Ramadán 1263/August-September 1847, the Babi sympathizer Mírzá 'Abdulláh Shírází struck a deadly blow to Muhammad Taqí's throat during dawn prayers, in his own mosque. The assassin, a Shírází baker (later camouflaged under a new name, Mírzá Sálih), was outraged by Muhammad Taqí's open enmity toward the Shaykhis. In reply to Mírzá 'Abdulláh's personal query concerning Ahsá'í, the mujtahid had declared: "Him as well as his followers I regard as the very embodiment of error."[148] This reply is given by most sources as the chief motivation for the assassination, but it is not unlikely that Mírzá 'Abdulláh was assisted in the act by Babi accomplices. Áqá Muhammad Hádí Farhádí, a militant merchant from Qazvin who was already involved in an earlier incident, cannot be ruled out.[149] However, all the evidence suggests that if there was a premeditated scheme, it was without Qurrat al-'Ayn's knowledge. In spite of her later endorsement of militant action in Badasht, it is highly unlikely that she would have sanctioned any act of violence against a member of her own family.

The assassination of Mullá Muhammad Taqí cost the Babis dearly. This was the earliest symptom of a militant mood prevailing over an active minority frustrated by the growing hostility, for which the 'ulama were held responsible. The shift from "the conveyance of the word" to active defiance, symbolized in the assassination of a high-ranking mujtahid, set the Babis on an irreversible path that eventually led them to the holy war of Tabarsí. It was the Babi rank and file who preceded the leadership in this transformation, and gradually forced it to the point of no return.

Immediately after the murder of Muhammad Taqí, most well-known Babis of Qazvin, then one of the largest groups in Iran, were rounded up. A wave of anti-Babi persecution followed. Mullá Muhammad, who considered the killing a Babi conspiracy led by Qurrat al-'Ayn, organized the joint forces of the tulláb, most notoriously Mullá Muhsin the Babi Killer (Bábí Kush), and the governor's agents to raid houses of the suspected Babis and to otherwise harass them.[150] Qurrat al-'Ayn herself, together with her maid Káfiya and another woman, was arrested and interrogated in the government house.[151] The severe punishment of the accused apparently persuaded the assassin, Mírzá 'Abdulláh, to surrender. The evidence he provided to support his confession was not convincing enough for Mullá Muhammad to release the detainees.[152] By insisting on the punishment of all alleged accomplices, the vengeful mujtahid hoped to eliminate the menace of the Shaykhi-Babi heresy once and for all.

In Tehran, where the accused were sent for further investigation, after much bargaining with the shah, Áqásí, and the minister's rival, Nasrulláh Sadr al-Mamálik Ardabílí,[153] Mullá Muhammad secured the death penalty for Shaykh Sálih Karímí, and Arab follower of Qurrat al-'Ayn, in revenge for the murder of his father. He was executed in Sabzih Maydán square.[154] Hájjí Asadulláh, the elder of the Farahádí family, also perished in detention.[155] Warning Sadr al-Mamálik that any clemency toward the Babis would "unloose a flood of calumny against those who are the chief repositories of the teaching and principles of our faith" and "embolden the enemies of Islam" to shatter the structure of clerical power, Mullá Muhammad persuaded the monarch to leave the rest of the Babi detainees in his charge.[156] Upon their return to Qazvin, contrary to earlier promises, two of the Babi activists—Mullá Ibráhím Mahallátí, a learned convert from the 'Atabát who apparently had challenged Mullá Muhammad Taqí on an earlier occasion, and Mullá Táhir Shírází, another follower of Qurrat al-'Ayn—were put to a long and cruel death in front of his house.[157] In spite of the government's pronounced unwillingness to permit the outbreak of violence, thereby involuntarily playing into the mujtahid's hands, those earliest executions marked the ominous start of an agonizing era of Babi killing that reached a climax in the executions of 1268/1852 and continued thereafter. The Qazvin executions, typical of many in later years, were carried out by the mob, incited by religious leaders. Either to accumulate rewards for the hereafter or to discharge their deep hatred for advocates of nonconformity and dissent, the participating crowd performed an act that was sanctified by mujtahids and increasingly tolerated by the state.

The adventurous Mírzá 'Abdulláh, however, survived and was bribed out of Tehran detention, only to be slain two years later in Tabarsí.[158] Qurrat al-'Ayn, only barely cleared of the charges against her, was ordered by Mullá Muhammad to be confined in his inner quarters. Shortly after, a perilous escape to Tehran set her free not only from the horrors of her birthplace, to which she never returned, but also of her father's house, where she was fearful of being poisoned by Mullá Muhammad's female agents.[159] In Tehran, under the protection of Mírzá Husayn 'Alí Núri, Bahá'u'lláh, the influential Babi in the capital, she spent several months in hiding in and out of the city.[160] Towards the middle of 1264/1848, following the general call for the Babis to assemble in Khurasan, she left Tehran and attended the Badasht gathering, where she played a major role in determining the movement's future.[161]

The assembly of Badasht was the culmination of Qurrat al-'Ayn's Babi career. Convinced of her own mission and free from family ties, she was more than ever determined to press home to the Babi audience her vision of religious independence and political revolt. The gathering also registered a new momentum in the history of the movement. The rising tides of persecution; highlighted by the Bab's captivity and the growing isolation imposed on the Babis by their opponents, gave rise to a new spirit of defiance. The Bab's call on his followers to gather in Khurasan, presumably in anticipation of the long-awaited Insurrection, was an implicit acknowledgement of this spirit.[162]

The conference was held between Rajab and mid-Sha'bán 1264/June-July 1848, in the hamlet of Badasht, east of Bastám, on the Khurasan-Mazandaran road. The eighty-one participants, mostly Babis of Khurasan, Mazandaran, and Qazvin, camped for three weeks in orchards on the hamlet's outskirts. The growing unrest in Mashhad had driven Quddús and his companions out of the city, forcing the wandering Babi group to hold its meeting en route at a location chosen purely by chance, where Qurrat al-'Ayn and other Babis traveling to Khurasan met other Babis returning from the province. Mullá Husayn's absence from Badasht became increasing significant in the course of the debates.163

If the choice of the location was spontaneous, the issues that made such a gathering urgent had for long troubled the eager participants. This was the first time that a mostly prominent group of the Babis could review—and as it turned out heatedly debate—a range of questions essential to the identity and the future strategy of the movement. Chief in the unwritten Babi agenda was the plight of the Bab, now incarcerated in a remote castle in Azerbaijan. There was an unchallenged consensus as to the binding duty of the Babis to rescue their spiritual leader. But any effort in this direction required an answer to a more pressing question concerning the Babis' future course of action. Moderation and prudence in the force of mounting hostility, radical Babis argued, could lead only to further suffering. Yet the final Insurrection against the forces of oppression would materialize only if the Qá'im made his advent unequivocally apparent. This in turn raise d questions as to the Bab's precise claim, and, even more crucial, the nature of his mission. Was the Bábíya merely an effort to rejuvenate Islam's inner truth? Or did it go beyond to establish a revelatory cycle altogether independent of Islam?164

Questions of such magnitude were bound to uncover strong differences of opinion within the embryonic body of converts whose loyalty to the founder of the movement was not yet translated into a consensus on the identity of his proposed creed. Moreover, the ideological polarization evident in Badasht could not have remained untouched by the equally agonizing problem of the movement's leadership and hierarchical order. The Bab had lately promoted Mullá Husayn to the rank of gateship and authorized him to lead the Babi forces into concerted action. But such delegation of power did not relieve the need for a charismatic leader while the prophet of Shiraz was absent from his flock. Both Qurrat al-'Ayn and Quddús were obvious candidates, and both were keen to register their self-avowed leadership.

It was only to be expected that Qurrat al-'Ayn, who had already challenged the Babi conservatives of the 'Atabát, would emerge as the chief representative of the radical tendency. Her antiorthodox positions became ever more clear when, in a symbolic act of defiance, she removed her veil in the middle of her speech to the

Badasht gathering; an act that turned some away from the movement forever and caused agony and despair to others. One Isfahání zealot cut his own throat. Unrepenting, Qurrat al-'Ayn proclaimed to the gathering: "Our days are the days of interregnum. Today all religious obligations are abrogated and such acts as prayer, fasting, and salutation [to the House of the Prophet] are futile. When the Bab conquers the seven kingdoms and unites different religions; he will bring a new sharí'a and entrust his Qur'án to the community. Whatever new obligations he ordains would then be compulsory to the people of the earth. Thus burden not yourselves with the worthless."[165] The abrogation of Islamic sharí'a, Qurrat al-'Ayn argued, was to be complemented with the active endeavor to remove the forces of disbelief and corruption. "I am the word that the Qá'im will utter," she claimed, "the word that shall put to flight the chiefs and nobles of the earth."[166]

With little hesitation in airing her views, Qurrat al-'Ayn was able to win over some of the more liberated participants, but at the expense of isolating others. Accusing her of "indiscreetly rejecting the time-honored traditions of the past"—charges already branded on her in the 'Atabát—a minority of the bewildered Babis turned to Quddús.[167] The rise to prominence of the Bab's young disciple was no accident. Earlier, in Mashhad, Mullá Husayn had displayed exceptional reverence for Quddús, presumably with the Bab's prior consent, and in effect treated him as a spiritual lieutenant to the captive prophet. Taking sides with the sharí'a-minded, Quddús criticized Qurrat al-'Ayn's radicalism, even denouncing her as "the author of heresy" and chastising her supporters as "victims of error."[168] This rejection of her doctrinal innovation reflected the misgivings of a number of prominent Babis present (including Muhammad Hádí and Muhammad 'Alí Nahrí, whose wife, Shams al-Duhá, had already fallen under Qurrat al-'Ayn's spell).

The doctrinal controversy, now transformed into a power struggle, was not relieved by Qurrat al-'Ayn's open challenge to her critics. Referring to Quddús as "a pupil" whom the Bab sent her to "edify and instruct,"[169] she rebuked him not only for having failed to raise the banners of Babi revolt in Mashhad but for his pietistic intransigence. On one occasion, she interrupted his prayers, sword in hand, declaring: "Wrap up this spectacle, the time for prayer and liturgy are over. Now is the time to prepare for the battlefields of sacrifice and dedication."[170] Later, defending herself against charges of blasphemy and the threat of punishment, she reminded her outraged opponents, perhaps, sarcastically, that as believers in Islamic sharí'a they must bring her, a woman heretic, back to the true path of religion only by the word, not the sword. It was therefore incumbent on them to prove her errors with arguments.

In the course of a debate requested by Qurrat al-'Ayn, however, it was she who managed to convince her chief rival, Quddús. Reiterating with passionate eloquence her antinomian stance, she tried to show the doctrinal weaknesses of the opposing party. Subsequently, in a daring act that perhaps challenged Quddús' meekness in the face of hostilities instigated by the Babis' archenemy, Sa'íd al-'Ulamá' (the mujtahid of Bárfurúsh), she perhaps tried to show symbolically that her radical commitments surpassed her male critics'. Dressed in men's clothing, unveiled and mounted, she waved her bare sword and cried: "Down with Sa'íd al-'Ulamá' and his followers!" The Babis responded: "Death to them all!" She repeated: "Down with this villain of all villains!" They replied: "Sudden death to all of them!"[171] No more effectively could she acquire the Babi mandate, thus outmaneuvering Quddús and silencing her critics. Other symbolic gestures by her supporters—discarding prayer rugs and breaking the prayer seals (equating them to idols)—were to further convey to the Babis the termination of the era of pietistic devotion and longing for otherworldly recompense.

To his followers' dismay, Quddús himself began to lean toward Qurrat al-'Ayn's position, an apparent curious shift not fully explicable by the enigmatic tone of the sources. The existence of a preconceived plan between the two leaders to introduce to the traditionally minded Babis the innovations of the new religion is too farfetched.[172] The differences were real. What could have tilted the balance in Qurrat al-'Ayn's favor, however, was Quddús' gradual disillusionment with acquiescence and suffering, which had inundated his earlier writings. The experience of Hajj, the persecutions of Shiraz, Kirman, Bárfurúsh, and most recently Mashhad, where once again he was forced to retreat, must have already eroded his conciliatory stance. Qurrat al-'Ayn's challenge only brought home the inevitability of armed struggle and its corollary, the unequivocal pronouncement of the independent Babi faith.

The role of Mírzá Husayn 'Alí Núrí, Bahá'ulláh, who after 1847 emerged as representative of a nascent tendency within the movement, should not be overlooked.[173] He tried, with some success, to bring about an uneasy understanding between the two conflicting factions. The earliest signs of an emerging third approach within Babism—that of a break with the past but nonviolent moderation in its implementation—can be seen in his very mediatory initiative.

The most obvious outcome of the Badasht debate was perhaps the prevalence of Qurrat al-'Ayn's views. They were undoubtedly decisive to the future of the movement. The Bab's claim to Qa'ímíya and the open pronouncement of a new prophetic cycle, as expressed in the Bayán and during the Tabriz tribunal, only reasserted her advocacy of religious renewal.[174] The Babi resistance in Tabarsí and other places proved the inevitability of confrontation. The gathering also brought to the surface the conflict between the traditional revivalists and the innovative revolutionaries; a conflict deeply rooted in the sociocultural diversity of the Babi structure.

No overall course of Babi policy was achieved beyond the acknowledgement of an urgent need for collective action. As a first pragmatic step in this direction, one can surmise, a march to Mazandaran was undertaken under the joint leadership of Qurrat al-'Ayn and Quddús, in order to establish a Babi foothold in his hometown, Bárfurúsh. This venture however, ended in total disaster when the Babis were raided by a band of villagers in the nearby Níyálá. The local mulla who led the aggressive crowd was apparently outraged by the sight of the unveiled Qurrat al-'Ayn sitting inside a howdah next to Quddús and chanting poems out loud, together with her companions. The assailants must have seen the Babi party as no more than a group of libertine infidels worthy of death. Even for the Babis, who witnessed with amazement, perhaps horror, the unrestrained conversation between a daring woman and her male traveling companion, perhaps even her unspoken affection for him, it was hard not to perceive the prevailing climate of emancipation as "abuse of liberty" and excesses from "bonds of moderation."[175] Reportedly, after hearing the news of Badasht, Mullá Husayn vowed that if he had been present he would have punished the transgressors with the sword.

The incident of Níyálá, the first fatal clash between Babis and a frenzied crowd, ended in several deaths and the dispersion of the confused Babi party in different directions. Quddús escaped in disguise to Bárfurúsh, while Qurrat al-'Ayn, accompanied by Bahá'ulláh, headed for his home region, Núr. It remained for Mullá Husayn and his companions to complete the march to Mazandaran.

After Badasht, between the end of 1264/1848 and the beginning of 1266/1850, Qurrat al-'Ayn wandered in Mazandaran. For a brief period during Ramadán 1264/September 1848, she was in Bárfurúsh in the house of pro-Babi Mullá Muhammad Hamza Sharí'atmadár, and even preached to his congregation.[176] Later, presumably before the arrival of the Babi party, she went into hiding in the Núr region, slipping from village to village. For about a year she took refuge in a farmhouse on the outskirts of the village of Váz, south of Ámul, where she was a guest of Áqá Nasrulláh Gílárdí.[177] She was hoping ultimately to join the Babis in Tabarsí,[178] but her hiding place was discovered by government secret agents, and she was arrested on charges of collaboration in the assassination of her uncle. Reportedly, she had already been listed by the government of Mírzá Taqí Khán Amír Kabír as a wanted Babi rebel.[179] She was brought to Tehran in Rabi al-Awwal 1266/January 1850, and after an interview with Amír Kabír[180] and a brief audience with the young monarch, Násir al-Dín Sháh,[181] was sentenced to imprisonment in the upper chamber of the house of Tehran's chief of police, Mahmúd Khán Kalántar, for the rest of her short life.

Even in detention in Kalántar's house, Qurrat al-'Ayn did not relinquish contacts with the Babis of Tehran, and continued to win new converts among the women of the capital.[182] Writing in Qazvíní dialect on grocery wrapping paper, using a pen made out of broom twigs and ink made of juice from green herbs, she used go-betweens to send out secret messages.[183] In late 1268/1852, after the unsuccessful attempt of the Babis on the life of the shah, her fate was eventually decided. She was first interrogated for several days by two senior mujtahids, Mullá 'Alí Kaní and Mullá Muhammad Andarmání.[184] What presumably could not have been decided on the ground of religious prohibition of the execution of female heretics was eventually settled when in Dhu al-Qa'da 1268/ September 1852, the mujtahids, apparently complying with government's wishes, passed a death sentence.[185] Remaining unrepentant throughout her interrogation, she refused their offer of clemency in exchange for recantation. Shortly after, she was brought in the middle of the night to Bágh Ílkhání, where she was strangled in secret by a drunken bodyguard. Her body was dumped in a shallow well at the back of the garden.[186]

Qurrat al-'Ayn's ideas and actions were decisive in the course of the movement toward independence and the conscious break that occurred with the dominant norms of Islam. In this respect she ranks equal to the Bab himself, at times even more determined than him and other leading Babis to register her rejection of the prevailing order. Having come from a clerical background, she revolted against traditions keenly revered by members of her own family. Exceptionally interesting is the way the messianic legacy; chiefly through the Shaykhi school, led to a full transformation of her Shi'ite outlook. She is perhaps the embodiment of what she calls a soul "enamoured with torment" (*shíftih-yi balá'*).[187] Such an outlook only made sense in a messianic culture where "proof of wisdom" and "intuitive endeavor" are to culminate in an historic cognition. Although one may partly agree with Browne that Babi thought was essentially Shi'ite in its Weltanschuung and that Babi history was a reenactment of the idealized Shi'ite past,[188] at the core of this preoccupation with suffering and martyrdom lay the seed of a dynamic future; a drive aptly encapsulated in the Babi maxim, "The time cycle is in progression." Qurrat al-'Ayn's abandonment of the Islamic sharí'a was the logical outcome of such an assumption. For her, cognition was a human responsibility that must be materialized in action. Abrogating prayers, whatever the theological justification, symbolized a divorce from the old notion of salvation through devotion. Instead, action was to be interpreted as "the conveyance of the word" and ultimately the establishment of the new Babi dispensation. Once the increasing pressure proved to Qurrat al-'Ayn, as to the other Babis, that action by the sword was unavoidable, martyrdom became the ultimate realization of the faith.

Qurrat al-'Ayn has sometimes been portrayed by posterity as a champion of women's rights. In her writings, however, she makes no direct reference to the position of women in her society. It is unlikely that she was ever aware of a suffragist movement or other trends in contemporary Europe. Indeed, her entire worldview differed fundamentally from the Western notion of women's emancipation as it first appeared in Iran after the Constitutional Revolution. Her outlook and motivation were primarily religious and remained so. But inevitably, being a Babi leader of high caliber with unconventional ideals, Qurrat al-'Ayn experienced dual disadvantages and deprivations, not only as an "outspoken heretic" but as a "rebellious woman." Both religious institutions and social norms sanctified women's subordination with stringent and jealously observed rules, infringements of which were severely punished. For Qurrat al-'Ayn not to be conscious of her disadvantages, and even more not to react to them, would have been impossible. Frustrations in her family life and persecutions in her Babi career both served as impetuses for inspirations that she transposed into a religious paradigm; what she terms "the state of primal truth." By assuming the symbolic role of Fátima, she envisaged a feminine model—a "primal truth," as she called it—that substantially differed from the role assigned to Fátima in the Islamic, more particularly Shi'ite, tradition as the daughter of the Prophet, the wife of 'Alí, and the mother of Hasan and Husayn; the role that guaranteed her sanctitude by lineage, marriage, and motherly love. Qurrat al-'Ayn's Fátima was one of independent will and action. The leadership she assumed in the 'Atabát and later in Badasht was the realization of this paradigm.

All the way back to Rábia al'Adawíya, the ninth-century Basran to whom Qurrat al-'Ayn probably looked as another role model, heterodox movements were often a breeding ground for women of vision and talent. This association should not be interpreted merely as an outlet for discharging frustration with the socioreligious order however. Qurrat al-'Ayn's religious convictions were almost inseparable from her feminine consciousness. The only solution she saw, for women and men alike, was a break with the past, and as the first step, a deliberate infringement of religious norms. To find her in the forefront of Babi radicalism and an advocate of progressive revelation is only logical. Her initiation into the Letters of the Living, on the other hand, was an acknowledgement of her equal place with men in the first unit of the ideal Babi order of All-Beings.

**Notes**
Reprinted from Amanat, Abbas, *Resurrection and Renewal: The Making of the Babi Movement in Iran, 1844-1850.* (Ithaca: Cornell University Press, 1989), Chapter 7.

1. Also titled Zakíya, according to Nabíl-i-A'zam, *The Dawn-Breakers: Nabíl's Narrative of the Early Days of the Bahá'í Revelation*; translated and edited by Shoghi Effendi (Wilmette: Bahá'í Publishing Committee, 1932) p. 628.

Mírzá Muhammad Taqí Sipihr, *Násikh al-Taváríkh: Sala'tin-i Qájár*, ed. by Muhammad Baqir Bihbúdí (Tehran: Intisharat-i Kitabfurushi-i, 1385/1965) Vol. 3, p. 220 is inaccurate on her titles.

2. In spite of a relatively large number of short biographies and other secondary sources, there is a lack of a scholarly account of Qurrat al-'Ayn's life, or an analysis of her ideas and her significance. Nearly all the histories of the Babi movement contain scattered references to her, sometimes a whole section. Shaykh Sultán Karbalá'í's "Maktúb," written in 1263/1847, in Mírzá Asadullah Fádili-i-Mázindaráni, *Tarikh-i-Zuhúru'l-Haqq* (Tehran: [s. n.], 1944) Vol. 3, pp. 245-59 and Haji Mírzá Jani, *Kitáb-i Nuqtatu'l-Káf, Being the Earliest History of the Bábís*; ed. by Edward G. Browne (Leyden: E. J. Brill; London: Luzac, 1910) are by far the earliest, though by no means the most comprehensive. Sipihr, *Násikh al-Taváríkh*, Vol. 3 and Rizá Qulí Khán Hidáyat, *Raudat al-Safá'yi Násirí*, 3rd ed. (Tehran, 1338-1339 Sh./1959-60) Vol. 10 suffer from their usual bigotry and inaccuracy, though they still contain valuable points. Aleksandr Kazem-Bek, "Bab et les Babis, ou Soulèvement politique et religieux, de 1845 à 1853," *Journal Asiatique* (Paris) Vol. 7 (1866) pp. 473-76 and Joseph Arthur, comte de Gobineau, *Les Religions et les Philosophies dans l'Asie Centrale* (Paris: Didier, 1866) pp. 167-69, 293-94 and other references, are heavily based on Sipihr, *Násikh al-Taváríkh*, but give a few new facts and even more myths and fictions that were in circulation as early as the 1860s. Later Babi-Bahá'í sources, Shaykh Kázim ibn Shaykh Muhammad Qazvíní, Samandar, "Táríkh-i Samandar" in 'Abd al-'Ali 'Alá'í, ed., *Táríkh-i Samandar va Mulhaqqát* (Tehran: [Bahá'í Publishing Committee], 131 Badí'/1975); Áqá Muhammad Mustafá ibn Shaykh Muhammad Shibl al-Baghdádí. "ar-Risalah al-Amiriyyah," appended to Ahmad Suhrab, *ar-Risalah at-Tis' 'Ashariyyih* (Cairo: Matba'at as-Sa'adah, 1338/1919); Nabíl-i-A'zam, *The Dawn-Breakers*; Mírzá Husain Hamadáni, *The Táríkh-i-Jadíd, or New History of Mírzá 'Alí Muhammad the Báb*, trans. Edward G. Browne (Cambridge: The University Press, 1893); and 'Abdu'l-Bahá, *Tadhkirat al-wafa' fi tarjumati hayati qudama'i 'l-ahibba'* (Haifa: 'Abbasiyya Press, 1342/1924) pp. 291-330, provide accounts that remained unrecorded up to a few decades later. Mullá Jafar Qazvíní's historical account (published in 'A. 'Alá'í, ed., *Táríkh-i Samandarí va Mulhaqqát*, pp. 446-500) and al-Qatíl al- Karbalá'í's "Risála" (in Fádil-i-Mázindaráni, *Tarikh-i-Zuhúru'l-Haqq*, appendix 2, pp.502-32), however, are surprisingly silent. Mírzá Abul-Fazl Gulpáyigání and Sayyid Mahdí Gulpáyigání, *Kashf al-Ghitá' 'an Hiyal al-A'dá* (Tashkent, [1919?]) pp. 92-111; Hájí Muhammad ibn 'Abd al-Baqi Mu'ín al-Saltana Tabrízí, *Táríkh-i Amr-i Bahá'í* (Tehran: Iran National Bahá'í Archives Library photostat publication, n.d.); 'Abdu'l-Husayn "'Avárih" Ayati, *Al-Kavákibu'd-Durriyyih fi Ma'áthiri'l al-Bahá'íyah* (Cairo: Matba`at as-Sa`adah, 1342/1923); and Fádil-i-Mázindaráni, *Tarikh-i-Zuhúru'l-Haqq* add few details to earlier accounts. A. L. M. Nicolas, *Seyyèd Ali Mohammed, dit le Bâb: histoire* (Paris: Dujarric, 1905), which seems to be based on oral reports (sometimes very similar to Qazvíní, Samandar), is the fullest in a European language, though far from complete. Some new details were also supplied by Browne in his notes to 'Abdu'l-Bahá, *A Traveller's*

*Narrative: Written to Illustrate the History of the Báb*, edited in the original Persian, and translated into English, with an introduction and explanatory notes by Edward G. Browne (Cambridge: The University Press, 1891). The few short works and poetry that were published by an anonymous Babi-Azalí for the centennial of her death, with the title *Bi-yád-i-Sadumín Sál-i-Shahádat-i-Qurratu'l-'Ayn Nábighih-i-Duwrán* (In commemoration of the centennial of the martyrdom of Qurratu'l-'Ayn, genius of the ages) (Tehran: [s. n.], 1949); and *Táhirah: Qurratu'l-'Ayn* by Husám Nuqabá'i ([Tehran: Bahá'í Publishing Committee], 128 Badí'/1972), is largely a collection of earlier accounts. Martha L. Root's *Táhirih, the Pure* ([Karachi: Root], 1938; 2nd ed. Los Angeles: Kalimát Press, 1981), is a short popular narrative. Denis M. MacEoin, "From Shaykhism to Babism: A Study in Charismatic Renewal in Shi'i Islam," Ph. D. diss., University of Cambridge, 1979 [forthcoming Kalimát Press], especially Chapter 6, pp. 194-196, provides a succinct account of her role in connection with the evolution of the Shaykhi community in the 'Atabát. Moojan Momen, *The Bábí and Bahá'í Religions, 1844-1944: Some Contemporary Western Accounts* (Oxford: George Ronald, 1981) provides some samples of lesser-known European accounts. 'Alí al-Wardí, *Lamahát Ijtimá'íya min Táríkh al-'Iráq al-Hadíth* (Baghdad: Mataba'at al-Irshad, 1971) Vol. 2, pp. 152-90, is the most comprehensive account in Arabic of Qurrat al-'Ayn's life. It contains fresh details on the Iraq period, chiefly based on two as-yet-unknown manuscripts: one by 'Abbúd Sálihí, a descendant of Mullá Muhammad Sálihí Baragháni, entitled "Qurratu'l-'Ayn, 'alá Haqíqatihá wa Wáqi'há" and the other by Mullá Ahmad Hisárí Khusrásaní, "'Aqá'id al-Shaykhíya." As late as 1974, new information emerged in Muhammad 'Alí Malik Khusraví, *Tárikh-i Shuhadá-yi Amr* (Tehran, 130 Badí'/1974) Vol. 3. Occasionally the Bab's writings or the writings of Qurrat al-'Ayn contain brief references to historical events. Some European accounts, such as Jakob Eduard Polak, *Persien: das Land und seine Bewohner* (Leipzig: F. A. Brockhaus, 1865) and other works, make brief references to her. Qurrat al-'Ayn's life was a source of inspiration for European writers, particularly for those who sought in her a heroine of women's emancipation. Izabella Grinevskaia's Russian play *Bab: Dramaticheskaia poema iz istorii Persii* (St. Petersburg: T-vo Khudozhestvennoi pechati, 1903) is one example. [See "Táhirih on the Russian Stage," by Jan Teofil Jasion in this volume, p. 273—Ed.]

3. Mírzá Muhammad ibn Sulaymán Tunkábuní, *Hadha kitab Qisas al'Ulamá* (Tehran: Habib 'Allah 'Ustad 'al-Mahir Mírzá, 1304/1886) pp. 19, 91; Muhammad Mushin Ághá Buzurg Tihrání, *Tabaqát A'lám al-Shí'ah* (An Najaf: 'al-Matab'ah 'al-'Ilmíyah, 1373-1388/1954-1968) Vol. 2, part 1, pp. 226-28, 660-61.

4. For the list of his works see 'Ághá Buzurg al-Tihrání, *Tabaqvát A'lám al-Shí'ah*, Vol. 2, part 2, pp. 660-61. Also Muhammad Mushin 'Ághá Buzurg al-Tihrání, *al-Dharí'a ilá Tasáníf al-Shí'ah* (al-Najaf: Matba'at 'al-Gharri; Tehran: Danishgah 1335-1398/1916-1978) Vol. 16, p. 71.

5. Tunkábuni, *Hadha kitab Qisas al'Ulamá*, p. 91.

6. Gobineau's reference (Gobineau, *Les Religions*, p. 167) to Mullá Muhammad Taqí as "Tradioniste femeux dans toute la Perse" could be interpreted as a

comment on his skill in traditions (akhbár) but not as a follower of Akhbárí school, as all evidence proves otherwise. He studied under the celebrated Usúlí Sayyid 'Alí Tabátabá'í (Tunkábuní, *Hadha kitab Qisas al'Ulamá*, p. 19). For his biography see Tunkábuní, *Hadha kitab Qisas al'Ulamá*, pp.19-44; Ághá Buzurg Tihrání, *Tabaqát A'lám al-Shí'ah*, Vol.1, part 1, pp. 226-228, and Muhammad 'Alí Mu'allim Habíbábádí, *Makárim al-asár dar ahvál-i rijál-i dawrah-i Qájár* (Isfahan: Nafa'is-i Makhtutat, 1377-1396/1958-1976) Vol. 5, pp. 1707-1716, and notes.
7. For his works both in prose and verse see Munzaví in Abul-Qásim ibn Zayn al'Ábidín Ibráhímí Kirmání [Sarká Áqá], *Fihrist-i Kutub-i Shaykh-i Ajall-i Auhad Marhúm-i Shaykh Ahmad Ahsá'í va Sá'ir-i Masháyikh-i 'Izá,.* 3rd ed. (Kirman, n.d.) Vol. 2, pp. 951, 1341, 1389, and 1396; Ághá Buzurg Tihrání, *al-Dharí'a*, Vol. 9, p. 317. His biography appears in Mu'allim Habíbábádí, *Makárim al-asár dar ahvál-i rijál-i dawrah-i Qájár,* Vol. 5, pp. 1707-1716, and in Muhammad 'Alí Mudarris, *Rayhánat al-Adab* (Tehran: Chapkhanah-i Sa'adi, 1326-1333 Sh./1947-1954) Vol. 1, p. 153.
8. Nicolas, *Seyyèd Ali Mohammed,* p. 273.
9. Sipihr, *Násikh al-Tavárikh*, Vol. 3, p. 219.
10. 'Abdu'l-Bahá, *Tadhkirat al-wafa' fi tarjumati hayati qudama'i 'l-ahibba'* , p. 291; and cf. Haji Mírzá Jani, *Kitáb-i Nuqtatu'l-Káf*, p. 142.
11. 'Abdu'l-Bahá, *Tadhkirat al-wafa' fi tarjumati hayati qudama'i 'l-ahibba'* , pp. 291-92.
12. al-Wardí, *Lamahát*, Vol. 2, p. 153 (citing Sálihí, "Qurratu'l-'Ayn, 'alá Haqíqatihá wa Wáqi'há").
13. Both sons later became mujtahids and Ismá'íl succeeded his father as imám jum'a. For their accounts see Ághá Buzurg Tihrání, *Tabaqát A'lám al-Shí'ah*, Vol. 1, pp. 23, 164. A third child, Isháq, was born in 1841 in Qazvin (al-Wardí, *Lamahát*, Vol.2, p. 153).
14. 'Abdu'l-Bahá. *Tadhkirat al-wafa' fi tarjumati hayati qudama'i 'l-ahibba'*, p. 292.
15. al-Wardí, *Lamahát*, Vol. 2, pp. 153-54.
16. 'Abdu'l-Bahá, *Tadhkirat al-wafa' fi tarjumati hayati qudama'i 'l-ahibba'*, p. 292; and Mu'ín al-Saltana, *Táríkh-i Amr-i Bahá'í*, p. 2.
17. Nabíl-i-A'zam, *The Dawn-Breakers*, p. 83; cf. Álúsí (see below, this chapter). The sentence *yá qurrat al-'ayní wa ruh al-fy'ádí* is originally from *qurrat a'yun* (heavenly recompense for the true believers, Qur'án 32: 17 and 25:74). *Qurrat'al-'ayn* is a common Arabic term of endearment sometimes given by the religious teachers to their favorite students.
18. Qazvíní, *Samandar*, p. 345.
19. For other examples of women mujtahids in the nineteenth century see MacEoin, "From Shaykhism to Babism," p. 194. For Shaykhi views on women, see Arthur, comte de Gobineau, *Trois ans en Asie*, 15 Ed. (Paris: B. Grasset, 1922, Vol. 2) p. 49.
20. See below, this chapter.
21. Qazvíní, *Samandar*, p. 344.
22. Possibly also accompanied by Mullá Muhammad 'Alí Qazvíní, her brother in law (Fádil-i-Mázindarání, *Tarikh-i-Zuhúru'l-Haqq*, p. 313).

23. 'Abdu'l-Bahá, *Tadhkirat al-wafa' fi tarjumati hayati qudama'i 'l-ahibba'*, p. 295, reports a "veracious dream" in which Qurrat al-'Ayn visited the Bab prior to his claims. This is another example of the way accounts of intuitive dreams were utilized to register anticipation for messianic Zuhúr or even allude to the claimant's identity.
24. Fádil-i-Mázindaráni, *Tarikh-i-Zuhúru'l-Haqq*, appendix 1, pp. 499-500.
25. 'Abdu'l-Bahá, *Tadhkirat al-wafa' fi tarjumati hayati qudama'i 'l-ahibba'*, p. 294, dates her arrival ten days after the death of Rashtí.
26. Mu'ín al-Saltana, *Táríkh-i Amr-i Bahá'í*, p. 46, without specifying his source.
27. Qazvíní, *Samandar*, p. 346. Cf. p. 78; 'Ávárih" Ayati, *Al-Kavákibu'd-Durriyyih*, Vol. 1, pp. 61-62.
28. Haji Mírzá Jani, *Kitáb-i Nuqtatu'l-Káf*, p. 140.
29. Mu'ín al-Saltana, *Táríkh-i Amr-i Bahá'í*, p. 3.
30. Shaykh Sultán Karbalá'í, "Maktúb," in Fádil-i-Mázindaráni, *Tarikh-i-Zuhúru'l-Haqq*, Vol. 3, p. 246.
31. See below, this chapter, for details.
32. al-Wardí, *Lamahát*, Vol. 2, pp. 156-157.
33. Haji Mírzá Jani, *Kitáb-i Nuqtatu'l-Káf*, p. 140; 'Ávárih" Ayati, *Al-Kavákibu'd-Durriyyih*, Vol. 1, p. 61.
34. al-Wardí, *Lamahát*, Vol. 2, pp. 155-156.
35. Moreover, the death of Rashtí's widow, who was a supporter of Qurrat al-'Ayn at the beginning of 1262/1846, gave new excuses to Mullá Ahmad Hisárí to press for the removal of Qurrat al-'Ayn and the return of the *Divan* to his control. Nabíl-i-A'zam, *The Dawn-Breakers*, p. 270; cf. Karbalá'í, "Maktúb," in Fádil-i-Mázindaráni, *Tarikh-i-Zuhúru'l-Haqq*, Vol. 3, p. 252, which implies that Mullá Ahmad was in collaboration with the "scum of the people" and "the riff-raff."
36. Ibid.
37. Ibid., citing an oral account from a resident of Kázimayn.
38. Fádil-i-Mázindaráni, *Tarikh-i-Zuhúru'l-Haqq*, Vol. 3, p. 314; cf. Gobineau. *Les Religions*, p. 167.
39. 'Abdu'l-Bahá, *Tadhkirat al-wafa'*, p. 295.
40. 'Ávárih" Ayati, *Al-Kavákibu'd-Durriyyih*, Vol. 1, p. 61.
41. Of the tracts, treatises, letters, poems, and prayers that she wrote, most either remain unidentified or have perished. Of her published works, besides her 1261/1845 "Risála" in Persian in reply to Mullá Jawád Valíyani (Qurratu'l-'Ayn, "Risála," in Mírza Asadullah Fádil-i-Mázandaráni, *Tarikh-i-Zuhúru'l-Haqq*, Vol. 3, 1944, appendix 1, pp. 484-501), Fádil-i-Mázindaráni, *Tarikh-i-Zuhúru'l-Haqq* produces six other works in prose: a letter to Mullá Husayn (in Arabic, pp. 334-338); two public addresses to Babis and the general public written circa 1263/1847 (pp. 338-365); a letter addressed to Álúsí (pp. 356-359); a tract in defense of the Bab (pp. 359-362); and two letters addressed to the Babis of Isfahan (pp. 362-366). The centennial volume: *Táhirih Qurratu'l-'Ayn, Bi-yád-i-Sadumín Sál-i-Shahádat-i-Qurratu'l-'Ayn Nábighih-i-Duwrán: Táhirih Centennial Volume* (Iran: [s. n.], 1949) pp. 36-52, produced six new Persian prayers and letters. Mírzá Abul-Fazl Gulpáyigání, *Kashf al-ghitá' 'an Hiyal al-A'dá* (Tashkent: [s. n.], [1919?])

appendix 2, pp. 1-21, added another long Arabic treatise and 'Ávárih Ayati, *Al-Kavákibu'd-Durriyyih,* Vol. 1, pp. 323-327, cited part of another apologia. Browne provided the text and translation of a letter addressed to Shaykh 'Alí Azím, in Mírzá Husain Hamadání, *The Táríkh-i-Jadíd,* appendix 4, pp. 434-441, and added useful notes. Of her poetry some samples were also printed in various sources. There is some degree of uncertainty on the authenticity of some of the pieces, arising from the fact that some of her poems are similar in style to those of Hátif Isfahání and Suhbat Lárí. Fádil-i-Mázindarání, *Tarikh-i-Zuhúru'l*-Haqq, produces seven poems (pp. 366-69) and the Centennial volume adds eight more (pp. 25-35). Edward G. Browne in *Materials for the Study of the Bábí Religion* (Cambridge: The University Press, 1918) gives the text and translation of three better-known poems and Ni'matulláh Dhuká'í Baydá'í, *Tádhkiríy-i-Shu'aráy-i-Qarn-i-Avval-i-Bahá'í* (Tehran: [Bahá'í Publishing Trust], 121-126 B.E./1965-1970) Vol. 3, pp. 107-32, gives an analysis of her style and produces some new poems. Two manuscripts in the Iran National Bahá'í Archives Library contain some further tracts and poetry.

42. Qurratu'l-'Ayn, "Risála," in Mírza Asadullah Fádil-i-Mázandarání, *Tarikh-i-Zuhúru'l-Haqq,* Vol. 3, appendix 1, p. 488.
43. Ibid.
44. Ibid., p. 493.
45. Ibid., pp. 486-87.
46. Ibid., p. 488.
47. Ibid., pp. 490-91.
48. Ibid., p. 491.
49. Ibid.
50. Ibid.
51. Ibid., p. 494.
52. The Bab, *Kitáb-i Bayán-i Fársí* (Tehran: [s. n., n. d.]) VI/2, pp. 30-32.
53. Haji Mírzá Jani, *Kitáb-i Nuqtatu'l-Káf,* pp. 140-41.
54. Ibid., p. 140.
55. Baghdádí, "Risála," p. 109. The author specifies that Qurrat al-'Ayn "appeared unveiled in the gatherings of believers, but in the gatherings of nonbelievers she spoke from behind a curtain."
56. al-Wardí, *Lamahát,* Vol. 2, p. 162; cf. Qazvíní, *Samandar,* p. 81, who calls them "women companions."
57. For her details, see Amanat, *Resurrection and Renewal,* Chap. 8.
58. Hasan Fu'ádí Bushrú'í, *Manázir-i Táríkhí-yi Nihzat-i Amr-i Bahá'í dar Khurásán* (Tehran: Iran National Bahá'í Archives photostat publication, n. d.) p. 23 ; cf. 'Abdu'l-Bahá, *Tadhkirat al-wafa',* p. 297.
59. Nabíl-i-A'zam, *The Dawn-Breakers,* pp. 270-71.
60. Qazvíní, *Samandar,* p. 358. Also known as Qánita, Haji Mírzá Jani, *Kitáb-i Nuqtatu'l-Káf,* p. 141.
61. See Amanat, Chap. 8. Other Babi women of Qazvin with special adherence to Qurrat al-'Ayn included the literate sister of Karbalá'í Lutf 'Alí Halláj (carder), the wife of Mullá Valíulláh Qazvíní, and the mother of Ibn Abhar (Qazvíní, *Samandar,* p. 370). The same source maintains that even before

1260/1844, Qurrat al-'Ayn was well known in women's circles of Qazvin and that the women relatives of traders, merchants, and notables referred to her as the "daughter of *áqá* and *khánum* (lady) (Qazvíní, *Samandar*, pp. 73, 345).
62. 'Ávárih Ayati, *Al-Kavákibu'd-Durriyyih*, Vol. 1, p. 117; cf. 'Abdu'l-Hamid Ishráq-Khávarí, *Táríkh-i Amrí-yi Hamadán* (Tehran: Iran National Bahá'í Archives photostat publication, n. d.) pp. 2-4 and Abul-Fazl Gulpáyigání, *Kashf al-ghitá'*, p. 105. Her details and some samples appear in Ahmad Mírzá 'Azud al-Daula, *Táríkh-i 'Azudí* (Tehran: [s. n.], 1355 Sh./1976) pp. 14-16.
63. 'Ávárih" Ayati, *Al-Kavákibu'd-Durriyyih*, Vol. 1, p. 117.
64. Dhuká'í Baydá'í, *Tádhkiríy-i-Shu'aráy-i-Qarn-i-Avval-i-Bahá'í*, pp. 167-202, gives an account of her life and some parts of her *masnaví*. The women of the household of Áqá Khán were also impressed by Qurrat al-'Ayn when she resided briefly in Núrí's house in Tehran in 1264/1848 (Mu'ín al-Saltana Tabrízí, p. 10; Polak, Vol. 1, p. 242). For impression on Shahrbánú, a woman in Dizvá in Núr region, see Malik-Khusraví, *Táríkh-i Shuhadá-yi Amr*, Vol. 3, p. 205.
65. al-Wardí, *Lamahát*, Vol. 2, p. 157.
66. Qazvíní, *Samandar*, pp. 78, 346-47.
67. Fádil-i-Mázindarání, *Tarikh-i-Zuhúru'l-Haqq*, pp. 337-38. See below this chapter, for his earliest conversion in Qazvin. See also MacEoin, "From Shaykhism to Babism," pp. 199-200
68. For Hisárí's later career see Amanat, Chap. 6.
69. Karbalá'í, "Maktúb," in Fádil-i-Mázindarání, *Tarikh-i-Zuhúru'l-Haqq*, pp. 245, 253, 256.
70. Ibid., p. 246.
71. Partially cited in al-Wardí, *Lamahát*, Vol. 2, pp. 159-63.
72. Karbalá'í, "Maktúb," in Fádil-i-Mázindarání, *Tarikh-i-Zuhúru'l-Haqq*, pp. 246-47; cf. al-Wardí. *Lamahát*, Vol. 2, p. 160, citing Hisárí, *'Aqa'id*
73. al-Wardí, *Lamahát*, Vol. 2, p. 161, citing Hisárí, *'Aqa'id*; cf. Karbalá'í, "Maktúb," in Fádil-i-Mázindarání, *Tarikh-i-Zuhúru'l-Haqq*, pp. 256-57.
74. Karbalá'í, "Maktúb," in Fádil-i-Mázindarání, *Tarikh-i-Zuhúru'l-Haqq*, pp. 245-59.
75. al-Wardí. *Lamahát*, Vol. 2, p. 161, citing Hisárí *'Aqa'id*; cf. Karbalá'í, "Maktúb," Fádil-i-Mázindarání, *Tarikh-i-Zuhúru'l-Haqq*, p. 257.
76. Baghdádí, "Risála," pp. 109-110.
77. The Bab's reply came from Mákú in mid-1261/1847, when Qurrat al-'Ayn was perhaps already out of the 'Atabát.
78. Baghdádí, "Risála," p.110. For an even stronger endorsement of Qurrat al-'Ayn's status by the Bab see passages from a letter cited in Fádil-i-Mázindarání, *Tarikh-i-Zuhúru'l-Haqq*, pp. 331-34, where she is praised as "the proof for all" (*hujja ala al-kull*), whose instructions are binding on all believers.
79. Baghdádí, "Risála," pp. 109-10. Of the Kázimayaní defectors, the author names five.
80. The Báb, *Tafsír al-hamd* (Tehran, 1970s) p. 127 (Iran National Bahá'í Archive Manuscript Collection, p. 69).
81. Fádil-i-Mázindarání, *Tarikh-i-Zuhúru'l-Haqq*, p. 333; trans. D. MacEoin "From Shaykhism to Babism," p. 207. For other passages and further discussion on the controversy, see pp. 206-07.

82. al-Wardí, *Lamahát,* Vol. 2 pp. 161-62, citing Hisárí, *'Aqa'id.*
83. Qazvíní, *Samandar*, p. 347; 'Ávárih" Ayati, *Al-Kavákibu'd-Durriyyih*, Vol. 1, p. 62.
84. al-Wardí, *Lamahát,* Vol. 2, p.162, citing Hisárí, *'Aqa'id.* It is not inconceivable that Mullá Ahmad also had a hand in the incident.
85. Haji Mírzá Jani, *Kitáb-i Nuqtatu'l-Káf,* p. 141; 'Abdu'l-Bahá, *Tadhkirat al-wafa'*, pp. 296-97.
86. Mírzá Husain Hamadání, *The Táríkh-i-Jadíd*, p. 272.
87. al-Wardí, *Lamahát,* Vol. 2, pp.162-63, citing Hisárí, *'Aqa'id*; cf. Haji Mírzá Jani, *Kitáb-i Nuqtatu'l-Káf*, p. 141.
88. Baghdádí maintains that "she was sent to Baghdad by order of válí," who probably had decided on this as a result of Shaykh Muhammad Shibl's intervention (Baghdádí, "Risála," p. 108).
89. Fádili-i-Mázindarání, *Tarikh-i-Zuhúru'l-Haqq*, p. 314, facsimile of Qurrat al-'Ayn's letters to her father. For reasons unknown, Mázindarání, ignoring repeated references in the letters to Qurrat al-'Ayn's father, identifies her uncle Mullá Muhammad Taqí as the addressee.
90. Ibid.
91. Ibid.
92. al-Wardí. *Lamahát,* Vol. 2, p.171; Nicolas, *Seyyèd Ali Mohammed, dit le Bâb*, pp. 274-76.
93. Shibl Baghdádí also provided three other quarters: one for Qurrat al-'Ayn's women companions, one for men, and the third for her teaching (al-Wardí, *Lamahát,* Vol. 2, p. 168, citing Abbúd Sálihí, "Qurratu'l-'Ayn").
94. al-Wardí, *Lamahát,* Vol. 2, pp. 168-69.
95. Qazvíní, *Samandar*, pp. 347-48.
96. Baghdádí, "Risála," p. 109; cf. Mírzá Husain Hamadani, *The Táríkh-i-Jadíd*, p. 272.
97. According to both Hanafi and Shii'ite law, a woman must be imprisoned until she again adopts Islam. See "Murtadd," in H. A. R. Gibb and J. H. Krammer, eds., *Shorter Encyclopaedia of Islam* (Leiden: E. J. Brill, 1953).
98. Cited in 'Ávárih Ayati, *Al-Kavákibu'd-Durriyyih*, Vol. 1, p. 64 and partly in Abul-Fazl Gulpáyigání, *Kashf al-ghitá'*, pp. 94-96, both without clear reference to the title of Álúsí's work. However, it is possible that this quotation is taken from Álúsí's incomplete and unpublished work *Nahj al-Saláma ila Mabáhith al-Imáma,* his last work written in 1270/1854 (MS no. B 4/678 in Library of Awqáf 'Ámma, Baghdad), in which according to Muhsin 'Abd al-Hamid, *al-Alusi mufassiran* (Baghdad: Matba'at 'al-Ma'arif, 1968) p. 125, he discussed Shaykhíya, Rashtíya, Bábíya, and Qurratíya with impartiality. For a slightly different version of Álúsí's comments cited in Mahmud Shukri Álúsí, *Mukhtasar al-Tuhfat al-Ithna 'Ashariya* (Cairo: [s. n.], 1373/1953) see al-Wardí, *Lamahát,* Vol. 2, pp. 169-70.
99. Part of this tablet cited in Jadid al-Islam, Hajji Husayn-Quli, *Minaj al-Talibin fi al-Radd 'ala al-Firqa tal-Halika al-Babiya* (Bombay: Matb'-i Gulzar Hasani, 1320/1902) pp. 342-346. A direct quotation in Abul-Fazl Gulpáyigání, *Kashf al-ghitá'*, p. 96, taken from a servant in Álúsí's house reports Álúsí as saying, "O Qurrat al-'Ayn! I swear by God that I share thy

belief. I am apprehensive, however, of the swords of the family of Uthmán," should be regarded as mere exaggeration. At most, it may point out Álúsí's sympathetic approach to her views.

100. Only Qazvíní, *Samandar,* pp. 348-49, reports of a certain Hakím Masíh, a Persian Babi of Jewish descent, who saw Qurrat al-'Ayn in Baghdad conversing with the Sunni 'ulama.
101. Shaykh Shináb al-Dín Mahmúd Álúsí, *Rúh al-Ma'ání fí Tafsír al-Qur'án al-'Azúm wa'l-Sab' al-Mathání.* (Egypt: [s. n.], 1301-1310/1883/1892) Vol. 7, pp. 22, 39. Other references can also be found in this work to Álúsí's discussion with Qurrat al-'Ayn.
102. al-Wardí, *Lamahát,* Vol. 2, p. 172, citing Abbúd Sálihí, "Qurratu'l-'Ayn," pp. 45-47. See also *Samandar,* p. 349 and Nicolas, *Seyyèd Ali Mohammed, dit le Bâb,* pp. 274-76 for references to Hammámí and his recollections.
103. The news of a number of her Arab and Persian mullas who accompanied her as far as Hamadan, and some to Qazvin, are given in Baghdádí, "Risála," p. 111 and Nabíl-i-A'zam, *The Dawn-Breakers,* p. 273.
104. Baghdádí, "Risála," pp. 111, 16. As a result of Qurrat al-'Ayn's preaching some of the inhabitants remained Babis for some time.
105. The militant mood of the people of Karand can be seen in their successive clashes with government forces. On one occasion in the early 1840s, the governor of Kirmánsháh, Hájj Shakí Khán, because of his "misconduct, immorality, excessive killing, numerous rapes," as well as "difference in religion," was killed in Karand along with two hundred of his troops. Hidáyat, *Raudat al-Safá'yi Násirí,* Vol. 10, p. 316.
106. Baghdádí, "Risála," p. 116.
107. Ibid., pp. 111-13.
108. Muhibb 'Alí must have been already informed of Qurrat al-'Ayn through the Persian agent in Baghdad. For his account see Amanat, Chap. 5.
109. Ághá Buzurg 'al-Tihrání, *Tabaqát A'lám al-Shí'ah,* Vol. 2, part 2, p. 774.
110. Baghdádí, "Risála," p. 113. According to this source, in 1263/1847 Qurrat al-'Ayn declared the purpose of her mission to be the conveyance of "the glad tiding of the advent of the promised Qá'im, the compassionate lord."
111. Ibid., pp. 114-15.
112. The above-mentioned Zubayda Khánum and the wife of Rustam Khán Qaraguzlú.
113. Mahdi Bamdad, *Sharh-i Hal-i Rijal Iran dar Qarn-i 12, 13, 14 Hijri* (Tehran: Kitabfurushi-i Zuvvar, 1347-1353 Sh. /1968-1974) Vol. 1, pp. 473-76.
114. Like many Persian cities, Hamadan was divided along sectarian lines. Though Usúlís were in ascendancy, the city was still regarded as one of the last footholds of declining Akhbárís, Gobineau, *Les Religions et les Philosophies dans l'Asie Centrale,* p. 30, of whom a good number turned to Shaykhism, Ayati Ávárih, *Al-Kavákibu'd-Durriyyih fí Ma'áthiri'l al-Bahá'íyah,* Vol. 1, p. 117. The Sufis, most significantly Ni'matulláhís and Kháksárs, were also represented.
115. Ishráq-Khávarí, *Táríkh-i Amrí-yi Hamadán,* p. 4; cf. Ayati Ávárih, *Al-Kavákibu'd-Durriyyih fí Ma'áthiri'l al-Bahá'íyah,* Vol. 1, pp. 117-18.
116. For his account, among other sources, see Mahdí Dirakhshán, *Buzurgán va*

*Sukhansaráyan-i Hamadán* (Tehran: Níkpú, 1341-42/1963-64) Vol. 2, pp. 80-81, and cited sources.
117. Ishráq-Khávarí, *Táríkh-i Amrí-yi Hamadán*, p. 4.
118. Ibid., pp. 1-4; cf. Abul-Fazl Gulpáyigání, *Kashf al-ghitá'*, citing Mullá Rizá Hamadání, son of 'Alí Naqí.
119. For Ni'matullahís, like many other later Sh'ite orders, the *qutb al-aqtáb* (pole of the poles) deputizes the Mahdi.
120. See Amanat, Chap. 2.
121. Possibly Mullá Husayn Razaví Hamadání, son of 'Abd al-Samad. 'Ághá Buzurg 'al-Tihrání, *Tabaqát A'lám al-Shí'ah*, Vol. 1, part 2, p. 596.
122. Possibly Sayyid 'Abd al-Samad Razavi Hamadání, who (according to Ághá Buzurg Tihrání, *Tabaqát A'lám al-Shí'ah*, Vol. 2, part 2, p. 738) was the religious judge of Hamadan, see also Vol. 1, part 2, p. 596.
123. Baghdádí, *Risála*, p. 117.
124. Ishráq-Khávarí, *Táríkh-i Amrí-yi Hamadán*, p. 3, citing a historical tract by Yuhaná Háfizí. Except for Hakím Masih, a Persian Jewish physician who saw Qurrat al-'Ayn at a gathering of the 'ulama in Baghdad and later became a Babi-Baha'i (Qazvíní, *Samandar*, p. 348), the above-mentioned Il'ázár (Lálizár) is the earliest-known Jewish convert. Another Jewish physician, Hakím Ílíyá, was an eyewitness to the Hamadan debate. His son Hakím Rahím (Rahamím) apparently became a Baha'i. It is difficult to believe that the above-mentioned Il'ázár is the same Mullá Lálizár Hamadání who helped Gobineau in his translation of Kant into Persian (Gobineau, *Les Religions et les Philosophies dans l'Asie Centrale*, p. 101) and possibly the Bab's Arabic *Bayán* into French. (Momen, *The Bábí and Bahá'í Religions,* pp. 18-19). Gobineau makes no reference to Qurrat al-'Ayn's visit to Hamadan. For other early Jewish converts in Khurasan, see Amanat, Chap. 8. Qurrat al-'Ayn's appeal to non-Muslim minorities—Jewish or Ahl-i-Haqq—once again illustrates the way the early Babis considered the new revelation not simply as a Shi'ite or Muslim affair.
125. Except for accompanying women, Baghdádí counts twelve of her chief adherents who followed Qurrat al-'Ayn to Qazvin. The remaining twenty-odd adherents returned to the 'Atabát. Haji Mírzá Jani, *Kitáb-i Nuqtatu'l-Káf*, maintains that Qurrat al-'Ayn's ultimate destination in her journey was Tehran, where she intended "to caution" Muhammad Sháh, presumably of the consequences of the Bab's incarceration in Mákú. Under family pressure, she canceled her plan.
126. 'Abdu'l-Bahá, *Tadhkirat al-wafa'fi*, p. 306.
127. Browne, *Materials for the Study of the Bábí Religion*, pp. 349-51, translated by E. G. Browne. "Am I not your Lord" is from Qur'an 7:171. Qazvíní, *Samandar*, p. 349; cf. Nabíl-i-A'zam, *The Dawn-Breakers*, pp. 81-82, dates this poem to the time prior to the Bab's open declaration of Qá'imiya. Muhammad Ma'sum Shirazi Ma'sum 'Alí Shah, *Tara'iq al-haqa'iq* (Tehran: Kitabkhanah-i Barani, 1960-1966) Vol. 3, p. 318, ascribes it to Suhbat Lárí, a contemporary of Qurrat al-'Ayn (d. 1251/1835 in Shiraz), who is said to have been acquainted with the Bab's family (Husám Nuqabá'I, *Bishárat-i Kutub-i Asimání* [s.l., s. n., 1970?], pp. 268-270). However, the mystical tone of the poem does not appear to be far from Qurrat al-'Ayn's outlook.

128. Baghdádí, "Risála," p. 117. One of them presumably is the same 'Abd al-Wahháb, whom Nicolas considers Qurrat al-'Ayn's brother. Nicolas, *Seyyèd Ali Mohammed, dit le Bâb*, p. 273.
129. Fádil-i-Mázandarání, *Tarikh-i-Zuhúru'l-Haqq*, p. 304; cf. Mullá Ja'far Qazvíní, "Tarikh" in 'Abd al-'Alí 'Alá'í, ed., *Tárikh-i Samandar, va Mulhaqqát* (Tehran: [Bahá'í Publishing Committee], 131Badí'/1975) p. 495.
130. Hidáyat, *Raudat al-Safá'yi Násirí*, Vol. 10, p. 345. At the age of eighty-three, in Najaf.
131. Fádil-i-Mázandarání, *Tarikh-i-Zuhúru'l-Haqq*, pp. 309-310, cites a testimony of recognition by Mullá 'Alí in which the author, in the cryptic language common to Shaykhis, acknowledges the Zikr and counts himself among his subordinates. In the end he wishes a hasty "relief" (*faraj*) for the "weak" who are anticipating the events of 1260. Both Tunkábuní, (*Qisas al'Ulamá*, p. 19) and Qazvíní (*Samandar*, p. 344), refer to his Shaykhi and then Babi beliefs, which are also confirmed by his own letter to the Bab cited in Iran National Bahá'í Archive Manuscript Collection, Vol. 98, pp. xxiii, 110-11. The Bab himself mentions him as one of his followers in The Báb, "al-Sahífa al-Rábi'a fi Sharh Du'á'ihi fi Zamán al-Ghayba," in *Majumu'ih-i Athar-i Hadrat-i A'la* (Teheran, 1977?) no. 13, pp. 150-154. (Iran National Bahá'í Archives Manuscript Collection; 60)
132. Haji Mírzá Jani, *Kitáb-i Nuqtatu'l-Káf*, p. 142; cf. Nabíl-i-A'zam, *The Dawn-Breakers*, pp. 273-76.
133. Qazvíní, "Tarikh," pp. 472-74.
134. For his account see Qazvíní, *Samandar*, pp. 15-54.
135. For the early Babis of Qazvin, see Qazvíní, *Samandar*, pp. 54-370; Fádil-i-Mázandarání, *Tarikh-i-Zuhúru'l-Haqq*, pp. 301-91; and Qazvíní, "Tarikh," pp. 447-52, 473-88, 494-98.
136. See Amanat, Chap. 8.
137. Baghdadi, "ar-Risalah al-Amiriyyah," pp. 118-19.
138. Mu'ín al-Saltana Tabrízí, *Tárikh-i Amr-i Bahá'í*, pp. 5-6.
139. Baghdadi, "ar-Risalah al-Amiriyyah," p. 109; al-Wardí, *Lamahát*, p. 156.
140. See above, this chapter. Also Ayati Ávárih, *Al-Kavákibu'd-Durriyyih fí Ma'áthiri'l al-Bahá'íyah*, Vol. 1, p. 110.
141. Polak, *Persien*, Vol. 1, p. 157.
142. The defamation campaign of Mullá Ahmad Hisárí and his allies in Karbalá' and his correspondence with the Shaykhis and non-Shaykhis of Iran and Iraq in defiance of Qurrat al-'Ayn must have affected her reputation. al-Wardí, *Lamahát*, Vol. 2, pp. 160-162, citing Mullá Ahmad's *'Aqa'id* and Shaykh Sultán Karbalá'í, "Maktúb," pp. 245-259.
143. Sipihr, *Násikh al-Tawárikh: Qájáríya*, Vol. 3, p. 219.
144. Ibid., p. 200. In his discussions with Gobineau, Siphir again repeated, this time in a sarcastic tone, the allegations concerning the followers of Qurrat al-'Ayn, who he believed were simply her lustful lovers. Gobineau, *Les Religions et les Philosophies dans l'Asie Centrale*, p. 180.
145. Qazvíní, *Samandar*, p. 75.
146. 'Ághá Buzurg 'al-Tihrání, *Tabaqát A'lám al-Shí'ah*, Vol. 2, part 2, p. 661.
147. Nabíl-i-A'zam, *The Dawn-Breakers*, p. 276; cf. Qazvíní, *Samandar*, pp. 354-56.
148. Nabíl-i-A'zam, *The Dawn-Breakers*, p. 276.

149. Mu'ín al-Saltana Tabrízí, *Tárikh-i Amr-i Bahá'í*, pp. 244-46, names two accomplices: Áqá Muhammad Hádí Farhádí and Sayyid Husayn Qazvíní, a Shaykhi. Tunkábuní, *Hadha kitab Qisas al'Ulamá*, p. 57, also speaks of few individuals. All other sources insist on Mírzá 'Abdulláh's personal initiative.
150. Vivid accounts of the persecutions appear in Qazvíní, *Samandar*, pp. 21-30 [under the biography of Mírzá Muhammad Qazvíní], pp. 73-76, 91-100, 354-56. After his murder, Mullá Muhammad Taqí came to be known in Shi'ite literature as the "Third Martyr" (*Shahíd thálith*), named after the two medieval Shi'ite martyrs from the 'ulama class.
151. Qazvíní, *Samandar*, pp. 357-58; cf. Mu'ín al-Saltana Tabrízí, *Tárikh-i Amr-i Bahá'í*, pp. 8-9.
152. Qazvíní, *Samandar*, pp. 358-59; Nabíl-i-A'zam, *The Dawn-Breakers*, pp. 277-78.
153. For his biography, see Bamdad, *Sharh-i Hal-i Rijal Iran*, Vol. 4, pp. 336-37.
154. Haji Mírzá Jani, *Kitáb-i Nuqtatu'l-Káf*, pp. 143-44; Nabíl-i-A'zam, *The Dawn-Breakers*, pp. 277-80; Baghdadi, "ar-Risalah al-Amiriyyah," p. 120. According to the *Nuqtatu'l-Káf*, p. 143, Mullá Mahmúd, the tolerant mujtahid of Tehran, refused to ratify the death sentence. For Shaykh Sálih, see Fádil-i-Mázandaráni, *Tarikh-i-Zuhúru'l-Haqq*, p. 261. According to an enigmatic reference in Nabíl-i-A'zam, *The Dawn-Breakers*, p. 271, Qurrat al-'Ayn was "so profuse in her praise of Shaykhi Sálih that a few suspected him of being equal in rank to Quddús."
155. Nabíl-i-A'zam, *The Dawn-Breakers*, pp. 281-82. For the Farhádís, see Amanat, Chap. 8.
156. Nabíl-i-A'zam, *The Dawn-Breakers*, p. 281.
157. Qazvíní, *Samandar*, pp. 111-13, cites a gruesome eyewitness account of the executions in Qazvin. After a severe beating with sticks, Shaykh Táhir, half burned, was dragged along and stoned to death by the mob. Mullá Ibráhím was first struck on the head with a hatchet by a passing carpenter, then stoned and burned.
158. He took refuge in the house of the Babi notable Rizá Khán Sardár (Nabíl-i-A'zam, *The Dawn-Breakers*, p. 287) and later in the house of Bahá'u'lláh (Qazvíní, *Samandar*, p. 366). He is presumably the same Mírzá 'Abdulláh who saved Qurrat al-'Ayn in the incident of Niyálá in 1264/1848 (Nabíl-i-A'zam, *The Dawn-Breakers*, p. 299). Haji Mírzá Jani, *Kitáb-i Nuqtatu'l-Káf*, pp. 143, 189, confirms his death at Tabarsí. For his justification of the assassination, see Qazvíní, *Samandar*, pp. 359, 361.
159. Qazvíní, *Samandar*, p. 362. For further details on her escape see Amanat, Chap. 8.
160. Ibid., pp. 364-66; Nabíl-i-A'zam, *The Dawn-Breakers*, pp. 286-87; Malik-Khusraví, *Tárikh-i Shuhadá-yi Amr*, pp. 190-191.
161. The assembly of Badasht, though covered by most Babi sources, remains shrouded in ambiguity. Nabíl-i-A'zam, *The Dawn-Breakers*, pp. 292-300 and Haji Mírzá Jani, *Kitáb-i Nuqtatu'l-Káf*, pp. 145-154, are both remarkable for their efforts to explain the radical conduct of Qurrat al-'Ayn. Mírzá Husain Hamadáni, *The Tárikh-i-Jadíd*, pp. 281-83; Gobineau, *Les Religions et les Philosophies dans l'Asie Centrale*, pp. 180-84; Nicolas, *Seyyèd Ali Mohammed, dit le Bâb*, pp. 277-87, and Ayati "Ávárih," Al-*Kavákibu'd-*

*Durriyyih,* pp. 127-31, among others add little to our knowledge. The attempts to put the events in a logical sequence are not always successful. Fádil-i-Mázandaráni, *Tarikh-i-Zuhúru'l-Haqq,* pp. 109-112 provides some new data.
162. See Amanat, Chap. 9.
163. For the events in Mashhad preceding Badasht see Nabíl-i-A'zam, *The Dawn-Breakers,* pp. 288-92, and Sayyid Muhammad Husayn "Mahjur Zavarih'I," *Vaqa'i'-i Mimiyyih: A Chronicle of the Babi Uprising at Fort Shaykh Tabarsi in Mazandaran* (East Lansing, Mich. H-Bahai, 2001. [Persian]) <http://www.h-net.msu.edu/~bahai/arabic/vol5/mimiyyih/mimiyyih.htm>. Mullá Husayn's reasons for staying behind are not entirely clear. Undeterred by the threats of the chief of the police, it is possible that he was still hoping to raise Babi recruits among the people of the city.
164. Gobineau, *Les Religions et les Philosophies dans l'Asie Centrale,* pp. 183-84 and Nicolas, *Seyyèd Ali Mohammed, dit le Bâb,* pp. 277-81.
165. Sipihr, *Násikh al-Tavárikh: Sala'tin-i Qájár,* Vol. 3, p. 239. Further on, Sipihr attributes to Qurrat al-'Ayn recommendations of sexual promiscuity and communistic beliefs—ancient charges common to most Islamic antiheretical literature. His allegations when Gobineau questioned him in 1865, remain unabated. Gobineau, *Les Religions et les Philosophies dans l'Asie Centrale,* p. 180.
166. Nabíl-i-A'zam, *The Dawn-Breakers,* p. 296.
167. Ibid., p. 293.
168. Ibid., p. 297.
169. Ibid.
170. Fádil-i-Mázandaráni, *Tarikh-i-Zuhúru'l-Haqq,* p. 325.
171. Ibid., pp. 325-26. Quoting an eyewitness account.
172. One example of such treatment is Nicolas, *Seyyèd Ali Mohammed, dit le Bâb,* pp. 280-83.
173. For Bahá'ulláh, see Amanat, Chap. 8.
174. See Amanat, Chap. 9.
175. Nabíl-i-A'zam, *The Dawn-Breakers,* p. 298.
176. Fádil-i-Mázandaráni, *Tarikh-i-Zuhúru'l-Haqq,* pp. 326-27.
177. While in Núr she gave her signet ring to a woman to be eventually sent to Quddús in Tabarsí. The verse on the signet ring read, "Lord of Táhira, remember her" (*rabb al-Táhira adrikhá*), Fádil-i-Mázandaráni, *Tarikh-i-Zuhúru'l-Haqq,* p. 327.
178. Malik-Khusraví, *Tárikh-i Shuhadá-yi Amr,* pp. 204-205.
179. Ibid., p. 206. Her host, Áqá Nasarulláh, was killed on the spot by government agents.
180. Qazvíní, *Samandar,* p. 368.
181. It has been reported that Násir al-Dín Sháh, after seeing Qurrat al-'Ayn, had said, "I like her look, leave her, and let her be," reported by Mírzá Yahyá Subh Azal to E. G. Browne. Browne, in 'Abdu'l-Bahá, *A Traveller's Narrative,* p. 313.
182. 'Abdu'l-Bahá, *Tadhkirat al-wafa',* p. 309. Of those who met her in the custody of Kalántar, the poetess Shams-i Jahán, daughter of Muhammad 'Alí

Mírzá, recorded her interview in her *masnaví* cited in Baydá'í, *Tádhkiríy-i-Shu'aráy-i-Qarn-i-Avval-i-Bahá'í*, Vol. 3, pp. 179-80; cf. Ayati Ávárih, *Al-Kavákibu'd-Durriyyih fí Ma'áthiri'l al-Bahá'íyah*, Vol. 1, pp. 309-311.

183. 'Alá'í, ed., *Táríkh-i* Qazvíní, *Samandar, va Mulhaqqát*, pp. 84, 368; Fádil-i-Mázandarání, *Tarikh-i-Zuhúru'l-Haqq*, p. 328.

184. Nicolas, *Seyyèd Ali Mohammed, dit le Bâb*, p. 449.

185. Mírzá Áqá Khán Núrí, the chief minister and the co-architect of the massacre of the Babis in Tehran, was himself on shaky ground. His wife, his sister, and other women of his harem were accused of being Qurrat al-'Ayn's sympathizers (Mu'ín al-Saltana Tabrízí, *Táríkh-i Amr-i Bahá'í*, p. 10; cf. Polak, *Persien*, Vol. 1, p. 353; and Malik-Khusraví, *Táríkh-i Shuhadá-yi Amr*, Vol. 3, p. 191). It is not therefore unlikely that Núrí himself, being anxious to clear himself of any charges, pressured the mujtahids to come up with Qurrat al-'Ayn's death sentence.

186. Accounts of Qurrat al-'Ayn's last days and her execution appear in Nabíl-i-A'zam, *The Dawn-Breakers*, pp. 621-28, and Nicolas, *Seyyèd Ali Mohammed, dit le Bâb*, pp. 446-52, both recording the recollections of Kalantar's wife. *The Times* of 13 Oct. 1852, also refers to the execution of the "Fair Prophetess of Kazoeen [Qazvin]" in an article titled "How They Punish Treason in Persia"; see Momen, *The Bábí and Bahá'í Religions,* p. 132. Polak in his *Persien*, Vol. 1, p. 353, claims to have been present at the event. Lady Sheil calls slaying Qurrat al-'Ayn a "cruel and useless deed." Lady Mary Sheil, *Glimpses of Life and Manners in Persia* (London: J. Murray, 1856) p. 281.

187. From a *ghazal* cited in the centennial volume Qurratu'l-'Ayn, *Bi-yád-i-Sadumín Sál-i-Shahádat-i-Qurratu'l-'Ayn Nábighih-i-Duwrán* (Tehran: [s. n.], 1949) p. 25.

188. Edward Granville Browne, *Literary History of Persia: Modern Times, 1500-1924* (Cambridge: The University Press, 1924) Vol. 4, p. 197.

# Becoming a Presence:
# Tahereh Qorratol'Ayn

by Farzaneh Milani

On a tombstone in the Shahzadeh Hossein Cemetery in the city of Qazvin is carved the gruesome image of a murder: a praying molla (a religious scholar) is being stabbed to death, from behind, by a masked man. A woman, semiconcealed behind a curtain, looks on. In her hand she holds a sheet of paper, incriminating evidence that she can read and write. The writings on the tombstone, carved over 150 years ago, make sure you understand what the image means: "Martyrdom of Molla Taqi by a Babi Heretic."

The woman behind the curtain, overseeing and presumably masterminding the molla's murder, is the nineteenth-century poet Fatemeh Baraghani, better known as Tahereh Qorratol 'Ayn. Her accuser, absent from the scene but pointing the finger through the image on the tombstone, is her husband and cousin, none other than the murdered molla's son. He remained unaffected by his wife's acquittal by a court of law, even after the confession of the real murderer.

It is unclear, given the iconography of the tombstone, which is the woman's greatest crime: the murder itself, whether she has masterminded it or is its more passive accomplice; or her usurpation of the written word, the evidence of which we find in her own hand: the paper. Or it might be that it doesn't really matter which: the writing on her hand is as good as the dagger in the assassin's hand for achieving the same lethal end: death of the patriarch.

In the society of mid-nineteenth-century Iran, knowledge, like a child was only legitimized if properly fathered by a man. In the hands of a woman, it became an unnecessary tool, a dangerous tool, even a sign of the end of time, of apocalypse. The murdered Molla Taqi was heard to have said words to this effect, with Tahereh in mind: "When the signs of the promised One appear, the Zindiq [heretic] of [the city of] Qazvin will also appear, and the words of the Zindiq will be the words of a woman's religion! Now this woman and her religion have appeared."[1] To avoid such a disaster, observed Mirza 'Abdol-Vahab, Tahereh's brother, "the clergy have prevented all women from studying lest they should become believers like Tahirih."[2]

Clearly, then as now, such views were not held by all the clergy. Actually, one of the first schools for girls, 'Effatiyeh (house of chastity), was founded in 1910 with the help and encouragement of a high-ranking mojtahed (one with a high theological status who is allowed independent legal judgments) Sheykh Mohammad Hossain Yazdi. But Tahereh's father-in-law and her husband blamed her book learning for destroying her life. Since that time others have also argued that her access to books—especially dissident, Sheykhi books—made her go "mad" and abandon the sanctity of motherhood and the sacredness of home. (Sheykhism is a school of theology that grew out of Shi'i Islam. With its pronounced messianic expectations, it is the theoretical foundation for Babism, a religious faith proclaimed in mid-nineteenth-century Iran that called for spiritual and moral reforms and a new sociopolitical order. "The Bab" [the gateway, or the intermediary, between the Hidden Imam and the believers] is the title given to the founder of Babism.)

E'tezadol-Saltaneh believes that "her persistent study of Sheykhi materials and inquiry into their books totally absorbed her and slowly changed her whole life. It ultimately made her leave her sacred matrimony to wander from place to place."[3] Moshir-Salimi is even more explicit in his diagnosis: Tahereh's "sustained examination of and curiosity about Sheykhi works changed her life to the point that she dumped her sacred and simple married life. Basically, she could no longer agree with her husband's views or her father-in-law/older uncle's reasoning and values. Their discussions led to physical fights. Finally, in spite of having three children, she left home and her married life."[4]

If education can threaten some women with the loss of their natural place and position in society, if it can cause violent disputes and eventually makes women leave their husbands, children, and the bliss of domestic life, it can also lead to women's madness. Kasravi, the famous historian, claims to know " the exact causes of Tahereh's insanity." While calling her a *Shir Zan* (a woman fearless and strong like a lion), or "one of the exceptional women of the whole world," he ultimately portrays her as a crazed woman, scurrying around caught in her own self-destructive messianic ethos but above all ruined by her extensive readings. "We know of all of her readings and her knowledge," he writes, "her poems clearly indicate what her brain was filled with. It is exactly these things that toppled her."[5]

Why should this woman's education have provoked such a strong reaction and intense hostility? It is true that most of Tahereh's detractors seem to object to her reading Sheykhi materials in particular, rather than to her pursuit of knowledge per se. But it is a fact that in her time, higher learning was basically a masculine prerogative. Women's reading was controlled if not discouraged. Even if unusual circumstances allowed a woman access to higher education, the outlets for public expression of such learning were severely limited. Women were excluded from the public domains of discourse. Theology was reserved for men. Most women neither had access to higher education nor were expected to learn Arabic, a necessary tool for the Islamic scholar. Their domestic confinement precluded that freedom to travel to centers of learning. Denied participation in disputation, they could not refine nor exchange points of view. Barred from the pulpit and public preaching, they had no audience and could not propagate their learning.

Obviously, some women before Tahereh had written and spoken out on religious issues. It was not uncommon for some daughters of the clerics or the privileged classes to be highly educated, especially in religious matters. But normally, such competence, its expression, and its audience were confined to the private and familial. Prayer books, books of religious instructions for women and children, were allowed; but sermons to men and doctrinal statements were not. Interpretative power was strictly a male prerogative. If in rare circumstances women attained the level of mojtahid, their decisions could not be binding on others. What was acceptable in the privacy of the home or in strictly female gatherings verged on insolence or even heresy when done in public. Women's learning could serve no public purpose. Silent in mosques and in mixed gatherings, women never preached or addressed "serious" religious matters beyond the home.

If a woman's place was only in the home as wife and mother, then Tahereh was never satisfied with her natural domain. Even though a wife and mother, she also busied herself in libraries and classes, with talks and debates. By becoming a public scholar, she penetrated a male preserve. She was not writing or speaking only on private, personal matters, in private; on the contrary, she addressed theological issues in public domain. She even challenged some of the most learned religious scholars of her time by inviting them to *Mojadeleh* (public rational argumentation). She assigned herself a public role and a public place. A triple transgression—verbal, spatial, and physical.

Tahereh refused to be trapped by stereotypes, images, ideals, and stories foisted upon her by tradition. She wanted to take charge, be mobile, subvert the master narratives of her culture, write her own story, control the plot, and orchestrate a public image for herself and perhaps for other women as well. She succeeded to a large extent. Just as she refused to be silenced or pinned down during her life, she has continued to defy silence or categorization after death. She has proven to be too enigmatic a presence to be dealt with neutrally or to be ignored altogether. Her life is probably the best documented of nineteenth-century Iranian women, although it is fact and fiction compressed into one. She is saint, whore, sorceress, martyr, and murderer. Invented and reinvented, she is honored and dishonored.

It is unfortunate that this woman who unveiled herself so many years ago still lives such a veiled life in the memory of her own people. Her life story represents, in more ways than one, a kind of fantasy literature, a literature that has absorbed in itself disparate materials from dreams and nightmares, fears and wishes, fascination and terror. It is hard to discern who she really was amid all the adulation and hatred that have surrounded her during and after her life. Extolled as a saint, an exceptional woman, a miracle, she is also denounced as a lunatic, a dangerous woman, a heretic.

On the one hand, there are those Babis and Baha'is, who have nothing but praise for her fervent involvement with and relentless advocacy of the Babi faith, her flawless character, and her martyrdom. They seem to miss or dismiss the moral and intellectual challenges posed by her personal life. They curiously ignore the significance of the private choices she made, such as leaving her husband and her three children, refusing to comply with prescribed norms of feminine comportment, and causing much agony to herself and to her immediate family, especially to her father and her children.[6] In a characteristic observation on her life, Edward G. Browne writes: "The appearance of such a woman as Kurratul'Ayn is in any country and age a rare phenomenon, but in such a country as Persia it is a prodigy—nay, almost a miracle. Alike in virtue of her marvelous beauty, her rare intellectual gifts, her fervid eloquence, her fearless devotion, and her glorious martyrdom, she stands forth incomparable and immortal amidst her countrywomen. Had the Babi religion on other claim to greatness, this were sufficient—that it produced a heroine like Kurratul'Ayn."[7]

On the other hand, there is a group that concentrates totally on its own version of Tahereh's private life and produces an avalanche of outrage against her personal choices. In *Baha'ism, Its Origins and Its Role*, she is claimed to put history to shame: "During 'Ali Mohammad Shirazi's [the Bab's] imprisonment, unpleasant events took place at the hands of Babis in [the cities of] Zanjan, Ghazvin and Mazandaran at foreign instigation and by the makings of people such as Mirza Hossein Ali [Baha'ullah] . . . as well as a prostitute by the name of Qaralein [Qorratol'Ayn]. History is ashamed to relate such events."[8] Presented as a blasphemer, Tahereh comes to be a symbol of spiritual and moral wickedness. Considered promiscuous, she is slandered as an advocate of promiscuity. Depicted with insatiable carnal desires, she is viewed as a woman with gargantuan sexual appetites, indulging indefatigably in earthly pleasures. The chronicler Mirza Muhammad Taqi Sepher, amazed that this beautiful "girl who had a moon-like face and hair like musk"[9] could also be so knowledgeable, gives his imagination free reign:

> She would decorate her assembly room like a bridal chamber and her body like a peacock of Paradise. Then she summoned the followers of the Báb and appeared unveiled in front of them. First she ascended a throne and like a pious preacher reminded them of Heaven and Hell and quoted amply

from the Qur'an and the Traditions. She would then tell them: "Whoever touches me, the intensity of Hell's fire would not affect him." The audience would then rise and come to her throne and kiss those lips of hers which put to shame the ruby of Ramman, and rub their faces against her breasts, which chagrined the pomegranates of the garden.[10]

Sepher not only attributes to Tahereh the familiar powers of the woman as a body, as a sex object, he also maintains that she "counseled the marriage of one woman to nine men."[11] Quoting Sepher, the historian Bastani-ye Parizi adds a zero to nine to increase the number of recommended husbands for each woman to "ninety" men.[12] It is as if, in not knowing what to say about such a remarkable woman, some historians just assumed she was promiscuous. What else could she be if she were beautiful and wished to appear before others?

Reactions to Tahereh have varied from repulsion to fascination, from horror to sympathy, from disgust to admiration. Any attempt to unveil her, to find the real woman beneath all the myths about her, inevitably leads to a struggle through a morass of contradictory information. Just as her dazzling complexity eluded her contemporaries, friends and foes alike, accounts of her life dissolve into legend. Now idealized, now demonized, now revered, now rejected, she provokes in her biographers and critics unrestrained creativity that often results in hagiography or demonology.

The mystery that shrouds Tahereh's life is quite different from the mystery she saw around her and tried to explain and understand. The first is like the veil she tried so hard to lift from her face. The second is the mysteries that impassioned her mind.

Snippets of information, sensational gossip that she has attracted through the years, haphazard interpretations of her poems, and rumors give Tahereh's life story an element of the fantastic, the surrealistic. Yet, although the information of her life is sketchy, often contradictory, underneath all the confusion and ambiguity one story emerges with clarity. It is the story of a woman who wanted voice, mobility, and visibility and succeeded in establishing and allocating her own space, the story of an absence who strove to become a presence.

Born Fatemeh Baraghani sometime in 1817, to a highly religious family, she was to have as many names as destinies. Om-e Salmeh, Hind, Zakiyeh, Noqteh (the point), Tuti (parrot), Zarrin Taj (crowned with gold), Qorrotol'Ayn (solace of the eye), Tahereh (the pure one),

Bent-e Taleh (daughter of evil) are only some of the acquired names, and perhaps a manifestation of attempts to make her disappear behind the veil of too many names. Ironically, the only daughter of this multinamed woman remains nameless. Islamic and, for that matter, Babi and Baha'i sources guard her name with silence. The only piece of information available on her is that "the girl died not long after the passing of her mother."[13] The life of this unnamed daughter, like that of almost all of her women companions, remains a mystery, an untold tale, a veiled story.

Owing to happy circumstances of birth, Tahereh received the finest education available. Her father, Molla Saleh, was a liberal and broadminded scholar of the Qor'an and the traditions and an influential high priest of his province. Her aunt, Mirza Nah-Sharaf Khanom, was so learned and accomplished in calligraphy that she "wrote most of the government's decrees in her beautiful hand."[14] First taught by her father, later by a tutor, Tahereh continued her studies in theology, Qor'anic exegesis, jurisprudence, and Persian and Arabic literature, an education quite unusual for a woman in those days. Pleased with the acuity of her insight mingled with her vast knowledge, Tahereh's father often discussed religious issues with her. But more importantly perhaps, he allowed her participation, from behind a curtain, in his classes and debating sessions.

Tahereh's thorough knowledge of scripture and the ease and eloquence with which she undertook theological discussions soon earned her a reputation. Her father, aware of the many restrictions placed upon women's access to religious authority, regretted his daughter's gender: "If she were a boy," he repeated, "she would have illumined my house and come to be my successor."[15] His successor Tahereh could not become, she could not even further her studies at a theological school because such schools were barred to women. Instead, she followed custom and was married, by arrangement, to her cousin, when she was barely fourteen. Her husband, the son of a paternal uncle, Molla Taqi, soon left for Iraq, accompanied by his wife, in order to pursue his religious studies. Abbas Amanat, a notable historian specializing in modern Iran, writes that: "for close to thirteen years the couple resided in Karbala (a shrine city in Iraq). Though Fatima (Tahereh) gave birth to sons, Ibrahim and Isma'il, it appears that almost from the start the marriage was not free from domestic quarrels."[16]

Tahereh grew up in an environment of passionate debates and absorbed the controversial points of theology of her day. In Iraq, she gained access to more Sheykhi materials and perhaps even attended classes of the Sheykhi leader, Seyyed Kazem Rashti.

Upon her return to Iran, Tahereh was more than just a female orator. She was a thinker in her own right. She was not only discussing and challenging religious issues with members of her extended family, she was now contradicting them. With a deeply held messianic vision of the world, she believed that a new era was in the making. Far from simply trespassing on male clerical terrain, she was challenging and subverting the dogma behind it. The orthodoxy of her family, especially her husband's, clashed bitterly with her reformist views. Consequently, she left her husband and her three children and, accompanied by her sister and her brother-in-law, she returned to Iraq to join Seyyed Kazem Rashti, who in appreciation of her scholarship had called her Qorratol'Ayn (solace of the eye). But by the time she reached her destination, Rashti had died. Tahereh stayed in his home and eventually took his place. From behind a curtain, she began to teach the many students of Rashti. But her radical views, her refusal to be secretive and practice Taqiyeh (dissimulation of faith), and above all, her unusual assumption of a traditionally masculine position disturbed many. And perhaps justifiably so. Even today, no woman in Iran occupies her position—that of a teacher and a leader in centers of higher learning for men.

In Iraq, Tahereh stepped beyond Islamic and Sheykhi theology and proposed a break with past religious legacy. Although the sole woman among the first eighteen disciples of the Bab and the only one who never met him face to face, she soon became one of the most influential and controversial figures of the movement. Openly advocating and preaching the new religious faith of Babism and appearing at times without her face veiled at gatherings of her followers, Tahereh threatened deep-seated cultural, social, and religious norms. Her fiery oratory, knife-edged and eloquent, and her knowledge, vast and radical, captivated and shocked her audiences. Many considered her a troublesome heretic overpowered by satanic temptations and inevitably licentious. In response to such allegations of immorality, she pleaded her case in a letter to her father. "I plead with you! This humblest of people is your daughter. You know her, and she has been brought up and educated under your supervision. If she had, or has, a worldly love, that could not have remained a secret to you. If you want to inquire into her affairs, God who holds the scale and is the remover of the veils would testify for her."[17]

Some Babi disciples saw Tahereh as a challenge to their faith. Her social vision was far beyond her time, too radical even for some Babi converts and sympathizers. Rebellious as they might have been as Babis, more widely prevalent cultural ideals of femininity colored all their beliefs. Objecting to her conduct and attempting to purify the new faith of her harmful innovations, they complained to the Bab. Disapproving of their consternation and of their allegations of immorality, the Bab defended Tahereh unequivocally and asked them "to accept without questions whatever she might pronounce, for they were not in a position to understand and appreciate her station."[18] He also bestowed upon her the title Jenab-e Tahereh (His Excellency, an honorific male title with the attribute of purity).

Put under surveillance in Iraq as a result of her activities, Tahereh was eventually deported and ordered to leave Ottoman territory. Followed by some thirty Babis, she left for Iran around 1847. Throughout her journey back home, she never stopped advocating the Babi faith, recruiting new members, and especially inviting highly respected theologians to public debates. In the city of Hamedan, one such gathering was convened. "Speaking from behind a curtain, Qurrat al'Ayn set three rules for disputation: reliance on prophecies; abstinence from smoking—a strict Babi prohibition; and most significantly, adopting decent language and avoiding abuse and execration. She unequivocally reiterated the basic themes of the early Babi doctrine: everlasting divine guidance, the progressive cycle of revelation, need for a new creed to meet the challenge of a changing age, and the legitimacy of the Bab as the sole recipient of divine inspiration."[19]

Tahereh's arrival in Qazvin caused an even greater controversy and a family feud. Her father and especially her father-in-law tried hard to convince her to stop proselytizing and to return to her husband. She refused both. All attempts to reconcile her with her husband proved ineffective, and she refused to give in to pressure to return home. Molla Mohammad eventually had to divorce her. It is around this time that Molla Taqi, Tahereh's father-in-law, who had intensified his public attacks on Sheykhis and Babis, was stabbed by a man named Mirza 'Abdullah Shirazi early one morning, while at prayer in his mosque. He died two days after the attack in September 1847. Accused of masterminding the murder of her father-in—law, Tahereh was arrested. Eventually released and put under house arrest, she soon escaped from her home and birthplace, never to return to either.

Spending almost a year in hiding in the capital city of Tehran, Tahereh left for Badasht in 1848, where she was to play a major and dramatic role in this first Babi convention. Before Badasht, no public claim had been made that the Bab was the inaugurator of a new faith. It was here, in northeastern Iran, that disciples superceded the Qor'an and Islamic rules publicly and collectively for the first time. They proclaimed Babism an independent faith rather than an offshoot of Islam. Actually, it was Tahereh who proclaimed the new faith and symbolically heralded the coming of the new era by her unveiling. In the words of 'Abdul Baha: "Tahirih, with her face unveiled, stepped from her garden, advancing to the pavilion of Baha'u'llah; and as she came, she shouted aloud these words: 'The trumpet is sounding! The great Trump is blown! The universal Advent is now proclaimed!' The believers gathered in that tent were panic struck, and each one asked himself, 'How can the Law be abrogated? How is it that this woman stands here without her veil?' . . . and thus was the new Dispensation announced and the great Resurrection made manifest."[20]

Tahereh's unveiling of her face in Badasht, however much an iconoclastic act, conformed with her expressed views before and after that gathering. It presented no dramatic break with her past. Not a metamorphosis or a sudden reaction, it was simply a culmination.[21] If her unveiling was interpreted as an invitation to lust, her words were viewed as the destruction of all religious values. Indeed, she did preach the elevation of the individual's conscience above all religious ordinances and exempted the believers from any Islamic laws. "All religious obligations are abrogated today," she said. "All prayers, fasting, and salutations are futile. When the Bab conquers the seven kingdoms and unites all religions, he will bring forth a new set of rules."[22] The assembly was set in an uproar. Many, enraged by her act, left the premises as well as their newly embraced faith. Some called her a heretic. One man wanted to strike her with a sword, while another, one 'Abdol Khaleq Esfahani, "aghast and deranged at the sight, cut his throat with his own hands."²³ Shattered by her heresy, he could not allow the sanctity of his eyes or honor to be defiled, nor his newly espoused faith to be defamed. Directing his anger against himself, "spattered with blood, and frantic with excitement, he fled away from her face."²⁴ The story of the first male casualty of woman's unveiling in Iran remains to be written.

The conference at Badasht, with eighty men and one woman present, was itself a novelty. Amazingly, it included a woman among its active participants. It is interesting to note that about the same time, on July 19, 1848, in another corner of the world, the first women's rights convention was convened. If in the small town of Seneca Falls, New York, women were busy working to amend the Constitution, in Iran, a woman was struggling to insert herself in the public sphere of debates. If the American feminists could seek women's active participation in their society and could try to change the terms of their social contract, their Iranian counterpart had to fight for the space to enter into the dialogue, for the privilege to be seen and to be heard in public.

Lady Sheil, the wife of the British ambassador, who visited Iran in those days, was so shocked by the total absence of women from the public scene that she hastily concluded: "In Persia a woman is nobody":

> Three easy stages over a very tolerable road, through valleys with mountains on both sides, sometimes near, sometimes more distant, brought us to [the city of] Tabriz on the 2nd of November. Here preparations on a grand scale were made for a solemn entry, from which I, however, as belonging to the inferior and ignoble class of womankind was excluded, though I was permitted to gaze on the scene at a distance. It was difficult to say how many thousand people had assembled, or what class of persons had come forth to do honor to the Queen of England's representative. There were princes and priests, and dervishes, and beggars; there were Koordish and Toork horsemen of the tribes, and soldiers, and Ghoolams; in short there was everything and everybody, but there was not a single woman, for in Persia a woman is nobody.²⁵

Normally, women contemporaries of Tahereh were not allowed to be in the presence of men, let alone to participate actively in debates and discussions and hold key leadership roles. Perhaps that is one reason why the convention at Badasht is remembered not only as a celebration of heresy but also as a shameful orgy of sinful lust. Tahereh's voice, her sermons, her unveiled face became signs of contamination, tokens of an unleashed sexuality that was deemed dangerous. "When all those assembled at Badasht accepted the new faith of licentiousness," writes E'tezadol-Saltaneh, "men and women mingled and lived the legend of the Epicurus Garden."[26]

After some twenty-one days, the gathering at Badasht was dispersed by nearby villagers. Tahereh wandered for a while from village to village, from one hiding place to another. She was finally arrested by government agents on charges of collaboration in the murder of Molla Taqi and sent to Tehran. There, she had an audience with the king, Nasser al-Din Shah, who is believed to have said: "I like her looks: leave her and let her be."[27] Some sources even maintain that the king wanted to marry her, should she stop believing in and advocating the new faith. Her reply was a definitive, even though poetic, no:

> Kingdom, wealth, and power for thee
> Beggary, exile, and loss for me
> If the former be good, it's thine
> If the latter is hard, it's mine.[28]

Despite the king's ordinance, leave her alone they did not. She was once again put under house arrest in the house of Tehran's chief of police. And when, in August 1852, an unsuccessful attempt was made on the life of the young monarch by three Babis, she was executed—a fate she shared with many men accused of being heretics. Whereas the execution of all other Babis was a public and publicized affair, that of Tahereh was shrouded in silence and secrecy. Consequently, accounts of her death are as conflicting as those of her life. Differing on details, however, they all agree on the broad outline: although in the Islamic precepts of apostasy a woman should not be executed but rather imprisoned until she regains her faith, she was executed by a governmental decree. There is also little doubt about the method of execution: one summer night, dressed in her best clothes, made up and perfumed, she was taken to a walled garden, strangled to death, and thrown in a well, followed by a heap of rocks. She was only thirty-six years of age.

The government of the time made a deliberate effort to conduct all Babi executions in public. Torturing and killing them in cities and villages soon became a commonplace event. According to one source, "not only the executioner and the common people took part in the massacre: sometimes Justice would present some of the unhappy Babis to various dignitaries and the Persian [recipient] would be well content, deeming it an honor to imbrue his own hands in the blood of the pinioned and defenseless victim. Infantry, cavalry, artillery, the ghulams or guards of the King, and the guilds of butchers, bakers, etc., all took their fair share in these bloody deeds."[29]

The Bab himself, executed two years earlier, did not fare any better than his followers. He was first carried around the city before being executed by a firing squad in public. Later, his body, along with that of his companion, was fastened to a ladder and dragged through the streets of the city of Tabriz.

Tahereh, the most outspoken, unrelenting, and controversial leader of this controversial movement, however, was handled quite differently. Concealed in a cloak of anonymity, her execution, like her life, was considered a private matter. In the society of her time, a woman's body—dead or alive—belonged to the privacy of the home. No forbidden eye was to be cast upon her. Even the body of an allegedly heretic woman could not escape this order of the day. Dead or alive, she had to remain concealed, hidden from prying eyes, privatized, veiled.

Accounts of Tahereh's death have an element of the fantastic to them. She seems to have died as she had lived, with an unswerving will and flamboyant originality. Lowell Johnson, quoting the son of the chief of police in whose house she was last imprisoned, writes:

> On the day she was secretly killed, it seemed as if she had been told it was going to happen. Tahirih bathed, changed all of her clothing and came downstairs to see the family . . .[She] called to me to go to the Chief of Police with a special request. "It seems that they wish to strangle me," she said, "Long ago, I set aside a silk handkerchief which I hoped would be used for this purpose. I deliver it into your hands and I want you to ask that drunkard to use it for the purpose of taking my life." When I went to the Chief of Police I found him completely drunk. He only shouted at me, "Don't interrupt our gay festival. Let that Babi woman be strangled and her body thrown into a hole." I was greatly surprised by such an order, because it was exactly what she had wanted. I did not ask him whether he would permit the murder to use the silk handkerchief. I just went to the two guards and they agreed that the handkerchief would be a good thing to use.[30]

Sources disagree on the logistics of Tahereh's strangulation.

Some believe that a handkerchief was used, while others write that she was choked by a silk scarf. Still others claim that the deadly weapon was the green turban of another executed Babi convert—Quddus—alleged to be her lover.[31] The strangulation itself, however, remains basically an undisputed fact, although some sources contend that she was not yet dead when thrown in the well.

But the Persian term for strangulation, *khafeh kardan,* also means to drown and more commonly conveys "suppressing, stifling, silencing." Unlike the Babis who were executed in public, the method of Tahereh's death suited her offense. Her voice was silenced because she shouldn't have spoken in the first place. Her body was hidden because she shouldn't have unveiled it. Perhaps the Friday prayer imam of Qazvin, Molla Taqi's replacement, knew better when he reproachfully warned Tahereh's father: "No glory remains on that house / From which hens crow like the cocks."[32]

The hen crowed like the cock; the private, the secret, leaked into the world of the public; the concealed became exposed; the absent became present; the seals dividing male/female, private/public broke down. Unveiling her face, as she unveiled her voice, Tahereh used her self as a medium, a text to break the silence. She asserted women's autonomy and distinctiveness in an age that demanded conformity and anonymity from its women. She wanted her face seen, her voice heard, her individuality known. She lifted the veil of secrecy and came out from behind the curtain.

Tahereh's contribution to the history of women's writing in Iran is invaluable: she proved that women could think, write, and reason like men—in public and for the public. Such actions set her apart from her contemporaries and confer upon her an inalienable precedence. The prominent women novelist Shahrnush Parsipur allies herself to a limited historical tradition that includes Tahereh. In a detailed enumeration of prominent figures, she considers Tahereh a precursor of women's modern literary tradition.[33]

The corpus of Tahereh's poetry, like accounts of her life, remains scattered and the subject of opposing views. A collection of Tahereh's poems was published for the first time more than a hundred years after her death. Although some question the authorship of certain poems ascribed to her, others claim that many of her poems were burned and lost to us. Still others maintain that some of her poems, coming as they did from the pen of a woman considered a heretic, were assigned to others. Their authorship disguised, her poems could more safely circulate from mouth to mouth. "It must be borne in mind that the odium which attaches to the name of Babi amongst Persian Muhammadans would render impossible the recitation by them of verses confessedly composed by her. If, therefore, she were actually the authoress of poems, the grace and beauty of which compelled an involuntary admiration even from her enemies, it would seem extremely probable that they should seek to justify their right to admire them by attributing them to some other writer." [34]

Major studies of poetry barely, if ever, deal with the work of Tahereh. Keshavarz-e Sadr and Moshir-Salimi include her among other women poets, assigning no special place to her. They provide cursory biographical notations and a few samples of her work. Whether because she has been deemed too offensive, too dangerous, or too minor a literary personage, no article, let alone a full-length book, has been written either on her work or on her life as a struggle for gaining a public voice.

Some of Tahereh's poems are difficult to understand. Their language is rich in abstractions. She not only mixes Arabic and Persian but also makes repeated allusions to Babi jargon and codes. Her religious convictions saturate her poetry and set her verse on fire. They glow in her poetry like a flame that burns every obstacle in its way. The erotic-mystical imagery and language she uses reveal an all-consuming love of and an intense devotion to a divine manifestation.

> In pursuit of your love, O darling,
> Enamored of afflictions, I am
> Why do you shun me so?
> Weary of your separation, I am.
> You've veiled your face
> You've disheveled your hair
> You've abandoned people
> Just as secluded, I am.
> You're the milk and you're the honey
> You're the tree and you're the fruit
> You are the sun and you are the moon
> A speck, an iota, I am.

> You're the palm and you're the date
> You are the nectar-lipped beloved
> A distinguished master, you, dear love,
> An insolent slave, I am.
> You are the Mecca and you are the One
> You're the temple and you're the shrine
> You're the beloved, the honored one
> The miserable lover, I am.
> "Come to me!"
> Love said alluringly
> "Free of pride and pretense,
> Manifestation of the One, I am."
>
> Tahereh is but floating dust at your feet
> Drunk by the wine of your face.
> Awaiting your blessing
> A confessing sinner, I am.[35]

Although the insignificance of the poetic persons is highlighted by juxtaposition to the virtues and holiness of the beloved, it is impossible to guess the sex of the beloved in this poem. Had it not been for the name Tahereh inserted in the last line, it would have been equally impossible to ascertain the gender of the poet. Ambiguity is compounded by the language itself, which is not gender marked. The second-person-singular pronoun *tow* used throughout the poem can be either masculine or feminine. The terms used to address the beloved make the task of the curious reader interested in deciphering the sex of the beloved no easier. *Sanam* (idol), *delbar* (sweetheart), *shahed* (beloved) can be addressed to both men and women.

In this poem and others like it, the gender of the poet cannot be ascertained. It is incidental to the major theme, or message, of the poem. The following poem is a first-person narrative that establishes in its first line the gender of the poet: "Should I unveil my scented hair." The following four lines further describe the narrator. In the last two lines, however, the poem takes a surprising turn. Characteristic of Tahereh's poetry, it dramatizes a theological conviction that becomes the very focus of the poem.

> Should I unveil my scented hair
> I'll captivate every gazelle

> Should I line my narcissus eyes
> I'll destroy the whole world with desire
> To see my face, every dawn
> Heaven lifts its golden mirror
>
> Should I chance to pass the church one day
> I'll convert all Christian girls.[36]

If self-assertion is a cardinal tenet of Tahereh's life, self-denial and self-effacement are key elements of her poetry. The themes of love, union, and ecstasy relate to mystic and spiritual experience. The object of love depicted is an abstraction rather than a concrete and palpable portrayal. It is ultimately divine love or its manifestation on earth. The desire and passion portrayed are merely starting points for spiritual realization, vehicles of expression in a long-established tradition of mystical love poetry. Perhaps nowhere does Tahereh depict more eloquently the Sufi theme of separation than in the following poem. This is the articulation of spiritual exile, imbued with fervor and intensity.

> I would explain all my grief
> Dot by dot, point by point
> If heart to heart we talk
> And face to face we meet.
>
> To catch a glimpse of thee
> I am wandering like a breeze
> From house to house, door to door
> Place to place, street to street.
> In separation from thee
> The blood of my heart gushes out of my eyes
> In torrent after torrent, river after river
> Wave after wave, stream after stream.
> This afflicted heart of mine
> Has woven your love
> To the stuff of life
> Strand by strand, thread to thread.[37]

Although modern notions of feminist writing might not be quite applicable to Tahereh's poetry—she does not overtly assert her gender or the rights of women—she nonetheless challenged the social and literary convention of her time. She questioned, problematized, and subverted the socially prescribed woman's place. She challenged the sharp separation between public and private, male and female, rational and emotional. She refused silence. By becoming her own public interpreter—a body with a voice and a voice with a body—she refused to slip away into silence. She defined the speaking subject as female and authorized for herself a public life. She earned herself an identity in ways both sexual and textual.

It is true that Tahereh's concerns were strictly along theological lines, but her explicit demand that she, a woman, be given the space to think for herself, to express her beliefs, and to use her voice publicly was significantly to question the validity of the place assigned to women. As an articulate theologian and poet, she challenged the silence and marginality that characterized the women of her era. Consciously or not, she dispensed with existing sex roles in order to create new ones.

It may be misleading to express Tahereh's religious aspirations in feminist terms. Whether she was a conscious champion of women's rights we don't know. Such a movement was not yet conceived of, let alone articulated.[38] Yet accounts of her life clearly indicate that even before her conversion to Babism, repeatedly and openly she challenged some of the most cherished and deep-seated norms of her society. Tahereh might not have espoused feminism (if we can use such an anachronistic term) as a cause, but she embodied it at every turn of her life. Her whole life story is indeed the expression of dissent and of dissatisfaction with the roles available to women. In fact, by her conduct, she subverted not only the established religion but the whole fabric of androcentric society. She rejected the traditional female occupations and the attributes of femininity by departing from existing gender roles. She eschewed the feminine virtues of submissiveness, domesticity, absence from the public view, and silence. Articulate rather than silent, transgressive rather than obedient, mobile rather than walled in, she challenged the prevailing norms of the established order.

Uninhibited by spatial constraints of femaleness, moving from one city to another, crossing boundaries between nations and cultures, she could not be pinned down. Now in Bagdad, now in Qazvin, returning to Iraq, visiting Kirmanshah, Hamedan, Nur, now in Tehran, now in Badasht, she embodied motion and vitality. In a culture that cements women to the private sphere through walls, veils, and their attendant customs, a culture so terrified by women's movement that even to this day a woman needs her husband's written permission to be granted a passport, a culture in which the word *harja'i* (straying about) becomes synonymous with *prostitute* when applied to a woman, Tahereh resisted any confinement.

Aversion and fear of women's mobility is not confined to any one culture or period. Perhaps the practice of footbinding in China best reflects the desire to confine a woman to the domestic sphere, to immobilize her. Or in the West, one of the major charges against witches concerned their ability to be mobile, to roam about. Condemned for their mysterious escapades, witches were thought to fly incredible distances through the air. "We," wrote the inquisitors in *Malleus Maleficarum*[39] (Hammer of Witches), "had credible . . . information from a young girl witch who had been converted . . . When she was asked whether it was only in imagination and fantastically that they rode, through as illusion of devils, she answered that they did so in both ways."[40] Dunking, a most common method of testing a witch, embodied society's fear of women's mobility: "The victim was stripped naked and bound with her thumb to her left toe, and was then cast into the pond or river. If she sank, she was frequently drowned; if she swam, she was declared guilty without any further evidence being required, and so escaped drowning to be hung or burned."[41]

Tahereh's physical mobility parallel's her metaphorical journey and her struggle to attain a voice of her own. Wherever she went, we are told, she attracted large audiences. Her physical presence, according to Babi/Baha'i and even Muslim sources, was irresistible. Her beauty, joined with her eloquence, it is said, was bewitching. She was endowed with personal magnetism. According to many, her power of persuasion caused many to convert to Babism despite the manifestly dangerous consequences of such a conversion. She was so charismatic a leader, it seems, that she not only recruited members but came to have a group of devoted followers known as the Qorratiyeh, that is, followers of Qorratol'Ayn.

Most sources claim that Tahereh's words did cast a spell. "In that small town of Kirand," writes Balyuzi, "her eloquence and the clarity of her disquisition so impressed the chiefs of that area that they offered to place twelve thousand men under her command, to follow her wherever she went."[42] According to Baha'u'llah [actually, 'Abdu'l-Bahá—

Ed.], in *Memorials of the Faithful*, her "sweet words" so mezmorized people that they preferred her talk to music in a wedding ceremony:

> It happened that there was a celebration at the Mayor's house for the marriage of his son; a nuptial banquet was prepared, and the house adorned. The flower of Tihran's ladies were invited, the princesses, the wives of vazirs and other great. A splendid wedding it was, with instrumental music and vocal melodies—by day and night the lute, the bells and songs. Then Tahirih began to speak; and so bewitched were the great ladies that they forsook the cistern and the drum and all the pleasures of the wedding feast, to crowd about Tahirih and listen to the sweet words of her mouth.[43]

The powers granted by Tahereh's eloquence were assumed astonishing for a woman, even for Babis themselves, for whom women's verbal expression was still a private matter. Although the Bab "allowed men and women members of an extended family to converse freely, he made it conditional on the topic being 'important and serious,' reducing the conversation to an exchange of no more than twenty-eight words if it was not."[44]

It is true that Tahereh's ideas provided mainly an alternative to the dominant religion. Yet, this stance allowed her further access to knowledge, organizational authority, and articulation of her ideas. It allowed her to reject some of the values of the dominant patriarchal society without giving up her strong and long-sustained religious beliefs.

The relationship between Babism and the women's movement has hardly been given an adequate treatment by historians. Though referred to in some works, it has not formed the focus of any extended research. Clouded by religious and political rhetoric, obscured by insufficient information about both movements, and somewhat crippled by a certain trivialization of both topics, the issue remains almost unexplored.[45] All one can say with certainty at this point is that Babism soon became a pejorative label used by antifeminist to justify their condemnation of those who struggled for equal rights and even for education for women. "In fact, the mullahs, led by Shaykh Fazlullah Nuri, a constitutionalist sympathizer who then became one of the most powerful opponents of the revolution," writes Bayat, "declared these schools and women's education in general, contrary to the Islamic law, hence *haram* (forbidden), and denounced the whole project as a Babi conspiracy."[46]

Taj-os Salteneh, who not only unveiled herself publicly but also used her autobiography to argue extensively against veiling, writes: "As I would start speaking my mind, mother said: 'You have turned Babi.' My relatives deprecated me. They avoided me and did not listen to me."[47] Taj-os Salteneh was thus conveniently branded a heretic and isolated. She was neither the first nor the last to be so treated. "The pioneers of women's militancy," says another early Iranian feminist, "made tremendous sacrifices. They exposed their breasts to arrows of accusation and reproach flung by women and men of the common people, who denounced them as 'wantons,' 'Babis,' and 'apostates.' "[48]

As for the scholarly writing on Tahereh, one of the its interesting features is the conspicuous lack of any major input by women—until almost a century after her death. The only woman contemporary who has written about her is a Westerner, Lady Mary Sheil. She spent a little over three years in Iran—from October 1849 to April 1853—and dedicated a paragraph to her in her book entitled *Glimpses of Life and Manners in Persia:* "There was still another victim. This was a young woman, the daughter of a moolla in [the Province of] Mazenderan, who, as well as her father, has adopted the tenets of Bab. The Babees venerated her as a prophetess; and she was styled Khooret-ool-eyn, which Arabic words are said to mean, Pupil of the eye. After the Babee insurrection had been subdued in the above province, she was brought to Tehran and imprisoned, but was well treated. When these executions took place she was strangled. This was a cruel and useless deed."[49]

Muslim sources about Tahereh's contribution to women's writing or to the women's movement differ from published materials by Babis and Baha'is. Generally speaking, Muslim sources, until recently, if not critical of her, basically relegated her to oblivion.[50] Although Babi/Baha'i sources have not delineated her specific contributions to the women's movement, they have, for the most part, considered her a "forerunner of the modern feminist movement"[51] and "a woman who gave her life for her sister women."[52] Her role as a precursor of Iranian women's literary tradition, however, remains neglected.

Paradoxically, after long years of silence by women writers about Tahereh's literary contribution, the novelist Shahrnush Parsipur, in the Islamic Republic of Iran, pays her tribute. In her novel *Tuba va Ma'na-ye Shab* (Tuba and the Sense of Night), published in 1989, Parsipur portrays Tahereh – without mentioning her name—as the first challenge to an age-old, male-centered, male-dominated belief system. "Haji thought to himself that women think. Unfortunately, they think. Not like ants or tree particles. Not like the specks of dust. But more or less like himself . . . After all didn't that rebellious woman cause a lot of trepidation and disorder during his childhood. They said she was a loose woman but a scholar too. A lot of rumors about her circulated around. He even recalled having heard a man tell his father that she is the Proof of the Age."[53]

Toward the end of her life, Tahereh lost faith in the efficacy of words to bring about the desired change. She became increasingly intolerant of views that differed from her own. Her desire to establish a dialogue, to challenge the established views through argumentation, proved too difficult to pursue, thwarted at each turn. Eventually, she realized words were too weak, unfit to guide, too soft, too ineffectual. According to Fazil Mazandari, the Baha'i historian: "Suddenly, Jenab-e Tahereh, a bare sword in her hand, appeared and with her characteristic eloquence, courage, and authority declared: 'wrap up this spectacle. The time for prayer and liturgy is over. Now is the time for devotion and sacrifice.' . . . She wanted to say forget words and enter the battlefield of bravery and self-sacrifice."[54]

The poet, disillusioned with words, finally resorted to cross-dressing and the sword. And how different is this picture from the tombstone carving. If Tahereh was destined to view life from behind a veil, if even in depicting her crime, her husband had to place her behind a curtain—immobile, hidden, and mute—Tahereh stepped forward—articulate, mobile, and ready to fight openly for her message.

> O slumbering one, the beloved has arrived, arise!
> Brush off the dust of sleep and self, arise!
>
> Behold, the good will has arrived,
> Come not before him with tears, arise!
>
> The mender of concerns has come to you,
> O heavy hearted one, arise!
>
> O one afflicted by separation,
> Behold the good tidings of the beloved's union, arise!

O you, withered by autumn,
Now, Spring has come, arise!

Behold, the New Year brings a fresh life,
O withered corps of yesteryear, up from your tomb, arise![55]

**Notes**

Reprinted from: Farzaneh Milani, "Becoming a Presence: Tahereh Qorratol'Ayn," *Veils and Worlds: The Emerging Voices of Iranian Women Writers* (Syracuse University Press, 1992) pp. 77-99.

1. Martha L. Root, *Táhirih the Pure, Iran's Greatest Woman*, 2nd ed. (Los Angeles: Kalimát Press, 1981) p. 102.
2. Ibid.
3. 'Alí Qulí Mírzá I'tizád al-Saltanah, *Fitnah-i Báb* (Bab's conspiracy), 2nd ed.; annotated by 'Abd al-Husayn Navá'í (Tehran: Babak, 1965) p. 168.
4. 'Alí Akbar Mushír Salímí, *Zanan-i Sukhanvar kih 'az yakhizar sal-i pish ta 'imruz bi zaban-i Farsi sukhan guftah'and* (Tehran: 'Ali Akbat 'Ilmi, 1337/1956) Vol. 2, p. 72.
5. Ahmad Kasravi, *Baha'igari* (Baha'ism) (Tehran: Mard-e Emruz, 1956) p. 81.
6. According to Abbas Amanat, *Resurrection and Renewal* (Ithaca, N.Y.: Cornell University Press, 1989), bitter reproaches "eventually forced him [Molla Saleh, Tahereh's father] to emigrate from Qazvin and retire in the 'Atabat [in Iraq], where he died in 1283/1866" (p. 322). As for the three children, Martha Root writes in Táhirih the Pure that in an interview with Tahereh's grandson, she was told the two sons "ran away from home because their father was not good to them; one went to Najaf [a city in Iraq] and the other went to live near Tehran; the girl died not long after the passing of her mother." Root, *Táhirih the Pure*, p. 51.
7. Edward Granville Browne, in 'Abdu'l-Bahá, *A Traveller's Narrative: Written to Illustrate the Episode of the Báb*; edited in the original Persian, and translated into English, with an introduction and explanatory notes by Edward G. Browne (Cambridge: The University Press, 1891) Vol. 2, p. 309.
8. *The Introduction to Bahaism, Its Origins and Its Role* [Hague: Nashr-e Farhang-e Eslami, 1978?].
9. Muhammad Sipihr [Lisán al-Mulk], *Násikh al-Taváríkh: Dawrah-i kamil tarikh-i Qájáríya*; ed. and annotated by Jahangir Qa'im'maqami (Tehran: Mu'assasah-'i Amir Kabir, 1337/1958) Vol. 3, p. 48.
10. Muhammad Sipihr, *Násikh al-Taváríkh: Sala'tin-i Qájár*, 1965, as quoted in Amanat, *Resurrection and Renewal*, p. 321.
11. Muhammad Sipihr, *Násikh al-Taváríkh*: Qájáríya, Vol. 3, p. 48.
12. Muhammad Ibráhím Bástání Parízúi, *Haft Sang* (Tehran: Intishárát-i Dánish, 1967) p. 357, n. 3.
13. Root, *Táhirih the Pure*, p. 51.
14. Badr ol-Moluk Bámdád, *From Darkness into Light: Women's Emancipation in Iran*; trans. F. R. C. Bagley (Hicksville, N.Y.: Exposition Press, 1977) p. 20.
15. Amanat, *Resurrection and Renewal*, p. 297.
16. Ibid.
17. Ibid., p. 309.

18. H. M. Balyuzi, *The Báb: The Herald of the Day of Days* (Oxford: George Ronald, 1974) p. 164.
19. Amanat, *Resurrection and Renewal*, p. 297.
20. 'Abdu'l-Bahá, *Memorials of the Faithful*; translated from the original Persian text and annotated by Marzeih Gail (Wilmette, Ill.: Bahá'í Publishing Trust, 1971) p. 201.
21. According to Browne, in *A Traveller's Narrative*, Vol. 2, p. 314, Subh-e Azal maintained that "when carried by her eloquence," Tahereh would allow her veil "to slip down her face, but she would always replace it after a few moments."
22. Muhammad Sipihr, *Násikh al-Tawáríkh*: Qájáríya, Vol. 3, p. 60.
23. Shoghi Effendi, *God Passes By* (Wilmette: Bahá'í Publishing Committee, 1944) p. 32.
24. Ibid.
25. Mary Sheil, *Glimpses of Life and Manners in Persia*, Reprint ed. (New York: Arno, 1973) p. 85.
26. I'tizád al-Saltanah, *Fitnah-i Báb*, p. 185. Epicurus is the ancient philosopher (341-271 B.C.) thought to have condoned pursuit of sensual gratification.
27. Browne, in *Traveller's Narrative*, Vol. 2, p. 313.
28. Husám Nuqabá'i, *Táhirah: Qurrat al-'Ayn*. ([Tehran: s. n.], 1983) p. 156.
29. Captain Alfred von Gumoens quoted in Moojan Momen, *The Bábí and Bahá'í Religions, 1844-1944: Some Contemporary Western Accounts* (Oxford: George Ronald, 1981) p. 133.
30. Lowell Johnson, *Táhirih* (Johannesburg: National Spiritual Assembly of the Bahá'ís of South and West Africa, 1982).
31. Dimitrii Marianoff and Marzieh Gail, "Thralls of Yearning Love," *World Order* (Summer 1972) pp. 7-42.
32. Amanat, *Resurrection and Renewal*, p. 322.
33. Shahrnú Pársíp'úr, "Why do you write?" (in Persian), *Dunya-yi Sukhan* (Tehran), no. 17 (March 1988), pp. 9-10.
34. Edward Granville Browne, *Selections from the Writings of E. G. Browne on the Bábí and Bahá'í Religions*; ed. Moojan Momen (Oxford: George Ronald, 1987) p. 241.
35. Mu'inu'd-Dín Mihrábí, *Qurrat'ul-Áyn Shá'riyeh Ázádíkháh va Millí-í Irán* (Nashr-i-Rúyesh, 1990) p. 148.
36. Nuqabá'i, *Táhereh Qurratu'l-Ayn*, p. 161.
37. Mihrábí, *Qurrat'ul-Áyn*, p. 149.
38. *In From Darkness into Light*, Bamdad claims that one of Tahereh's close associates, the wife of "Seyyed Kazem Rashti, had invited a number of enlightened ladies to her house to discuss the disastrous condition of the country and the deplorable status of its women." This meeting led to the foundation of "an organized body called the National Ladies Society." Bámdád, From Darkness into Light, p. 34.
39. Heinrich Institirius, Malleus Maleficarum; translated with an introduction, bibliography and notes, by the Rev. Montague Summers (London: J. Rodker, 1928).
40. Quoted in Selma R. Williams and Pamela J. Williams, *Riding the Nightmare: Women & Witchcraft* (New York: Atheneum, 1978).
41. Cecil Henry l'Estrange Ewen, *Witch Hunting and Witch Trials: The*

*Indictments from the Records of 1373 Assizes held for the Home Circuit A.D. 1559-1736* (London: K. Paul, Trench, Trubner, 1929) p. 68.
42. H. M. Balyuzi, The Báb: *The Herald of the Day of Days* (Oxford: George Ronald, 1974) p. 164.
43. 'Abdu'l-Bahá, *Memorials of the Faithful*, p. 202.
44. Quoted in Mangol Bayat, *Mysticism and Dissent; Socioreligious Thought in Qajar Iran* (Syracuse: Syracuse University Press, 1982) p. 116.
45. Baharieh Rouhani Ma'ani maintains that "the painful plight of many early Babi and Bahá'í women has escaped even the keen eye and the critical pen of Bahá'í historians, whose attitudes were so conditioned by the customary practices and unjust traditions of the time that they did not notice the struggles of most of the early women believers; or if they did, these appeared so insignificant to them that they did not warrant professional historical treatment." Baharieh Rouhani Ma'ani, "Religion and the Myth of Male Superiority," Peggy Canton, ed., *Equal Circles, Women and Men in the Bahá'í Community* (Los Angeles: Kalimát Press, 1987) p. 23.
46. Mangol Bayat, "Women and Revolution in Iran, 1905-1911," Lois Beck and Nikki Keddie, ed., *Women in the Muslim World* (Cambridge, Mass.: Harvard University Press, 1978) p. 300.
47. Taj al- Saltanah, *Khaterat-i Taj al- Saltanah* (Taj-os Saltaneh's memoir), ed. Mansurah Itteihadiyah and Sirus Sa'dvandiyan (Tehran: Nashr-i Tarikh-i Iran, 1362/1983) p. 109.
48. Bámdád, *From Darkness into Light*, p. 39.
49. Sheil, *Glimpses of Life and Manners in Persia*, p. 281.
50. Some prominent women historians in recent years have celebrated and acknowledged Tahereh's contribution to women's awakening in Iran. In "The Beginnings of Religious Clerics' Economic and Political Power," Homa Nateq believes that "in the history of constitutional and liberation movements in Iran, the role of Qorratol'Ayn as a freedom-loving ideologue and poet is unique" *Alifba* (Paris), no. 2, n.s., (Spring 1983) p. 43. Bayat, in *Mysticism and Dissent* writes "For Qorratol-'Ayn, a woman of great vision and intellectual abilities who resented the traditional milieu in which she was unable to move at will, Babism proved a unique chance to achieve emancipation. She took advantage of the movement to free herself from the bonds Islam imposed upon her. Her rejection of the veil symbolizes her defiant attitude towards the traditional social customs pertaining to women." (p. 115). Guity Nashat considers her "the most unusual woman of nineteenth-century Iran" and "the first woman in the modern history of Iran to openly rebel against the conventions of her time." Guity Nashat, "Women in Pre-Revolutionary Iran: A Historical Overview," in Guity Nashat, ed., *Women and Revolution in Iran* (Boulder, Colo.: Westview Press, 1983) p. 19.
51. Allesandro Bausani, "Babis," *The Encyclopedia of Religion*; ed. Mircea Eliade et al (New York: Macmillan, 1987) Vol. 2, pp. 32-34.
52. Root, *Tahira the Pure*, p. 34.
53. Shahrnú Pársíp'úr, *Túbáva ma'ana-yi shah* (Tehran: Intishárát'i Ispark, 1367 [1988/89]).
54. Mírza Asadullah Fádil-i-Mázandarání, *Tarikh-i-Zuhúru'l-Haqq* (Tehran: [n. p.]) Vol. 3, 1944, p. 325.
55. Nuqabá'i, *Táhereh Qurratu'l-Ayn*, p. 160.

A GROUP OF KURDISH GIRLS, c. 1892.

# Táhirih:
# A Religious Paradigm of Womanhood

by Susan Stiles Maneck

Every historically minded religion begins as a reform movement whose interest is to change the very fabric of society. It begins, therefore, with a vision and ideals. Ideals are what we set before us: they are what we strive to attain. It is important that as ideals are approached they continue to recede and change if they are to give us fresh scope for future advances. When surpassed, the ideal ceases to be an ideal. When cleaved to, it becomes a mere convention that stifles and impedes progress. Among the paradigms each religion has propagated is the ideal of the perfect woman.

Each religion has had its paradigm of the ideal woman. In Hinduism this has been Sita, the perfect wife who remains faithful to her husband at all costs. In Christianity the most eminent woman is the Virgin Mary, symbol of motherhood who, though devoted to her son, remained discreetly aloof from his ministry. There is Fátimih, the daughter of Muhammad, who figures in the role model of mother, wife, and daughter together.

Táhirih, the most well-known woman in Bábí-Bahá'í history, presents a startling contrast to the former models.[1] This gifted poet of nineteenth-century Iran, far from being a dutiful daughter, continually opposed the theological positions of her father Mullá Sálih, a prominent Muslim cleric of Qazvín. Neither is she admired for her success as a mother and a wife, since her estrangement from her husband (also a cleric) resulted in her forced separation from her children as well. Little wonder that to Muslims she is a paradigm of the dangers of allowing women to much freedom! This paper seeks to understand the significance of Táhirih, as an historical and literary figure, and as a symbol of womanhood, for all who felt impelled to take note of her, be they Bahá'ís or non-Bahá'ís, Easterners or Westerners.

## Biography

> How could it be that a woman, in Persia where woman is considered so weak a creature, and above all in a city like Qazvin, where the clergy possessed so great an influence, where the Ulamas, by their number and importance attracted the attention of the government and of the people—how could it be that there, precisely under such untoward circumstances, a woman could have organized so strong a group of heretics? There lies a question which puzzles even the Persian historian, Sipihr, for such an occurrence was without precedent![2]

Táhirih's background was certainly inauspicious for one who would later emerge as a preeminent leader of the militantly anticlerical Bábí religion and who would become, in Shoghi Effendi's words, "the first woman suffrage martyr."[3] Fátimih Zarrín Táj Baraghání, known to Bahá'ís by her titles Qurratu'l-'Ayn and Táhirih, was born to the most prominent family of 'ulamá of Qazvín (circa A.H. 1233/ A.D. 1817-18). Her father, Mullá Muhammad Sálih, along with her uncle Mullá Muhammad Taqí, had established their dominance over the more than one-hundred ecclesiastics who lived in the city. Mullá Muhammad Sálih was renowned for his commentaries on the Qur'an (*tasfir*). In exercising religious law, he had a reputation for rigidity and firmness. His brother Mullá Muhammad Taqí had achieved his position by his ruthless denunciation of rivals, particularly those sympathetic to the Shaykhí school,[4] which he declared to be a dangerous heresy and whose leader, Siyyid Kazím, he had excommunicated. A younger brother accepted the Shaykhí views and became a firm follower of Siyyid Kazím Rashtí.

Táhirih and her younger sister Marziyih were brought up in a strictly religious yet affluent environment. Her father, recognizing Táhirih's extraordinary abilities, had permitted her to continue her studies beyond the elementary level that was expected of a woman of her station. She far surpassed her brothers[5] in theological and juridical knowledge.

At the age of thirteen, Táhirih was married to the eldest son of her uncle Mullá Muhammad Taqí. She bore three children from that marriage, two sons[6] and a daughter. Family tensions soon developed after Táhirih became attracted to the teachings of the Shaykhís. Her father, husband, and uncle all tried to dissuade her from supporting the views of Siyyid Kazím Rashtí, but to no avail. Through her Shaykhí relatives she corresponded with the leader of that school and wrote a treatise vindicating it. Siyyid Kazím, delighted to have such a talented supporter within the immediate family of his arch-enemy Muhammad Taqí, bestowed upon her the name Qurratu'l-'Ayn (Solace of the Eyes). Táhirih's relations with her husband quickly deteriorated, and after her father-in-law publicly began to denounce the Shaykhís from his pulpit, she decided to leave her husband and children and return to her father's house. Shortly afterwards she set out for Karbilá and joined the circle of Shaykhís there.

She arrived in Karbilá around 1843, only to find that Siyyid Kazím Rashtí had passed away just a few days earlier. At the time of her arrival, a controversy had erupted within the Shaykhí community between those who stressed the charismatic and mystical aspects of the teachings of Shaykhism, and the more conservative Shaykhís who wished to preserve their legitimacy within Shí'í orthodoxy. The "radical" Shaykhís held that the central tenet of Shaykhism was the belief in the imminent appearance of the Qurratu'l-'Ayn or Mihdí, the Promised One who would appear at the end of time. Táhirih sided with the radicals, and by allying herself with Siyyid Kazím's widow, she won the support of the Shaykhí women in Karbilá as well as that of other students and adherents of the late Siyyid. Taking up residence in Siyyid Kazím's house, she held classes in place of those that had been offered by the Shaykhí leader, this much to the chagrin of Kazím's son Mullá Ahmad who wished to succeed his father.

When the Báb arose claiming to be the Promised One, Táhirih immediately accepted his claim and persuaded most of the Shaykhí community of Karbilá to do the same. The Báb appointed her as one of his chief disciples, one of the nineteen "Letters of the Living." [7] Her commitment to the Báb came, not so much out of extensive investigation of the Bábí beliefs, but rather seems to have been a result of a revelatory experience.[8]

The surviving samples of her work[9] from this period demonstrate her considerable ability in using the Qur'án, *hadíth*, and *tafsír* to argue for God's continuing revelation in history. At the same time, she insisted that to recognize God's activity, particularly as manifested in the person of Prophets, one must possess an inner awareness of God's purpose (*sunnat-i illahi*).

Claiming that much of Islamic law was no longer binding upon Bábís, she refused to perform the daily ritual prayers. At the same time, she instituted a number of innovations within the Bábí community at Karbilá. Her most dangerous and unconventional act was appearing unveiled at Karbilá in a gathering of believers.

Abbas Amanat suggests that this was probably the first time an Iranian woman had considered unveiling on her own initiative.[10] The circle of women who gathered around her (both in Karbilá and later in Qazvín, Hamadán, Baghdad, and Tehran) appears to have formed one of the earliest group of female Iranians to attain awareness of their deprivations as women. Yet Táhirih's activities did not represent a woman's liberation movement in the modern sense of the word. Táhirih clearly saw the unveiling of women as an act of religious innovation. Neither the writings of Táhirih nor those of the Báb concern the issue of women's rights as such.[11] Apparently Táhirih experienced the Báb's revelation as liberating, whether or not it specifically addressed the status of women *per se*.

Táhirih's activities became quite controversial, even within the Bábí community. Many Bábís did not view the Báb's revelation as a total split with the past or with Islamic law. They regarded Táhirih's behavior as scandalous and unchaste. For this reason, in answer to complaints about Táhirih, the Báb gave her the title by which she is now known, Táhirih, meaning "the Pure One."[12] As a result of his response, many of the more conservative Bábís left the fold, although most accepted the Báb's judgment.

The opposition of the non-Bábí ulama went even deeper. Much of Táhirih's poetry written during this period was virulently anti-clerical. She frequently issued challenges to debate the 'ulamá. During the month of Muharram 1847, while Shiite Muslims donned mourning clothes to commemorate the martyrdom of the Imám Husayn, Táhirih deliberately excited their reaction by dressing in gay colors and appearing unveiled. She urged the Bábís to celebrate the Báb's birthday, which fell on the first day of that month.[13] The enraged 'ulamá incited a mob to attack Siyyid Kazím's house. Finally, the governor of Karbilá intervened and had Táhirih placed under house arrest for three months before allowing her to be sent to Baghdad.

Accompanied by the leading Bábí women of Karbilá, along with a number of Shaykhís who were her devoted followers, Táhirih set out for Baghdad, where she continued her activities, offering public lectures from behind a curtain.[14] Often the 'ulamá would attend these lectures to refute her. On one of these occasions the Shah's Jewish physician, then accompanying the Shah on pilgrimage to Karbilá, was present and became thoroughly convinced of the validity of Táhirih's message. This physician, Dr. Hakím Masih, became the first Bábí convert of Jewish origin.[15]

This conversion aroused further opposition and caused Táhirih to be imprisoned in the house of the Muftí of Baghdad Ibn Álúsí. Ibn Álúsí later wrote these observations in regards to Táhirih.

> Some people alleged that Qurrat al-'Ayn believes in the total abolition of the duties, but I do not see any truth in this though she stayed in my house about two months and so many discussions took place between me and her in which there was no taqíya [dissimulation] or apprehension. Verily, I saw in her such a degree of merit and accomplishment as I rarely saw in men. She was a wise and decent woman who was unique in virtue and chastity. I have referred to my discussions with her on another occasion; if one became aware of them, one would realize that there is no doubt about her knowledge. It became obvious to me that Bábíya [Babis] and Qurratíya [Qurratis] are the same. They believe that the time for five times obligatory prayers is over and that revelation is unsuspended and therefore the Perfect [Man] will have [further] revelations. However, these revelations are not canonical.[16]

Táhirih was not tried for apostasy, since the usual penalty for that crime (death) could not be applied to women. Meanwhile, her family in Qazvín was quite disturbed by her activities. Her unveiling, in particular, led to rumors of immorality. Táhirih's father dispatched a relative to Iraq who induced the governor to order her deportation to Iran.[17] Wherever she traveled en route, more excitement was raised. In the village of Karand some 1200 people immediately offered her their allegiance. In Kirmánsháh, however, her activities caused such an uproar that the Bábís were attacked by a mob and driven out of the city, but not before Táhirih had been able to expound the teachings before the leading women of Kirmánsháh, among them the governor's wife, who had long been a patron of the Shaykhís.[18] In Hamadán, Táhirih met with both the leading 'ulamá and the most notable women of the city, whose number included members of the royal family.

On her arrival in Qazvín, her husband Mullá Muhammad, from whom she had been longed estranged, urged her to return to his household. She replied:

> If your desire had really been to be a faithful mate and companion to me, you would have hastened to meet me in Karbilá and would on foot have guided my howdah all the way to Qazvín. I would, while journeying with you, have aroused you from your sleep of heedlessness and would have shown you the way of truth. But this was not to be. Three years have elapsed since our separation. Neither in this world nor in the next can I ever be associated with you. I have cast you out of my life forever.[19]

Táhirih's uncle and father-in-law, Muhammad Taqí, had a reputation for being virulently opposed to both the Bábís and the Shaykhís. On numerous occasions he incited mob violence against them. After one of these incidents, Mullá 'Abdu'lláh, a Shaykhí and a Bábí sympathizer, decided to retaliate. When Mullá Taqí appeared in the local mosque to offer his dawn prayers, Mullá 'Abdu'lláh fatally stabbed him and fled.[20] This led to the arrest and torture of many of the Bábís of Qazvín. Táhirih was implicated as well. To stop this orgy of violence, Mullá 'Abdu'lláh surrendered himself. Despite this, the other Bábís were not released, and many were executed. Táhirih escaped with the assistance of Bahá'u'lláh, who hid her in his home in Tehran.[21] 'Abdu'l-Bahá recalled those days:

> When word of this spread throughout Tihrán, the Government hunted for her high and low; nevertheless, the friends[22] kept arriving to see her, in a steady stream, and Táhirih, seated behind a curtain, would converse with them. One day the great Siyyid Yahyá, surnamed Vahíd, was present there. As he sat without, Táhirih listened to him from behind the veil. I was then a child, and was sitting on her lap. With eloquence and fervor, Vahíd was discoursing on the signs and verses that bore witness to the advent of the new Manifestation. She suddenly interrupted him and, raising her voice, vehemently declared: "O Yahyá! Let deeds, not words, testify to thy faith, if thou art a man of true learning. Cease idly repeating the traditions of the past, for the day of service, of steadfast action, is come. Now is the time to show forth the true signs of God, to rend asunder the veils of idle fancy, to promote the Word of God, and to sacrifice ourselves in His path. Let deeds, not words, be our adorning!"[23]

Later, following a general call upon the Bábís to gather in Khurásán, both Táhirih and Bahá'u'lláh travelled to a place called Badasht where eighty-one Bábí leaders had gathered to decide how they might effect the release of the Báb from imprisonment and to discuss the future direction of the Bábí community. At the meeting tension developed between Táhirih (who headed the more radical Bábís advocating a complete break with Islam, as well as the militant defence of their community) and the more conservative Quddús (who initially favored policies aimed at the rejuvenation of Islam and prudent accommodation with religious and secular power). Bábís generally accepted Quddús as the chief of the Báb's disciples. Táhirih is reported to have said in regards to the latter, "I deem him . . . a pupil whom the Báb has sent me to edify and instruct. I regard him in no other light." Quddús, for his part, denounced Táhirih as "the author of heresy."[24] At one time when Quddús was rapt in devotions, Táhirih rushed out of her tent brandishing a sword. "Now is not the time for prayers and prostrations," she declared, "rather on to the field of love and sacrifice!"[25]

But her most startling act was to appear before the assembled believers unveiled. Shoghi Effendi vividly describes the scene:

> . . . Táhirih, regarded as the fair and spotless emblem of chastity and the incarnation of the holy Fátimih, appeared suddenly, adorned yet unveiled, before the assembled companions, seated herself on the right-hand of the affrightened and infuriated Quddús, and, tearing through her fiery words the veils guarding the sanctity of the ordinances of Islám, sounded the clarion call, and proclaimed the inauguration, of a new Dispensation. The effect was electric and instantaneous. She, of such stainless purity, so reverenced that even to gaze at her shadow was deemed an improper act, appeared for a moment, in the eyes of her scandalized beholders, to have defamed herself, shamed the Faith she had espoused, and sullied the immortal Countenance she symbolized. Fear, anger, bewilderment, swept their inmost souls, and stunned their faculties. 'Abdu'l-Kháliq-i-Isfahání, aghast and deranged at such a sight, cut his throat with his own hands. Spattered with blood, and frantic with excitement, he fled away from her face.[26]

Unperturbed, Táhirih declared, "I am the Word which the Qá'im is to utter, the Word which shall put to flight the chiefs and nobles of the earth!"[27]

Táhirih, much to the dismay of many Bábís, finally won over Quddús to her point of view.[28] Quddús conceded that the Islamic law had been abrogated. So complete was their reconciliation that the two departed from Badasht riding in the same howdah. When they neared the village of Níyálá, the local mullá, outraged at seeing the unveiled woman sitting next to a man and chanting poems aloud, led a mob against them. Several people died in the resulting clash, and the Bábís dispersed in different directions.[29]

From 1848-1850, pitched battles raged between the Bábís and government forces in Mázandarán, Zanján, and Nayríz. Táhirih remained in hiding, moving from village to village for about a year.[30] Around 1849, authorities arrested her on charges of complicity in the assassination of her uncle. They brought her to Tehran where they imprisoned her in the house of the Kalántar (Mayor). The Kalántar's wife became very attached to Táhirih, and women again flocked to hear Táhirih's discourses.[31]

On July 9, 1850, the Báb was executed in Tabríz by order of the Shah. Two years later a small group of Bábís sought to take revenge by assassinating the Shah. The attempt failed, and a general massacre of the Bábís then ensued. The government decided to execute Táhirih as well. According to one European observer,[32] before her execution was ratified, Táhirih was taken before Násiri'd-Dín Sháh. He proposed marrying Táhirih on condition that she recant her heretical beliefs. Táhirih's most famous poem was written as a blunt refusal of his proposal. After being interrogated by two senior *mujtahids*, Mullá 'Alí Kaní and Mullá Muhammad Andirmání, Táhirih dressed herself in wedding attire for her martyrdom. She was taken to a garden in September 1852,[33] strangled, and thrown down a well.[34] Her last words are reported to be: "You can kill me as soon as you like, but you can not stop the emancipation of women."[35]

## Poetry

Táhirih's uniqueness as a female religious leader can be seen in the dynamism of her poetry. Before examining these poems, however, we have first to determine which of those poems credited to her are likely authentic. Most of the early Bábí documents were destroyed in the massacres of 1852, so Táhirih's poetry was often preserved only orally and thus was subject to all the revisions and variations which that process involves. Some of the poems credited to her were in fact written by others. For instance, Táhirih is said to have written one poem and sent it to the Báb after she recognized his station through a vision. E. G. Browne has translated a part of this poem as follows:

> The effulgence of thy face flashed forth and
> the rays of thy visage arose on high;
> Then speak the word, "Am I not your Lord?"
> and "Thou art, Thou art!" we will all reply.³⁶

However, Muslim scholars have determined that this poem was the original composition of an earlier poet Muhammad Báqir Suhbat of Lar in whose collection the whole poem (with certain variants) occurs.³⁷ Táhirih may well have quoted this when writing to the Báb, but it does not seem to have been her original composition. Another *ghazal* (untranslated) credited to Táhirih by these same Muslim scholars, according to Noghabai is the work of Ta'ir Isfahání.³⁸ Táhirih's poetry is often confused with the work of the Bahá'í historian and poet Nabíl as well.

Because so little of Táhirih's poetry has been translated into English or compiled in any sort of anthology, I will quote some poems at length.³⁹ Most of her poems are *ghazals* written in the *kamil* meter. Táhirih wrote in a very classical and difficult style, using rare Arabic phrases frequently. Modern writers have sometimes criticized her for being bombastic. However, none of these phrases interrupt the spontaneous flow of her poetry. Her poems are often ecstatic and inspiring, with graceful rhythm and excellent diction. The general themes of her poetry include her ecstatic love for God and his Manifestation, the Báb (and perhaps Bahá'u'lláh); her fascination with suffering and martyrdom; her messianic fervor and apocalyptic expectations for renewal of the social order; her hostility towards traditional clergy. The latter two themes are reflected in the following poem, which also expresses her high regard for the intellectual freedom she expects the new dispensation to bring. Such strong revolutionary and anticlerical themes were unprecedented in Iranian poetry—whether written by male or female—prior to the outpouring of such literature during the Constitutional Revolution more than fifty years later.

> Truly, the Morn of Guidance commands the breeze to begin
> All the world has been illuminated; every horizon; every people
> No more sits the Shaykh in the seat of hypocrisy
> No more becomes the mosque a shop dispensing holiness

> The tie of the turban will be cut at its source
> No Shaykh will remain, neither glitter nor secrecy
> The world will be free from superstition and vain imaginings
> The people free from deception and temptation
> Tyranny is destined for the arm of justice
> Ignorance will be defeated by perception
> The carpet of justice will be outspread to everywhere
> And the seeds of friendship and unity will be spread throughout
> The false commands eradicated from the earth
> The principle of opposition changed to that of unity[40]

The next poem, written in a style similar to Rúmí's *Divan-i Shams-i Tabríz,* conveys the ecstatic quality of Táhirih's poetry. I quote a small portion of it:

> In the path of your love, O Idol,[41]
>     I am enaoured with torment
> How long will you ignore me, I am grief-stricken
> My face veiled, my hair torn out
> I have separated myself from all creation
> You are the light, you are the veil, you are the moon,
>     you are the horizon.[42]

The following poem expresses Táhirih's longing for martyrdom:

> In the land of your love I remain, finding no favor from anyone
> See what a stranger I am, Thou who art King of the land?
> Is it a sin, O Idol, that my every breath breathes the mystery of your love?
> Separate me, kill me, take me unjustly
> The time of patience has ended, how long should I stand separation?
> When every piece of my being, like a hollow reed, tells a sad tale
> Reason cannot apprehend you, souls die of your thought
> All the door of existence are nothing, you are ultimate
> When the zephyr passes by bringing news of their destruction
> Making pale the faces and the eyes weep, what would be your loss?
> You step to my bed in the morning out of compassion, I fly with both
>     wings and hands
> When you rescue one from this place, you will take her to the
>     placeless place
> Then I will let go of the soul of the world, for you are the creator
>     of all souls.[43]

E. G. Browne has translated Táhirih's most famous *ghazal*, which was written in answer to Násiri'd-Dín Sháh's marriage proposal.[44] The first section is addressed to the Báb as the Beloved. The second is Táhirih's answer to the Shah.

> The thralls of yearning love constrain the bonds of pain and calamity.
> These broken-hearted lovers of thine to yield their lives in their
> zeal for thee.
> Though with sword in hand my Darling stand with intent to slay
> though I sinless be,
> If it pleases him, this tyrant's whim, I am well content with his tyranny.
> As in sleep I lay at the break of day that cruel charmer came to me,
> And in the grace of his form and face the dawn of the morn I
> seem to see.
> The musk of Cathay might perfume gain from the scent of those
> fragrant tresses rain.
> While his eyes demolish a faith in vain attacked by the pagans
> of Tartary.[45]
> With you, who condemn both love and wine for the hermit's cell and
> the zealot's shrine,[46]
> What can I do, for our Faith divine you hold as a thing of infamy?
> The tangled curls of thy darling's hair, and thy saddle and steed
> are thy only care;
> In thy heart the Absolute hath no share, nor thought of the poor
> man's poverty.
> Sikandar's pomp and display be thine, the *Qalandar's* habit and
> way be mine;
> That, if it please thee, I resign, while this, though bad, is enough for me.
> Pass from the station of "I" and "We," and choose for thy home Nonentity,
> For when thou has done the like of this, thou shall reach the supreme
> Felicity.

The next poem is probably the last one written by Táhirih. It refers to her interrogation by the two *mujtahids* who signed her death warrant. The poem reflects disappointment but not despair, disillusionment but no loss of vision. I quote only a portion of it:

> At the corner of the lip, a single beauty mark and two black tresses
> Alas, for the bird of the heart, a single grain and two snares
> A constable, a shaykh and I; the talk is of love.
> How can I reply to them; one boiled and two raw?
> From the face and the locks of the Idol my days are as nights.
> Alas, for my days; day is one, night two . . . .[47]

## Táhirih as Paradigm

In the introduction, I suggested that Táhirih was for the Bahá'ís the religious paradigm of womanhood, comparable to the figures of Sita, Fátimih, and the Virgin Mary. But non-Bahá'ís as well have often seen her as a figure bigger than life. Long before the Bahá'í Faith had made its way West, Europeans were inspired and fascinated by her. Lord Curzon called her life "one of the most affecting episodes in modern history."[48] Marie von Najmajer, the gifted Austrian poet, heard of Táhirih in 1870, and was inspired to write her greatest poem on Táhirih's life. Marianna Hainisch, mother of an Austrian president and founder of the New Woman Movement for Austria, claimed to have been inspired that same year. She stated in 1925, "The greatest ideal of womanhood all my life has been Táhirih . . . of Qazvín, Iran. I was only seventeen years old when I heard of her life and her martyrdom, but I said, 'I shall try to do for the women of Austria what Táhirih gave her life to do for the women of Persia.' "[49]

Sarah Bernhart, the famous actress, requested the playwright Catulle Mendes to write a dramatized version of Táhirih's life. He referred to Táhirih as "the Persian Joan of Arc, the leader of emancipation of women of the Orient . . . who bore resemblance both to the medieval Heloise and the neo-platonic Hypatia . . ."[50]

Edward Granville Browne wrote of Táhirih:

> The appearance of such a woman as Kurratu'l-'Ayn is in any country and any age a rare phenomenon, but in such a country as Persia it is a prodigy—nay, almost a miracle. Alike in virtue of her marvelous beauty, her rare intellectual gifts, her fervid eloquence, her fearless devotion, and her glorious martyrdom, she stands forth incomparable and immortal amidst her countrywomen. Had the Babi religion no other claim to greatness, this were sufficient—that it produced a heroine like Kurratu'l-'Ayn.[51]

To the Muslim polemicists, Táhirih is often an archetype of a different sort. For them she is the paradigm of the dangerous and seductive whore, an object lesson in the dangers of allowing women too much freedom. One such writer describes her story in these terms:

> It seems God created women as a sort of test for men. As it is forbidden to go near the wine, so it is forbidden to go near the other, women. When beautiful women discard their modesty they bring rains of devastation. There was such a woman Qurratul Ayn in Iran . . . .
>
> Qurratul Ayn was an extremely beautiful woman. She was well educated and oration was her special art. She coul compose poetry in Persian language.

A RELIGIOUS PARADIGM OF WOMANHOOD ❋ 197

> When she came to know that Ali Mohamad Baab had in vated a new religion; she not only accepted the religion but also became a preacher. To lure the people into the fold of new religion she renounced Pardah and began to mix up with people showing her beauty and preaching the new relgion. She succeeded in gaining hold over a large number of people on account of her beauty. She was opposed by her family, but she did not yield. She feared her uncle's wrath, hence she directed her lovers to murder the holy soul. Several of her lover's went in search of her uncle, they learnt that he was in some Mosque offering prayer, they went there and martyred the Mujtahed in the state of prayer.
>
> When her prime opponent was removed she became bold enough to preach her hedonism with more gusto . . . Tension prevailed in Iran due to her activities . . . The Emperor [*sic*] of Iran sent his army to capture her . . . When the mischievous Qurratul Ayn was brought to the Royal court, she came bare faced the king bent his head down but others began to look at the marvelous beauty stealthily . . . [52]

No other single Bábí or Bahá'í hero or heroine has captured the imagination of Western Bahá'ís as has Táhirih. Numerous novels have been written about her.[53] This may partly be due to the fact that women have largely dominated the Faith in the West. Yet strangely, these accounts tone Táhirih down considerably. For instance, Táhirih's leadership within the Shaykhí community of Karbilá has been largely ignored. The story of Táhirih brandishing a sword and disturbing Quddús's devotions cannot be found in Western accounts. This may be partly attriable to the tendency of Bahá'ís to minimize the militant aspects of the Bábí religion in keeping with their present-day political quietism. But the over-all result is that Táhirih appears as a more forceful personality in Persian Bahá'í sources than she does to Western Bahá'ís.

But if Táhirih provides a paradigmatic ideal of womanhood for Bahá'ís, we would do well to examine what qualities are therefore being commended and which ones are largely absent. This paradigm suggests that women are encouraged to be assertive, intelligent, eloquent, passionately devoted to causes, and yet, still beautiful. Absent are many of those qualities generally found in other feminine ideals: devotion to family, modesty, gentleness, and submissiveness.

How do the qualities Táhirih exemplified affect the lives of Bahá'í women, particularly those living in a cultural context that does not reinforce these qualities? Yazd is a city situated in central Iran with a reputation for conservatism and religious fanaticism. Anthropologist Judith Goldstein did field work on the religious communities of Yazd between 1973-1975. She observed that Bahá'í women, unlike the women of other communities, associated freely with men and participated nearly equally in religious gatherings. The principle of the equality of men and women was a frequent topic of discussion, used to establish the superiority of the Bahá'í teachings. Noting that for Bahá'ís "eloquence is a cultivated virtue; one might argue that it becomes a substitute for public, communal ritual,"[54] she goes on to say:

> Bahai women conduct religious discussions in a manner quite different from the style of more traditional women's conversation. The skillful use of metaphor and command of argument can be seen . . . The Bahai women's active stance is expressed in eloquence.[55]

As Dr. Goldstein points out, the model for the articulate Bahá'í woman is the immortal heroine Táhirih. Yet this model would not go unchallenged. Other women, such as Bahíyyih Khánum, are often held up as models of women playing more traditional "supporting roles." Yet the figure of Táhirih presents a paradigm truly unique in religious history. Ultimately, only the future will tell if the Bahá'í community will exploit the potentialities of this paradigm.

**Notes**

An earlier version of this paper was presented for a seminar on women in Middle Eastern and South Asian literature directed by Dr. Leslie Flemming at the University of Arizona. The author wishes to thank Dr. Fleming for her helpful comments on this work, which received an award from the American Academy of Religion, Western Region.

1. In the theological sense, Táhirih is not the most important woman in the Bahá'í Faith: that distinction belongs to Navváb, the wife of Bahá'u'lláh, and to Bahíyyih Khánum, his eldest daughter. Of the first figure, however, very little has been written in English, or to my knowledge in Persian. Bahíyyih Khánum is much better known, since she served as the de facto head of the Bahá'í community several times. She has usually been depicted as playing a supportive role in relation to 'Abdu'l-Bahá and Shoghi Effendi, although in the opinion of this writer she was much more of an independent actor. She has not attracted nearly as much popular attention within the Bahá'í community as has Táhirih. Táhirih plays, in this sense, a much more important role for she has become a legend. Both in Iran and America, her name is the most popular one given to Bahá'í girls.
2. Aleksandr Kazem-Bek, "Bab et les Babis, ou Soulèvement politique et religieux, de 1845 à 1853," *Journal Asiatique* (Paris), Vol. 7 (1866) p. 474. English trans-

lation in Emily McBride Perigord, *Translation of the French Foot Notes of the Dawn Breakers* (Wilmette, Ill.: Bahá'í Publishing Trust, 1977) p. 39.
3. Shoghi Effendi, *God Passes By* (Wilmette, Ill.: Bahá'í Publishing Trust, 1974) p. 75.
4. The Shaykhí school was founded by Shaykh Ahmad-i-Ahsá'í (d. 1824). He held that there was a material body and soul and a spiritual body and soul and that only the latter would be raised in the resurrection. He also held that Muhammad's Night Journey was not to be taken literally. He was known for his extreme veneration of the Imáms and for his belief in the imminent appearance of the Hidden Imám.
5. Her brother 'Abdu'l-Vahháb said of her, "None of us, her brothers or her cousins dared to speak in her presence, her learning intimidated us, and if we ventured to express some hypothesis on a disputed point of doctrine, she demonstrated in such a clear, precise and conclusive manner that we were going astray, that we instantly withdrew confused." (A. L. M. Nicolas, Seyyèd, *Ali Mohammed, dit le Bâb: histoire* (Paris: Dujarric, 1905) pp. 273-74. English translation in Perigord, Translation of the French Foot Notes, p. 13.)
6. Her two sons Ibráhím and Isma'il later became mujtahids. The latter succeeded his father as the Imám-Jum'ih of Qazvín. Abbas Amanat, "The Early Years of the Babi Movement, Background and Development." D.Phil. dissertation, University of Oxford, 1981, p. 255.
7. The term Letters of the Living refers to nineteen Arabic letters comprising the opening verse of surihs of the Qur'án (except the nineteenth): "In the name of God the Merciful, the Compassionate." The Báb plus his disciples total nineteen Letters of the Living.
8. According to 'Abdu'l-Bahá, she recognized the Báb through a dream: "One night when it was getting along toward dawn she laid her head on her pillow, lost all awareness of this earthly life, and dreamed a dream; in her vision a youth, a Siyyid, wearing a black cloak and a green turban, appeared to her in the heavens; he was standing in the air, reciting verses and praying with his hands upraised. At once, she memorized one of these verses, and wrote it down in her notebook when she awoke. After the Báb had declared his mission, and His first book, 'The Best of Stories,' was circulated, Táhirih was reading a section of the text one day, and she came upon that same verse, which she had noted down from the dream. Instantly offering thanks, she fell upon her knees and bowed her forehead to the ground, convinced that the Báb's message was truth." 'Abdu'l-Bahá, *Memorials of the Faithful* (Wilmette, Ill.: Bahá'í Publishing Trust, 1971) p. 193.
9. Among her known works still extant are a letter written to her cousin Mullá Javad Valiyani who at first became a Bábí and then rejected the Bábí Faith. Six other works are produced in Mírza Asadullah Fádil-i-Mázandarání, *Tarikh-i-Zuhúru'l-Haqq*, Vol. 3 (Tehran: [s. n.], 1944) which includes a letter to Mullá Husayn in Arabic; two public addresses; a letter addressed to the Muftí of Baghdad, Ibn Álúsí; an apologetic tract written in defense of the Báb; and two letters addressed to the Bábís of Isfahán. A centennial volume written by Azalí Bábís in 1949, and entitled *Táhirih Qurratu'l-'Ayn Bi-yád-i-Sadumín Sál-i-Shahádat-i-Qurratu'l-'Ayn Nábighih-i-Duwrán* provides six other prayers and letters. Mírzá Abul-Fazl Gulpáyigání, *Kashf al-ghitá' 'an Hiyal al-A'dá* (Ashkhabad: [s. n.], 1334/1916) contains a long Arabic treatise. E. G. Browne gives the text and translation of a letter written to Shaykh Alí 'Azím in an

appendix of Mírzá Husain Hamadání, *The Táríkh-i-Jadíd, or New History of Mírzá 'Alí Muhammad the Báb*; trans. Edward Granville Browne (Cambridge: The University Press, 1893). Táhirih's poetry will be discussed later.
10. Abbas Amanat, *Resurrection and Renewal: The Making of the Babi Movement in Iran, 1844-1850* (Ithaca: Cornell University Press, 1989) pp. 305-307.
11. The Báb's teachings certainly aimed at improving the condition of women by abolishing the temporary marriage allowable in Shiite Islam as well as the practice of instant divorce, but women's position could hardly be regarded as equal.
12. Amanat, *Resurrection*, p. 307. Shoghi Effendi, *God Passes By*, p. 32; 'Abdu'l-Bahá, *Memorials*, p. 192; Martha L. Root, *Táhirih the Pure, Iran's Greatest Woman*. 2nd ed. (Los Angeles: Kalimát Press, 1981) p. 44; and Nabíl-i-A'zam, *The Dawn-Breakers: Nabíl's Narrative of the Early Days of the Bahá'í Revelation*. 2nd ed. (Wilmette, Ill.: Bahá'í Publishing Trust, 1970) p. 293 indicate more specifically that Bahá'u'lláh gave Táhirih her title at the conference at Badasht and that the Báb subsequently approved it.
13. Amanat, *Resurrection*, p. 305.
14. Táhirih would, under normal circumstances, remain veiled. She unveiled only when she had a particular point to make, no doubt because of its shock appeal.
15. Root, *Táhirih*, p. 62.
16. Cited in Amanat, *Resurrection*, p. 310. Amanat lists a couple of secondary sources for this quote, which he translates but is not certain of the title of Álúsís's work here. He speculates it is from Álúsís's incomplete and unpublished work *Nahj al-salama ila mabaahith al-Islamama*, Álúsís's last work, written in 1270 A.H.
17. Amanat, *Resurrection*, p. 309.
18. Nabíl-i-Azam, *Dawn-Breakers*, p. 272.
19. Quoted in Ibid., pp. 273 and 275.
20. After describing this incident, 'Abdu'l-Bahá remarks, "These things would take place before the reality of this Cause was revealed and all was made plain. For in those days no one knew that the Manifestation of the Báb would culminate in the Manifestation of the Blessed Beauty [Bahá'u'lláh] and that the law of retaliation would be done away with, and the foundation-principle of the Law of God would be this, that 'It is better for you to be killed than to kill'; that discord and contention would cease, and the rule of war and butchery would fall away. In those days, that sort of thing would happen." *Memorials of the Faithful*, pp. 198-99.
21. *Dawn-Breakers*, pp. 285-86. Táhirih's father remained convinced of her innocence as well as her chastity, but the accusations caused him untold grief. At one point, the prayer leader at the Friday mosque of Qazvín read a verse mocking Mullá Sálih: "No glory remains on that house / From which the hens crow like the cocks." Mullá Sálih was said to have remained silent, as tears ran down his face. Amanat, *Resurrection*, p. 322.
22. Bábís.
23. *Memorials of the Faithful*, p. 200.
24. *Dawn-Breakers*, p. 297.
25. Husám Nuqabá'i, *Táhirah: Qurrat al-'Ayn* (Tehran: Bahá'í Publishing Committee, 128 Badi'/1972) p. 60.
26. Shoghi Effendi, *God Passes By*, p. 32.

27. Ibid., pp. 32-33.
28. Bahá'u'lláh apparently proved instrumental in bringing about a reconciliation. His subsequent actions show that, while advocating a total break with Islam, He believed in nonviolent means for attaining that end.
29. Amanat, *Resurrection*, p. 328.
30. Ibid., p. 329.
31. *Dawn-Breakers*, p. 622.
32. Jakob Eduard Polak, *Persien: das Land und seine Bewohner* (Leipzig: F. A. Brockhaus, 1865) Vol. 1, p. 352.
33. Amanat, *Resurrection*, p. 329.
34. *Dawn-Breakers*, pp. 626-27.
35. Shoghi Effendi, *God Passes By*, p. 75.
36. Edward Granville Browne, *Materials for the Study of the Bábí Religion* (Cambridge: The University Press, 1918) p. 350.
37. Mohammad Ishaque, "Qurratu'l-'Ayn: A Bábí Martyr," *Four Eminent Poetesses of Iran* (Calcutta: Iran Society, 1950) p. 32.
38. Nuqabá'i, *Táhirah*, p. 157.
39. Where not otherwise stated, these rough translations, intended only to convey Táhirih's general meaning, were done by this author with the assistance of Farzad Nakhai.
40. Nuqabá'i, *Táhirah*, p. 152.
41. "Idol" is sometimes used poetically to refer to an object of extreme devotion.
42. Nuqabá'i, *Táhirah*, p. 154.
43. Ibid., p. 159.
44. Browne, *Materials*, pp. 348-49.
45. Táhirih is here suggesting that Islam, which survived the Mongols' invasions, has fallen before the Báb.
46. "Love and wine" are to be understood in the mystical sense.
47. Nuqabá'i, *Táhirah*, p. 152.
48. George Nathaniel Curzon, *Persia and the Persian Question* (London: Longmans, Green, 1892) Vol. 1, p. 497, n.2
49. Root, *Táhirih*, p. 112.
50. Shoghi Effendi, *God Passes By*, p. 76.
51. Edward Granville Browne, quoted in 'Abdu'l-Bahá, *A Traveller's Narrative: Written to Illustrate the Episode of the Báb*; trans. by Edward G. Browne (New York: Bahá'í Publishing Committee, 1930) p. 309.
52. Ghulamali Ismail Naji, *Zehra Bano*; translator, Raza Husain Baroywal (Karachi: Peermahomed Ebrahim Trust, 1973) pp. 100-101.
53. Among these are *Táhirih* by Clara Edge (Grand Rapids, Mich.: Edgeway Publisher, 1964), *From behind the Veil* by Kathleen Jemison Demas (Wilmette, Ill.: Bahá'í Publishing Trust, 1983), and a short story appearing in *World Order* entitled, "Thralls of Yearning Love" by Dimitrii Marianoff and Marzieh Gail (World Order [Wilmette, Ill.] Vol. 6, no. 4 [Summer 1972] pp. 7-42).
54. Judith Goldstein, "Interwoven Identities: Religious Communities in Yazd, Iran.," Ph.D. dissertation, Princeton University, 1975, p. 206.
55. Ibid., p. 227.

**A GIRL IN THE TRIBAL DRESS** of the Shah Savan, c. 1890. Women's clothing in tribal areas was quite different than that in the towns and cities.

# Ruptured Spaces and Effective Histories: The Unveiling of the Bábí Poetess Qurrat al-'Ayn-Táhirih in the Gardens of Badasht

by Negar Mottahedeh

> But if Goethe was right to assert that when we cultivate our virtues, we at the same time cultivate our faults, and if, as everyone knows, a hypertrophied virtue—such as the historical sense of our age appears to be—can ruin a nation just as effectively as a hypertrophied vice: then there can be no harm in indulging me for this once.
> —*Friedrich Nietzsche, On the Uses and the Disadvantages of History for Life*

> The French Revolution viewed itself as Rome reincarnate. It evoked ancient Rome the way fashion evokes costumes of the past.
> —*Walter Benjamin, Theses on the Philosophy of History*

The Bábí movement, established in 1844, in Persia by Siyyid 'Alí Muhammad, entitled the Báb (the Gate), is known as a messianic movement aimed at the transformation of a society conditioned by Twelver Shi'ism in a land governed by the corrupt despotic rule of the Qájár dynasty.[1] Persisting a mere decade, owing in part to an extensive and comprehensive persecution of its membership by the Shiah clergy and the Qájár despot's representatives, the movement affected a variety of sectors in Persian society. In contemporary historiography, the Bábí movement is, however, chiefly renowned for its egalitarianism and particularly for its impact on the status of women in Iran. This is perhaps because of the public visibility of one of the Bábí movement's female leaders, the poetess Qurrat al-'Ayn—Táhirih.

The vast majority of the Báb's early followers, including Qurrat al-'Ayn, were learned scholars in Shiah Islamic jurisprudence and the Islamic traditions. The Báb's followers, each in their own particular way, accepted his social and religious teachings and acknowledged his ultimate claim to be the return of the twelfth Imam—a figure important to the constitution of Twelver Shi'ism in Islam. After the Báb's cruel murder, most of the Bábís who survived the ensuing fierce attacks by the clergy and the government forces acknowledged the claims of the prophet-founder of the Bahá'í Faith—Bahá'u'lláh and recognized him as the successor of the Báb.[2]

The manner in which the term "Bábí" gained currency as a way to denote a peculiar kind of modernity in *common parlance* in late-nineteenth-century to early-twentieth-century Iran is no less worthy of note. For as derogatory as its resonances were, they seem to be imbedded, more often than not, within a context of sartorial innovation. The term "Bábí," was used as a stereotypic attachment to any gesture of resistance to traditional Shiah Islamic values. It was a simplification, of course, and like most stereotypes, an arrested and fixed type of representation that masqueraded in an untold carnival of images of foreignness, of modernist innovation, of nihilism, and of irreligiosity.[3] As such this stereotype was a memory in miniature constructed on the basis of events that took place at the specific time in Persian history in which the Bábí movement emerged, while simultaneously detached, reformulated, and recovered to illuminate other times and places. One may, along with historian Huchang Chehabi, speculate on the role played by the Bábí poetess Qurrat al-'Ayn's public unveiling at the Bábí conference in Badasht in the association between sartorial innovation and heresy.[4]

The Bábí conference in Badasht was held in the summer of 1848. Although significant in history as a moment that designates Babism's complete break with Islam, it has received little focused attention in contemporary Iranian historiography. This is perhaps due to the lack of consistent information on the specifics of the gathering.

One can relate this paucity of detail in the early renditions of the Badasht conference to the way in which some of the particulars of the proceedings were perceived by the conference participants. Significantly, to be sure, is the occasion of Qurrat al-'Ayn's unveiled appearance recorded in Nábil's Narrative as recollected by Shaykh Abú Turab. Female unveiling in the public sphere before the turn of the century in Iran was not only rare, but for a Shiah populace such as that assembled in Badasht, it was a gesture of relentless revolt. For that reason alone, perhaps, the act was perceived as unseemly for a comely woman who was venerated as an emblem of purity and infallibility among the followers of the Báb.

In this paper I will attempt to unpack the function of revolutions as forces that introduce discontinuity in history, problematizing thereby the writing of a comprehensive and continuous history. More specifically, I address the ways in which the Bábí revolt in Badasht introduced a rupture in Islamic history. Pried open by the unveiled appearance of Qurrat al-'Ayn in the public and male domain of the Badasht gardens, I will argue, the historical discourses on Islamic space are reconfigured and disarticulated, affecting the very heart of Islamic notions of selfhood and identity. By positioning the reading of this moment of unveiling on the problematic figure of Shaykh Abú Turab in Nábil's Narrative, I will discuss how the necessary configuration of human agency in an effective history reintroduces continuity into the historicity of revolt. In doing so, human agency problematizes the relation between the discontinuous character of revolutions and the "patient and continuous" development of history.

## Foucault, Genealogy, and Effective History

Writing in 1971, Michel Foucault elaborated his position on traditional historiographic practices in an homage to his mentor Jean Hyppolite in an essay called "Nietzsche, Genealogy, History." In formulating his thoughts about the direction of his own historiographic practice, Foucault refers to Nietzsche's conception of genealogy as an effective history. Drawing on Nietzsche's uses of the notion of origin, Foucault maintains that the foundation of any event depends not on a single originary gesture, but on a discontinuous multitude of events and attitudes for its emergence. History writing therefore must take a second look at the bedrock for its claims. For if events are not formed on the basis of continuous progress and development, historiography can in no way support its current practice which purports to be a dry affirmation of facts and figures, which merely recognize specific originary moments and mirror them so to enable mankind's rediscovery of a lost and uniform self.

> The traditional devices for constructing a comprehensive view of history and for retracing the past as a patient and continuous development must be systematically dismantled. Necessarily, we must dismiss those tendencies that encourage the consoling play of recognitions. Knowledge even under the banner of history, does not depend on "rediscovery," and it emphatically excludes the "rediscovery of ourselves." History becomes "effective" to the degree that it introduces discontinuity into our very being—as it divides our emotions, dramatizes our instincts, multiplies our body and sets it against itself. Effective history deprives the self of the reassuring stability of life and nature, and it will not permit itself to be transported by a voiceless obstinacy toward a millennial ending. It will uproot traditional foundations and relentlessly disrupt its pretended continuity. This is because knowledge is not made for understanding; it is made for cutting.[5]

The writing of history, then, must take on new forms. Forms that question in their very conception, notions of the unitary subject, that interrogate the affirmations of stability at the base of nature and culture, and that disrupt practices preoccupied with the tracing of uninterrupted progress in human history. An effective history must therefore question the unity of authorship and authority behind the formulation of cultural life, because it recognizes chance as the originator of intent. Effective history thereby cuts any notion of continuity at the heart of tradition.

Shaykh Abú Turab's recollections of the unveiled Bábí poetess Qurrat al-'Ayn's appearance in a garden in Badasht emerge as significant when measured in the balance of this historical force field. For in their very formulation, these recollections introduce a rupture within the traditional historical Islamic discourses on space—spatial discourses which purport to be the very foundation for Islamic notions of selfhood and identity.

It is precisely on the basis of Abú Turab's recollections that we can argue that the Bábí revolt at the Badasht Conference constituted an event which in Foucault's own formulations was neither "a decision," "a treaty," "a reign," or "a battle," but "the reversal of forces," "the usurpation of power," "the appropriation of a vocabulary turned against those who once used it," and ironically, "the entry of a masked 'other,'" into the realm of traditional history.⁶

## The Bábí Revolt in Badasht

The Bábí Conference in Badasht was held for three weeks between June and July of 1848. Quddús, one of the first people to join the Bábí movement and his companions (who were among the Conference's participants) had intended on raising the Black Standard in Mashhad.⁷ They were, however, forced out of the city of Mashhad due to heightened anti-Bábí fervor, and were wandering on horseback in the northeastern corner of Iran. Qurrat al-'Ayn and her companions, traveling from Tehran, were on their way to the region of Khurasan to join Quddús' forces and to ride under the Black Standard. They met the group of wandering Bábís en route on the Mazandaran-Khurasan road and from all accounts decided to change their destination. Despite the turn of events, the two groups joined and decided to rent three gardens in which they could contemplate their fate and review a range of questions regarding the identity of the movement and its future strategy.

The group's charismatic leader Siyyid 'Alí Muhammad—surnamed the Báb—had claimed (in 1844) to be "the Gate" to the Qá'im who would usher forth a new era in religious history. Due to his claim, which traditionally would imply the imminent relinquishment of power by both the Shiah clergy and the Qájár dynasty, the Báb was imprisoned by the authorities in a remote castle-prison in Azerbaijan. The prime agenda of this group of eighty-one Bábís, therefore, was the plight of the Báb. They were anxious to find a way to rescue him. Any effort in this direction, however, was contingent on a plan of future action. "Moderation and prudence in the face of mounting hostility, radical Bábís argued, could lead only to further suffering. Yet the final Insurrection against the forces of oppression would materialize only if the Qá'im made his advent unequivocally apparent."⁸This raised the question of the Báb's precise claim and the nature of his mission. Who was the Báb? Was he the Qá'im—the Messiah who they had been expecting for hundreds of years? Was his message a rejuvenation of the Islamic truth? Or did he intend to establish a new and independent religion? These pressing questions, unrelated to the question of loyalty to the Founder, were meant to establish the status of the movement and the identity of its participants.

Of the three gardens, one was assigned to the famous poetess and Bábí leader Qurrat al-'Ayn—surnamed Táhirih (the Pure One) at the Conference. The second was assigned to Quddús. A man later known by the title Bahá, who had rented the properties, reserved a third garden for himself.[9] The rest of the participants camped on the grounds surrounding these Bábí leaders.

The narratives and histories of the events differ slightly concerning the manner in which the events took place. Most agree on the following points: 1) that the poet/leader Qurrat al- 'Ayn appeared unveiled before the conference participants[10]; 2) that she argued for a definite break with the tradition of Islam; 3) that confusion and contention followed, leading to the denial of Faith on the part of several of the participants; and 4) that the gathering affected the further development of the movement and affected a radical change in the rituals and actions undertaken by its participants.

Qurrat al-'Ayn, the poetess, took on the leading role at the conference, arguing for a definitive break with the old Islamic traditions. Some sources maintain that Quddús rejected her as a radical and "the author of heresy." She, on the other hand, questioned Quddús' claims to leadership, having failed to raise the banner of Bábí revolt in Mashhad.[11] This radical split between the two leaders is claimed by most parties to have determined the dynamics of the Badasht Conference.

## Shaykh Abú Turab Recollects: Qurrat al-'Ayn's Unveiling

Shaykh Abú-Turab, who the Bábí historian Nábil introduces as the "best-informed as to the nature of the developments in Badasht," is reported to have related the following incidents:

> Illness, one day confined Bahá'u'lláh to His bed. Quddús, as soon as he heard of His indisposition, hastened to visit Him... The rest of the companions were gradually admitted to His presence and grouped themselves around Him. No sooner had they assembled than . . . the messenger of [Qurrat al-'Ayn] . . . suddenly came in and conveyed to Quddús a pressing invitation from [Qurrat al-'Ayn] to visit her in her own garden. "I have

severed myself entirely from her," he boldly and decisively replied. I refuse to meet her."

... [S]uddenly the figure of [Qurrat al-'Ayn], adorned and unveiled appeared before the eyes of the assembled companions. Consternation immediately seized the entire gathering. All stood aghast before this sudden and most unexpected apparition. To behold her face unveiled was to them inconceivable. Even to gaze at her shadow was a thing which they deemed improper, inasmuch as they regarded her as the incarnation of Fatimih, the noblest emblem of chastity in their eyes . . .

That sudden revelation seemed to have stunned their faculties. [One of the participants] was so gravely shaken that he cut his throat with his own hands. Covered with blood and shrieking with excitement, he fled away from the face of [Qurrat al-'Ayn]. A few, following his example, abandoned their companions and forsook their Faith . . .[12]

Historians fascinated by the sight of Qurrat al-'Ayn's unveiled appearance have either applauded this gesture as the originary moment of women's liberation in Iran or, in absolute disgust for this act of heresy, claimed this gesture to be the foundation for, as well as the fundamental proof of, the deserved ill repute and false motives of the Bábí movement. Seldom have they stayed in the garden to witness what Shaykh Abú Turab claims to have followed. Nábil's informant goes on to report that Qurrat al-'Ayn who had seated herself next to Quddús:

... rose from her seat and, undeterred by the tumult that she had raised in the hearts of her companions, began to address the remnant of the assembly. Without the least premeditation, and in language that bore striking resemblance to that of the Qur'an, she delivered her appeal with matchless eloquence and profound fervor. She concluded her address with this verse from the Qur'an: "Verily, amid gardens and rivers shall the pious dwell in the seat of truth, in the presence of the potent King."[13] ... Immediately after, she declared: "I am the Word which the Qá'im is to utter, the Word which shall put to flight the chiefs and nobles of the earth."[14]

The Shaykh's lucid recollection of the moment of Qurrat al-'Ayn's usurpation of power is unequaled in the annals of early Bábí historiography. Yet, before I go on to discuss the specific ways in which I think this recollection of the events at Badasht "cuts" (to paraphrase Foucault) our knowledge of Islamic history and disarms its notion of a unified subjectivity as well as its sense of historical continuity, I would like to briefly discuss the Islamic discourses on space and their effects on the historiography of the Islamic garden. For it is against these practices, I will argue, that Qurrat al-'Ayn's radical critique is aimed.

## Islam and Spatiality

It is said that in the early days of the religion of Islam the Prophet Muhammad used space and orientation as a way to establish the fundamental nature of Islam. He did this first to distinguish his newborn revelation from paganisms by aligning the new religion with other extant monotheistic religions. Every day he would turn in prayer towards Jerusalem—the Qibla of Judaism and Christianity. For the followers of the new religion, this corporal gesture became a sign of difference from the surrounding religious practices—affiliating, through the orientation of the body in space, the religion of Islam with the other two monotheistic religions. Then one day, it is said, his followers realized that he no longer was turning in that direction, but that he now was turning towards Mecca, changing the direction of his prayer in order to establish the unique and independent nature of Islam within the context of monotheism.[15] Spatiality thus gained relevance for the identity of the pious Muslim through these doctrinal and ritual practices of the body.

Spatial practices in most Islamic countries today function similarly to constitute a national and a personal identity. They are enforced as doctrines or laws to distinguish the realm of the public from the private. Spatial discourses directly superimpose the differential place of women and men upon this private/public split. These practices are significantly and hermeneutically linked to verse 53, of Sura 33, of the Qur'an on the issue of the *hijab*, which in Arabic literally means to hide something from sight, to separate or establish a threshold, or to forbid.[16] Thus linked, the verse of the *hijab* is construed as a prohibition that concerns space, and is more commonly associated with the practice of veiling.

Verse 53 of sura 33 of the Qur'an reads as follows:

> O ye who believe! Enter not the dwelling of the Prophet for a meal without waiting for the proper time, unless permission be granted you. But if ye are invited, enter, and, when your meal is ended, then disperse. Linger not for conversation. Lo! That would cause annoyance to the Prophet, and he

would be shy of (asking) you (to go); but Allah is not shy of the truth. And when ye ask of them (the wives of the Prophet) anything, ask it of them from behind a curtain. This is purer for your hearts and for their hearts.[17]

Traditionally, when the question of the relevance of a certain verse arises, Islamic scholars turn towards memory or recollection.[18] The *hadith* have constituted this memory for posterity, through the (re)collection of the various stories told by the associates and the family of the Prophet. Among the thousands of these hadith there is *one* significant story that relates to the Qur'anic verse on the question of veiling and which, according to the Moroccan feminist scholar Fatima Mernissi, gets lost in the shuffle. This misplacement, which should more relevantly be called "dissimulation" (because of the word's close association with the act of veiling), has instituted a rather skewed impression of the context of the verse, and suggested that the Prophet ordered the separation of the sexes with it.[19] The political and cultural context for the descent of the verse on the *hijab* as constituted by al-Bukhari's version of Anas's recollections of this incident would prove such a view far from the mark.

## The Prophet's Wedding Night: The Institution of the Veil

In his collection of hadiths, the historian Al-Bukhari writes that on the night when the Prophet celebrated his marriage to Zaynab, Muhammad became frustrated with his guests. The whole city of Medina had been invited to the celebrations and despite the show of impatience on the part of the Prophet, the guests would not leave. Finally, standing on the threshold of the wedding chamber, he recited the verse of the *hijab* (quoted above) while drawing a curtain between himself and his companion, Anas.[20] In effect this act of drawing the curtain not only separated the space between the sublime and the profane (the space between the Prophet and his disciples), but also the space *between two men*. This act and the verse of the *hijab*, situated above all the identity of the two men as separate and established a hierarchical division of power between the two through a spatial division.

In the period that followed, the verse revealed on the Prophet's wedding night became a handy tool for a confused community in civil war in Medina. The wedding of Zaynab and the Prophet took place during a period of instability in which the Prophet attempted to gain a foothold in Medina. The Muslims were constantly under attack by the surrounding community, and it was obvious that one of the most powerful ways to weaken an already unsettled community was through attacking the Muslim women. The verse of the *hijab* gave the Muslim community a solution to a whole network of problems.[21] The act of veiling was introduced into the Muslim community as a way to distinguish between the wives of the Prophet (to whom the Medinese were forced to show respect) and the female slaves.[22] Veiling, then, derived from the act of drawing the curtain *between two men*, was introduced into the Muslim community in Medina as a sign of hierarchical differentiation, *now between women*. In the midst of civil war, the wives of the Prophet adopted the veil to protect themselves from molestation and the community from vigilant attacks.

During this war, the streets of Medina (i.e., public space) became male space, and if women of higher status wanted to enter into this space, they were to do this on the condition that they pull a piece of clothing over their heads and bodies.[23]

Mernissi argues that the institution of this act in the Medinese period marked the beginning of women's repression in Islam—a religion which from its inception was an egalitarian community.[24] To agree with her on this point, one would have to disregard the more recent history of Muslim women, who in the struggle for independence in the Algerian War of Independence (1954-1962), and in the struggle against imperialism in Iran during the Islamic Revolution (1978-1979), chose to don the veil as a gesture of difference from the West. In other words, they chose to veil as a gesture that would position them against the perceived "repression" of colonial and imperialist power.[25]

So, rather than argue that the veil is essentially repressive on the one hand, or essentially liberating on other hand, I would suggest based on this reading of history, that the verse of the *hijab* revealed on the Prophet's wedding night entered into an apparatus of power and knowledge. It did so as a point of communal identity at a restless moment in Islamic history. The female body was construed as the focal point of this identity. As such, it was given the task of protecting Muslim communal identity by protecting its own. Islamic identity was thus constituted on a problematic rupture divided on this body's gendered split between nature and culture—and again on its historically hierarchized social divide—a body culturally constituted as vulnerable and perceived as naturally harmful.[26] Having entered into the apparatus of power and knowledge at this level, the verse of the *hijab* marked a problem for closure within Islamic discourses on space. Its fluctuations within the contending recollections/knowledges that surrounded it and the political discourses that activated it, further problematized the constitution of a unified and continuous Islamic identity, despite all efforts to construe it as otherwise. The veil as a representation of this fragmented identity came to function both positively and negatively within the dynamics of power. As a point of identity, it became an arena of constant struggle and domination for the future Muslim communities. It functioned therefore as a screen behind which the mysterious, the feared, the stereotypical and sexually potent Muslim female figure could lay dormant, always ready to erupt into the uncertain domain of the public.

Space and its gendered partitioning, as we have already observed, is fundamental in several ways to both the doctrine and the practice of Islam. Before we return to the discussion of its disarticulation in the gardens of Badasht, I would like to move our attention to a consideration of a particularly potent public space, which has for centuries fired the imagination of indigenous Muslim poets and geographers alike. This is the space of the garden.

## The Islamic Garden

We can imagine that in the context of the ecological conditions of the area "conquered" by Islamic thought, the garden could be seen as a way to ameliorate the often life-denying, arid, and monotonous conditions of the land. People of high and low economic status incorporated a life-sustaining oasis into their own properties, carefully sheltered away with a wall in order to (one can only assume) shut out the hustle-bustle and odors of the city. This is clearly depicted, even if we only cast a passing glance on the various collections of images that have been handed down through Mogul arts, and ancient Persian miniatures and carpets. It would seem, from a cursory study of the vegetal imagery introduced into the carpet tradition during the Abbasid period in Iran, that the garden was so greatly valued that it was important to construct a never-fading image of it onto a transportable medium such as the carpet. This would introduce the garden's verdant quality to interior spaces.

A brief study the life style and practices of the Iranian nobility, as depicted especially by the grand narratives of royal history and Iranian (mystical) poetry, may allow us to reach similar conclusions. We learn that gardens were always incorporated into the structures of dynastic residences for the pleasure and traditional rituals of the ruling class. These tales situate the royal garden as a site of romance and hedonistic pleasure, and as spaces where the king would hold court and celebrate his weddings. In allegories of the garden, the space of the garden represents and activates the dynast's dreams, desires, and nightmares. The garden not only enables his daily and ritual activities, it is an integral part of his physical and phantasmagoric realities.[27]

Traditional historiographic practice claims the garden's main function to be the spatial reflection of the Paradise of the Qur'an. Its structure in the form of the Persian Chahar Bagh, for example, is said to directly represent the Garden of paradise described by the Prophet Muhammad himself in this following verse:

> And besides these shall be two gardens,
> green green pastures,
> therein two fountains of gushing water
> therein fruits, and palm-trees and pomegranates
> therein maidens good and comely . . .
> houris, cloistered in cool pavilions . . .[28]

This description of Paradise is regularly interrupted by the refrain:

> O which of your Lord's bounties will you and you deny?

thereby giving room for detailed attempts to figure out a geography of Paradise in the form of two times two gardens, a quadrangular layout of many royal Persian gardens called the Chahar Bagh—"Four Gardens."

Echoing theocratic narratives, historians of the garden return to similar Qur'anic verses about Paradise as a source that unquestionably situates the origin and the homogenous nature of the Islamic garden for all time. Historians of the Islamic garden place the garden in the grand narrative of Muslim life and attribute its very structure and continuity to the authority of the Prophet.

What is sorely missing from these historical accounts is a sense of discontinuity and change that leaves open to further research the construal of a variety of other influences in the making of the material paradise on earth: considerations for irrigation and traditional horticultural practices are examples of these. Other considerations for instance for the ease of hunting, for aesthetics, and architecture may also be the reasons behind the garden's present form. What is denied in the traditional historical analyses of the Islamic garden, then, is an *analytics* of the social and historical contexts which may signal various sources of authorship and historical influence, not to mention deeply embedded pre-Islamic associations with the garden and its beauties, as external conditions for the emergence of such a discourse.[29]

## The Prophet's Wedding Chamber and the Gardens of Badasht

It is precisely against this kind of historiography that assumes a "suprahistorical" perspective and discourse that I have launched Shaykh Abú Turab's memory of the revolt in Badasht.[30] The event, or rather, the critical practice I attribute to it, presupposes four methodological principles identified by Michel Foucault in his 1970 inaugural lecture at the Collège de France "The Order of Discourse": the principle of reversal, wherein the origin, tradition and authority of the Islamic discourse on space is put into question; the principle of discontinuity, which recognizes the discontinuity of discursive practices on space, their crossing, juxtaposition, and exclusion; the principle of specificity which recognizes the violence of discourse done on things—here Islamic space; and finally, the principle of exteriority, which identifies the external conditions of possibility for such a discourse.

In my reading, Shaykh Abú Turab's recollections of the proceedings of the Badasht Conference are remarkable, because they situate, for the first time in close to twelve centuries, a female unveiled in Islamic public space. Beyond this, they are remarkable, because of the place that they claim that such an event took place, and finally because of the striking rhetoric that is associated with this provocative gesture in a garden.

Although twelve centuries apart, (al-Bukhari's version of) Anas's recollections of the event of the descent of the verse of the *hijab* on the threshold of the Prophet's wedding chamber and Shaykh

Abú Turab's recollections of the moment of Qurrat al- 'Ayn's unveiling in the gardens of Badasht have similar although inverse effects in their appropriation by traditional historical practice. Whereas in the case of the Prophet Muhammad, the rhetoric—that is the Qur'anic verse—is preserved in historical memory over and above the act of drawing a curtain between two men; in the case of Badasht, the act of a female's unveiled appearance, rather than Qurrat al-'Ayn's powerful address, is remembered.

In the case of one, the preservation of the word enabled the opportunity for men to regain control over the liberated woman folk of Mecca and Medina, while in the case of the other, the act of unveiling was seized as a figurative construct that would reinforce the Bábí discourse on equality.[31] Both of these historiographic practices, though dealing with events that are separated by many centuries, are examples of the ways in which discourse is a violence done to things. A critical stance against this kind of discursive violence is evident in Qurrat al-'Ayn's own rhetorical practices as recollected by Shaykh Abú Turab.

**The Order of Discourse**

If we consider the gestures and rhetorics that are said to have occurred at Badasht together as a co-determining whole, we are struck by the recognition and the awareness Qurrat al-'Ayn herself professed of the place in which she spoke, not only as a public space that is exclusively reserved as a male domain, but also as the space of the garden which for centuries had been associated with the space of the Islamic paradise. In sustaining this recognition, I will propose that the gesture of unveiling by Qurrat al-'Ayn signaled a critical analytics on two fronts and an acknowledgment of a violence done to space by discourse on two levels.

On the one hand we see that in the simple act of appropriating the Qur'anic verse, "Amongst gardens and rivers . . ." Qurrat al-'Ayn's speech acknowledged the structural imposition of the discourse of the Qur'anic Paradise on the space of the garden. On the other, her appearance unveiled in a traditional public domain questioned the imposition of Islamic territorial partitioning upon an otherwise undifferentiated public space. In both cases, she questioned the structural imposition of a so-called Islamic discourse on space.

Her use of Qur'anic language at once supported the authority of the Qur'an while simultaneously undoing its *meaning* through a specifically gendered mode of enunciation in the public sphere. She thus appropriated a vocabulary and "turned it against those who had once used it." In this act of appropriation, Qurrat al-'Ayn effectively resituated paradise and hell on earth. She did so by suggesting that those sitting in the garden, in that very tent, *were* the pious assembled before the potent King. In her speech and action, Qurrat al-'Ayn thus reintroduced human agency within the context of history and positioned authority and change within the realm of human activity. She questioned thereby the contiguous character of historical unfolding prefigured and guided by a Divine hand.

Qurrat al-'Ayn's address at Badasht questioned the homogenous unity established as the source of authorship of the Islamic garden and of the social division of space. In other words, her speech and her act of unveiling in the public domain reconfigured the disjunction between the doer and the deed—a disjunction which ironically presupposes a continuity between the Author of Islam and "his" work/people on earth. Put differently, whereas before it had been a given that it was Allah's will that Islamic space was to be divided by the believers into two territories, and that the garden should be divided into four, to reflect Qur'anic Paradise, Qurrat al-'Ayn's action and speech now clearly posited *human activity* as the external condition of possibility for spatial discourse in Islam. Human activity was the only party responsible for this determination.

Because of the imbrication of spatiality and veiling in Islam, one can additionally say that if she could unveil despite the so-called injunction to veil (exemplified by the appropriation of the Qur'anic verse), then others could appropriate the veil without that injunction in mind. Human activity alone could therefore be held responsible for the construal of a gendered space and the constitution and the authorship of the garden as the Qur'anic paradise.

Her act and her speech introduced a disjunction between the Islamic discourses on space, "cutting" them off from their assumed Qur'anic injunctions. Qurrat al-'Ayn thus situated the deed and doer within the same discursive matrix. In effect, her gesture and speech proposed the possibility of a reversal in the meaning of that space through the force of rhetorical and practical juxtaposition. The garden previously regarded as the space of paradisical and poetical musings, was thus redressed as a space of activity and resistance.

Her appearance unveiled in the public and gendered space of the garden also questioned the hierarchical structure imposed on the space of the garden as space of piety, as well as that of nobility. In questioning this hierarchical structure, Qurrat al-'Ayn claimed that her presence in the garden as the word spoken by the Qá'im would put to flight "the chiefs and nobles of the earth." Although physically unveiled, her speech re-veiled her (so to speak) as the Word spoken by the Qá'im himself, the charismatic leader who according to Shi'ite tradition was to abrogate the Islamic sharia (law) and establish the reign of a new era in religious and political history. Her gesture thus introduced a "foreign other" into the realm dominated by the rhetorics of authority and power formerly attributed to her sexual counterpart. As such she launched a frontal attack on (Islamic) hierarchical and otherworldly discourse, introducing human activity as the only basis for social progress.

In the days that followed this historical speech each of the participants at the conference took on a new name, thereby signaling their rebirth into a new era in time. Then, as if to acknowledge Qurrat al-'Ayn's gesture, the participants discarded their prayer rugs (which by design orient the pietistic body towards Mecca) and broke their prayer seals, equating them to idols, in a gesture not unlike Muhammad's when he, in the Holy City, tried to convey the definite break with an era of paganistic devotion by destroying the objects of idol worship. The space of Islam was confronted by a discourse of antagonism at the Badasht Conference, thereby creating the conditions for a new discourse on space and a new era in (religious) history.[32]

## Shaykh Abú Turab's Recollections

By positioning my own historiographic intervention (in the Islamic discourses on space) on Shaykh Abú Turab's recollections of the events that took place at the Badasht Conference, I have been able to reconstruct a consistent, continuous, and antagonistic portrait of a revolutionary movement that, through the gestures and words of one of its renowned female representatives, "introduced discontinuity into the life of the Islamic mind." In appropriating these recollections, I have been able to argue that the Bábí movement (read through the moment of its self-recognition in Badasht) was a revolutionary movement, that "cut" our knowledge of Islamic history, disarmed its notion of a unified subjectivity, and questioned its sense of historical continuity in the figure of the authorial Word of its Prophet. Ironically, this claim was only possible by the appropriation of an undivided subjectivity informed by Shaykh Abú Turab's recollections of Qurrat al-'Ayn.

For if we look at other accounts of Qurrat al-'Ayn, there is reason to believe that matters are not as straightforward as they seem. The British Orientalist Edward Browne's collections of various historical materials suggest that in one of his conversation with a well-known Bábí it was remarked that Qurrat al-'Ayn never intentionally took off the veil.[33] Browne comments that *if he can remember* the conversation correctly, this Bábí responded to the question of Qurrat al-'Ayn's discarding of the veil in the following words:

> It is not true that she laid aside the veil. Sometimes when carried away by her eloquence, she allowed it to slip down off her face, but she would always replace it after a few moments.[34]

## Nábil's Narrative, Agency, and Effective History

The positioning of my historiography of the Bábí revolt in Badasht on the recollections of Abú Turab is rather precarious in the context of Bábí history, since no one seems to elaborate on who Abú Turab is. Browne suggests that Abú Turab was one of the earliest disciples of the Báb and that he was married to one of Qurrat al-'Ayn's female students, a woman of "extraordinary virtue and piety."[35] Nábil, on the other hand, introduces Abú Turab as a Shaykhí who never really acknowledged the Báb's claims until much later in the Báb's career.[36] According to Nábil, he apparently died in the Tehran prison where he was held captive with some well known Bábí leaders including Bahá'u'lláh.[37] There appears to be no other reference to Abú Turab anywhere else.

To add more complexity to the matter, Abú Turab seemingly plays *the* most insignificant role in the grand, and at times grotesque, history of the Bábí movement as presented in Nábil's Narrative. He appears only four times in the more than seventy years of history narrated by Nábil. Once as the chronicler of the Badasht conference,[38] a second time as Qurrat al-'Ayn's bodyguard after the

Conference,[39] a third time as the harbinger of glad tidings at Shaykh Tabarsí,[40] and finally as a character witness against Haji Mírzá Karím Khán Kirmani in his recollections of Siyyid Kazím.[41]

It this the latter moment that I would like to pause and reflect on since here, once again, Abú Turab's unfailing recollections are drawn upon to elucidate a critical situation.[42] In Nábil's historiography, Abú Turab's recollection of Karím Khán is brought into the picture only paragraphs before Siyyid Kazím Rashti's death is characterized. This is obviously a moment that if not negotiated carefully would create a potential crisis for Babism's legitimacy as a religious movement.

Siyyid Kazím was known as the religious leader of the Shaykhí school, a heterodoxy of Shiah Islam situated in Karbala (Iraq). According to most accounts, the Báb's initial claim of Mahdihood were directed at Siyyid Kazím's students, many of whom accepted it after the teacher's death and became active participants in the movement.[43] Shaykh Abú Turab is claimed to be one of Siyyid Kazím's prominent students who late in the Báb's career accepted the latter's claim to Mahdihood. Qurrat al-'Ayn and Quddús were among other students who accepted this claim.

Siyyid Kazím had for years, according to most sources, taught the Return of the Twelfth Imam and prepared his students to investigate this claim were it to occur in their lifetime. In 1844, when the Báb proclaimed his mission a great many of Siyyid Kazím's students recognized this claim. In effect the Báb took on "the successorship" of the Shaykhí school after the teacher's death.

The positioning of Abú Turab's recollection in the context of Nábil's historiography becomes clear, if we consider the role played by the third party (Haji Mirza Karím Khán Kirmani) of this recollection in relation to the development of the Bábí movement. Karím Khán, another prominent student of Siyyid Kazím, left the Shaykhí school some years before the death of its leader (Siyyid Kazím) and established himself in Kirman where he started his own branch of the school (called the Kirmani school). Although familiar with the Báb's claims, Kirmani whole-heartedly rejected the Báb and was for years involved in the agitation of the remainder of Siyyid Kazím's students against the Báb and his followers.

Abú Turab's recollections, situated (in textual terms) only

moments before Siyyid Kazím's death in Nábil's Narrative give his words a highly charged task: to recall a moment in which Siyyid Kazím rejects his own student, Karím Khán. In Abú Turab's recollection of this conversation Siyyid Kazím is said to have referred to Karím Khán as one "accursed," whose doctrines are "heretical" and "atheistic" and "who has grievously erred in his judgment."[44] Abú Turab's recollection of this conversation with his own teacher can be read as a self-serving character assassination. But its strategic positioning at a crisis point in Nábil's historiography, clearly situates its contents in a historiographic place that rids the reader of any doubt as to the successorship of Siyyid Kazím before the historical crisis even occurs (in historiographic terms). For Nábil, Abú Turab's recollections situate the necessary continuity of his narrative of the Bábí movement's revolutionary history and its legitimacy.

But why is this important? What relevance does this textual positioning have for a revolutionary history that relentlessly posits human agency as the driving force of social progress, and that uses strategy in the face of chance to disrupt the foundations of Islamic thought through introducing discontinuity in history?

Abú Turab's character role, although infinitesimal in Nábil's narration of Babism revolutionary history, is played on a measured field of continuity and discontinuity. Abú Turab's recollections of Badasht in the Narrative launch an account of the movement's discontinuity with Islamic traditions and values, forcing a break between Islam and Babism in the figure of the Conference. Turab's recollections of Qurrat al-'Ayn's actions and words in Badasht, much like his portrayed role as her body guard after the Conference suture the necessary subjectivity that would then posit human agency and action up against the "scrambled" identity of Islam. His recollection thus situates a continuous subjectivity against the decrepit identity that is Islam's. (The Conference participant's collective appropriation of new names, we should note, is important in the configuration of this identity.) For Nábil, this still leaves the question of the movement's legitimacy unanswered.

In drawing on Abú Turab's recollections, Nábil situates the Bábí movement's legitimacy in Siyyid Kazím's rejection of his pupil Karím Khán. He does this more importantly before the teacher's death. Indeed, through this rejection (and almost fortuitously) he posits the Báb as the legitimate claimant to Siyyid Kazím's successorship. Thus he creates, through Abú Turab's memory, a continuity between the two schools of thought. Legitimacy is established in the face of every claim directed at the movement from it opponents.

The figure of Abú Turab must be seen as a problematic one then. Divided on the juncture between insignificance and infinite signification; split on the critical line dividing continuity and change; and called upon to bear witness to the movement's legitimacy and Qurrat al-'Ayn's illegitimate gesture, Abú Turab represents the figure of the Bábí movement as such. For as Fischer and Abedi remark, the Bábí movement as a revolutionary movement was a "mixture of progressive ideas and initiatives and reactionary theocratic ones," often encountered on a rhetorical level (at least) within the body of Islamic and especially Shiah heterodoxies.

If we are to rely to some extent on the implicit mirror that I have placed between the early days of the Islamic religion and the events at Badasht, it is clear that the historicity of revolt is not only in its innovations or, in Foucault's phraseology, in the introduction of "discontinuity" or "interruptions" in history. Revolts are, to a limited extent, moments that harken back, not only to establish their legitimacy, or to construe a unified subjectivity in the face of danger, but to animate the moments of the present with the life force of a distant and desirable past. As such, they constitute and activate moments of the past within the present moment of the everyday. This is an instance of Walter Benjamin's notion of *der Jugste Tag*—where the chronicler's most recent day is also and inevitably the messianic Day of Judgment.[45]

In this light, Edward Browne is not far from the mark when he notes that the Bábí movement was essentially Shiah in its *Weltanschauung* and that Bábí history was a reenactment of the idealized Shiah past.[46] Nonetheless, we can see within the fruit of this memory of an idealized past, the seed of "a dynamic future." Qurrat al-'Ayn's constitution of individual agency and human responsibility as the force that must by necessity be materialized into action can only be seen in this light in the context of religious history.

**Notes**
Originally published in *Bahá'í Library Online* at:
<http://bahai-library.org/articles/rupture.html> Many thanks to the *UCLA Journal of History* readers of the first draft whose extensive comments helped in the formula-

tion of this version of the essay. Also my deepest appreciation and thanks to Jacob Krauss without whose long distance faxes, encouragement and critiques, this paper wouldn't have taken shape.

1. Twelver Shiism is a derivation of Islam which distinguishes itself in the belief in the familial successorship of the Prophet Muhammad by Twelve Imams. The last of these successors is 'Abu'l-Qasim Muhammad who, according to the traditions, went into Occultation in 874 A.D., due to the hostility of the enemies of the Imam. The Hidden Imam has many titles including Mahdi, Sahib az-Zaman, Qa'im. His return is believed to mark the end of time and the reign of peace on earth
2. For a detailed account of the life and writings of Bahá'u'lláh, consult H. M. Balyuzi, Bahá'u'lláh, *The King of Glory* (Oxford: George Ronald, 1980).
3. The British Orientalist E. G. Browne's reflections on the clothes he had acquired for his travels from Yazd to Kerman in his travelogue dated 1887-1888, may suggest the possible relation and confusion of the "Bábí" term's stereotypic connotations. This anecdote relates a scene in which an abridged memory connected to the term "Babi" is recalled, illuminating the present moment of Browne's vogue: "I had arrayed myself in a new suit of clothes made by a Yezdi tailor, of white shawl-stuff, on the pattern of an English suit. These were cool, comfortable, and neat; and though they would probably have been regarded as somewhat eccentric in England, I reflected that no one at Yezd or Kirm would doubt that they were the ordinary summer attire of an English gentleman. Haji Safar [Browne's young Persian assistant], indeed, laughingly remarked that people would say I had turned Bábí (I suppose because early Bábís were wont to wear white raiment), but otherwise expressed the fullest approval." (Browne, *A Year Among the Persians* [Cambridge: The University Press, 1927] p. 452)

The term "Babi" in this anecdote is not only addressed to the eccentricity of the foreign other, but to the wearing of an extraordinary configuration of clothing, the color of which may connote an act of dissent. The anecdote represents not only what Browne as a British Orientalist associates with his suit, but fortuitously reveals an assumption about the Yazdi and Kirmani mind. Although Browne was extremely interested and driven to understand the Persians and moreover the Babis, he failed to grasp the historical connection (made by his travel companion) between what he was wearing and the perceived role of the Babi in innovating fashions in Iranian culture.

The unveiled Qajar princess, Taj al Saltanih's memoirs (1884-1914) situate the connotative values of the term "Babi" quite illustratively within the context of modern education, naturalism, and irreligiosity. Speaking of the effects of her education on the development of her mature identity she writes: "Right up to my eighteenth year, I had held beliefs taught to me by my nanny that the heavens were pulled by a chain in an angel's hand, or that when God's wrath was incurred, the sound of thunder came . . . As I progressed in my studies day by day, my irreligiosity grew until I was a complete naturalist myself. Since these ideas were new to me, I was eager to impart them to my mother, my relatives, and my children. As I would begin to talk, however, my mother would curse at me, 'You have turned Babi!' My relatives would invoke God's forgiveness and keep their distance, refusing to listen." (Taj al-Saltanah, *Crowning Anguish: Memoirs of a Persian Princess from the Harem to Modernity*, 1844-1914, ed. by Abbas Amanat, trans. by Anna Vanzan and Amin Nesati [Washington, D.C.: Mage Publishers, 1993] p. 309)

Taj's memoir as a whole constructs clear connections between her modern education, her unveiling, women's liberation, and her desire and respect for European ideals as encountered by her in various French literatures and philosophies. Yet in this brief anecdote set in the chamber of familiarity the term "Babi," and not "Imperialism," arises to suture the connection between her modern subjectivities and her alleged naturalism and irreligiosity.

Another literary reference to the derogatory term "Babi" is found in a short story by Rasul Parvizi which humorously relates the effects of the panoptic enforcement of modern clothing policies under the Reza Shah (1925-1941) in the young man's home town of Shiraz. As is well known, the Pahlavi monarch Reza Shah's legacy in Iranian history falls within the realm of modernization in his enforcement of European clothing and the forced injunction to the unveiling of Iranian women in the late 1930s and early 1940s. Houchang Chehabi sketches this "progressive move" from the institution of the Pahlavi hat (similar to the French kepi) as the official hat for all Iranian men in 1927, to the decree in 1935 that established the chapeaux in an effort to construe an Iranian Westernization. (Houchang Chehabi, "Staging the Emperor's New Clothes: Dress Codes and Nation Building under Reza Shah," *Iranian Studies* [Los Angeles], Vol. 26 [Fall 1993] pp. 212, 215) Chehabi notes the violent reproach by the general populace towards these new policies which reluctantly moved them from a complex diversity of cultural practices in clothing towards the mobilization of a national front through the forced uniformity of dress. This done, the institution of new policies in the 1930s, and especially the injunction to unveil, introduced "the people" into an international system of clothing and etiquettes that would ultimately distinguish them from others in bordering countries.

The panoptic enforcement of the rules of clothing through the active engagement of the police force, the school system, the traffic comptrollers, and even undercover agents in bathhouses to monitor compliance, especially with respect to the rule to appear unveiled in public places, strikes one as almost surreal. The general reaction towards this totalized foreign mimicry enforced by the disciplinary institutions of the state resonates in the young Shirazi's chant, in Rasoul Parvizi's story, as he walks around town knocking off people's Pahlavi hats and ripping them to pieces:

> We don't want a blue hanky,
> We don't want a Babi guv'nor,
> We don't want a foreign hat.
> (Chehabi, "New Clothes," p. 230)

The survival of the stereotype "Babi" in this piece of prose, three quarters of a century after the collapse of the Babi movement, is remarkably linked not only to the enforced introduction of foreign values and internationalism, but to a variety of associations with a change of clothing.

The stereotypical denotation "Babi" as a memory in miniature in these brief anecdotes ambivalently joins the two poles of outside appearance and personal identity—the traditional realms of the *zaher* and the *baten* in the ordinary and everyday speech of the Iranian people: "You have turned Babi!" Remarkably, it conflicts with the official attempts to dissociate the two realms during the reign of Reza Shah whose counter-imposition of the veil on prostitutes was meant to prevent "the association of unveiling with unwholesome mores." Chehabi remarks that despite the efforts to elucidate the intentions of the policy, "traditional Iranians saw it as an attempt to turn a virtue into a vice." (Chehabi, "New Clothes," p. 219)
4. Chehabi, "New Clothes," p. 210.
5. Michel Foucault, "Nietzsche, Genealogy, History," in *Foucault Reader*, ed. by Paul Rabinow (New York: Pantheon, 1984) p. 88.
6. Ibid.
7. In July 1848, the Bábí leader of this upspring, Mulla Husayn Bushrui, the first disciple of the Báb, raised the Black Standard in Mashhad and set off westward. The implications of this gesture for the government and the religious hierarchy alike were obvious. In Shiah Islam, there is a well-known tradition attributed to the Prophet that suggests, that should one see the Black Standard coming from Khurasan, then one should go to it. The Mahdi, the religious leader who went into hiding in the early days of Islam according to this Tradition, will be there.

More importantly, however, the raising of the Black Standard in Khurasan was an act imbued with historical and contra-dynastic significance. The raising of the Black Standard is historically known as the gesture that inaugurated the final overthrow of the Umayyad dynasty by the Abbasids. This symbolic act not only signaled an impending attack on the existing religious order by the coming of the Mahdi, but posed a definitive threat for the existing dynasty. Although, ironically, the importance of this challenge got buried under the confusion of the government caused by the death of Muhammad Shah, the populace of Barfurush en route confronted the Bábís traveling under Mulla Husayn's banner, forcing them to take up positions around the Shrine of Shaykh Tabarsi. The conflict between the two groups lasted from mid-October 1848 to early May 1849.
8. Abbas Amanat, *Resurrection and Renewal: The Making of the Babi Movement in Iran* 1844-1850 (Ithaca: Cornell University Press, 1989) p. 325.
9. Bahá (or Bahá'u'lláh) would in 1863 establish the Bahá'í Faith.
10. Some of these sources use very vague language that could allow for an interpretation of her action as the gesture of physical unveiling, or of the unveiling the truth of a matter, or of the unveiling one's true intentions or opinions, thus making the issue somewhat more ambiguous.
11. Amanat, *Resurrection and Renewal*, p. 326.
12. Nabíl-i-A'zam, The Dawn-Breakers: *Nabil's Narrative of the Early Days of the Bahá'í Revelation*; translated and edited by Shoghi Effendi (Wilmette, Ill.: Bahá'í Publishing Trust, 1932) pp. 293-95

13. "The object of the conference was to correct a widespread misunderstanding. There were many who thought that the new leader came, in the most literal sense to fulfill the Islamic Law . . . [Qurrat al- 'Ayn] had her own characteristic solution to the problem . . . It is said . . . that [Qurrat al- 'Ayn] herself attended the conference with a veil on. If so, she lost no time in discarding it, and broke out into the fervid exclamation, 'I am the blast of the trumpet, I am the call of the bugle,' i.e. 'Like Gabriel, I would awaken sleeping souls.' It is said, too, that this short speech of the brave woman was followed by the recitation by Baha'u'llah of the Surih of the Resurrection. Such recitations often have an overpowering effect. The inner meaning of this was that mankind was about to pass into a new cosmic cycle, for which a new set of laws and customs would be indispensable." (T.K. Cheyne, *The Reconciliation of Races and Religions* [London: A. & C. Black, 1914] p.103)
14. Nabíl-i-A'zam, *The Dawn-Breakers*, pp. 295-96.
15. Fatima Mernissi, *The Veil and the Male Elite: A Feminist Interpretation of Women's Rights in Islam; trans.* Mary Jo Lakeland (Reading, Mass.: Addison Weslley, 1991) pp. 65-70.
16. Ibid., p. 93.
17. Ibid., p. 85.
18. This practices situates a significant difference between Western perceptions of stories and memories, where often times the latter are considered mere fables and thus disabling in an effort to constitute Truth and Knowledge.
19. For other references to hadiths related to this verse, consult Leila Ahmed's *Women and Gender in Islam: Historical Roots of a Modern Debate* (New Haven: Yale University Press, 1992) chapter 3.
20. Mernissi, *The Veil and the Male Elite*, p. 100.
21. Ibid., p. 92.
22. Ahmed suggests other circumstances for the institution of the veil, drawing from Ibn Sa'd's (re)collections. See Leila Ahmed, *Women and Gender in Islam*, p. 54.
23. In this particular context I am referring to the Prophet's wives, since his wives were the only ones that came along on the expedition.
24. Fatima Mernissi suggests this event as a symbolic expression of "regression on sexual equality" commingled with a "regression in social equality," but the coincidental imagery of the descent of the hijab over all women for the "fifteen centuries that followed" in this paragraph and her subsequent discussions strongly suggests the above reading (pp. 178-79).
25. See Fanon's discussion of the veil: "Algeria Unveiled" in Franz Fanon, *A Dying Colonialism*; trans. by Haakon Chevalier (New York: Grove Press, 1967) and Faegheh Shirazi-Mahajan's discussion of the role of the veil in the Iranian Islamic revolution in, "The Politics of Clothing in the Middle East: The Case of Hijab in Post-Revolutionary Iran," *in Critique: Critical Middle Eastern Studies* (Abingdon, Eng.), no. 2 (Spring 1993) pp. 54-63.
26. We have come to learn that sexuality, in the context of Islam, is territorial (Fatima Mernissi, *Beyond the Veil*, p. 81). Sexuality is mapped, as it were, unto the specific topology of the public and the private. In this context, female veiling is formulated as a way to ensure the purity of the public

sphere, generally designated as male, and the protection of the female, in the same context, through a gesture of dissimulation. As such, this construction permits the definition of female identity, in this context, as split. On the one hand, in the context of the perception of her natural constitution, the female is seen as a distraction, an invasion or intervention to the male's formulation of his identity as pious or divine. Her presence as a "natural"/sexual being in the public sphere, in other words, interferes with the Muslim man's relation with his God. On the other hand, in the context of her cultural status in Muslim history and as the embodiment of the community's identity as such, the female is seen as weak—indeed, in need of protection in the male domain. The veil thus covers over her constitutional split, creating a unified or whole subject that is both dangerous by nature and incapable of defending herself or the Muslim community's identity within the social domain. Without the veil, this dual and dangerous quality is thought to come to the fore, unveiling a "scrambled" identity, dangerous and mutilated.

27. This reading stems from Nezami Ganjavi, *The Haft Paikar* (The Seven Beauties); trans. C. E. Wilson, 2 vols. (London : A. Probsthain, 1924). But also see Julie Scott Meisami's essay "Allegorical Gardens in the Persian poetic tradition: Nezami, Rumi, Hafez," in *International Journal of Middle Eastern Studies* (London), Vol. 17 (1985) pp. 229-60.
28. From the Qur'an 55:46-75.
29. As noted by G. Marçias in the Encyclopedia of Islam, "Persian horticulture flourished long before the birth of Islam and was associated with princely life," from "Bustan," *Encyclopedia of Islam*; ed. J. H. Krammers, et al., new ed. (Leiden: Brill, 1960).
30. Friedrich Nietzsche in his *Untimely Meditations*, ed. by Daniel Breazeale; trans. by R. J. Hollingdale ( Cambridge University Press, 1997) uses the term "suprahistorical" to reject a history that perceives the present as the end of time and the events of the past as a history which has completed its development. This traditional conception of history is supported by the idea of an external controlling force, of an eternal truth, of a continuous and uniform identity that is always conscious of and identical to itself.
31. This forgetting on the part of Bábí historiography constituted the foundation for the appropriation of that discourse for future feminist purposes. Consult, for example, the section on Táhirih Qurrat al 'Ayn in Farzaneh Milani's *Veils and Words: The Emerging Voices of Iranian Women Writers* (Syracuse University Press, 1992, pp. 77-99, and reprinted in this volume) where Qurrat al-'Ayn is placed as the first in the line of liberated/liberating women's voices in Iran. Also see Abbas Amanat in his introduction to *Taj al- Saltanah, Crowning Anguish*, p. 59, where he places her within a similar trajectory. Amanat also rejects these views in an earlier book *Resurrection and Renewal*, p. 330. (It is interesting to note how, in an effort to remain objective, historians often forget what they have already said differently.) Also for a delightfully utopic and early account of the coincidence between Qurrat al-'Ayn's "originary" gestures and the concomitant development of the women's movement in the West, see Martha Root's *Táhirih the Pure*, 2nd ed. (Los Angeles: Kalimát Press, 1981).

32. Amanat, *Resurrection and Renewal*, p. 327.
33. This statement may of course be understood in terms of the way in which the notion of female unveiling is conceptualized in Islamic ideology. Unveiling has at different times and spaces been understood as a gesture of female nudity. Its citation therefore is incriminating to the woman and to the pious in Islam. According to Amanat's assertions, many sources claim that Qurrat al-'Ayn did indeed unveil in public. Most say, however, that she only did so in the gathering of "believers." And while most sources agree that she never unveiled publicly before the Badasht conference, others even doubt that she did so on that occasion. (Amanat, *Resurrection and Renewal*, pp. 295-316). A double disavowal takes place in the reconfiguration of these various narratives, wherein firstly none but the "believers" are incriminated by this public violation; and secondly, no one is whatsoever.
34. Edward G. Browne in 'Abdu'l-Bahá, *A Traveller's Narrative: Written to Illustrate the Episode of the Báb*, 2nd ed. (Amsterdam: Philo Press, 1975) p. 314.
35. Ibid., p. 247.
36. A Shaykhí is a student of the Shaykhí school, a heresy of Shiah Islam established in the middle of the nineteenth century in Karbala, Iraq. This is a school from which the Báb drew many of his early adherents.
37. Nabíl-i-A'zam, *The Dawn-Breakers*, p. 30 .
38. Ibid., p. 211.
39. Ibid., p. 216.
40. Ibid pp. 29-31. For a discussion of the Shaykh Tabarsí uprisrings, also known as the Mazandaran upheavals, see Moojan Momen "The Social Basis of the Babi Upheavals in Iran: A Preliminary Analysis," in *International Journal of Middle Eastern Studies*, Vol. 15 (1983) pp. 157-83.
41. Nabíl-i-A'zam, *The Dawn-Breakers*, pp. 29-31 .
42. Ibid.
43. For a more detailed account of the movement and its history, see Mangol Bayat, *Mysticism and Dissent: Socioreligious Thought in Qajar Iran* (Syracuse University Press, 1982).
44. Nabíl-i-A'zam, *The Dawn-Breakers*, p. 29 .
45. For an excellent discussion of Benjamin's Jetztzeit, see Ian Balfour's "Reversal Quotation (Benjamin's History)," MLN , Vol. 106 (1991) pp. 622-45.
46. Edward Granville Browne, *Literary History of Persia: Modern Times* (1500-1924) (Cambridge: The University Press, 1924) Vol. 4, p. 197.

**RUSSIAN ACTRESS AS TÁHIRIH**
Nadezhda Nikolaevna Muzil-Borozdinaas in costume for the play *Bab* that was successfully produced in St. Petersberg, 1904, before being banned by the censors

# Táhirih on the Russian Stage

by Jan Teofil Jasion

St. Petersburg, Russia–23 January 1904—The Literary Artistic Theatre. At 7:30 in the evening, a spectacle was presented from the fabled Orient. It was advertised as a being taken from Persian history. It presented the audiences with a glimpse of Persian life—salons with rich carpets and cushions, street life with its vendors, hawkers and turbaned inhabitants, oriental music and dances. The play *Báb*[1] played to a packed audience. It was the most extraordinary play of the season. The stage design, the colorful costumes, the native dances and music, and above all the very uplifting moral and ethical message that touched everybody's inner being. After every act, and there where five of them, the audience stood and applauded and called out the author and showered her with flowers at the end. The papers were filled with reviews, even before the staging, when the book first appeared six or seven months earlier. Many of the reviews published in 1903, stated that the play must be staged, for its effect on the whole of society would be uplifting. The reviews of the play were very positive. Of course, they criticized minor points in the performance or in the script or its deviation from history, but overall the press was enthusiastic.

The roles of the Báb and Táhirih were very well played, they all stated. Even photographs from the play appeared in some of the newspapers. The play so successfully portrayed its message of peace, love, tolerance, and the brotherhood of all people that, after four performances, it received a five-year ban from the Czar's censor.

The author of the play was Izabella Arkadev'na Grinevskaia (1852-1942), a Polish-born writer who lived in St. Petersburg and wrote in Russian. We do not know when Izabella Grinevskaia first heard of Táhira or of the Báb. Perhaps it was from Ivan S. Turgenev (1818-1883), the Russian novelist and dramatist. Benjamin Jowett (1817-1893), professor of Greek at Oxford, related that he often heard Turgenev speak about the Báb. We know from Grinevskaia, that she wrote an essay on her personal impressions of Turgenev, which was published in *Teatr i Iskusstvo*.

Her interest in the Middle East, and especially in the region of the Caucasus, must have begun sometime in the 1890s, or maybe even earlier. She wrote several poems on Oriental themes, versified songs from the Persian; she even learned Georgian and Armenian, to the point where she could translate poems of some of the more famous poets. Her interest continued all her life. As late as 1925, she was asked to declaim a poem by a famous Georgian writer at one of the academic societies.

Her other important works touching on the Orient included, besides the play *Báb*, the play *Bekha Ullah*, a lengthy essay on Russian studies, and publications on the Bábí and Bahá'í Faiths which were published twenty-years after her passing in Asuncion, Paraguay. The other literary works which she wrote included plays, essays, poems, monologues, and translations. As a translator, she translated into Russian from Polish, German, French, Italian, English, Armenian, and Georgian. She taught at a drama school connected with a theatre. She also lectured for ten years in philosophy in St. Petersburg.

It was about 1900 that she began to write the play *Bab*. By this time, there was a large body of published research on both the Báb and Bahá'u'lláh in Russia. In fact, the first book on the history of the Báb in a Western language was published in Russian in 1865, by Aleksandr Kazem-Bek (1802-1870), a professor of Oriental studies at St. Petersburg. He was followed by others, such as Viktor Romanovich Rozen (1849-1908), Jean-Albert-Bernard Dorn (1885-1881), Aleksandr Grigor'evich Tumanskii (d. 1920), Valentin Alekseevich Zhukovskii (1858-1918), and Georgii Batiushkov. Their research was greatly facilitated by the cooperation of various Russian officials at diplomatic missions in the Middle East, who gathered not only information but also manuscripts. In his epic survey of Western accounts of the Bahá'í Faith, Moojan Momen states that "Georgy Batyushkov, who was Russian Con.-Gen. in Beirut and traveled in Persia, wrote with the help of [Ivan G.] Grigorovich an article entitled 'Babidy: Persidskaya Sekta.' He also collected a copy of the *Kitábu'l-Aqdas* and a manuscript of Táhirih's works for the Asiatic Museum."[2]

The play was produced by Aleksei Sergeevich Suvorin (1834-1912), the editor of a publishing empire centered on the newspaper *Novoe Vremia* and owner of the Literary-Artistic Theatre. The director was Evtikhii Pavlovich Karpov (1857-1926). He later successfully produced Checkhov's *Cherry Orchard*. Iakov Sergeevich Tinskii (1862-1922) played the role of the Báb and Nadezhda Nikolaevna Muzhi'l-Borozdina played Tahirih, or Khuret as she is known in the play. Muzhi'l-Borozdina was a member of the theatre company and would act in other plays by Grinevskaia, namely *Renessans* in 1908, and *Shuty* in 1909. This was a large production, the script called for eighty-one actors, plus musicians and dancers. The scenes take place in Shiraz and Tabriz, and in the country near Persipolis. A review written by Aleksandr Alekseevich Izmailov (1873-1921) (writing under the pseudonym of Smolenskii) and published in the newspaper *Birzheviia vedomosti* is typical of many and is worth quoting since it provides us with a short pen sketch of the play:

> From town to town, he was expelled because his speeches were like "manna from heaven"—and then they judged and tried him. Thus in three verses is the essence of the history of the Báb, Al-Muhammad, the head of the renowned Persian sect of the Bábís, the history of which inspired Mrs. Grinevskaya to write this dramatic poem.
>
> This is an extremely interesting, full, and deeply tragic play. Persia—far-flung skies and distant customs and ways. It seemed that such a faraway country would be unable to interest a Russian audience in such a theme. But there are people and histories of universal character. And the history of the Báb is one of these. It can stir and move a Russian as well as a Persian. It is almost strange that in our literature no one has come to write about such a wonderful, true-to-life tragedy. Obviously, it required from the author very significant work and study of the material. Obviously, it required great effort in its production. If all this work and effort had not been met with the sympathetic appreciation of the audience, it would have been pitiful. But appreciation was full and complete: Beginning the evalu-

ation of the success—the theatre was full to overflowing, though the prices were raised. The audience began calling out the author after the first act and continued doing so after every act, right up to the end of the performance, when they covered the author with flowers. Obviously, the audience greatly appreciated this consistent, stylistic play. Performers were also called out; in short, there were all the signs of success.

It is hardly necessary to relate the history of the Báb. It has entered all the encyclopedias. The author followed the history and made use of all the effective moments in the life of Ali. In front of viewers passed the romantic incident of the daughter of the mujtahid, Khuret, with her idealistic love for the courageous reformer; pictures of teaching of multitudes by the Báb; the struggle of his followers with the representatives of formalistic, bureaucratic orthodoxy; the trial of Ali and his followers and their incarceration, resulting in their execution.

Some of the scenes are extremely effective, beautiful, and imbued with national coloring. The beautiful, bored maid Khuret, in her father's house, esteemed and in luxury, spends her time watching beautiful slaves dance and sing in their colorful attire.

A square in Shiraz, full of people, is seething with life, wonderfully picturesque and lively,—a motley gathering of people; guttural cries of vendors and the sound of the call-to-prayer by the muezzin. A powerful mood of expectation is built up at the moment of Ali's entrance, when suddenly everyone is silent and alert in an atmosphere of prayerful, reverent expectation of he who was the talk of Shiraz.

Equally effective was the scene of the religiously performed wedding of Ali and Khuret; the vow of fidelity by the Bábís in the pale light of the moon; the Báb's torment in the dungeon and his last tender talk with his beloved bride-wife; finally his answers to the judges before his sentence of death. As living pictures, Persian life passes before the viewers. The smallest detail of the artistic production is sustained with excellence. Teasing the eyes are the brazenly bright costumes of the performers. Artistic new scenery was created by the artist S. N. Vorobyev. The author and the performers have grasped its significance. The producer, director, and scenery designer-artist also ought to be mentioned here—give them their due. The abundance of damatic moments in the play and the introduction into it of singing, music, and dancing suggests that it would make wonderful material for an opera. The plot of this dramatic poem and its obvious high style seem to confirm this idea.

The play of Mrs. I. A. Grinevskaya was imbued with noble idealism. It was written in a complete rhythmical verse, but regrettably often diffuse and verbose. Generally, the performance would have gained had it been shortened in some parts. Even with all the sympathetic understanding of the Báb's idealistic speeches, it was sometimes wearisome to listen to his enormous monologues. Very likely these abridgements will be made in future performances and will eliminate the necessity of starting the performance a half hour earlier.

Mr. Tinsky portrays a handsome Ali in outward appearance, with full, manly, and inspired beauty. A force of genuine idealism, strength of purity, and conviction emanate from his personality and his speeches. His pathos is reserved and without exaggeration. One can easily understand why multitudes follow him and even give their lives for him. Beautiful was Mrs. Muzil-Borozdina—"the light of the eyes" and the daughter of mujtahid Salih. But into the portrayal of idealism and spirituality of this outstanding daughter of Persia, something seemed to creep in her voice, something of a trivial note, and occasionally the manner of common ingénue, which clashed with the general high tone of the play.

From among the other performers, the following stood out: Mrs. Korsak, Messrs. Bastunov, Khvorostav, and Sudbanin. Mr. Charnov performed rather well in the role of the judge—Haji Bakir. General casting and faultless knowledge of their parts, on the part of all the performers, made good impression.

Plenty of flowers were given to Mrs. Muzil-Borozdina and to the author. Curtain calls were noisy and prolonged.[3]

Grinevskaia herself states that she purposefully deviated from true historical facts in order to make the play more acceptable to a Russian audience which was unfamiliar with the history of the new religion or with Islamic tradition. Therefore, in the play, Tahirih not only meets the Báb but falls in love with him.

Here are two of her speeches, the first to her father, and the second to the Báb:

> My father, listen, Ali has wealth untold;
> Richer is he than many kings of might,
> He doth but speak, and I am garbed in light,
> My dwelling place is burnished o'er with gold.
> There is no Shah can bring such a dower,
> Much may we give, yet his be not the debt,
> Each word he uttereth is fraught with power
> And sparkles like a diamond richly set.
> Before the splendor of his speech, the sky,
> Spreading yon starry canopy o'er Shiraz, pales.
> Are we enhanced by our jeweled veils?
> Upon our husbands' merits we rely

> And they adorn us. Now am I afraid
> To grasp a beggar's staff. In Ali's heart
> No bitterness, nor malice, hath a part
> Low minds alone by evil thoughts are swayed.[4]

Then there is a speech by Khouret addressed to Ali (i.e., the Báb):

> Before thee do I stand, bereft of voice,
> Thy speech doth sound as from another sphere,
> Dumb am I, Ali, when thy voice I hear!
> Ali, my bridegroom, husband of my choice
> And sovereign of my will—that will, I lay
> Into thy hands! As God, as God alone Thou guidest me.
> And thou shalt point the way
> To my desire. All that I am I own
> Is thine, forever thine: each thought, each breath,
> Ali husband and lord, is thine till death.
> I would speak in the tempests roar
> Yet be held in thy silent thrall!
> As a mighty cloud I would soar
> But for thee like the dew to fall.
> As the birds of the air were I free
> Thy chains, beloved were more sweet
> And were I a Queen—I would be
> A slave at thy feet.[5]

These speeches bear some similarity to the poems of Táhirih. Perhaps this indicates that Grinevskaia had access to the manuscripts of Táhirih's writings that were in St. Petersburg or she had access to the works of the British Orientalist Edward Granville Browne. The nobility of the personages of the Báb and Tahirih were very well depicted.

Unfortunately, the play had a very short run. Four more performances were held on 26 and 30 of January, 22 February, and 12 March. Then the censor put a five-year ban on its production. The reasons are not clear; perhaps, as Grinevskaia herself states, it was too "pacifist" for the times. The Russo-Japanese War had just broken out. However, there was praise for the play coming from a meeting held at the office of the censor.[6] The actions of the censor's office seem to have been irrational. They permitted the play to be published as a book, and reviews about the book as well were permitted. The play was permitted to be staged, advertisements announcing the staging of the play were widely decimated in the press. Then "they" placed a ban on the play after a very successful but short run.

Nonetheless, "they" permitted reviews, even lengthy reviews, of the stage production to appear even months afterwards—some even with photographs. Boleslav Viktorovich Grodzkii (1865-?) was able to take a poem out of the play *Bab* and set it to music; the *Pesnia Assady* (Assad's song) was published in 1904.[7] It seems that the ban on the play was limited to St. Petersburg, since it was reported that in December it was successfully staged in Astrakhan.[8]

But then the whole nature of censorship is irrational and schizophrenic. What happened to Grinevskaia's work was typical of most writers in Russia. Of her interactions with the office of the censor, she stated:

> There was no censorship hindrance when publishing my works, but when they were staged, I had a lot of difficulties of this sort. For example, in the play that I translated, "Druzia," that was in the Mikhailovsky Theatre, I had to exclude a few passages. First the censors did not allow shouts that were supposed to be done by the seller of the newspaper *Svoboda* [Freedom] (in the play). At that time this word was considered unquotable, but I managed to defend it, as well as some dogmas of co-operative associations.
>
> These words and phrases were so new in those recent times that publishers found this drama, in which elections, cooperative associations, and discussions about "freedom" were featured, very alien. I had to fight for both "Bab" and *"Surovye dni"* [Severe days][9] to be staged. The censorship would always concede to well-grounded arguments and did not at all act as if it necessarily "forbids" everything[10]

In 1917, a second edition was published and it was staged at the People's Theatre in Petrograd (formerly St. Petersburg). The actress who played Táhirih was Truze. It too was warmly received.

The play was later translated into German by Feodor Fedorovich Fidler [German: Friedrich Fedor Fiedler] (1859-1917), into French by Nina Halpérine-Kaminsky (d. 1925/26), and into Tartar by an unnamed poet. But it was neither published nor staged in any of these languages. The last performance of the play for which this author has any information was in 1922, in Ashkhabad under the direction of Orlov. This is how 'Alí-Akbar Furútan, (1905-2003), a Persian teacher living in Russia, remembers this performance:

> In 1922, a group of well-known Russian actors came to 'Ishqabad to perform in the famous Gigant Theatre of that city. The director of this group, also a famous actor, was a certain Orlov whose wife was an established actress. On the suggestion of a number of Bahá'ís, this group decided to

stage Isabel Grinevskaya's poetic drama *The Bab*, and with financial assistance from some of the Bahá'ís and many rehearsals, the play was prepared. On the night of the performance, a large audience of Bahá'ís and non-Bahá'ís gathered in the theatre, but at the climax of the play when interest was at its highest, the theatre was suddenly enveloped in darkness. Fortunately, the interruption did not last long, and after a few minutes the electricity was restored. It was later found that a few unsympathetic individuals had cut the main power cables on the street to express their hostility in this way. The play, however, continued and was most favorably received.[11]

**Notes**
Based on a forthcoming biography: *The Literary Steps of Izabella Arkadev'na Grinevskaia, 1854-1944*.

1. Izabella Arkadev'na Grinevskaia. *Bab. Dramaticheskaia poema iz istorii Persii v 5-ti deistviiakh i 6-ti kartinakh*. (The Báb. Dramatic poem from the history of Persia in 5 acts and 6 scenes) (St. Petersburg: T-vo Khudozhestvennoi pechati, 1903) p. 148.
2. Moojan Momen, *The Bábí and Bahá'í Religions 1844-1944: Some Contemporary Accounts* (Oxford: George Ronald, 1981) p. 41n.
3. Smolenskii [Aleksandr Alekseevich Izmailov], Literary-Artistic Theatre Association, "Bab"—Dramatic Poem by I. A. Grinevsaya, *Birzhevyya Vyedomosti* (SPb), no. 42 (24/01/1904) p. 3," unpublished ms. translation by Alex P. Powell (Tseplayaoff).
4. Quoted in Gabriel de Wesselitsky, *A New Great Russian Poet: An Address* (South Kensington: Lamley, 1907) pp. 8-9. Translation by Mrs. A. Grein.
5. Ibid., p. 9.
6. *Otzyvy pechati o dramaticheskoi poem "Bab" (Iz persidskoi zhizn). Izabelly Grinevskoi sostavil I. Sh* .(Responses of reviews to the dramatic poem "Bab" (from Persian life), by Izzabella Grinevskaia; compiled by I. Sh.) (St. Petersburg: Elektropechatnia K A Chetverikova, 1910) pp. 39-40.

   For further information on this very important aspect of literary life in Russia, see: Marek Tobera, "Cenzura prasy w Cesarstwie Rosyjskiem na przeomie XIX i XX w.," (Censorship of newspapers in Imperial Russia at the end of the 19th, beginning of the 20th cent.) in *Piœmiennictwo-systemy kontroli-obiegi alternatywne* (Literature—systems of control and alternative publications) (Warsaw: Biblioteka Narodowa, 1992) t. I, pp. 175-223.
7. *Pesnia Assady* (Assad's song); set to music by Boleslav Viktorovich Grodzkii (St. Petersburg: Seliverstov, 1904). [*Bab*, p. 124.].
8. *Teatral'naia gazeta* (St. Petersburg) (1 Jan., 1905) no. 1, p. 23.
9. *Surovye dni, Dramatichskaia poema Pugachevshchiny v 5-ti deistviiakh, 6 stikhakh* (St. Petersburg: Mir, V. L. Bolgushevskogo, 1909) p. 238. It was staged that same year and received many good reviews.
10. Izabella Arkadev'na Grinevzkaia, "Izabella Arkadev'na Grinevskaia's First Literary Steps," translated from the Russian by Irina Essinova; introduction and notes by Jan Teofil Jasion, Dec. 16, 2003, typescript, p. 20.

# TÁHIRIH IN HISTORY
## The Writings of Qurratu'l-'Ayn

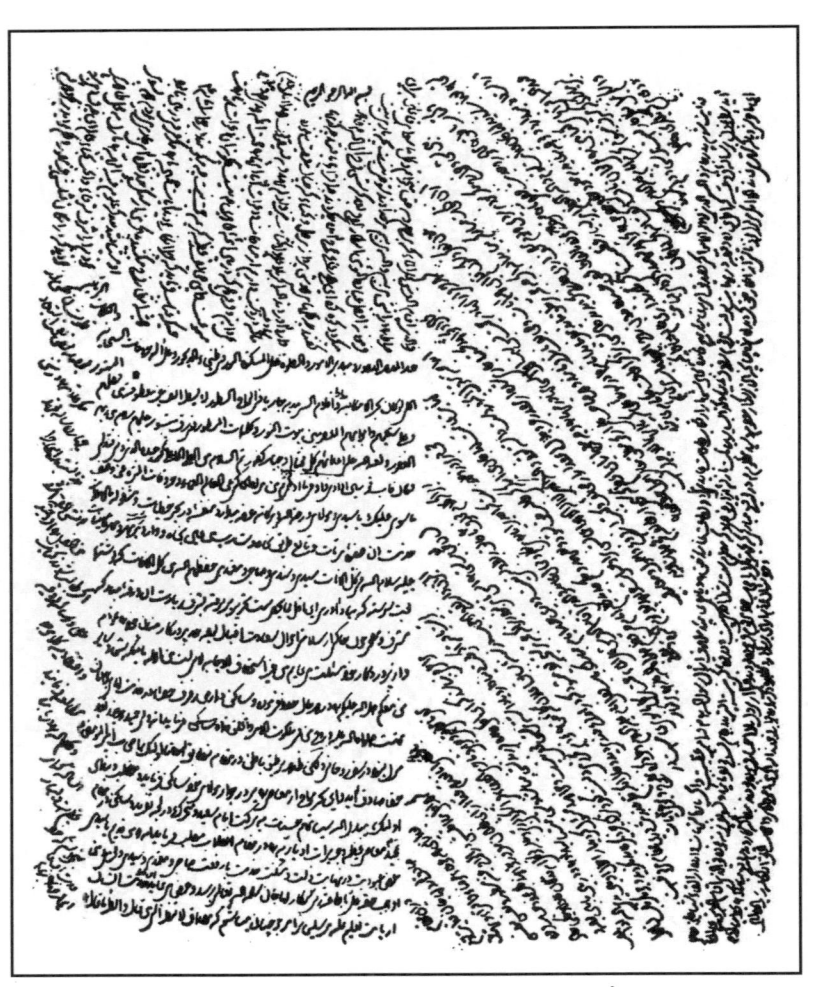

AN EXAMPLE OF THE HANDWRITING OF TÁHIRIH

# The Writings of
# Qurrat al-'Ayn Qazvini (Táhira)

by Denis MacEoin

The writings of Qurrat al'Ayn deserve close attention in view of her central role in the creation of a distinct Bábí doctrine . . . Of particular interest are the controversies which focused on her in Karbala, Baghdad, Qazvin, and Badasht. A study of these controversies, her role in generating them, and the reasons for the success of her views provide us with a singularly clear picture of the way in which Bábí doctrine developed in the earliest period outside the pronouncements and speculations of the Báb.[1]

References to these rifts within the Bábí community (if we may use so concrete a term) are to be found in a number of sources. Chief among these are two letters written by Shaykh Sultan al-Karbalá'í and Mullá Ahmad Mu'allim Hisárí respectively; three letters by the Báb printed in *Zuhúr al-haqq*[2]; and several letters written in Qurrat al-'Ayn's own hand.

Gobineau stated mistakenly that *"Il ne parait pas que Gourret-oul-Ayn, la Consolation-des-Yeux, ait rien composé, du moins je n'en ai pas connaisance, ou, si elle a écrit, son œuvre est peu considérable."* [It does not seem that Qurrat al-'Ayn, the Consolation-of-the-Eyes, ever composed anything, at least I have no knowledge of it, or, if she has written, her works are few.][3] The reason for this error appears a few lines later when he goes on to say "*Mais une autre personne, aujourd'hui vivante, moins éminente sans doute que la Consolation-des-Yeux, mais qui occupe pour tant, parmi les religionnaires, un rang très élevé et que l'on désigne par le titre de 'Son Excellence la Purifiée', Djenâb Moteherreh, a composé un ouvrage qui est la avidement par tous les bâbys.*" [But another person, who is alive today, surely less famous than the Consolation-of-the-Eyes, but who occupies a very high rank among the religionists, and that one is referred to by the title "Her Excellency the Purified," Jináb-i Mutahhara, has composed a work that is read with great eagerness by the Bábís.][4]

It is evident that Gobineau was misled by the existence of two titles, Qurrat al-'Ayn and Jináb-i Mutahhara (which I take to be a confusion or duplication for Jináb-i Táhira). These do not, of course, refer to two individuals but one.[5]

Qurrat al-'Ayn is known to have written a large number of *risálas*, prayers, homilies, and, above all, poems, many of which are still extant. The earliest of her works of which any record exists is a treatise written in support of the doctrines of al-Ahsá'í, in response to a general request by Sayyid Kázim Rashtí for Shaykhí ulama to write in this vein.[6] This seems to have been written and sent to Rashtí between her first visit to Karbala' (at an unspecified date) and her second visit at the very beginning of 1844, a mere ten days before the Sayyid's death.

The fate of this treatise is now unknown; it may have been among the large number of papers lost after Rashtí's death, when his house in Karbala' was sacked.[7] If it could be discovered and identified, it might prove of particular value in providing us with a reliable picture of this woman's beliefs prior to her conversion to Babism.

Shaykh Kázim Samandar has remarked that the earliest poetry composed by her consisted of elegies (*maráthí*) on the sufferings of the imams (perhaps under the influence of her father, who wrote much on this subject).[8] These too appear to have been lost.

We have already referred to a treatise entitled *Sab'-mi'a*, written by Qurrat al-'Ayn in defense of Babism. It appears that she wrote this in response to a request from the Báb himself that she compose "an account of 'the matter' (or 'the cause') in a book written according to seven hundred (*sab'-mi'a*)." This request was made in a letter written to her around the time of the schism among the Bábís of Karbala (about 1262-1263/1846-1847).[9]

This treatise has also been lost, nor do we possess any record of its precise contents. I would surmise that it was simply a collection of seven hundred Shi'ite *akhbár* touching on the appearance of the Qá'im similar to the collections entitled *Arba'ín*, containing forty traditions.[10] There is evidence that such compilations were made by Bábí clerics. . . .

A number of treatises by Qurrat al-'Ayn have survived. The earliest of these seems to be the *risála* referred to by Hamadání, who says that she wrote some two to three thousand verses in reply to questions posed by two Shaykhí ulama, Mullá 'Abd al-'Alí and Mullá Jawád [Vilyání?].[11] I discovered a copy of this treatise in the manuscript collection INBA [Iran National Bahá'í Archives] 6003C, running from p. 332 to p. 379. The colophon at the end of the letter is dated 1262/1846, but the letter itself seems to have been written from Karbala' as early as 1261/1845: this is indicated at the top of a printed copy of the major part of the *risála* contained in *Zuhúr al-haqq*.[12] Mázandarání did not use the INBA 6003C manuscript as the basis for his text (there are minor variations between the two), so I assume his earlier date is taken from another manuscript.

The autograph manuscript of an important treatise by Qurrat al-'Ayn is in the possession of an Azalí Bábí living in Tehran. A Xerox copy is kept by the present writer. Forty-two pages in length, this letter is one of the longest of her extant writings and provides detailed discussions of several important doctrinal issues. It is particularly concerned with the theme of the cyclical appearance of the Divine Will in the prophets and the concept of an age of inner truth that has just begun. There is a useful discussion of the Shaykhí theory of the Fourth Pillar (*rukn-i rábi'*), suggestive of an early date of composition. The author also addresses herself to the issue of the Báb's claims, in particular the notion that his writings represented divine revelation (*wahy*). She advances a moderate view that is of considerable value in helping us understand how these claims may have been regarded by leading Bábís (even radical ones like herself) in the early period.

Although he nowhere indicates the provenance, date, or current location of any of the manuscripts used by him, Mázandarání prints several other treatises by Qurrat al-'Ayn in *Zuhúr al-haqq*. These are:

(i) A letter to Mullá Husayn Bushrú'í, pp. 334-38
(ii) A general letter written after her departure from Karbala' pp. 338-52
(iii) A general letter addressed to non-Bábí Shi'ites, also written after her departure from Karbala', pp. 352-56
(iv) A letter addressed to Sunni Muslims, replying to doubts expressed by the Mufti of Baghdad, Shaykh Mahmúd al-Álúsí, pp. 356-59
(v) A letter replying to slanders levelled by other Bábís, written partly in Persian, pp. 359-66.

Mázandarání also prints facsimiles of two letters written to her uncle Hajj Mullá Muhammad Taqí between pages 314 and 315.

An Arabic apologia for Babism written by Qurrat al-'Ayn is published as an appendix to the Gulpáygánís' *Kashf al-ghitá' 'an hiyal al-a'dá'*. In the text of the book itself, it is explained that two copies of this risála were sent to Mírzá Abu'l-Fadl Gulpáygání. One came from a merchant in Iskandarún whose father had lived in Baghdad, where he had copied it from the original. The other was sent by a Mírzá 'Abd Alláh 'Iráqí, who had copied it himself but forwarded a different transcript in the hand of a scribe called Habíb Alláh.[13]

It is not clear what happened to the copies in Gulpáygání's possession. On his death, the Bahá'í leader 'Abbás Effendi ['Abdu'l-Bahá] ordered his papers to be collected. These were then taken by Áqá Shaykh Muhammad 'Alí (a nephew and son-in-law of the Bahá'í cleric Nabíl-i Akbar) to Ashkhabad, from whence they were removed to Tehran. It seems that they were then handed over to Gulpáygání's nephew, Sayyid Mahdí, who completed the writing of the *Kashf al-ghitá'*, which he had printed in Ashkhabad.[14] After that, the trail goes cold. An alternative account states that some at least of these papers were delivered by 'Abbás Effendi to Nabíl-i Qa'in'í.[15] I would surmise that the papers, including at least one copy of this risála, are in the possession of Sayyid Mahdí's descendants, or in the Iran National Bahá'í archives in Tehran, or in Haifa.

Unfortunately, there is good reason to believe that most of Qurrat al-'Ayn's considerable output of apologetic writing has been destroyed or lost. Something of the extent of this output is indicated by Muhammad Mustafá al-Baghdádí. He says that, when she was in Kirmánsháh in 1263/1847, letters would arrive for her every day from ulama and other enquirers. She would write rapid replies to all of these.[16] The anonymous Azalí history, *Qurrat al-'Ayn: bi-yád-i sadumin sál-i shahádatI*, states that, while under house arrest in Tehran, 'lzziyya Khánum, Subh-i Azal's eldest sister, would send her younger sister Fatimá to visit her, Fatimá then being eight or nine years old. The little girl would bring letters for Qurrat al-'Ayn concealed in her pocket and would take replies away in the same manner.[17] Many prayers, poems, homilies, and other pieces reached the Bábís in this way, and many of the originals are still extant.[18] These copies may be in the possession of 'Izziyya Khánum's family,[19] but it is possible that some are in Bahá'í hands as well.[20]

The above-mentioned Azalí publication contains some twenty-eight pages of poems and prayers by Qurrat al-'Ayn. Hussám Nuqabá'í, the Bahá'í editor of a book entitled *Táhira-Qurrat al-'Ayn*,[21] claims that most of these are "suspect" (*mashkúk*),[22] although he does not provide any grounds for these suspicions. Indeed, in the present state of our knowledge of Qurrat al-'Ayn's writings, I cannot see on what basis such a claim could be reasonably founded. I think it quite possible that some of these pieces, particularly the poems, are works written during her Tehran confinement (about 1849 to 1852).

A number of these pieces are, in fact, found in a manuscript supplied to me in 1977 by a descendant of Hájj Mullá Muhammad Taqí Baraghání, Qurrat al-'Ayn's paternal uncle. This manuscript, written in 1339/1921, consists of 150 pages and contains about thirteen pieces of prose and over eighty poems. Altogether, it is one of the largest extant manuscripts of works by Qurrat al-'Ayn, particularly in respect of her poetry. Its importance is underscored by the fact that pages 56 to the end were, according to a statement in the text, copied from a manuscript in the author's own hand. The scribe states that he has taken pains to change nothing, even where words have dropped out and so on.

Even more important is a manuscript in the Tehran Bahá'í Archives, INBA 5045E. This is a small manuscript of exactly 10x6 cms., consisting of one hundred and two folios. It is written in a very fine, minute *shikastanasta'líq hand* on variously coloured paper. Clearly of some age, the manuscript has, unfortunately, lost its last pages, and contains little to indicate the actual date or to identify the scribe. The heading on the first page, however, uses the phrase *'alayhá 'l-bahá'* ("upon her be the beauty") following the sobriquet Táhira, a clear indication that the scribe was a Bahá'í. This collection contains some 46 prose pieces, many of them letters to individuals. If its authenticity could be assured, there is no doubt that it would provide an indispensable source for the views of Qurrat al-'Ayn, as expressed to her fellow-converts.

The collection of early Bábí writings issued as INBMC 80 under the title *Nivishtiját wa áthár-i ashάb-i awwaliyya-yi amr-i a'lá* contains (pp. 212-82) a reproduction of a manuscript which may be tentatively ascribed to Qurrat al-'Ayn. The style is certainly consistent with that of other materials more definitely known to have been written by her, and the contents which include detailed references to the controversies between her and other Bábís in Iraq, described here as "what took place between me and some of the brethren,"[23] —lend support to the supposition of her authorship. In particular, there is a personal reference on page 278, where the writer says: *yá ikhwání . . . lá thanú hádhihi 'l-aqallata min al-dharra* (O my brethren . . . do not praise this creature who is less than an atom), using the feminine *hádhihi 'l-aqalla* rather than the masculine *hádha 'l-aqall*.

Apart from its references to the disputes between Qurrat al-'Ayn and Mullá Ahmad Mu'allim Hisárí, this letter is valuable for its brief account of the issue between the Báb and Mullá Jawád Vilyání, its defence of the role and position of the Letters of the Living (*al-sábiqún*), particularly Mullá Husayn Bushrú'í, and its use of quotations from early writings of the Báb. It is particularly interesting for its rejection of rational proofs,[24] its condemnation of traditional knowledge,[25] its use of the concept of the organ of the heart in reaching true understanding,[26] and the emphasis it places on spiritual love as a prerequisite for gnosis (*ma'rifa*).[27]

At present, only one other manuscript collection (in this case, exclusively poetry) is definitely known to contain work by Qurrat al-'Ayn. This is a manuscript in the possession of the Bahá'í writer, Ni'mat Alláh Dhuká'í Baydá'í, who discovered it in 1319-1320 Sh./1941-1942, when living in Shíráz. Thanks to his generosity, I was provided with a copy of this manuscript in 1977. The collection contains 73 pages with 475 *bayts* in eight sections, two of which are clearly the work of Bihjat-iQazvíní.[28] The manuscript was transcribed by the Bahá'í calligrapher Abu'l-Hasan Nayrízí in

1341/1922-1923 from a copy dated 20 Sha'bán 1267/20 June 1851 (when Qurrat al-'Ayn. was still alive). There is no name for the scribe responsible for the original manuscript.[29]

The present author has heard of the existence of a number of other manuscript collections of works by Qurrat al-'Ayn, all of them described as *díwáns* of her poetry in her own hand. Should these exist and should they prove to be genuine, their importance would be considerable. For the benefit of future scholars, let me place on record what I know of these supposed collections. They are: 1) a *díwán* said to be in the possession of a Mrs. Taván̄gar, a descendant of Mírzá Mustafá, Browne's Azalí scribe; 2) a *díwán* owned by Hajj Shaykh 'Abbúd al-Sálihí, a Muslim descendant of one of Qurrat al-'Ayn's brothers, who has told me that it is among his family papers in Karbala'; and 3) a *díwán* in the possession of a Muslim friend of Mr. al-Sálihí, Dr. Qásimí.

A few manuscripts of Qurrat al-'Ayn's writings—mainly poems have found their way to Europe. E. G. Browne possessed a small number, including a letter from Qurrat al-'Ayn, to Mullá Shaykh 'Alí Turshízí, transcribed by Subh-i Azal. This may be found in the Browne Collection, F.66* (item 12a). The original letter, in the hand of Qurrat al-'Ayn, was known to have been in Browne's possession at one time, since he reproduced it in facsimile in his editions of the *Táríkh-i jadíd* and the *Nuqtat al-káf*.[30] It was lost for many years until identified by the present author in Folder 3 of the Browne Collection.

That same folder also contains the original of what is alleged to be an autograph *mathnaví* by Qurrat al-'Ayn, This was sent to Browne on 24 September 1892 by Shaykh Abmad Rúhí Kirmání. It is reproduced in *Materials*.[31] Comparison of the handwriting of this item with that in several other pieces known to be in Qurrat al-'Ayn's hand shows clearly that it is not an autograph. Although I would be reluctant to make a firm statement at this stage, my feeling is that the poem itself may be a forgery, since it is in a style rather different to that of other poems definitely known to be the work of Qurrat al-'Ayn, Manuscript F.22 in the Browne Collection contains more poems, including a long *mathnaví*. Some of these are attributed to Qurrat al-'Ayn, Another poem ascribed to her may be found in Folder 2, of which it forms part of item [42].

The only other manuscripts in the West are two poems and a letter once in the possession of A. L. M. Nicolas (109), but now of unknown location. According to Momen, the Russian Consul-General in Beirut, Georgy Batyushkov, who at one time traveled in Iran, collected a manuscript of Qurrat al-'Ayn's works for the Asiatic Museum in the St. Petersburg Academy of Sciences.[32] Momen also refers to an article by the Russian orientalist V. A. Zhukovski, in which he mentions various papers collected by the Russian consul at Astarábád, F. A. Bakulin; these included some writings by Qurrat al-'Ayn.[33] E. G. Browne refers to copies of several more Bábí poems, possibly containing some by Qurrat al-'Ayn, which were contained in a manuscript with the class-mark P.92, lent him by the late Charles Schefer.[34] Of the present whereabouts of Schefer's manuscript, I have, I regret, no idea. . . .

In his account of [the *Qayyúm al-asmá'* by the Báb], the Bahá'í writer Shoghi Effendi states that its "entire text was translated into Persian by the brilliant and gifted Táhirih [i.e., Qurrat al-'Ayn]."[35] Since this author never provides references for his remarks, it is impossible to know on what grounds he makes this statement. But I am certainly unaware of any such translation, nor have I found any reference to Qurrat al'Ayn having produced a translation of the *Qayyúm al-asmá'* in any of the numerous documents I have consulted on her life.[36] . . .

In general, there is a serious problem of authenticity in the case of Qurrat al-'Ayn's writings, particularly her poetry. A number of poems have been attributed to her which are, in fact, by other poets, including the early nineteenth-century Súfí poet of Shíráz, Mullá Muhammad Báqir, better known as Suhbat-i Lárí (1162-1251/1749-1835-36).[37]

A version of the well-known poem beginning: *lamahátu wajhika 'shraqat wa shi'á'u tal'atika 'talá*[38] appears in the *Díwán* of Suhbat-i Lárí.[39] Suhbat himself seems to have been imitating a poem by Jámí, beginning: *nafahátu waslika awqadat jumaráti shawqika fi 'l-mashá'*.

A *mukhammas* beginning: *ay bi-sar-i zulf-i tu súdá-yi man / va'z gham-i hijrán-i tu ghúghá-yi man* which appears in *Qurrat al-'Ayn*,[40] has also been attributed to the Bábí martyr Hájj Sulaymán Khán Tabrízí.[41] A *ghazal* beginning: *khál bi-kunj-i lab yakí turra-yi mushkfám du* raises different problems. There is a very similar *ghazal* (identical in one line) by Sakína 'Ufat Shíráziyya, and Wafá-yi Qummí has at least two lines very close to its opening stanzas.[42]

Hájí Fath Alláh Maftún Yazdí, however, attributes this *ghazal* to Umm Hání (d.1236/1820-1821), a daughter of Hájí 'Abd al-Rahím Khán Yazdí.[43]

One of Qurrat al-'Ayn's best-known and most attractive poems is a *rubá'í* beginning: *gar bi-tu uftadam nazar chihra bi-chihra rú bi-rú*. According to Yazdí, this piece appears in old collections and is variously attributed to Nazírí[44] or 'Atá'í. Baydá'í, however, attributes it to yet another poet of the Safaví period, Táhirí Kashfí, known in the Deccan as Sháh Táhir Dakhaní.[45] It is also worth comparing two lines in the version attributed to Qurrat al-'Ayn with two lines from a poem by Qásim al-Anwár quoted by Browne.[46] The authenticity of several other poems has been challenged without firm attribution to other writers.[47]

Apart from those just mentioned, the texts of numerous poems attributed to Qurrat al-'Ayn have appeared in several publications.[48]

**Notes**
Excerpts reprinted from: *The Sources for Early Bábí Doctrine and History: A Survey* (Leiden: E. J. Brill, 1992) pp. 107-116.

1. A basic outline of these controversies and an analysis of their implications may be found in Denis M MacEoin, "From Shaykhism to Babism: A Study in Charismatic Renewal in Shí'í Islam." Ph. D. dissertation, University of Cambridge, 1979, pp. 203-207 [forthcoming, Kalimát Press]. See also Abbas Amanat, *Resurrection and Renewal: The Making of the Babi Movement in Iran, 1844-1850 (*Ithaca: Cornell University Press, 1989) Chap. 7.
2. Mírza Asadullah Fádil-i-Mázandarání, *Tarikh-i-Zuhúru'l-Haqq* (Tehran: [s. n.], 1944) Vol. 3, pp. 332-333, 333, 333-334.
3. Joseph Arthur, comte de Gobineau, *Les Religions et les Philosophies dans l'Asie Centrale* (Paris: Didier, 1865) p. 280. Translation by Ed.
4. Ibid.
5. Gobineau repeats this mistake on pp. 293-94: "... *ce n'est pas l'Unité tout entière, qui se compose encore de dix-huit autres individualités, parmi lesquelles doit de toute nécessité se trouver une femme. Cétait, au début, la Conslotion-des-Yeux ; aujourd'hui, c'est Son Excellence la Purifiée.*" [ ... it is not the complete (or whole) Unity, which is composed of eighteen other individuals, among whom must necessarily be found one woman. It was, at the beginning, the Consolation-for-the-Eyes; nowadays, it is Her Excellency the Purified.] It is not clear to me which work of Qurrat al-'Ayn's could have been so avidly read by the Bábís in Gobineau's day.
6. Nabíl-i-A'zam (Mullá Muhammad-i-Zarandí), *The Dawn-Breakers: Nabíl's Narrative of the Early Days of the Bahá'í Revelation;* translated and edited by Shoghi Effendi (Wilmette, Ill.: Bahá'í Publishing Committee, 1932) p. 83; Mázandarání, *Tarikh-i-Zuhúru'l-Haqq*, Vol. 3, p. 312. It was in approval of

this *risala* that Rashtí first addressed her by the phrase that was to become the basis of her main sobriquet, Qurrat al-'Ayn.
7. See Abul-Qásim ibn Zayn al'Ábidín Ibráhímí Kirmání [Sarká Áqá], *Fihrist-i Kutub-i Shaykh-i Ajall-i Auhad Marhúm-i Shaykh Ahmad Ahsá'í va Sá'ir-i Masháyikh-i 'Izám*. 3rd ed. (Kirman, [n.p., n.d.]) part 1, p. 625.
8. Shaykh Kázim ibn Shaykh Muhammad Qazvíní, "Táríkh-i Samandar," in 'Abd al-'Ali 'Alá'í, ed. *Táríkh-i Samandar va Mulhaqqát* (Tehran: [Bahá'í Publishing Committee], 131 Badí'/1975) p. 345.
9. Letter quoted in Mázandarání, *Tarikh-i-Zuhúru'l-Haqq*, Vol. 3, pp. 333-34; this quotation appears on p. 334.
10. So named in response to a tradition attributed to Im·m Ja'far al-Sádiq: "Whoever of our followers shall preserve forty traditions, God shall raise him up on the day of judgement as an *'álim* and a *faqíh*, nor shall he be punished (for his sins)." Numerous such collections have been made. Among the best known are the *Arba'ín* of Shaykh Bahá' al-Dín al-'Ámilí and Muhammad Báqir Majlisí.
11. Mírzá Husain Hamadání, *The Táríkh-i-Jadíd, or New History of Mírzá 'Alí Muhammad the Báb*; trans. Edward Granville Browne (Cambridge: The University Press, 1893) p. 283.
12. Vol. 3, pp. 483-501.
13. Mírzá Abul-Fazl Gulpáyigání and Sayyid Mahdí Gulpáyigání, *Kashf al-Ghitá' 'an Hiyal al-A'dá*. (Tashkent: [n.p.1919?]) p. 110.
14. Ibid., pp. 3-6.
15. Fadl Alláh Subhí Muhtadí, *Khátirát-i Subhí dar bára-yi Bábígarí wa Bahá'ígarí*. 5th ed. (Qum, 1354 Sh./1975) p. 85.
16. Muhammad Mustafa al-Baghdadi, "ar-Risalah al-Amiriyyah," appended to Ahmad Suhrab, *ar-Risalah at-Tis' 'Ashariyyih* (Cairo: Matba'at as-Sa'adah, 1338/1919) p. 112.
17. Táhirih (Qurratu'l-'Ayn), *Bi-yád-i-Sadumín Sál-i-Shahádat-i-Qurratu'l-'Ayn Nábighih-i-Duwrán* (In Commemoration of the centennial of the martyrdom of Qurratu'l-'Ayn, genius of the ages) (Tehran: [s. n.], 1949) p. 12.
18. Ibid., p. 11.
19. Ibid., p. 25
20. Mázandarání, *Tarikh-i-Zuhúru'l-Haqq*, Vol. 3, p. 328, refers to letters from this period.
21. This work contains selections from a number of published historical works (regardless of quality) and several poems and letters by Qurrat al-'Ayn, some of historical interest.
22. Husám Nuqabá'i, *Táhirah: Qurrat al-'Ayn* ([Tehran: Bahá'í Publishing Committee.], 128 Badi'/1972) p. 73.
23. *Nivishtijaf wa athar-i ashab-i awwaliyya-yi amr-i a'la* (Tehran: National Spiritual Assembly of the Bahá'ís of Iran, 1970s) p. 225. (Iran National Bahá'í Manuscript Collection, 80).
24. Ibid., p. 217
25. Ibid., p. 244
26. Ibid., p. 246
27. Ibid., p. 293.

28. Karim Khan Mafi, a cousin of Husayn Quli Khan Nizam al-Saltana, was a poet who wrote under the *takhallus* of Bihjat. He corresponded with Qurrat al-'Ayn while she was confined in Tehran. See Mazandarani, *Zuhur al-haqq*, Vol. 3, p. 385; Ni'matulláh Dhuká'í Baydá'í, *Tádhkiríy-i-Shu'aráy-i-Qarn-i-Avval-i-Bahá'í*. 3 vols. (Tehran: [Bahá'í Publishing Trust], 121-26 B.E./1965-1970) Vol. 1, pp. 217-22.
29. The original colophon contains an interesting statement: "The day of the great martyrdom is near, after the martyrdom of the Point [i.e., the Bab], there shall be no further respite for anyone." This is an unusually eloquent comment on the mood of the Babis at this critical juncture.
30. Hamadání, *The Tárikh-i-Jadíd*, facing p. 434. The text is printed on pp. 434-37, and a translation of part one on pp. 437-41. Háji Mirza Jáni, *Kitáb-i Nuqtatu'l-Káf, Being the Earliest History of the Bábís*; ed. Edward Granville Browne (Leyden: E. J. Brill; London: Luzac, 1910.) facing p. 140 of the Persian text.
31. Edward Granville Browne, *Materials for the Study of the Bábí Religion* (Cambridge: The University Press, 1918) facing p. 344. The text is printed on pp. 343-47.
32. Moojan Momen, *The Bábí and Bahá'í Religions, 1844-1944: Some Contemporary Western Accounts* (Oxford: George Ronald, 1981) p. 41n.
33. Ibid., p. 43
34. Browne. *Materials*, p. 352
35. Shoghi Effendi, *God Passes By.* Rev. Ed. (Wilmette: Bahá'í Publishing Trust, 1944 [1974]) p. 23. Cf. p. 74.
36. This paragraph has been inserted here from page 56 of the original work.—Ed.
37. On Suhbat, see Mahdi Bamdad, *Sharh-i Hal-i Rijal Iran dar Qarn-i 12, 13, 14 Hijri* (Tehran: Kitabfurushi-i Zuvvar, 1347-1353 Sh. /1968-1974) Vol. 6, pp. 211-212; introduction to Muhammad Báqir Suhbat Lárí, *Dívan-i Suhbat Lárí*. 4th ed. (Shiraz, 1354 Sh./1975-76) pp. ix-xix.
38. Published by Browne in 'Abdu'l-Bahá, *A Traveller's Narrative: Written to Illustrate the Episode of the Báb*; edited in the original Persian, and translated into English, with an introduction and explanatory notes by Edward G. Browne (Cambridge: The University Press, 1891) Vol. 2, pp. 314-316 and in his *Materials*, pp. 349-51.
39. Suhbat Lárí, *Dívan*, pp. 129-130. On this, see also Edward Granville Browne, "The Bábís of Persia. II. Their Literature and Doctrines," *Journal of the Royal Asiatic Society* (London), vol. 21 (1889) pp. 240-41.
40. Táhirih (Qurratu'l-'Ayn), *Bi-yád-i-Sadumín*, pp. 26-27.
41. Muhammad-'Ali Malik-Khusraví, *Tárikh-i Shuhadá-yi Amr* (Tehran: n.p., 130 Badí'/1974) Vol. 3, p. 228.
42. Ma'sum 'Ali Shah, Muhammad Ma'sum Shirazi, *Tara'iq al-haqa'iq* (Tehran: Kitabkhanah-i Barani, 1960-1966) p. 235.
43. Haji Fath Allah Maftun Yazdi, *Bab wa Bahard bishinasid* (Hyderabad, n.d.) p. 271.
44. Naziri of Nishapur, d. 1021/1612-13. See Edward Granville Browne, *Literary History of Persia: Modern Times (1500-1924)* (Cambridge: The University Press, 1924) p. 252.
45. Baydá'í, *Tádhkiríy-i-Shu'aráy*, Vol. 3, pp. 111-12. Bayda'i bases this attribu-

tion on a miscellany in his possession containing this poem. The collection is, he maintains, over one hundred and fifty years old.
46. Edward Granville Browne, *Literary History of Persia* (Cambridge: The University Press, 1920-24) Vol. 3, p. 480.
47. Baydá'í, *Tádhkiríy-i-Shu'aráy,* Vol. 3, pp. 102, 109-110, 132.
48. Mázandarání, *Tarikh-i-Zuhúru'l-Haqq*, Vol. 3, pp. 366-69; Nuqabá'i, *Táhirah*, pp. 139-97; 'Alí Akbar Dihkhudá, *Lughat'náma* (Tehran: Chápkhánah-'i Majlis, 1325-52 Sh./1946-74) under "Táhira"; 'Alí Akbar Mushír Salímí, *Zanan-i Sukhanvar kih 'az yakhizar sal-i pish ta 'imruz bi zaban-i Farsi sukhan guftah'and* (Tehran: 'Ali Akbat 'Ilmi, 1337/1956) Vol. 2, pp. 82-98; Táhirih (Qurratu'l-'Ayn), *Tuhfah-i Tahirah*; ed. by Isfandyár Bakhtiyárí. [2nd. ed.] (Karachi: Bakhtiyárí, [Delhi: Jayyi Barqi Press] 1933) pp. 28-47; Mirza Mahdi Shirazi, *Tadhkirat al-khawatin* (Bombay, 1306/1889) under "Qurrat al-'Ayn"; (Sa'id) Mahmúd Khayrí, *Farhang-i sukhanvarán va saráyandagan-i Qazvín* (Qazvín: Intishárát-i Tahah, 1370/1991) Vol. 1, pp. 131-136; Baydá'í, *Tádhkiríy-i-Shu'aráy*, Vol. 3, pp. 121-130; Browne, *Materials*, pp. 347-48; Browne, "Babis of Persia II," p. 297; Martha L. Root, *Táhirih the Pure, Iran's Greatest Woman*. 2nd ed. (Los Angeles: Kalimát Press, 1981 [2000]) between pp. 94 and 95. [More recently John S. Hatcher and Amrollah Hemmat, trans., *The Poetry of Táhirih* (Oxford: George Ronald, 2002) and *Táhirih: A Poetic Vision* by Ivan Lloyd (Eloy, Ariz;: Desert Rose Publications, 1999; also this volume).—Ed.]

# A Prayer

by Táhirih Qurratu'l-'Ayn

O Thou to Whose pure and unique quintessence praise is owed:
Only from the Word that issued from Thy holy and exalted Being does honor come.

O eternal adored One, O goal of the mystics:
What world have you created, which is purified above the description of anyone else, and what handiwork have you invented, which is sanctified above the praise of the people of the divine creation!

This world could not exist by means of the splendor of anyone save Thee, and this lofty and exalted station belongs to no one but Thee. I bear witness by the visible eye fashioned from the light of utterance that thou art the maker of this world, and that aside from Thee all have been burned up by a drop from the spray of the radiance of that command; and that Thou art the fashioner of this universe and aside from Thee all have been annihilated by a reflection of the flickering of the gleam of that decree.

God is Great!

Where is there a seeing eye, a hearing ear, a perceptive heart, a supportive breast? For what station is higher and greater than this, that the Creator of being hath created it anew? And what world is more exalted or holier than the one that the fashioner of beneficence hath made manifest afresh? And what a pure, mind-clearing call has issued from the most noble talisman, the honored temple, the embellished emblem, the most straight scale, in the sanctuary of hearts—upon the horizon of Sinai and the dawning-place of manifestation! All the divine ones shed their haughtiness, and by means of the cry, "This is he!" they enthralled all the spirits who subsisted in the realm of power. And what a fresh, soul-nourishing breeze hath been brought into existence by the potency of the Omnipotent, the Inaccessible, such that all those who dwell on the plane of the invisible essence have departed the realm of outward illumination for that complete serenity.

God is Most Powerful!

By one glance from among those wondrous glances—by that blessed and exalted glance that was higher than even the "B" of "Be!" that derived from the light of glory—being would be bestowed on me, even though it was undeserved (indeed, it was pure effulgence and kindness). And I am melted by Thy divine assistance, Lord of munificence, for that radiant and glorious aid is identical to the exalted and illumined light. I am melted, my God, by that mercy whereby Thou didst create me at a time when nothing existed save it. I was formed whirling, after a pattern that no one besides Thee had fashioned, so that Thou mightest set me in motion. Thus might I be brought out of the world of the veils of glory by the attraction exercised by Thy preexistent essence, and thus might I transcend the station of allusions by means of love for Thy shining countenance.

My God, I bear witness to that which Thou has wrought.

I accept that which Thou hast given, shall bring forth what Thou didst desire, and shall choose that station which Thou didst bestow upon me. Thus might I gaze upon a beauty that is none other but Thee:

No God is there but Him. And I am effaced. I seek a splendor that could not exist by means of any save Thee.

No God is there but Thee! And I become sober.

My God, Thine imperative is the answer to my call; Thy "perhaps" is the salve for my misery, and Thine advent is the decree of my religion and the success of my Cause.

Verily, Thou art He who created me for the sake of all that, and by virtue of what exists there Thou didst fashion me. Verily, Thou art the best of witnesses, the most merciful of the merciful, and the most generous of the generous. Thou dost answer the call of the distressed.

And praise be to Thy Self, lord of the worlds.

**Notes**
Juan R. I. Cole, translator

Source: *Qurratu'l-`Ayn: Bi-yad-i sadumin sal-i shahadat* (Tehran, 1949), pp. 36-37.
Published in: *Translations of Shaykhi, Babi and Baha'i Texts* (East Lansing), no. 6, August 1997. <http://www.h-net.msu.edu/~bahai/trans/tahir1.htm>

**ROYAL WOMEN**
Two wives (or close relatives) of the king living in the harem at the palace. The photograph was probably taken by the shah himself, c. 1863. Note the rich silks and brochades of the indoor garments.

# A Gathering of the Poems of Táhirih

Translated by the various authors found in this volume

## The Song of Tahira*

Translated by: Arthur J. Arberry

> *If ever confronting face to face my glance should alight on you*
> *I will describe to you my sorrow for you in minutest detail.*
> *That I may behold your cheek, like the zephyr I have visited house by*
> *house, door by door, lane by lane, street by street.*
> *Through separation from you my heart's blood is flowing from my eyes*
> *river by river, sea by sea, fountain by fountain, stream by stream.*
> *My sorrowful heart wove your love into the fabric of my soul thread by*
> *thread, thrum by thrum, warp by warp, woof by woof.*
> *Tahira repaired to her own heart, and saw none but you page by page,*
> *fold by fold, veil by veil, curtain by curtain.*

Translated by: Masudu'l Hasan

> *O Beloved, if I am admitted to your presence*
> *I will tell Thee in detail of the grief that I suffer because of*
> *Thy separation,*
> *In order to get a glimpse of your face, I am moving like zephyr*
> *From door to door, and street to street*

---

\* Táhirih did not give titles to her poems. For easier identification, each poem here has been given an arbitrary title taken from the text of a translation.

*Because of Thy separation the blood of my heart flows as tears*
   *From my eyes, like fountains, streams and rivers;*
*Your love is woven into the fabric of my soul;*
   *Thread by thread, warp by warp, and woof by woof.*
*In the book of my heart, there is nought but you*
   *In every word, every sentence, and every page.*

## Translated by Farzaneh Milani:

*I would explain all my grief*
*Dot by dot, point by point*
*If heart to heart we talk*
*And face to face we meet.*

*To catch a glimpse of thee*
*I am wandering like a breeze*
*From house to house, door to door*
*Place to place, street to street.*

*In separation from thee*
*The blood of my heart gushes out of my eyes*
*In torrent after torrent, river after river*
*Wave after wave, stream after stream.*

*This afflicted heart of mine*
*Has woven your love*
*To the stuff of life*
*Strand by strand, thread to thread.*

## Translated by Mohammad Ishaque:

*If I happen to see thee before me face to face, I shall tell thee of my pangs in minute details;*
*To see thy face, like unto Zephyr I passed from house to house, door to door, street to street, lane to lane;*
*The circuit of thy tiny mouth and thy cheeks with down of ambergris (are luxuriant) with buds, roses, tulips and fragrance;*
*On account of thy separation, my heart's blood flows forth from my eyes (like) many a Tigris, many a sea, many a brooklet, many a stream.*
*The dejected heart hath knit thy love on the web of life thread by thread, fibre by fibre, warp by warp, woof by woof;*
*Táhirah entered her heart and found nothing save thee (searching) page by page, fold by fold, screen by screen, layer by layer.*

## The Effulgence of Thy Face . . .

### Translated by Edward Granville Browne:[1]

> The effulgence of thy face flashed forth and the rays of thy visage arose on high;
> Then speak the word, "Am I not your Lord?" and "Thou art, Thou art!" we will all reply.[2]
> The trumpet-call "Am I not?" to greet how loud the drums of affliction[3] beat!
> At the gates of my heart there tramp the feet and camp the hosts of calamity.
> That fair moon's love is enough, I trow, for me, for he laughed at the hail[4] of woe,
> And triumphant cried, as he sunk below, "The Martyr of Karbalá am I.[5]
> When he heard my death-dirge drear, for me he prepared, and arranged my gear for me;
> He advanced to mourn at my bier for me, and o'er me wept right bitterly.
> What harm if thou wilt the fire of amaze should'st set my Sinai-heart ablaze,
> Which thou first mad'st fast in a hundred ways but to shake and shatter so ruthlessly?
> To convene the guests to his feast of love all night from the angel host above
> Peals forth this summons ineffable, "Hail, sorrow-stricken fraternity!"
> Can a scale of the fish of amaze like thee aspire to enquire of Being's Sea?
> Sit mute like Táhira, hearkening to the whale of "No" and its ceaseless sigh.[6]

## The Morn of Guidance

### Translated by Susan Stiles Maneck and Farzad Nakhai:

> Truly, the Morn of Guidance commands the breeze to begin
> All the world has been illuminated; every horizon; every people
> No more sits the Shaykh in the seat of hypocrisy
> No more becomes the mosque a shop dispensing holiness
> The tie of the turban will be cut at its source
> No Shaykh will remain, neither glitter nor secrecy
> The world will be free from superstition and vain imaginings
> The people free from deception and temptation
> Tyranny is destined for the arm of justice
> Ignorance will be defeated by perception

*The carpet of justice will be outspread to everywhere
And the seeds of friendship and unity will be spread throughout
The false commands eradicated from the earth
The principle of opposition changed to that of unity.*

## Awaiting Your Blessing

## Translated by Susan Stiles Maneck and Farzad Nakhai:

*In the path of your love, O Idol, I am enamoured with torment
How long will you ignore me, I am grief-stricken
My face veiled, my hair torn out
I have separated myself from all creation
You are the light, you are the veil, you are the moon, you are the horizon. . .*

## Translated by Farzaneh Milani:

*In pursuit of your love, O darling,
Enamored of afflictions, I am
Why do you shun me so?
Weary of your separation, I am.
You've veiled your face
You've disheveled your hair
You've abandoned people
Just as secluded, I am.*

*You're the milk and you're the honey
You're the tree and you're the fruit
You are the sun and you are the moon
A speck, an iota, I am.*

*You're the palm and you're the date
You are the nectar-lipped beloved
A distinguished master, you, dear love,
An insolent slave, I am.
You are the Mecca and you are the One
You're the temple and you're the shrine
You're the beloved, the honored one
The miserable lover, I am.
"Come to me!"
Love said alluringly
"Free of pride and pretense,
Manifestation of the One, I am."*

> Tahereh is but floating dust at your feet
> Drunk by the wine of your face.
> Awaiting your blessing
> A confessing sinner, I am.

## In the Land of Your Love

## Translated by Susan Stiles Maneck and Farzad Nakhai:

> In the land of your love I remain, finding no favor from anyone
> See what a stranger I am, Thou who art King of the land?
> Is it a sin, O Idol, that my every breath breathes the mystery of your love?
> Separate me, kill me, take me unjustly
> The time of patience has ended, how long should I stand separation?
> When every piece of my being, like a hollow reed, tells a sad tale
> Reason cannot apprehend you, souls die of your thought
> All the door of existence are nothing, you are ultimate
> When the zephyr passes by bringing news of their destruction
> Making pale the faces and the eyes weep, what would be your loss?
> You step to my bed in the morning out of compassion, I fly with both wings and hands
> When you rescue one from this place, you will take her to the placeless place
> Then I will let go of the soul of the world, for you are the creator of all souls.

## Yearning Love

## Translated by Edward Granville Browne:[7]

> The thralls of yearning love constrain the bonds of pain and calamity.
> These broken-hearted lovers of thine to yield their lives in their zeal for thee.[8]
> Though with sword in hand my Darling stand with intent to slay though I sinless be,
> If it pleases him, this tyrant's whim, I am well content with his tyranny.
> As in sleep I lay at the break of day that cruel charmer came to me,
> And in the grace of his form and face the dawn of the morn I seem to see.
> The musk of Cathay might perfume gain from the scent of those fragrant tresses rain.
> While his eyes demolish a faith in vain attacked by the pagans of Tartary.[9]

> With you, who condemn both love and wine[10] for the hermit's cell and
>    the zealot's shrine,
> What can I do, for our Faith divine you hold as a thing of infamy?
> The tangled curls of thy darling's hair, and thy saddle and steed are thy
>    only care;
> In thy heart the Absolute hath no share, nor thought of the poor man's
>    poverty.
> Sikandar's[11] pomp and display be thine, the Qalandar's[12] habit and
>    way be mine;
> That, if it please thee, I resign, while this, though bad, is enough for me.
> Pass from the station of "I" and "We," and choose for thy home Nonen
>    tity,
> For when thou has done the like of this, thou shall reach the supreme
>    Felicity.

## Translated by Farzaneh Milani:

> Kingdom, wealth, and power for thee
> Beggary, exile, and loss for me
> If the former be good, it's thine
> If the latter is hard, it's mine.

## Translated by Masudu'l Hasan:

> You are fond of power and empire;
> I am fond of faith and poverty;
> If power and empire are to be preferred
> Be blessed with them.
> And if the way of the Dervish is to be deprecated
> I don't mind the punishment.

# A Beauty Mark . . .

## Translated by Susan Stiles Maneck and Farzad Nakhai:

> At the corner of the lip, a single beauty mark and two black tresses
> Alas, for the bird of the heart, a single grain and two snares
> A constable, a shaykh and I; the talk is of love.
> How can I reply to them; one boiled and two raw?
> From the face and the locks of the Idol my days are as nights.
> Alas, for my days; day is one, night two. . .

## Should I Uuveil . . .

## Translated by Farzaneh Milani:

> *Should I unveil my scented hair*
> *I'll captivate every gazelle*
>
> *Should I line my narcissus eyes*
> *I'll destroy the whole world with desire*
>
> *To see my face, every dawn*
> *Heaven lifts its golden mirror*
>
> *Should I chance to pass the church one day*
> *I'll convert all Christian girls*

## Arise!

## Translated by Farzaneh Milani:

> *O slumbering one, the beloved has arrived, arise!*
> *Brush off the dust of sleep and self, arise!*
>
> *Behold, the good will has arrived,*
> *Come not before him with tears, arise!*
>
> *The mender of concerns has come to you,*
> *O heavy hearted one, arise!*
>
> *O one afflicted by separation,*
> *Behold the good tidings of the beloved's union, arise!*
>
> *O you, withered by autumn,*
> *Now, Spring has come, arise!*
>
> *Behold, the New Year brings a fresh life,*
> *O withered corps of yesteryear, up from your tomb, arise!*

## If Anyone Walks In My Path

## Translated by Edward Grandville Browne:[13]

> *If anyone walks in my path I will cry to him that he may be warned*
> *That whoever becomes my lover shall not escape from sorrow and affliction.*

*If anyone obeys me not and does not grasp the cord of my protection[14]*
*I will drive him far from my sanctuary, I will cast him in wrath to the winds of "No." [15]*
*I am Eternal from the Everlasting World; I am the One from the Realms of the Limitless;*
*I am come [to seek for] the people of the Spirit, and towards me indeed do they advance.[16]*

1. Browne's footnotes are taken from his publication of this poem in E. G. Browne, comp. *Materials for the Study of the Bábí Religion* (Cambridge University Press, 1918) p. 249.
2. See Qur'an vii, 171. The meaning is, "If you claim to be God, we will all accept your claim."—E.G.B.
3. There is a play on the word *balá*, which means "yea" and also "affliction."—E.G.B.
4. *Salá*, which I have translated "hail," means a general invitation or summons.—E.G.B.
5. i.e., the Imám Husayn, of whom several of the Bábí leaders claimed to be a "Return."—E.G.B.
6. i.e., "Thou art a mere tiny scale on the smallest fish of the Ocean of Being, and even the Leviathans of that Ocean can but proclaim their own insignificance and non-existence."—E.G.B.
7. Browne's footnotes are taken from his publication of this poem in E. G. Browne, comp., *Materials for the Study of the Bábí Religion,* p. 249.
8. This poem is presumably addressed to the Báb.—E.G.B.
9. *i.e.* the religion of Islám, which, having survived the terrible Tartar or Mongol invasion of the thirteenth century, fell before the Báb.—E.G.B.
10. "Love and wine" are to be understood here in a mystical sense.—E.G.B.
11. Alexander the Great.—E.G.B.
12. A *Qalandar* is a kind of darwish or religious mendicant.—E.G.B.
13. Though not included among the poems quoted in this volume, the following fragment was translated by Browne and is worth including here. He attributed the poem only doubtfully to Táhirih, however.
14. Or Saintship, for *Wiláyat* has both meanings. Amongst the Arabs he who would seek the protection of some great Shaykh or Amir catches hold of one of the cords of his tent, crying *Aná dakhíluk!* "I place myself under thy protection!"—E.G.B.
15. Not-Being, or Negation, or Annihilation.—E.G.B.
16. The Arabic words with which this line concludes are, as is to often the case with the Bábís, hopelessly ungrammatical.—E.G.B.

# Bibliography

'Abd al-Hamid, Muhsin. *al-Alusi mufassiran*. Baghdad: Matba'at 'al-Ma'arif, 1968.

'Abdu'l-Bahá. *Memorials of the Faithful*; translated from the original Persian text and annotated by Marzeih Gail. Wilmette, Ill.: Bahá'í Publishing Trust, 1971.

---------. *Tadhkirat al-wafa' fi tarjumati hayati qudama'i 'l-ahibba'* (Memorials of the faithful). Haifa: 'Abbasiyya Press, 1342/1924.

---------. *A Traveller's Narrative: Written to Illustrate the Episode of the Báb*; edited in the original Persian, and translated into English, with an introduction and explanatory notes by Edward G. Browne. 2 Vols. (Persian and English). Cambridge: The University Press, 1891. Reprint: New York: Bahá'í Publishing Committee, 1930 (Vol. 2 only). Reprint: Amsterdam: Philo Press, 1975 (Persian and English). Reprint: Los Angeles: Kalimát Press, 2004 (the 1930 edition).

Abul-Fazl Gulpáyigání, Mírzá. *Kashf al-ghitá' 'an Hiyal al-A'dá*. Ashkhabad: [s. n.], 1334/1916.

--------- and Sayyid Mahdí Gulpáyigání. *Kashf al-Ghitá' 'an Hiyal al-A'dá*. Tashkent: [s. n.], [1919?].

Afaqi, Sabir. *Khátún-i 'ajam*. Lahore: Maqbál Akai'damí, 1995.

---------. "Khatun-i 'ajam and Iqbal," 1993.

---------. *Najm-i-Durri*. Karachi: Bahá'í Publishing Trust, 1964.

---------. *Talu-i-Sahtar*. Karachi: Bahá'í Publishing Trust, 1985.

---------. "Qurratu'l-'Ayn Táhirih," *Nigár-í Pákistán* (Karachi), April 1986., pp. 54-67.

Afnan, Abu'l-Qasim, comp. *Chahár Risálih-i-Tárikhí Dar Báriyih-i-Táhirih Qurratu'l-'Ayn*. Weinacht, Switz.: Landegg Academy, 1991.

Afza, Khanum Asmat. "*Iqbal kay fikri nazam maen aurat ka maqam*" (The perspective of women in the ideological system of Iqbal), paper, University of the Punjab (Lahore), n.d.

'Ághá Buzurg 'al-Tihrání, Muhammad Mushin. *al-Dharí'a ilá Tasánif al-Shí'ah*. 25 vols. An-Najaf: Matba'at 'al-Gharri; Tehran: Danishgah 1335-1398/1916-1978.

---------. *Tabaqát A'lám al- Shí'ah*. 2 vols. in 5 parts. An-Najaf: 'al-Matab'ah 'al-'Ilmíyah, 1373-1388/1954-1968.

Ahmad, Aziz. "Zarrin Taj," *Savera* (Lahore), n.d.

Ahmad, Sohail. *Tarfain*. Lahore: Sang-i-meel, n.d.

Ahmed, Leila. *Women and Gender in Islam: Historical Roots of a Modern Debate*. New Haven: Yale University Press, 1992.

Akhtar Hussain Rá'epúrí. *Gard-i Ráh: Khvud navisht, mutála'ah, musháhadah*. Karachi: Maktabah-yi Afkár, 1984.

'Alá'í, 'Abd al-'Ali, ed. *Tárikh-i Samandar va Mulhaqqát*. Tehran: [Bahá'í Publishing Committee], 131Badí'/1975.
Altaf, Siyyid Amjad. "Sham-o-Sahar," *Naqsh Sani* (Lahore), Jan.-Feb. 1982, p. 20.
Álúsí, Mahmud Shukri. *Mukhtasar al-Tuhfat al-Ithna 'Ashariya*. Cairo, n.p., 1373/1953.
Álúsí, Mahmúd ibn 'Abd Allah. *Rúh al-Ma'ání fí Tafsír al-Qur'án al-'Azim wa-al-Sab' al-Matháni*. Bulaq, Egypt: [s. n.], 1301-1310/1883/1892.
'Amili, Baha' al-Din Muhammad ibn Husayn. *Al-Arba'un hadithan*. Beirut: Dar al-Rasul al-Akram, 1992.
Amanat, Abbas. "The Changing World of Taj al-Saltana," introduction to Taj al- Saltanah. *Crowning Anguish: Memoirs of a Persian Princess from the Harem to Modernity, 1844-1914*; ed. by Abbas Amanat; trans. by Anna Vanzan and Amin Nesati. Washington, D.C.: Mage Publishers, 1993.
_____. "The Early Years of the Babi Movement: Background and Development." D. Phil. dissertation, University of Oxford, 1981.
_____. *Resurrection and Renewal: The Making of the Babi Movement in Iran, 1844-1850*. Ithaca: Cornell University Press, 1989.
Andreas, Friedrich Carl. *Die Babi's in Persien*. Leipzig: Verlag der Akademischen Buchhandlung (W. Taber), 1896.
Ariyanpur, Yahyá. *Az Sabá Tá Nímá*. Vol. 1. Tehran: Intishárát-i Zavvár, 1971.
*Aspects of Iqbal*. Lahore: Quami Kutub Khano, 1938.
Ayati "Ávárih," 'Abdu'l-Husayn. *Al-Kavákibu'd-Durriyyih fí Ma'áthiri'l al-Bahá'iyah*. 2 vols. Cairo: Matba`at as-Sa`adah, 1342/1923.
_____. *Kashfu'l-Hiyal*. 3 Vols. in 1. Tehran: Kitabfurushi-yi `Ilmi, 1346/1947.
Azad, Jagannath. *Kolambas ke das men: Safar námah*. New Delhi: Maktabah-yi Jámi'ah, 1987.
Aziz, Akhtar. *Larkian Jo Mashhoor Hu'in*. Lahore: [s. n., n. d.].
'Azud al-Daula, Ahmad Mírzá. *Tárikh-i 'Azudí*. Tehran: [s. n.], 1355 Sh./1976.
The Báb. "Excerpts from the Qayyumu'l-Asma," *Selections from the Writings of the Báb*; compiled by the Research Department of the Universal House of Justice; translated by Habib Taherzadeh. Haifa: Bahá'í World Centre, 1982.
_____. *Kitáb-i Bayán-i Fársí*. Tehran: [s. n., n. d.].
_____. "al-Sahífa al-Rábi'a fi Sharh Du'á'ihi fi Zamán al-Ghayba," in *Majumu'ih-i Athar-i Hadrat-i A'la*. Tehran, [c. 1977], no. 13, pp. 150-154. (Iran National Bahá'í Manuscript Collection; 60)
_____."Tafsir Surat al-Hamd," in *Majumu'ih-i Athar-i Hadrat-i A'la*. Teheran: [c. 1977], pp. 120-155. (Iran National Bahá'í Manuscript Collection; 69)
Badakhsháni, Maqbúl Beg. *Adab námah-yi Írán*. Vol. 1. Lahore: Nígárishát, 1989.

Badayuni, Abr Ahsani Ginnauri, [poem on Tahirih], *Bahá'í Magazine* (Lahore), July 1972.
Badayuni, Zia Ahmad. *Samanzaar-i-Sher Farsi wa Hind*. Delhi: Anjuman-i Taraqqi-i Urdu, n. d.
al-Baghdadi, Muhammad Mustafa. "ar-Risalah al-Amiriyyah," appended to Ahmad Suhrab, *ar-Risalah at-Tis' 'Ashariyyih*. Cairo: Matba'at as-Sa'adah, 1338/1919. Pp. 102-128. Reprinted, Lansing, Mich.: H-Bahai, 1998. Available at < /~bahai/areprint/vol2/baghdadi/risalah19.htm>
*Bahaism: Its Origins and Its Role*. [The Hague: Nashr-i Farhang-i Inqiláb Islámí, 1978?].
Balfour, Ian. "Reversal Quotations (Benjamin's History)," *MLN* (Baltimore), Vol. 106 (1991) pp. 622-45.
Baloch, A. D. "Iqbal Aur Iran." Master's thesis, University of the Punjab. Lahore: n. d.
Balyuzi, Hasan M. *The Bab: The Herald of the Day of Days*. Oxford: George Ronald, 1974.
_____. *Bahá'u'lláh: The King of Glory*. Oxford: George Ronald, 1980.
Bámdád, Badr ol-Moluk. *From Darkness into Light: Women's Emancipation in Iran*; trans. by F. R. Bagley. Hicksville, N.Y.: Exposition Press, 1977.
Bamdad, Mahdi. *Sharh-i Hal-i Rijal Iran dar Qarn-i 12, 13, 14 Hijri*. 6 vols. Tehran: Kitabfurushi-i Zuvvar, 1347-1353 Sh./1968-1974.
Barney, Laura Clifford. *God's Heroes, a Drama in Five Acts*. London: K. Paul, Trench, Trübner, 1910.
_____. *Hasr badaman: Qurratul'ain ke 'uruj o zaval kikarbnak tamsil*; [trans. by] Sadiqulkhair. Karachi: Shahnaz Buk Klab, 1986. [God's heroes. Urdu]
Bástání Párízí, Muhammad Ibráhím. *Haft Sang*. Tehran: Intishárát-i Dánish, 1967.
Bausani, Alessandro. "Babis," *The Encyclopedia of Religion*; ed. by Mircea Eliade, et al. New York: Macmillan, 1987, Vol. 2, pp. 32-34.
_____. *Persia religiosa: da Zaratustra a Bahá'u'lláh*. Milan: Il saggiatore, 1959.
Bayat, Mangol. *Mysticism and Dissent; Socioreligious Thought in Qajar Iran*. Syracuse University Press, 1982.
_____. "Women and Revolution in Iran, 1905-1911," in Lois Beck and Nikki Keddie, eds., *Women in the Muslim World*. Cambridge: Harvard University Press, 1978.
Baydá'í, Ni'matulláh Dhuká'í. *Tádhkiríy-i-Shu'aráy-i-Qarn-i-Avval-i-Bahá'í*. 3 vols. Tehran: [Bahá'í Publishing Trust], 121-126 B.E./1965-1970.
Beg, Abdulla Anwar. *The Poet of the East: The Life and Work of Dr. Sheikh Sir Muhammad Iqbal, the Poet-Philosopher, with a Critical Survey of His Philosophy, Poetical Works and Teachings*. Lahore: Quami Kutub Khana, 1939.

Benjamin, Walter. "Theses on the Philosophy of History," in Walter Benjamin, *Illuminations*; ed. by Hannah Arendt; trans. by Harry Zohn. New York: Schoken Books, 1968.
Bois, Jules. "Babism and Bahaism," *Forum* (Concord, N.H.), Vol. 74 (July 1925) pp. 1-10.
Browne, Edward Granville. "The Bábís of Persia. II. Their Literature and Doctrines," *Journal of the Royal Asiatic Society* (London), Vol. 21 (1889) pp. 881-1009.
―――――. *Literary History of Persia*. 4 vols. London: T. F. Unwin, Vols. 1-2, 1902-04; Cambridge: The University Press, Vols. 3-4, 1920-24.
―――――. *Literary History of Persia: Modern Times (1500-1924)*. Cambridge: The University Press, 1924; 1959. (*A Literary History of Persia*; 4 Vols.)
―――――. *Materials for the Study of the Bábí Religion*. Cambridge: The University Press, 1918.
―――――. *A Persian Anthology*; ed. by E. Dennison Ross. London: Methuen, 1927.
―――――. "Personal Reminiscences of the Bábí Insurrection at Zanján in 1850," *Journal of the Royal Asiatic Society* (London), vol. 29 (1897) pp. 761-827.
―――――. *Selections from the Writings of E. G. Browne on the Bábí and Bahá'í Religions*, ed. by Moojan Momen. Oxford: George Ronald, 1987.
―――――. *A Year Among the Persians*. Cambridge: The University Press, 1927.
Burke, Martyn. "Tahirih," in Tahirih Khododoust Foroughi, comp., *'My Calamity is My Providence.'* Wilmette, Ill.: Foroughi, 1984.
'Căfărzadă, Aziză. *Zărr'intac Tah'ită*. Baku: Göytürk, 1996.

Chehabi, Houchang. "Staging the Emperor's New Clothes: Dress Codes and Nation Building under Reza Shah," *Iranian Studies* (Los Angeles), Vol. 26 (Fall 1993) pp. 209-233.
Cheyne, T. K. [Thomas Kelly]. *The Reconcilliation of Races and Religions*. London: A. & C. Black, 1914.
Chirol, Valentin. *The Middle Eastern Question; or, Some Political Problems of Indian Defence*. London: J. Murray, 1903.
Cobb, Stanwood. "The World-Wide Influence of Qurratu'l-'Ayn," *Bahá'í World, Vol. 2, 1929-1928*. New York: Bahá'í Publishing Committee, 1928, pp. 257-62.
Curzon, George Nathaniel. *Persia and the Persian Question*. 2 vols. London: Longmans, Green, 1892.
Dar, Bashir Ahmad. *A Study in Iqbal's Philosophy*. Lahore: Sh. M. Ashraf, 1944.
Dará Shikúh, Prince. *Safinat-ul-Auliya*. Cawnpore: [s. n.], 1884.
Dawudi, Maqbood Anwar. *Matalib-i-Iqbal*. Lahore: Feroze Sons, 1984.
Demas, Kathleen Jemison. *From Behind the Veil: A Novel About Tahirih*. Wilmette, Ill.: Bahá'í Publishing Trust, 1983.

Dhahabí, Muhammad ibn Ahmad. *Tárikh-al Islám wa-wafayát al-masháhrwaír-wa-al-'lám.* 38 vols. Beirut: Dár al-Kitáb al-Arabí, 1987-1993.
Dihkhudá, 'Alí Akbar. *Lughat'náma.* 38 vols. in 51. Tehran: Chápkhánah-'i Majlis, 1325-52 Sh./1946-74.
Dilávarí, 'Abúlqásim Rafíq. *Á'imah-yi tablís.* Lahore: Maktabab-yi Ta'imír Insáyyat, Vol. 2, 1978.
Dirakhshán, Mahdí. *Buzurgán va Sukhansaráyan-i Hamadán.* 2 vols. Tehran: Níkpú, 1341-42/1963-64.
Eastwick, Edward Backhouse. *Journal of a Diplomat's Three Years' Residence in Persia.* London: Smith, Elder and Co., 1864.
Edge, Clara A. *Tahirih.* Grand Rapids, Mich.: Edgeway Publisher, 1964.
_____. *Qurrat'ul-Ayn Tahirih*, [translated by] Shamsheer Ali. Lahore: Sputnik, 1998. [Urdu]
Elahi, Manzoor. "Qurrat'ul-Ayn," *Naqoosh* (Lahore), no. 140 (1965) p. 532.
_____. "Qurrat'ul-Ayn," *Dard-e-Dilkusha.* Lahore.
Eliyá, Jaun. *Sháyad.* Karachi: Eliyá Akádimyá, 1990.
Enver; Ishrat Hasan. *The Metaphysics of Iqbal.* Lahore: Sh. M. Ashraf, 1963.
Ewen, Cecil Henry l'Estrange. *Witch Hunting and Witch Trials: The Indictments from the Records of 1373 Assizes held for the Home Circuit A.D. 1559-1736.* London: K. Paul, Trench, Trübner, 1929.
Fádil-i Mázandaráni, Mírza Asadullah. *Taríkh-i Zuhúru'l-Haqq.* Vol. 3. Tehran: [s. n.], 1944.
Fanon, Franz. *A Dying Colonialism*, trans. by Haakon Chevalier. New York: Grove Press, 1967.
Fáruq, Es. Em. 'Umar. *Tavásín-i-Iqbál.* 3 vols. in 2. Lahore: Iqbál Akádimí Pákistán, 1987.
Farzánah, Nílam. *Urdú adab kí ahmkhavátín návil nigár.* Aligarh: Ejúkeshanal Buk Há'ús, 1992. [Urdu]
Fischer, Michael M. J. and Mehdi Abedi. *Debating Muslims: Cultural Dialogues in Postmodernity and Tradition.* Madison: University of Wisconsin Press, 1990.
Foucault, Michel. "Nietzsche, Genealogy, History," in Michael Foucault, *The Foucault Reader*; ed. by Paul Rabinow. New York: Pantheon Books, 1984.
_____. "The Order of Discourse," in *Untying the Text: A Post-Structuralist Reader*; ed. by Robert Young. Boston: Routledge & Kegan Paul, 1981.
Fu'ádí Bushrú'í, Hasan. *Manázir-i Táríkhí-yi Nihzat-i Amr-i Bahá'í dar Khurásán.* [Tehran: Iran National Bahá'í Archives photostat publication], n.d.
Furútan, 'Alí-Akbar. *The Story of My Heart*, trans. by Mahnaz Aflatooni Javid. Oxford: George Ronald, 1984.
Gail, Marzieh. *Dawn Over Mount Hira and Other Essays.* Oxford: George Ronald, 1976.

———. *The Sheltering Branch*. Oxford: George Ronald, 1959.
———. "The White Silk Dress," *World Order* (Wilmette, Ill.), Vol. 7 (Nov. 1941) no. 8, pp. 261-74. Reprinted in: *The Bahá'í World, Vol. 9: 1940-1944*. Wilmette, Ill.: Bahá'í Publishing Committee, 1945, pp. 814-21; and a revised version in Marzieh Gail, *Dawn Over Mount Hira and Other Essays*. Oxford: George Ronald, 1976, pp. 80-90.
Ghalib. *Diwan-e-Ghalib*. Aligarh: Maktaba-e-Alfaaz, 1981.
Gibb, H. A. R. and J. H. Krammer, eds. *Shorter Encyclopaedia of Islam*. Leiden: E. J. Brill, 1953.
Gobineau, Joseph Arthur, comte de. *Les Religions et les Philosophies dans l'Asie Centrale*. Paris: Didier, 1865.
———. *Trois ans en Asie*. 15 éd. 2 vols. Paris: B. Grasset, 1922.
Goldstein, Judith. "Interwoven Identities: Religious Communities in Yazd, Iran." Ph.D. dissertation, Princeton University, 1975.
Grinevskaia, Izabella Arkadev'na. *Bab: Dramaticheskaia poema iz istorii Persii*. St. Petersburg: T-vo Khudozhestvennoi pechati, 1903.
Gulriz, Muhammad 'Ali. *Minu-Dar: Ya Bab al-Janna-yi Qazvin*. Tehran: Danishgah-i Tihran, 1337/1958.
Habíb Jalib. *Harf-i sar-idár*. Lahore: Vanguard, 1987. [Urdu and Punjabi]
Hadí, Hasan, comp. *Hadi Hasan's A Golden Treasury of Persian Poetry*; trans. M. S. Israel. 2nd rev. ed. New Delhi: Indian Council for Cultural Relations, 1972.
al-Hallaj, al-Husayn ibn Mansur. *The Tawasin of Mansur al-Hallaj*, trans. by Aisha Abd ar-Rahman at-Tarjumana. Berkeley: Divan Press, 1974.
Hasan, Masudul. "Qurratu'l-Ayn Tahira," in *Stories and Biographies from Iqbal*. Lahore: Ferozsans, 1978, pp. 167-69.
Hatcher, John S. *A Sense of History: A Collection of Poems*. Oxford: George Ronald, 1990.
Hazeen, Saqib. *Babi wa Baha'i*. Peshawar: [s. n., n. d.].
Hidáyat, Rizá Qulí Khán. *Raudat al-Safá'yi Násirí*. 3rd ed. Tehran: [s. n.], 1338-1339 Sh./1959-60, Vol. 8-10.
———. *Tazkirah-'i Riyaz al-'arifín*. Tehran: Kitabfurush-i Mahmudi, 1965.
Hidayat Hosain, M. "A Female Martyr of the Babi Faith," in *Proceedings of the Idara-i-Maarif-i-Islmia*. Lahore: [s. n.], 1933.
"How They Punish Treason in Persia," *The Times* (London), 13 Oct. 1852, p. 4, col. 4.
Huart, Clément. *La Religion de Bab, réformateur persan du XIXe siècle*. Paris: Ernest Leroux, 1889.
Husain, Hamadání, Mírzá. *The Táríkh-i-Jadíd, or New History of Mírzá 'Alí Muhammad the Báb*, trans. by Edward Granville Browne. Cambridge: The University Press, 1893.
Ibráhímí Kirmání, Abul-Qásim ibn Zayn al'Ábidín [Sarká Áqá]. *Fihrist-i*

*Kutub-i Shaykh-i Ajall-i Auhad Marhúm-i Shaykh Ahmad Ahsá'í va Sá'ir-i Masháyikh-i 'Izám.* 3rd ed. 2 vols. in 1. Kirman, n.p., n.d..

'Ilmí, Sayyid Mahfúzlhaq. *Tajalli.* Lahore: Bahá'í Publishing Trust, 1972.

Institirius, Heinrich. *Malleus Maleficarum*; translated with an introduction, bibliography and notes, by the Rev. Montague Summers. London: J. Rodker, 1928.

Iqbal, Muhammad. *Asrár-i khudí.* Lahore: [s. n.], 1915.

_____. *Das Buch der Ewigkeit*; Aus dem Persischen übersetz von Annemarie Schimmel. Munich: Max Hueber, 1957. [*Javidnama.* German]

_____. *The Development of Metaphysics in Persia.* London: Luzac, 1908.

_____. *The Development of Metaphysics in Persia.* Lahore: Bazm-Iqbal, [1930?].

_____. *Iqbal's Javid Nama*, versified English rendering by A. Q. Niaz. Lahore: Iqbal Academy Pakistan, 1984.

_____. *Javidnama.* Lahore: [s. n.], 1932.

_____. *Javid-nama: ma'ahu farhang.* Hyderabad: [s. n.], 1946. [With Persian-Urdu glossary]

_____. *Javid-nama*, translated from the Persian by Arthur J. Arberry. London: Allen & Unwin, 1966.

_____. *Kulliyát-i-Iqbál Urdú.* Lahore: Ghulam Ali & Sons, 1973.

_____. *Le Livre de l'éternité*, trans. by Eva Meyerovich et Mohammed Mokri. Paris: A. Michel, 1962. [*Javidnama.* French]

_____. "McTaggart's Philosophy," in Muhammad Iqbal, *Speeches, Writings and Statements of Iqbal.* 3rd ed. Lahore: Iqbal Academy Pakistan, 1977, pp. 143-51.

_____. *A Messenger from the East*, trans. by M. Hadi Hussain. 2nd ed. Lahore: Iqbal Acdemy Pakistan, 1977. [*Payam-i mashriq.* English]

_____. *The Mosque of Cordoba: English Rendering with Comparative Urdu Text*; trans. by Saleem A. Gilani. Lahore: Iqbal Acdamy Pakistan, 1995.

_____. *Payam-i mashriq.* Lahore: [s. n.], 1923. [Persian]

_____. *Persian Psalms;* trans. by Arthur J. Arberry. Lahore: Sh. M. Ashraf, 1961. [*Zabur-i 'ajam.* English]

_____. *The Pilgrimage of Eternity, being an English Translation of Muhammad Iqbal's Javidnama*, trans. by Shaikh Mahmud Ahmad. Lahore: Institute of Islamic Culture, 1961.

_____. *Il Poema Celeste*; traduzione del testo persiano e note del Alessandro Bausani. Rome: Instituto Italiano per il Medio ed Estremo Oriente, 1952. [*Javidnama.* Italian]

_____. *The Secrets of the Self (Asrir-i khudí): A Philosophical Poem*; trans. with introduction and notes by Reynold A. Nicholson. London: Macmillan, 1920.

_____. *Six Lectures on the Reconstruction of Religious Thought in Islam.* Lahore: Kapur Art Print. Works, 1930.

_____. *Zabur-i 'ajam*. Lahore: Maqbul 'Am Pris, [1932?].
*Iqbal as a Thinker: Essays by Eminent Scholars*. Lahore: Sh. M. Ashraf, 1944.
*Iran National Bahá'í Manuscript Collection*. 103 vols. Tehran: National Spiritual Assembly of the Bahá'ís of Iran, [1970s].
Irshad, Mohammad. "Du Aahu-i-Tishna Dar Nanakzar—Habatia and Qurrat'ul-Ayn," *Fanun* (Lahore), Nov.-Dec. 1986.
Ishaque, Mohammad. "Qurratu'l-'Ayn: A Bábí Martyr," *Four Eminent Poetesses of Iran*. Calcutta: Iran Society, 1950, pp. 28-35.
_____. *Sukhanvarán-i Irán dar 'Asr-i Házir*. 2 vols. Calcutta: Ishaque, 1933-1937.
Ishráq-Khávarí, 'Abdu'l-Hamid. *Táríkh-i Amrí-yi Hamadán*. [Tehran: Iran National Baha'i Archives photostat publication], n.d.
I'tizád al-Saltanah, 'Alí Qulí Mírzá. *Fitnah-i Báb* (Bab's conspiracy)., ed. by 'Abd al-Husayn Navá'í. 2nd ed. Tehran: Babak, 1974.
Jadid al-Islam, Hajji Husayn-Quli. *Minaj al-Talibin fi al-Radd 'ala al-Firqa al-Halika al-Babiya*. Bombay: Matb'-i Gulzar Hasani, 1320/1902.
Já'isí, Kabír Ahmad. *Jadid Taik i Shu'ara*. Aligarh: Idarah-yi 'Ulum-i Islamiyah. 'Aligarh Muslim Yunivarsiti, 1990.
Jalál al-Dín Rúmí. *The Mathnawí of Jalálu'ddín Rúmí*; ed. with critical notes, translation & commentary by Reynold A. Nicholson. 8 vols. London: Luzac, 1925-1940.
Jamílah Háshmí. *Chihra bachihrah rúbarú*. Lahore: Rá'i'tarz Buk Klab, 1977.
Jáni, Háji Mirza. *Kitáb-i Nuqtatu'l-Káf, Being the Earliest History of the Bábís*, ed. by Edward Granville Browne. Leyden: E. J. Brill; London: Luzac, 1910.
Jáved, Khádim 'Alí. *Iqbal Aur Aorat*. Lahore:n.p., n.d.
Javed, Masaud. "Khatoon-i-Ajam," *Rujhan* (Karachi), 1991.
Johnson, Lowell. *Táhirih*. Johannesburg: National Spiritual Assembly of the Bahá'ís of South and West Africa, 1982.
Kaosar, Inam'ul-Haque. "Qurrat'ul-Ayn Tahirih," *Imroze* (Lahore), 23 April 1966.
Karbalá'í, Shaykh Sultán. "Maktúb," in Mírza Asadullah Fádil-I Mázandaráni. *Tarikh-i-Zuhúru'l-Haqq*. Vol. 3, Tehran: n.p., 1944, pp. 245-259.
Kashmiri, Maulana Anwar Shah, in *Dar al-'Ulum* (Deoband number), 1957.
Kashmiri, Shad, [eulogy in the memory of Tahirih], *Nawa-i-Kashmir* (Gujranwala).
Kasravi, Ahmad. *Baha'igari* (Bahaism). Tehran: Mard-e Emruz, 1956.
Kayvan Qazvini, 'A. 'A. *'Irfan Namih*. Tehran: [s. n.], 1348/1929.
Kazem-Bek, Aleksandr. "Bab et les Babis, ou Soulèvement politique et religieux, de 1845 à 1853," *Journal Asiatique* (Paris), Vol. 7 (1866) pp. 329-84, 457-522; Vol. 8 (1866) pp. 196-252, 357-400, 473-507.
Khán, Hájí Mírzá Huseyn. *Tanbíhu'l-Atfá*. Constantinople, 1298 /1881.
Khayrí, (Sa'id) Mahmúd. *Farhang-i sukhanvarán va saráyandagan-i Qazvín*. Qazvín: Intishárát-i Tahah, 1370/1991.

Kirmani, Aneesa. "Zarrin Taj – Qurratu'l-'Ayn," *The Bahá'í Magazine* (Lahore).
Lloyd, Ivan. *Táhirih: A Poetic Vision.* Elroy, Ariz.: Desert Rose Publications, 1999.
Ma'ani, Baharieh Rouhani. "Religion and the Myth of Male Superiority," in Peggy Canton, ed. *Equal Circle: Women and Men in the Bahá'í Community.* Los Angeles: Kalimát Press, 1987, pp. 3-32.
MacEoin, Denis M. "From Shaykhism to Babism: A Study in Charismatic Renewal in Shí'í Islam." Ph. D. diss., University of Cambridge, 1979. [Los Angeles: Kalimát Press, forthcoming]
―――――. *The Sources for Early Bábí Doctrine and History: A Survey.* Leiden: E. J. Brill, 1992.
Majlis, Muhammad Baqir ibn Muhammad Taqi. *Kitab al-Arba'in.* Qum: al-Matba'ah al-'Ilwiyah, 1399/1978-79.
Malcolm, Sir John. *A History of Persia, from the Most Early Period to the Present Time.* 2 vols. London: J. Murray, 1815.
―――――. *A Sketch of Persia.* London: J. Murray, 1827.
Malcolm, Napier. *Five Years in a Persian Town.* London: Murray, 1905.
Malik-Khusraví, Muhammad-'Ali. *Tárikh-i Shuhadá-yi Amr.* 3 vols. Tehran: n.p., 130 Badí'/1974.
Maneck, Susan Stiles. "Tahirih: A Religious Paradigm of Womanhood," *Journal of Bahá'í Studies* (Ottawa), Vol. 2 (1989) no. 2, pp. 39-54.
Marçias, G. "Bustan," in *The Encyclopedia of Islam*; ed. by J. H. Krammers, et al. New ed. Leiden: Brill, 1960.
Marianoff, Dimitrii and Marzieh Gail. "Thralls of Yearning Love," *World Order* (Wilmette, Ill.), Vol. 6 (Summer 1972) no. 4, pp. 7-42.
Masud, Khwaja. "The Cry of Tahira," *The News* (Rawalpindi), 13 November 1995.
Ma'sum 'Ali Shah, Muhammad Ma'sum Shirazi. *Tara'iq al-haqa'iq.* 3 vols. Tehran: Kitabkhanah-i Barani, 1960-1966.
Mehr, Ghulam Rasul. *Matalib-i Zarb-i Kalim.* Lahore: Shaikh Ghulam 'Ali, 1976.
Meisami, Julie Scott. "Allegorical Gardens in Persian Poetic Tradition: Nezami, Rumi, Hafez," *International Journal of Middle Eastern Studies* (London), Vol. 17 (1985) pp. 229-60.
Mernissi, Fatima. *Beyond the Veil: Male-Female Dynamics in a Modern Muslim Society.* New York: John Wiley, 1975.
―――――. *The Veil and the Male Elite: A Feminist Interpretation of Women's Rights in Islam*; trans. by Mary Jo Lakeland. Reading, Mass.: Addison Weslley, 1991.
Mihrábí, Mu'inu'd-Dín. *Qurratu'l-'Ayn Shá'riyeh Ázádíkháh va Millí-í Irán.* Cologne: Nashr-I Rúyesh, 1990.
Milani, Farzaneh. "Becoming a Presence: Tahereh Qorratol'Ayn," *Veils and*

*Words: The Emerging Voices of Iranian Women Writers*. Syracuse University Press, 1992, pp. 77-99.

Momen, Moojan. *The Bábí and Bahá'í Religions, 1844-1944: Some Contemporary Western Accounts*. Oxford: George Ronald, 1981.

_____. "The Family and Early Life of Tahirih Qurrat al-'Ayn." *Baha'i Studies Review* (London), Vol. 11 (2003) pp. 35-52.

_____. "The Social Basis of the Babi Upheavals in Iran: A Preliminary Analysis," *International Journal of Middle Eastern Studies* (Cambridge), Vol. 15 (1983) pp. 157-83.

Mottahedeh, Negar. "Ruptured Spaces and Effective Histories: The Unveiling of the Babi Poetess Qurrat al-'Ayn-Tahirih in the Gardens of Badasht," *Bahá'í Library Online*. [s. l.]: Jonah Winters, [5 Dec. 2002]. Available at <http://bahai-library.org/articles/rupture.html>

Mu'allim Habíbábádí, Muhammad 'Alí. *Makárim al-asár dar ahvál-i rijál-i dawrah-i Qájár.* 5 vols. Isfahan: Nafa'is-i Makhtutat,1377-1396/1958-1976.

Mudarris, Muhammad 'Alí. *Rayhánat al-Adab*. 6 vols. Tehran: Chapkhanah-i Sa'adi, 1326-1333 Sh./1947-1954; 2nd revised ed., Tehran [s. n.], 1335/1957.

Mudarrisi Chahardihi, Mutraza. *Shaykhigari va Babigari az Nazar-i Falsafa, Tarikh, Ijtima.* 2nd ed. Tehran: [s. n.],1351 Sh./1972.

Muhtadi, Fadl Allah. *Khatirat-i Subhi dar bar-yi Babigari wa Baha'igari*. 5th ed. Qum, 1354 Sh./1975.

Mu'ín al-Saltana Tabrízí, Hájí Muhammad ibn 'Abd al-Baqi. *Táríkh-i Amr-i Bahá'í*. [Tehran: Iran National Bahá'í Archives Library photostat publication, n.d.].

Mu'ínurrahmán, Sayyid. *Jámi'át men Iqbál kátahqíqí and tanqídímutála'ah*. Lahore: Iqbál Akádmí, 1977.

Nabíl-i-A'zam (Mullá Muhammad-i- Zarandí). *The Dawn-Breakers: Nabíl's Narrative of the Early Days of the Bahá'í Revelation;* translated and edited by Shoghi Effendi. Wilmette, Ill.: Bahá'í Publishing Committee, 1932; 2nd ed., Wilmette, Ill.: Bahá'í Publishing Trust, 1970.

_____. *The Dawn-Breakers: Nabíl's Narrative of the Early Days of the Bahá'í Revelation*, translated and edited by Shoghi Effendi. London: Bahá'í Publishing Trust, 1953.

Naji, Ghulamali Ismail. *Zihra Bano*. Karachi: n.p., 1972.

_____. *Zehra Bano*, trans. by Raza Husain Baroywal. Karachi: Peermahomed Ebrahim Trust, 1973.

Najmajer, Marie von. *Gurret-ül-Eyn. Ein Bild aus Persiens Neuzeit in 6 Gesängen*. Vienna: Rosner, 1871.

Nashat, Guity. "Women in Pre-Revolutionary Iran: A Historical Overview," in Guity Nashat, ed., *Women and Revolution in Iran*. Boulder, Colo.: Westview Press, 1983.

Nasím Amrohví. *Farhang-i Iqbál.* Lahore: Izhár Sanz, 1984.
Nassakh, 'Abdulghafur. *Tazkratu'l-Ma'asareen.* Calcutta: n.p., n.d.
Nateq, Homa. "The Beginnings of Religious Clerics' Economic and Political Power," (in Persian) *Alifba* (Paris), no. 2, n.s. (Spring 1983) pp. 40-57.
Nazif, Süleyman. *Nasireddin Sah ve Babiler.* Istanbul: Kanaat Kitaphare ve Matbaasi, 1923.
_____. "Translation of Passages on Tahirih . . ." appendix to Necati Alkan, "Süleyman Nazif's *Nasiruddin Shah ve Babiler*: An Ottoman Source on Babi-Baha'i History," *Research Notes in Shaykhi, Babi and Baha'i Studies* (East Lansing), Vol. 4, no. 2 (November, 2000). Available at <http://www.h-net.org/~bahai/notes/vol4/nazif.htm>
Nezami Ganjavi. *The Haft Paikar (The Seven Beauties),* trans. by C. E. Wilson. 2 vols. London: A. Probsthain, 1924.
Nicolas, A.-L.-M. *Seyyèd Ali Mohammed, dit le Bâb: histoire.* Paris: Dujarric, 1905.
Nietzsche, Friedrich. "On the Uses and Disadvantages of History for Life," in *Untimely Meditations*; ed. by Daniel Breazeale; trans. by R. J. Hollingdale. Cambridge University Press, 1997.
Nizami, Siraj. "Táhirih," *Saiyara Digest* (Lahore), August 1968.
_____. [article on Qurratu'l-'Ayn], in *Saiyara Digest* (Lahore), Aug. 1968.
*Nivishtijaf wa athar-i ashab-i awwaliyya-yi amr-i a'la.* Tehran: National Spiritual Assembly of the Bahá'ís of Iran, 1970s. (*Iran National Bahá'í Manuscript Collection*; 80)
Nuqabá'i, Husám. *Bishárat-i Kutub-i Asimání* [s.l., s. n., 1970?].
_____. *Táhirah: Qurrat al-'Ayn.* [Tehran: Bahá'í Publishing Committee.], 128 Badi'/1972.
Pársíp'úr, Shahrnú. *Túbáva ma'ana-yi shah.* Tehran: Intishárát'i Ispark, 1367/1988-1989.
_____. [article on Qurratu'l-'Ayn], in *Saiyara Digest* (Lahore), Aug. 1968.
_____. "Why do you write?" (in Persian) *Dunya-yi Sukhan* (Tehran), no. 17 (March 1988) pp. 9-10.
Perigord, Emily McBride. *Translation of French Foot-Notes of the Dawn-Breakers.* Wilmette, Ill.: Bahá'í Publishing Trust, 1977.
Phelps, Myron Henry. *Life and Teachings of Abbas Effendi.* New York; London: G. P. Putnam's, 1903.
Polak, Jakob Eduard. *Persie: Bericht.* Vienna: Verlag d. K. K. Hof-u Staatsdr., 1873 (Officieller Ausstellungs-Bericht; 14).
_____. [article on Qurratu'l-'Ayn], in *Saiyara Digest* (Lahore), Aug. 1968.
_____. *Persien: das Land und seine Bewohner.* 2 vols. Leipzig: F. A. Brockhaus, 1865.
Qamar Hashmi, Sayiyid. *Tamasha Talab Aazaar.* Karachi: [s. n.], 1988. al-Qatíl

al-Karbalá'í. "Risála," in Mírza Asadullah Fádil-i Mázandaráni. *Tarikh-i Zuhúru'l-Haqq.* Vol. 3. Tehran: n.p., 1944, appendix 2, pp. 502-32.

Qazvíní, Mullá Jafar. "Tarikh," in 'Abd al-'Ali 'Alá'í, ed., *Táríkh-i Samandar va Mulhaqqát.* Tehran: [Bahá'í Publishing Committee], 131Badí'/1975, pp. 446-500.

[Qur'án] *The Koran Interpreted*; translated by Arthur J. Arberry. Oxford: University Press, 1964.

[Qur'án] *The Koran*; translated by Revised J. M. Rodwell. London: J. M. Dent, 1933. (various editions)

[Qur'án] *The Koran, commonly called the Alkoran*; trans. George Sale. London: Thomas Tegg, 1825. (various editions)

Qureshi, Altaf Ali. "Charaghan-i-Rafta," *Qaomi Digest* (Lahore), Aug. 1994.

Qureshi, Azim. [Article], in *Mahnama Ihsas* (Peshawar), 1962.

Quershi, Hakim Matiur Rahman. "Tazmeen bar Qurrat'ul-Ayn Baha'i," *Al-Ilm* (Karachi), April, 1980, p. 12.

"Qurratu'l-'Ayn," in *Urdú insá'iklopídiya.* 3rd ed. Lahore: Firozsanz, 1984.

Raipuri, Akhtar Hussain. *Gard-i-Rah.* Karachi: Af Kaar, 1989.

Ra'is Amrahi. *Kulliyat-i Ra'is Amlrahvi.* Karachi: Velkam Buk Port, 1995.

Razmí, Sáqib. *Ázádí-yi nisvánkánayá saverá.* Lahore: Maqb-ul Ikaidamí, 1991. [Urdu]

Renan, Ernest. *The Apostles.* New York: Carleton, 1866.

_____. [Article on Qurratu'l-'Ayn], in *Saiyara Digest* (Lahore), Aug. 1968.

_____. *Les Apôtre.* Paris: Calmann Levy, 1866.

Riyáz, Muhammad. *Jávednáma: Tahqíq o tauzíh.* Lahore: Iqbál Akádimí Pákstán, 1988.

Romani, Shanam. [Poem in praise of Tahirih], in Sabir Afaqi, *Khátún-i 'ajam.* Lahore: Maqbál Akai'dami, 1995..

Root, Martha L. *Táhirih the Pure, Iran's Greatest Woman.* [Karachi: Root], 1938.

_____. [article on Qurratu'l-'Ayn], in *Saiyara Digest* (Lahore), Aug. 1968.

_____. *Táhirih the Pure, Iran's Greatest Woman.* 2nd ed. Los Angeles: Kalimát Press, 1981.

_____. *Táhirih, Qurratu'l-'ayn*; translated by Abbas Ali Butt. Delhi, n.d. [Urdu]; 2nd ed. Karachi: Bahá'í Publishing Trust, 1966; 3rd ed., 1974. [Urdu].

Rozen, Viktor. "Manuscrits Arabes," *Collections Scientifiques de l'Institut des Langues Orientales du Ministère des Affaires Etrangères* (St. Petersburg), 1877, Vol. 1, pp. 179-212.

_____. "Manuscrits Persans," *Collections Scientifiques de l'Institut des Langues Orientales du Ministère des Affaires Etrangères* (St. Petersburg), 1886, vol. 3, pp. 1-51.

Ruhe, David S. *Robe of Light: The Persian Years of the Supreme Prophet Bahá'u'lláh, 1817-1853.* Oxford: George Ronald, 1994.

Rypka, Jan. *D?jiny perské a tád?ické literatury.* Prague, 1956.

Sahbá'í, Asim, [poem in praise of Tahirih], in Sabir Afaqi. *Khátún-i 'ajam.* Lahore: Maqbál Akai'damí, 1995.

Saiyidain, Khwaja Ghulam. *Iqbal's Educational Philosophy.* Revised ed. Lahore: Shaikh Muhammad Ashraf, 1942.

Sálihí, Abbúd. "Qurratu'l-'Ayn, 'alá Haqíqatihá wa Wáqi'há," cited in 'Alí Wardí, *Lamahát Ijtimá'iyah min Táríkh al-'Iráq al-Hadíth.* Vol. 2. Baghdad: Mataba'at al-Irshad, 1971

Salímí, 'Alí Akbar Mushír. *Zanan-i Sukhanvar kih 'az yakhizar sal-i pish ta 'imruz bi zaban-i Farsi sukhan guftah'and..* 3 vols. Tehran: 'Ali Akbat 'Ilmi, 1337/1956.

Samandar Qazvíní, Shaykh Kázim ibn Shaykh Muhammad. "Táríkh-i Samandar," in 'Abd al-'Ali 'Alá'í, ed., *Táríkh-i Samandar va Mulhaqqát.* Tehran: [Bahá'í Publishing Committee], 131 Badí'/1975.

Schimmel, Annemarie. *Gabriel's Wing: A Study into the Religious Ideas of Sir Muhammad Iqbal.* Leiden: E. J. Brill, 1963.

―――――. "Iqbal and the Babi-Baha'i Faith," *The Baha'i Faith and Islam: Proceedings of a Symposium, McGill University, March 23-25, 1984*; edited by Heshmat Moayyad. Ottawa: Association for Bahá'í Studies, 1990, pp. 111-19.

―――――. "Qurrat al-Ayn Tahirih," *The Encyclopedia of Religion.* Volume 12. New York: MacMillan Publishing Company, pp. 179-80.

Sears, William. *Release the Sun.* Wilmette: Bahá'í Publishing Trust, 1968.

Shah, Chiragh Hussain. *Iqbal Aur Qurratu'l-Ayn.* Peshawar: n.p., n.d.

Sharar, 'Abdulhalím. *Qurratu'l-'Ayn.* Lucknow: Dilgudaz Press, 1923. [Urdu]

―――――. *Táhirah.* Lahore: Nazír, 1991.

Sharíf, Khálid. *Nárasá'í.* Lahore: Mávará, 1989.

Sheil, Mary. *Glimpses of Life and Manners in Persia.* London: J. Murray, 1856. Reprint: New York: Arno, 1973.

Shirazi, Mirza Mahdi. *Tadhkirat al-khawatin.* Bombay, 1306/1889.

Shirazi-Mahajan, Faegheh. "The Politics of Clothing in the Middle East: The Case of Hijab in Post-Revolutionary Iran," *Critique: Critical Middle Eastern Studies* (Abingdon, Eng.), no. 2, Spring 1993, pp. 54-63.

Shoghi Effendi. *God Passes By.* Wilmette: Bahá'í Publishing Committee, 1944. (Revised Ed. 1970; Revised ed., 1974.)

Siddiqui, Mohammad Ali. "Qurratu'l-Ayn: A Profile in Courage," *Dawn* (Karachi), 4 March 1973.

Singh, Iqbal. *The Ardent Pilgrim: An Introduction to the Life and Work of Mohammed Iqbal.* London: Longmans, Green, 1951.

Sinha, Sachchindananda. *Iqbal: The Poet and His Message.* Allahabad: R. N. Lal, 1947.

Sipihr, Muhammad [Lisán al-Mulk]. *Násikh al-Taváríkh: Dawrah-i kamil tarikh-i Qájaríya*; ed. and annotated by Jahangir Qa'im'maqami. 3 vols. in 1. Tehran: Mu'assasah-'i Amir Kabir, 1337/1958.

_____. *Násikh al-Taváríkh: Sala'tin-i Qájár*; ed. by Muhammad Baqir Bihbúdí. 4 vols. Tehran: Intisharat-i Kitabfurushi-i, 1344/1965.

_____. *Tarikh-i Qajariyah'oz mujulladat-i Nasikh'al-tavarikh.* Tabriz: Matba'ah ah-i 'Aga 'Ali Ashghar, 1319/1901.

Suhbat Lárí, Muhammad Báqir. *Dívan-i Suhbat Lárí.* Tehran: Shirkat-i taba-i kitab, 1317/1938-39.

Sultana, Sayyeda Akhtar. "Makalamat-e-Iqbal Ka Tajzia." Master's thesis, University of the Punjab, (Lahore), n.d.

Sykes, Percy Molesworth. *A History of Persia.* 2 Vols. London: Macmillan, 1915.

Táhirih (Qurratu'l-'Ayn). *Bi-yád-i-Sadumín Sál-i-Shahádat-i-Qurratu'l-'Ayn Nábighih-i-Duwrán* ( In commemoration of the centennial of the martyrdom of Qurratu'l-'Ayn, genius of the ages). Tehran: [s. n.], 1949; also digitally printed by H-Bahai at:
<http://www.hnet.msu.edu/~bahai/areprint/tahirih/sadumin/sadumin.htm>

_____. *Ishraq-i Rabbani* (Divine effulgence) [digitally published]. East Lansing, Mich.: H-Bahai, 2000. Available at:
<http://www.h-net.msu.edu/~bahai/areprint/tahirih/ishraq/ishraq.htm>

_____. *The Poetry of Táhirih,* [trans.] by John S. Hatcher and Amrollah Hemmat. Oxford: George Ronald, 2000.

_____. "A Prayer by Tahirih Qurratu'l-'Ayn," trans. Juan R. I. Cole. *Translations of Shaykhi, Babi and Baha'i Texts* (East Lansing), no. 6, August 1997, at <http://www.h-net.msu.edu/~bahai/trans/tahir1.htm>

_____. "Risála," in Mírza Asadullah Fádil-I Mázandarání. *Tarikh-I Zuhúru'l-Haqq.* Vol. 3, Tehran: [n.p.], 1944, appendix 1, pp. 484-501.

_____. "Risalih," in Abul-Fazl Gulpáyigání, Mírzá and Sayyid Mahdí Gulpáyigání. *Kashf al-Ghitá' 'an Hiyal al-A'dá.* Tashkent: [s. n.], [1919?], Appendix I.

_____. *Risalih* (Treatise appended to Mirza Abu'l-Fadl's Kashf al-Ghita) [digitally reprinted]. East Lansing, Mich.: H-Bahai, 1997-98. Available at <http://www.h-net.msu.edu/~bahai/areprint/tahirih/kg1.htm>

_____. *Risalih dar Javab-i Mulla Javad-i Qazvini* (Refutation of Mulla Javad Qazvini) [digitally reprinted]. East Lansing, Mich.: H-Bahai, 1998. Available at <http://www.h-net.msu.edu/~bahai/areprint/tahirih/radd.htm>

_____. *Tuhfah-i Tahirah*; ed. by Isfandyár Bakhtiyárí. Karachi: Bakhtiyárí, 1930. 2nd ed. Dehli: Jayyi Barqi Press, 1933. [Persian]

*Tajalli.* Lahore: The Bahá'í Community of Lahore, April 1974.

*Crowning Anguish: Memoirs of a Persian Princess from the Harem to Modernity, 1844-1914*; ed. by Abbas Amanat; trans. by Anna Vanzan and Amin Nesati. Washington, D.C.: Mage Publishers, 1993.

Taj al- Saltanah. *Khaterat-i Taj al- Saltanah* (Taj-os Saltaneh's memoir); ed. by Mansurah Itteihadiyah and Sirus Sa'dvandiyan. Tehran: Nashr-i Tarikh-i Iran, 1362/1983.

Tunkábuní, Muhammad ibn Sulaymán. *Hadha kitab Qisas al'Ulamá*. Tehran: Habib 'Allah 'Ustad 'al-Mahir Mirza, 1304/1886.
*Urdu Encyclopedia of Islam* (*Urdu da'irah-i ma'arif-i Islamiya*). 20 vols. Lahore: Punjab University, 1964.
Ussher, John. *A Journey from London to Persepolis, including Wanderings in Dagestan, Georgia, Armenia, Kurdistan, Mesopotamia and Persia*. London: Hurst and Blackett, 1865.
Vahid, Syed 'Abdul. *Iqbal: His Art and Thought*. Revised ed. London: John Murray, 1959.
Vambery, Arminius. *Reise in Mittelasien von Teheran durch die Turkmanische Wöste an der ostköste des Kaspischen Meeres nach Chiwa, Bochara und Samarkand*. 2. aufl. Leipzig, F. A. Brockhaus, 1873.
Vasti, Shaukat. *Kahta hun sac*. Islamabad: al-Qalam, 1995.
Vijdani, Mukhlis, [translated poem by Tahirih], *Wah Karigar*, June 1969.
al-Wardí, 'Alí. *Lamahát Ijtimá'íyah min Táríkh al-'Iráq al-Hadíth*. Vol. 2. Baghdad: Mataba'at al-Irshad, 1971.
Wasti, Pervez, [poem], *Sang-i meel* (Karachi), 1964.
Wasti, Shaukat. *Kahta hun Sac*. Islamabad: Idara-I Ilmwar Fun, 1981.
Wesselitsky, Gabriel de. *A New Great Russian Poet: An Address*. South Kensington: Lamley, 1907.
Williams, Selma R. and Pamela J. Williams. *Riding the Nightmare: Women & Witchcraft*. New York: Atheneum, 1978.
Yazdi, Haji Fath Allah Maftun. *Bab wa Bahá-ra bisnasid*. Hyderabad: [s.n.], n.d.
Younghusband, Sir Francis Edward. *The Gleam*. London: J. Murray, 1923.
Zavarih'i, Sayyid Muhammad Husayn "Mahjur." *Vaqa'i'-i Mimiyyih: A Chronicle of the Babi Uprising at Fort Shaykh Tabarsi in Mazandaran*. East Lansing, Mich. H-Bahai, 2001. [Persian] Available at: <http://www.h-net.msu.edu/~bahai/arabic/vol5/mimiyyih/mimiyyih.htm>

# Contributors

**'Abdu'l-Bahá** (1844-1921), head of the Bahá'í Faith, 1892-1921; appointed by Bahá'u'lláh as the "Center of the Covenant."

**Sabir Afaqi**, Former Head of the Urdu and Persian Departments at Azad Kashmir University, Muzaffarabad, Pakistan.

**Abbas Amanat**, Professor of History, Yale University, New Haven, Connecticut.

**Masud'l Hasan**, author.

**M. Hidayat Hosain**, Persian scholar, associated with the Royal Asiatic Society of Bengal, 1910-1941.

**Muhammad Iqbal** (1873-1938), philosopher, major Urdu poet, and political leader of what later became Pakistan.

**Mohammad Ishaque**, educator, author.

**Jan Teofil Jasion,** author, editor.

**Anthony A. Lee,** Instructor, West Los Angeles College; author, editor, poet.

**Susan Stiles Maneck**, Associate Professor, Jackson State University, Jackson, Mississippi.

**Khwaja Masoud**, Former Principal of Gordon College, Rawalpindi, Pakistan.

**Farzaneh Milani**, Associate Professor of Studies in Women and Gender, and of Persian, University of Virginia, Charlottesville.

**Negar Motahedeh**, Assistant Professor, Program in Literature at Duke University, Durham, North Carolina.

**A.-L.-M. Nicolas** (1864-1939), Orientalist and French consular official to Iran.

**Süleyman Nazif** (1869-1922), Turkish poet and Orientalist.

**Shoghi Effendi**, (1897-1957), Guardian of the Bahá'í Faith (1921-1957); author and translator.

**Mohammad Ali Siddiqui**, former Director of Quaid-i Azam Academy, currently associated with Hamdard University, Pakistan.

# Translators

**Necati Alkan**, Ph. D. candidate Ruhr-Universität Bochum, Germany.

**Arthur John Arberry** (1905-1969), former Professor of Arabic at Cambridge University.

**Edward Granville Browne** (1862-1926), former Professor of Arabic at Cambridge University.

**Juan R. I. Cole**, Professor of Modern Middle East and South Asian History at University of Michigan, Ann Arbor.

**Farhad Nakhai**, artist, Tucson, Arizona.

**Peter Terry**, author, independent scholar.

# TÁHIRIH IN HISTORY
## The Poems of Táhirih in the Original Languages
### Calligraphy by Rasheed Butt

بخیالت ای نکو رو به مرام باشد این دل
بجمالت ای نکو خو، بکلام باشد این دل
چو نموده‌ای بافسون، بدل حزین پر خون
که مسلسل از نظاره به هیام باشد این دل
بجمال حسن رویت، بتتار مشک مویت
بهسار بزم کویت، بمرام باشد این دل
چو نمایش به محضر، بریش بعزّ منظر
بجلال و شوکت و فرّ بنظام باشد این دل
چو بجذب رُوی مهوشش شده‌ام غریق آتش
نشود دگر که سرخوش بغنام باشد این دل
به تلطّف و تکرّم، به تعطّف و ترحّم
بر بازماتو هم، کهام باشد این دل
چو زما سوی برانی، ز خودش بخود رسانی
ز بلاء خود چشاینی، بدوام باشد این دل
ز دلم شراره بارد که نسب ز نار دارد
ز چه روشن نیارد که بکام باشد این دل

جوانی چه آورد و پیری چه برد
بُتِ خورد سال و می سال خورد
بت خورد سالی که یک جلوه‌اش
ببرد از دل اندیشه خواب و خورد
می سال خورد یکه یک قطره‌اش
نخورد آنگه مرد و گر آنگه خورد
ز یک خم دهد ساقی روزگار
تراصاف و مراد ردّه درد
هزاران اسیر وبند و یکی
عنبار علائق ز قلبش سترد
نه بازی است رفتن به میدان عشق
که از صد هزاران یکی پا فشرد
ز طوطی دعا دعوی از مدّعی است
ببینیم تا گوی میدان که برد

سجود و جهک فرضاً علی فی الصلواتی
تراپرستم اگر فی المثل جولات و مناتی
بچشم خویش نظر کن مرا گو زچه مستی
در آئینهٔ رخ خود بین مرا پرس زچه ماتی
نرفته در عتبات زهر کعبهٔ رویت
روان زچشمهٔ چشم من است شط فراتی
خدای عالم و آدم مربّی همه اشیاء
ترا وفا بدهد یا مرا زغصه نجاتی
حیات من نه زجان و ممات من نه زمرگ است
من الوصال حیاتی من الهراق مماتی
بوقت مرگ کشودی زپرستم لب شیرین
چنانکه بازبمانم ز نو دمیده حیاتی

اگر باد دهم زلف عنبر آسا را
اسیر خویش کنم آهوان صحرا را
وگر به نرگس شهلای خویش سرمه کشم
بروز تیره نشانم تمام دنیا را
برای دیدن رویم سپهر هر دم صبح
برون برآورد آئینهٔ مطلا را
گذار من بکلیسا اگر فتد روزی
بدین خویش برم دختران ترسا را

چو ظهور آن شه معروف عظمت شئون جلاله
بجهان جان شد از شرف حسنت وعزت مقاله
همه جان جملهٔ انس و جان شد در قدومی ارغان
به تعشق آمده عاشقان قبل سبیل وصاله
طلع البهاء و شهرت ظهر البهاء و اللمعة
قلل الوجود نیرت فلکاً لوجه جماله
همه آیه های مسلسله زلسان او شده نازله
همه انبیاء مهر وله متبرجاً بجماله

لمعاتِ وجهك اشرقت و شعاعُ طلعتِك اعتلا
نچہ رو است برنجم زنی بزن کہ بلّے بلی
بجواطبجبل الست تو زولا چو کس بلا زدم
ہم خیمہ زد بدردِ دل سپہِ غم و چشمِ بلا
من و عشقِ آں مہ خوبرو کہ چو زد صلای بلا بر او
بہ نشاط و قہقہہ شد فدا کہ انا الشہید بہ کربلا
چو شنید نالۂ مرگِ من پے سازِ من شد و برگِ من
فشی الی مہد لا و بکٰے علی مجلجلا
چہ شود کہ آتشِ حیرتی زنیم بجملۂ طور دل
خشگشگتہ و دگشگتہ متمد کہ کا مترنزلا

پے خوانِ دعوتِ عشق او ہمہ شب زنیل کردہ بیاں
رسد این صفیرِ ہمہمی کہ گروہ غمزدہ اصلا
تو کہ فلس ہی حیرتی چہ زنی زنجرِ وجود دم
بنشین چو طاہرہ دمبدم بشنو فروشِ تنگ لا

باختہ جاں بوفایش ہمہ شاہد باشید
ایستادہ بوفایش ہمہ شاہد باشید
روز اول کہ رسیدیم بمقامِ ازلی
محو نمودہ سوایش ہمہ شاہد باشید
دور ہا کز دہ ایں چرخِ مدّور چیں
ایستادم بوفایش ہمہ شاہد باشید
نیست مقصود مرا غیرِ رضائش اللہ
آدم عین رضایش ہمہ شاہد باشید
قرۃ العین نگر با نظرِ پاک صفا
کیست منظورِ بہایش ہمہ شاہد باشید
خواہم از فضلِ خداوندِ قیومِ قدیم
ریزم خوں بہ بہایش ہمہ شاہد باشید

## POEMS OF TÁHIRIH IN THE ORIGINAL LANGUAGES * 285

خال بکنج لب یکی طرّهٔ مشک فام دو
وای بحال مرغ دل دانه یکی و دام دو
محتسب است و شیخ و من صحبت عشق در میان
از چه کنم مجابشان پخته یکی و خام دو
از رخ و زلف آن صنم روز من است همچو شب
وای بروزگار من روز یکی و شام دو
ساقی ماه روی من از چه شدستِ غافلی
باده بیار می بده نفت یکی و دام دو
مست دو چشم دلربا همچو ترا به پُرّه‌ای
در کف ترکِ مست بین باده یکی و جام دو
کشتهٔ تیغ ابروتِ گشته هزار همچو من
بستهٔ چشم جادویت میم یکی و لام دو
وعده وصل میدهی لیک وفا نمی کنی
من بجهان ندیده ام مرو یکی و کام دو
گاه بجانِ سگ درت گاه کمینه چاکرت
فرق نمی کند مرا بنده یکی و نام دو

هان صبح هدی افسرمود آغازِ تنفس !
روشن همه عالم شد ز آفاق و ز انفس
دیگر ننشیند شیخ بر مسندِ تزویر
دیگر نه شود مسجد دکّانِ تقدّس
ببریده شود رشتهٔ تختِ الحنک ازهم
نه شیخ بجا ماند، نه زرق و تدلّس
آزاد شود دهر ز اوهام و خرافات
آسوده شود خلق ز تخییل و توسوس
محکوم شود ظلم بازوئے مساوات
معدوم شود جهل ز نیروئے تفرّس
گسترده شود در همه جا فرشِ عدالت
افشانده شود در همه جا تخم توئنس
مرفع شود حکمِ خلاف از همه آفاق
تبدیل شود اصل تباین بتجانس

## POEMS OF TÁHIRIH IN THE ORIGINAL LANGUAGES

ای خفته رسید یار برخیز  از خود نشان غبار برخیز
هین بر سر مهر و لطف آمد  ای عاشق زار یار برخیز
آمد بر تو طبیب غم خوار  ای خسته دل نزار برخیز
ای آنکه خمار یار داری  آمد مه غم گسار برخیز
ای آنکه به هجر مبتلائی  شد موسم وصل یار برخیز
ای آنکه خزان فسرده کردت  اینک آمد بهار برخیز
هان سال نو و حیات تازه هست
ای مرده لاش پار برخیز

در وصل تویم زنده اجاب  فافتح یا مفتح الابواب
چه شود گر بر تو ره یابند  کم یقوا ناظرین خلف الباب
تا کی از حضرت و صبر و شکیب  طال طول همو رار حجاب
در پس پرده تا به حسرت  از هم نظرة بلا جلباب
از تو غیر از تو مدعائی نیست  مالدیهم سوی لقاک ثواب
سگردانیفی هولئ ثم صوا  ما لهم من لدی سواک مآب
از سبب ها گذشت از حجب  فرقوا الحجب دار تقول الاسباب
بنما آفتاب را بی ابر  بگشا از جمال خویش نقاب
تا بمانند عاشقان حیران  خشگ مغزان شوند اولوالالباب
باخود آینه سجود آن هوا  هوشیاران شوند مست و خرآب
بنده و خواجه درهم آویزند
لاعبید یُری ولا ارباب

پادشه عشق ندا میکند  در ره معشوق صدا میکند
در صفت طلعت انوارش  خامه توصیف حیا میکند
هر که زهر ذره‌ای آگه شود  لاجرش جان بفدا میکند
شمس که در روز ضیا نور رخش  ذره پر از نور جلا میکند
سوی غمش رقص کنان میرود  هر که تمنای لقا میکند
دیدن رویش فقر آرام ام  غرقه دریای فنا میکند
این نه منم مادح رویش ولا  جمله ذرات ثنا میکند
هر که زلالآی شوه آگه شود
خویش در این مرحله لا میکند

چشم مستش کرد عالم را خراب
هر که دید افتاد اندر پیچ و تاب
گردش چشم وی اندر هر نظر
می‌رباید حبّهٔ اهل اللباب
گو چه آید زین دل مجنون محض
کو زده در خیمهٔ لیلی قباب
خیمهٔ آتش نشینان پُر شرر
آتش با شعله زد در هر حجاب
گر نه باشد نار موسی در ظهور
از چه کُل محو و اندر اضطراب
خواهم از ساقی بجبّ‌ام طفحه‌ای
تا بگویم با تو سرّ ما اجاب
هان نگر بر ما بعین باصره
تا ببینی وجه حق را بے‌نقاب
آمد از مظهر عمایی در نزول
با تجلّی رخی چون آفتاب

ای صبا بگو از من آن عزیز بهائی را
اینچنین بودا باشد طلعت بهائی را
ابر لطف آن محبوب تشنه رشحه میبارد
بر هیاکل مطروح مجسترهائی را
نسمهٔ عراقیش میوزد بسی روحا
زنده می‌نماید او بهیکل سوائی را
باب را بکن غرّ بیش شد مفتح ابواب
لطف او شده سائل اهل فتح طائی را
بابیان نوریه جبلگی برون آئید
از حجاب بهائی عزّ بنگر یدِ فائی را
طلعت مبین ناگه طالع از حجاب عزّ
مشنوای عزیز من نطق ابن ترائی را

ایا عاشقان ایا عاشقان شد آشکار رب حق
رفع حجب گردید هان از قدرت رب فلق
خیزید کایم دم بابها، ظاهر شده وجه خدا
بنگر بصد لطف و صفا، آن روی روشن چون شفق
یعنی زه خلاق زمان شد ایمان جسم جهان
روز قیام است ای بهان هر دم شدید ال غسق
آمد زمان راستی، کژی شد اندر کاستی
آن شد که آن می خواستی از عدل و قسط و نسق
شد از میان جور و ستم هنگام لطف است و کرم
ایدون بجای شهر ستم شد جانشین قوت و رمق
علم حقیقی شد عیان شد جهل معدوم از میان
برگو بشیخ اندر زمان بر خیز و بهم زن ورق
بو دار چه عمری از گون وضع جهان از چند چون
هان شیر آمد جای خون باید بجر دل نی طبق
گرچه باند از ململ طاهر شده شاه و دول
لکن بلطف لم یزل بر هاند از ایشان علق

در ره عشقت ای صنم شیفته بلا منم
چند معایرت کنی با غمت آشنا منم
پرده بروی بسته ای زلف بهم شکسته ای
از همه خلق رسته ای از همگان جدا منم
نور توئی تتق توئی ماه توئی افق توئی
خوان مرا قنق توئی شاخه هما دامنم
شیر توئی شکر توئی شاخه توئی ثمر توئی
شمس توئی قمر توئی ذره منم هما منم
نخل توئی رطب توئی لعبت نوش لب تجئی
خواجه با ادب توئی بنده بی حیا منم
کعبه توئی صنم توئی دیر توئی حرم توئی
دلبر محرم توئی بی عاشق بی نوا منم
من زیم تو نیم هم نی زکم و ز بیش هم
چون بتو متصل شدم بی حد و انتها منم
شاهد شوخ دلبرا گفت بسوی من بیا
رسته ز کبر و از ریا مظهر کبریا منم
طاهره خاکپای توست می گفت ای لقای تو
منتظر عطای تو معترف خطا منم

جذبات شوقك الجمّت بسلاسل الغمّ والبلا
همه عاشقان شکسته دل که دهند جان بره ولا
اگر آن صنم زره ستم پی کشتنم نهد قدم
لقد استقام بسیفه فلقد رضیت بما رضی
سحر آن نگار ستمگرم قدمی نهاد به بسترم
فاذا رایت جماله طلع الصباح کما نما
نه چو زلف غالیه بار او نه چو چشم فتنه شعار او
شده نافۀ به همه ختن شده کافری به همه ختن
تو که غافل از می و شاهدی بی مرّوا بذا زاهدی
چه کنم که کافر و جاحدی ز خلوص نیّت اصفیا
تو و ملک و جاه و سکندری من و رسم و راه قلندری
اگر آن نیکوست تو در خوری و گر این بد است مرا سزا
به مراد زلف معلّقی پی اسپ و زین معنبری
همه عمر منکر مطلقی ز صفیر فارغ بی نوا
بگذر ز منزل ما و من بگزین به ملک فنا وطن
فاذا فعلت بمثل ذا فلقد بلغت بما تشا

هلمّ ای گروه عمّانیان بجشید هلهله دلا
که ظهور دلبر ما عیان شد فاش و ظاهر بر ملا
برنید نفخ ز هر طرف که ز وجه طلعت با عرف
رفع الغطاء ت و کشف ظلم اللیال قد انجلی
برسید با سپه طرب صنمی عجیب صمدی عرب
بدمید شمس ز ما غرب بدو یدالیمنی ولا
فوران نار ز ارض فانوران و زیشطر طا
طهران روح ز شطر ها و لقد علا و قد اعتلا
طیری ای تکفکف ورق البها تصفصفت
دیک الضیاء تذ و رقت مجمل متجلّلا
ز ظهور آن شه آله ز الست آن مده ما له
شده آلهه همه الهتی بغنیّات بلی بلی

بتموّج آمد آن یمّی که بجز بلاشش بحر نشمے
منظهر است بهر دمی دو هزار وادی کربلا
ز کمان آن رخ پر ولع ز کمند آن مه ده دله
دو هزار فتنه و سلسله متفرّقه متّسلا!
همه موسیان عمایش همه عیسیان بهمایش
همه لبّان بجائیش متوطّن تنزّلا
بحر الوجود تموّجت بلعل الشهود تلجّت
شفق النجوم تلجلجت بلغت اوج تجلّا
هیکل جمال زطلعتش، قلاج جلال زرفعتش
دول جلال ز سطوتش متخفّی تمنزّلا
دلم از دو زلف سیاه او و زفراق روی چو ماه او
بترابه تهدّم راه او و شده خون من تسبّلا
زغم توای مه مهربان ز فراقت آشو دلبران
شد روح هیکل جسمیان متخفّفاً متخفّلا
توآن تش شعشع روی خود تو آن ملمّع موی خود
که رسانیم توبکو سے خود متعرض تعجّلا

صمدم ز عالم سرمدم احدم ز منبع لاحدم
پی اهل افئده آمدم هلمّوا إلیّ لمقبل
قبسات ناری شیتی انا ذا ألست برّبکم
بگذر ز ساحت قدسیان بشنو صغیر بلی بلی
منم آن ظهور مسیحیی، منم آن منیّت کلّی منی!
منم آن سفینهٔ ایمنی و لقد ظهرت مجلجلا
شجر مرتفع جان منم، ثمر عیان و نهان منم
ملک الملوک جهان منم، ولی البیان قد علا
شهدائی طلعت نار من بدوید سوی دیار من
سر جان کنید نثار من که منم شهنشه کربلا

مهر تو را دل حزین بافته بر قماش جان
رشته به رشته نخ به نخ تار به تار پو به پو
در دل خویش طاهره گشت و ندید جز تو را
صفحه به صفحه لا به لا پرده به پرده تو به تو

بدیار عشق تو مانده ام زکسی ندیده عنایتی!
بغیر بیم نظری فکن که تو پادشاه ولایتی
گنهی بود مگر ای صنم که زسر عشق تو دم زنم
فهجرتنی و قتلتنی و احندتنی بجنایتی
شده راه طاقت وصبر طی بچشم فراق تو تا بکی
همه بند بند مرا چو نی بود از غم تو حکایتی
عجز العقول لدرک هلاک النفوس لوهمه
بکمال تو که برد رهی نبود بجز بجز تو نهایتی
چو صبا برت گذر آورد ز بلاکشان خبر آورد
رخ زرد و چشم تر آورد چه شود کنی تو عنایتی

قدمی نهی تو به بسترم سحری ز فیض خود از کرم
بهوای قرب تو برپرم به دو بال هم بجناحتی
برهانیم چو از این مکان بکشانیم سوی لامکان
گذرم زجان و جهانیان که تو جان و جان ده خلقتی

طلعاتِ قدسِ سبحانی شراراتی که جمالِ حق شده برملا
بزن ای صبا تو بر آتش بجگر ده غمزه غمزه ده غمزدگان صلا
هله ای طواف منتظر! ز عنایتِ شهِ مقتدر
مهِ مستتر شده مشتهر متجلّیا یا تجلّا
شده طلعتِ صمدی عیان که به پاکنف علم بیان
ز گمان دهم جهانیان جبروتِ اقدسِ عصمت را
بسرِ عزّت فرزشان نشستن آن شهِ بی‌نشان
بزد ای صلا به ملاء شان که گرد مدّعی الولا
چو کسی طریقتِ مرا رود کمنش ندا که خبر شود
که هرآنکه عاشقِ من بود، نرَهَد ز محنت و ابتلا
کسی آنکه را اطاعتم، نه گرفت حبل ولایتم
کمنش بعید ز ساحتم دهمش بقَهر با بلا

گر بتو افتدم نظر چهره بچهره رو برو
شرحِ دهم غمِ تو را نکته به نکته مو بمو
از پی دیدن رخت همچو صبا فتاده‌ام
خانه به خانه در بدر کوچه به کوچه کو بکو
می‌رود از فراقِ تو خونِ دل از دو دیده‌ام
دجله بدجله بلکه‌ام به یم چشمه به چشمه جو بجو
دورِ دهانِ تنگِ تو عارضِ عنبرین خطت
غنچه به غنچه گل به گل لاله به لاله بو ببو
ابرو و چشم و خالِ تو صید نموده مرغِ دل
طبع بطبع دل بدل مهر بمهر خو بخو